A CATALOGUE OF EARLY ISLAMIC GLASS STAMPS IN THE BRITISH MUSEUM

A CATALOGUE OF EARLY ISLAMIC GLASS STAMPS IN THE BRITISH MUSEUM

A.H. MORTON

BMP

Published for the Trustees of the British Museum by
BRITISH MUSEUM PUBLICATIONS

Published by British Museum Publications,
46 Bloomsbury Street, London WC1B 3QQ

British Library Cataloguing in Publication Date

British Museum
A catalogue of early Islamic glass stamps
in the British Museum.
1. Glass weights – Catalogs
2. Glassware, Islamic – Catalogs
I. Title II. Morton, A.H.
748.8 CJ3413

ISBN 0-7141-1413-8

Printed in Great Britain
Text by The Paradigm Press, Gateshead
Plates by The University Press, Oxford

CONTENTS

Acknowledgements

The writer's thanks go in the first place to the authorities of the British Museum for accepting and providing for the compilation of the present work. Within the Department of Oriental Antiquities, by which the project was originally put forward for approval, the Keeper, Lawrence Smith, and Deputy Keeper, Jessica Rawson, have uncomplainingly backed it in spite of the delay with which it has finally been completed. Much is due to Dr J.M. Rogers, Assistant Keeper in charge of Islamic objects, for his kindly interest and unfailing support. The former Keeper of the Department of Coins and Medals, R.A.G. Carson, agreed to the inclusion of the material in that Department and arranged for it to provide the large number of casts required, a task that was carried out most satisfactorily by David Owen. N.M. Lowick, of the same Department, gave advice and information on the items in his care with his customary readiness. The photography of the rather refractory material was patiently and successfully completed by Victor Bowlie of the Museum's Photographic Department. Successive Managing Editors of British Museum Publications, Peter Clayton and Celia Clear, have been consistently encouraging and helpful, while the tedious task of editing has been carried out uncomplainingly by Jenny Chattington. Among others who have provided information or given advice - the latter not necessarily taken - the following call for special mention: the late Dr Paul Balog, Michael Bates of the American Numismatic Society, R.J. Charleston, Dr D.O. Morgan, J.F. Morton, Dr Yasin Safadi and, finally, T.R. Volk of the Fitzwilliam Museum, who was also responsible for awakening a dormant interest in glass stamps at an opportune moment.

Note on the Catalogue

The objects described are in either the Department of Coins and Medals or that of Oriental Antiquities. The accessions registers of both, like the main registers of other Departments, are arranged in the same way; the accession number consists of the date of accession expressed in figures, followed by a serial number (e.g. 1978 11-15 1). For accessions made in the nineteenth century it is usual to omit the figures for the century. The catalogue indicates which items are in the Department of Coins and Medals. A few pieces, now transferred from the Departments of Western Asiatic and Egyptian Antiquities to that of Oriental Antiquities, retain their original accession numbers, as noted. The registers of objects in the Department of Oriental Antiquities itself begin from the creation of the separate Department in 1921. Other previously acquired material was accessioned in those now held by the Department of Medieval and Later Antiquities: unless otherwise specified, earlier accession numbers refer to that series. Items which lacked individual accession numbers have recently been incorporated in a supplementary series of Oriental Antiquities registers and given serial numbers with the prefix OA +. A number prefixed S. refers to an item from the Slade bequest.

An equals sign (=) between two references indicates that both refer to the same piece.

In the Arabic texts the following conventions are used:

Brackets [ ] enclose illegible and restored portions.
Parentheses ( ) enclose emendations.
Braces { } enclose superflous letters.

Provenances

The registers very rarely have information about where pieces were originally found. There are a number of references to Egypt as a provenance though it is not always clear whether it is a record of fact or a deduction. More precise locations have been mentioned in the commentaries on a few pieces (Nos 397, 540, 553, 555). In addition the following items are said to have come from the Fayyum: Nos 144, 227, 345, 429, 433, 544.

The Plates

The illustrations are life size and mostly taken from plaster casts. With some deeply sunk or curved stamps, the casts made by the conventional method used were not satisfactory and for these and certain fragile and decayed pieces direct photography was employed. Ordinary methods of lighting do not usually reveal the inscriptions of well-preserved stamps adequately and a special technique is required: the main or only source of light is placed close to the camera lens and the piece slightly tilted so that light reflects off the smooth background of the stamp into the lens. The legend and design then stand out against the highlighted background in the photograph. The results are often as good as or better than those obtained from casts but the image is of course slightly foreshortened. The occasional blurred-looking illustrations reproduce the blurring of the original stamps which can give an impression very like that of a photograph that is out of focus.

Preface

The objects included in the present work may all be described as glass stamps, that is pieces of glass stamped in the course of manufacture with one or more impressions. The material thus defined includes disparate types serving different and in some cases unexplained purposes but the great majority of the pieces in this and similar collections belong to a single series and it is this group that gives the study of early Islamic glass stamps its main interest and importance. Of the 556 items described here three-quarters and more belong to this main series, which was produced by the office of weights and measures in Egypt in the eighth and ninth centuries AD. The group itself falls into three main categories, known as coin weights, heavy weights and vessel stamps, the last being stamps applied to measures of capacity. The unique feature of the group is that a high proportion carry legends which clearly state what they are for and who issued them. The latter is unusual on weights and measures of all periods and understandably so, for it is not what is written on commercial weights and measures that ensures their honest use but the simultaneous existence of an efficient system for the supervision of the market-place; the people on the spot do not need to be told who the authorities are. For whatever reasons, the Egyptian government of the period was exceptionally informative and as a result has provided us with the opportunity of studying a large body of metrological material securely documented as coming from a single and undoubtedly official source. There are of course many problems when it comes to interpreting it but it gives us a fuller picture of how the supervision of weights and measures was organized in a particular society than is available anywhere else until much later. We are also fortunate, incidentally, in the kind of glass used at the beginning of the period. With Ụmayyad and early Abbasid pieces, however much breaking or chipping may have occurred, the original surface of the glass is hardly ever worn or devitrified at all; many retain the fire glaze from the time they were made. A study carried out by Matson has shown that this is due to the unusually durable composition of the glass. It is also apparent, though scientific tests have not been carried out to confirm it, that towards the end of the eighth century glass of a different and less durable sort began to be used, for pieces in good condition come to be exceptional and on many the surface has more or less decayed away.

The first datable stamps known from Egypt after the Islamic conquest are of the early eighth century AD; very soon afterwards the employment of stamps on weights and measures reached its greatest degree of elaboration; from then on the system can be seen to continue without interruption, though with a general trend towards simplicity, into the second half of the ninth century. The early Islamic system derives eventually from that in use in pre-Islamic Egypt, for Byzantine glass pieces of the three main categories are known. They, however, are much less informative; they lack denominations and the issuing authority is identified in most cases simply by a monogram. After the ninth century as well, glass stamps, mainly in the form of small disks, continued to be produced in Egypt under the Fatimid, Ayyubid and Mamluk dynasties, that is until the fourteenth or fifteenth centuries, but again the legends are less explicit, so much so that debate continues over whether the disks are weights or not. These later series differ from the earlier ones in other respects, perhaps owing to changes introduced by the Fatimids on their conquest of Egypt in 969; though the tradition of glass stamps continued, there is a distinct break in continuity between the early and the later systems. AD 900 therefore provides a convenient terminal date for the catalogue.

The British Museum's holdings of Islamic glass stamps are divided into a smaller group, consisting almost entirely of coin weights and other small disks, in the Department of Coins and Medals and a larger one, containing all types, in that of Oriental Antiquities. For the early period the former has contributed 84 items. The first acquisitions of glass stamps appear to have been made in 1853, when the Coin Department received a few in the numismatic collection of Ignatius Pietraszewki, formed earlier in Constantinople where its owner was employed in the Russian Service. Not long afterwards a few were included in the bequest made by Felix Slade of his great collection of glass. Slade's executors later presented others. From the eighteen-seventies to the eighteen-nineties the main source was the Rev. Greville J. Chester, an energetic provider of all kinds of Egyptian antiquities for the museums of England. A number of lots were acquired from him by purchase or gift. Between 1889 and 1895 groups of stamps were included in the extensive donations made by the British Museum's Director, A.W., later Sir Augustus, Franks. Smaller acquisitions were and have continued to be made but in this century the holdings have been greatly strengthened by the gift of two private collections. One, formed in Egypt before 1920 by the Rev. W.R.W. Gardiner, was given in 1966 by Miss Mabel Adamson. Gardiner's collection contained 348 pieces of all periods including a good group of early ones. More important, however, is the collection of Dr Llewellyn Phillips, presented by his widow in 1933 in memory of her husband. The collection was made in Cairo where Dr Llewellyn Phillips was in medical practice. As the Museum received it it amounted to 821 pieces, again of all periods, but with a very strong representation of early ones, which its owner had evidently concentrated on. It is largely thanks to Mrs Llewellyn Phillips's generosity that the British Museum's collection is of major importance. Though much smaller than those of the American Numismatic Society and the Museum of Islamic Art in Cairo, so far as can be told it is considerably larger than all others, large enough to contain examples of all the major categories as well as many rarities. A catalogue by Stanley Lane-Poole of the Islamic glass stamps then in the Museum was published in 1891. Eighty of the pieces he described qualify for inclusion here, which shows how the collection has grown. The debt owed to Lane-Poole and all others who have written on the subject before and after him will be abundantly apparent from the pages that follow.

Introduction

1. PEOPLE NAMED ON THE STAMPS

Within the main Egyptian series there are some stamps with dates but otherwise the dating of particular types depends almost entirely on the names of the individuals which appear on them. The higher-ranking people are almost all known from literary sources and elsewhere; nearly all the others are only identifiable in the sense that their names are found on the glass associated with those of people who are known. Such associations have by now to a great extent been listed and the chronological implications worked out, though there are a few people named on official-looking stamps whose exact place in the series is still uncertain. The people named, with a handful of possible exceptions, fall into five groups which are discussed separately below, as is the question of the names which appear on stamps outside the main series.

Caliphs

The ultimate ruler of Egypt in the eighth and ninth centuries AD was the Caliph, the sovereign, at the beginning of the period, of the undivided Islamic Empire and, later, of the early Empire's territories with the exception of Spain. The Caliphs, belonging first to the Umayyad and then to the Abbasid dynasty, did not reside in Egypt and very rarely visited it. However, they effectively controlled it and the Governors of Egypt were regularly appointed from outside the province, until in the second half of the ninth century, one of them, Aḥmad b. Ṭūlūn, became too strong to be dismissed and for some time rule over Egypt became hereditary among his descendents. However, though the Tulunids may be regarded as an independent dynasty, they did not wholly reject the Caliph's suzerainty. The Caliph's name was not a standard part of the legend of the official glass stamps in the early period, as it was later under the Fatimids, but it is found in a few cases. The Umayyad Yazīd II is named on a small group of vessel stamps in association with Egyptian Finance Directors. Weights and measures of all the then current types, except *fals* weights, are known in the name of the second Abbasid Caliph, al-Manṣūr but it is clear that they were all issued during a small part of his reign. Under his successor al-Mahdī, on the other hand, *dīnār*-system weights were issued in the Caliph's name through most of the reign, but measures and heavy weights were all in the names of subordinate officials. Stamps with Caliphs' names next appear in the ninth century when, for a time, they were used on the larger *raṭl*-systems weights in conjunction with officials' stamps and, presumably in a similar fashion, on measures. Specimens are recorded of the Caliphs al-Wāthiq, al-Muʿtaṣim and al-Mutawakkil.

Besides the vessel stamps of Yazīd II already mentioned there are a few other stamps with the names of Umayyad Caliphs, but it seems probable that they do not belong to the Egyptian series. In some cases, notably those of the heavy weights published by Abdel-Kader (1935) and Ettinghausen, there are reasons to believe that they are of Syrian manufacture and possibly the whole group was produced in Syria. (See also No. 532)

Governors and Finance Directors

From early Umayyad times the administration of Egypt, like that of other provinces, was seen as having two main aspects, that of security, combined with religious and 'Arab' affairs, and that of the collection of the revenue. Responsibility for the former lay with the official whom modern writers call the .Governor but whom the early sources usually speak of simply as being 'in charge of prayer' (*ʿalā al-ṣalāt*), or sometimes more fully as 'in charge of war and prayer' (*ʿalā al-ḥarb wal-ṣalāt*). Taxation was the province of the Finance Director, usually similarly described as being 'in charge of taxes' (*ʿalā al-kharāj*), occasionally as 'master of the taxes' or 'agent' (*ṣāḥib al-kharāj*, *ʿāmil*). As was first clearly pointed out by Casanova (1891, 95-6; 1893, p. 343), the issue of glass weights and measures was originally part of the duties of the Finance Director, and not of the Governor. However, as he also noted, both offices could be, and often were, combined, a single person being appointed for both 'prayer' and taxes (*ʿalā al-ṣalāt wal-kharāj*). (It is often convenient, when referring both to Governors with control of finances and Finance Directors proper, to refer to the two categories together as Finance Directors.)

In the early period the names of Governors who had responsibility for finances occur on the stamps; those of ones only appointed for 'prayer' do not. The Finance Director was undoubtedly an influential figure: ʿUbaydallāh b. al-Ḥabḥāb was able to have two Governors dismissed in quick succession. Nevertheless, the Governor certainly outranked him in theory and in the first two decades in which the stamps were issued only the Governor bore the title *al-Amīr*. The glass provides clear evidence that the issue of glass stamps went with control of finances until well into the Abbasid period but from the last quarter of the second century AH the picture is rather obscure. The distinction between the two functions is still occasionally referred to in Kindī's *Book of Governors of Egypt*, but it is possible that it was less rigorously maintained, for in some cases, that of Aḥmad b. Ṭūlūn for instance, people who are named on the stamps are only described as in charge of 'prayer'. On the other hand, it is also possible that Kindī's data are less complete or accurate in this respect for the late second and third centuries AH.

Kindī is the main literary source for the Governors and Finance Directors of Egypt. He provides a complete list of the Governors with their dates, the accuracy of which has received a considerable degree of confirmation from a variety of evidence, including that of the glass stamps themselves. He usually makes it clear whether a particular Governor had control of the finances or not and though, as has just been said, his information in this respect is somewhat puzzling for the late second and third centuries AH, it stands up very well for the earlier period. Unfortunately for the study of glass stamps, it was not part of his purpose to tell us about Finance Directors who were not also Governors and they are only mentioned incidentally, if at all. Some of both classes of officials are also known from other literary sources, coins and papyri. There is no doubt in the majority of cases about where their stamps belong in the series. The most thorough examination of the evidence for most such officials is that of Grohmann (1924) which is the chief source of much later work, notably the useful summaries of careers presented in the works of Miles. In the present catalogue the official position and dates of the Governors and Finance Directors who appear on the stamps in the collection are given without comment, except in a few cases where received views seem to need correction or explanation.

Overlords

In the second quarter of the ninth century AD it ceased to be the usual practice for the Caliph to appoint the Governor of Egypt directly. Instead, the governorship was granted to one of the influential figures at the Court of Baghdad who proceeded to appoint the actual governor on his own behalf. The earliest case of such a grant was that given by the Caliph al-Ma'mūn to his brother Abū Isḥāq in AH 213/AD 829 (Kindī, 185). The system came to an end with Aḥmad b. Ṭūlūn's independence. The grantees of this type have been called Viceroys, but since none of them appears to have ever visited Egypt while in control of the appointment of the Governor, Overlord seems a more appropriate term. The names of some of the Overlords occur on stamps, examples in the present collection being Ashinās and possibly Ītākh.

Executives

One of the largest groups named on the stamps is that of a type of official evidently subordinate to the Finance Director. Such names are usually introduced by the 'executive formula', *ʿalā yaday* ('at the hands of'), though the formula itself is sometimes found with names of other categories. In the recent English-language literature such officials are generally referred to as Prefects, presumably on the assumption that they were actually in charge of the issue of weights and measures. They may indeed have had some such responsibility but since the legends merely represent them as carrying out the orders of their superiors, the word executive has been preferred for them here.

The earliest executive whose name we have is Junāda b. Maysara, who appears on a series of stamps of ʿUbaydallāh b. al-Ḥabḥāb dated 111/729-30 (e.g. No. 54). However, as is shown below (p. 38), the activities of even earlier executives are attested by a series of anonymous counterstamps going back to the time of Usāma b. Zayd. When named executives first appear, their names follow those of the Finance Directors on the same stamp; a little later, under Ḥafṣ b. al-Walīd, the first separate executive stamps, those of Yazīd b. Abī Yazīd, occur. Nothing is known of most of the executives beyond the fact that their names appear on the stamps in certain situations. In a few cases identifications have been proposed with people mentioned in literary works but, even if they are correct, the identifications reveal very little. The only executive who appears to have any more substantial identity is Yazīd b. Abī Yazīd, who is likely to be the person of the same name who acted as Finance Director fifteen years before he first appeared in the lesser role of executive. However, even in this case, a coincidence of names is not impossible.

The evidence for the Umayyad period seems to indicate that the executives' names never stood alone on the original weights and measures. From quite early in the Abbasid period, however, their names do sometimes appear alone on certain types of pieces, usually those which can reasonably be regarded as being of little prestige: *fals* weights, small *raṭl*-system weights, commodity stamps and, later, fractional *dīnār*-system weights. Even on these the name of the executive is most commonly introduced by the executive formula, indicating that the status of the executive had not greatly changed. Though the last part of the series is not yet fully known, executives continue to appear on stamps until about AH 220. After that date there are almost no names found which can be taken to be those of executives.

Artisans

The last group of people named on the stamps of the main series is a very small one. Their names occur in the centres of the reverses of coin weights in the early Abbasid period, from shortly before the reign of al-Manṣūr, and are introduced by a formula here read as *ṭabʿa* ('stamping of ...', i.e. stamped by so-and-so). Among them there is one odd-man-out, al-Muhājir, who is in fact the latest in date. His name appears on a coin-weight reverse die after *ṭabʿa*, but also on ordinary executive stamps; both types belong to the same short period, the finance directorship of Muḥammad b. Sulaymān (see Nos 290-1, 294, 298, 306-7). It is possible that al-Muhājir combined the duties of an executive with those of the members of the smaller group, but it is perhaps more probable that he was simply an executive whose name on the coin-weight reverse appears in an exceptional position introduced in an exceptional way.

The remainder of the group seems to consist of only three people, Chael, Severus and Kāmil, though in some cases the reading of the last name presents problems. It is noteworthy that two of the names show that their possessors were Copts, or at least of Coptic origin. It is clear that the three were not executives; their names only occur in the centres of coin-weight reverses, the margins of which are occupied by a second name, either of an executive or a Finance Director. All three are found associated in this way with known executives. It makes little difference whether the introductory formula is read *ṭabʿa* or, as is certainly possible and has been preferred by some, *ṣanʿa*, 'making' (or *ṭabaʿahu* or *ṣanaʿahu*. See pp. 42 f below). The members of this category are evidently of lower status than the executives and presumably in some way concerned with the actual manufacture of the coin weights (and, very probably, the other weights and measures on which their names do not appear). Whether they were actually the craftsmen or played a supervisory role in the workshop cannot be determined but in this catalogue they have been called artisans. The interpretation of their position put forward here is essentially that first suggested by Casanova (1893, p. 349), who, however, read *ṣanʿa* rather than *ṭabʿa*.

Others

With a few exceptions, nearly all belonging to the third century AH, for which the evidence is less complete, the people named on the stamps of the main Egyptian series fit into the classification given above. Outside the main series there are two very small groups of stamps which name identifiable people. The first, which has already been referred to above, bears the names of Umayyad Caliphs and was probably produced in Syria. On two of the heavy weights in this group a second name follows that of the Caliph, in one case that of an Umayyad Prince, in the other that of a Finance Director of Damascus (Abdel-Kader 1935, 1; Ettinghausen). The second group consists of coin weights with the names of rulers of the Aghlabid dynasty of western North Africa; it is represented in the collection by No. 373 (*q.v.*). There is little that can be said about the remaining names. There are many of them, but they occur on a wide range of types few of which at present can be classified as belonging to series or groups of any size. Some of them are accompanied by titulature, most commonly the title Amir, which certainly indicates a personage of some standing, but though occasionally, as in the cases of Zakariyy b. Yahyā and his associates (see Nos 383, 387) and ʿAlī b. Muḥammad (No. 397), it is possible to suggest not implausible identifications, they remain tentative.

2. COIN WEIGHTS AND OTHER SMALL DISKS

Coin weights

The legends on many of the smaller pieces in this and similar collections state that they are weights for *dīnārs*, *dirhams* or *falses*. Fractional weights also occur. Other types with less explicit legends can be assigned to the same three categories. *Dīnār*, *dirham* and *fals* are, of course, the words used at the period for gold, silver and copper coins respectively and they appear in the legends of the actual coins. Ever since Castiglioni, and later Rogers, correctly read the words for weight in the legends, such pieces have normally, and understandably, been referred to as coin weights. There are, however, as will be shown, still unsolved metrological and other problems which make it difficult to see how some of the *dirham* weights and all the *fals* weights in fact correspond to the silver and copper currency and, in the case of some of the *dirham* weights at least, it is conceivable that they were not intended for weighing coins. Nevertheless, while final judgement remains to some extent suspended, it is still convenient to call them all coin weights. From the relative abundance of the official coin weights and the parallel examples of the vessel stamps and *raṭl*-system weights it can be assumed that they were distributed to retailers.

In an article that appeared when this introduction was largely written Michael Bates (1981), discussing the later glass disks of the Fatimid and Ayyubid periods, which he, unlike Balog (1981 and elsewhere), takes to be coin weights, has presented a challenge to an assumption which, as he says, underlies much past writing on the subject, the assumption that coin weights were used to check the accuracy of coins one by one. On the basis of literary and other evidence he argues that they were used for weighing out quantities of coinage of a known, or generally accepted, standard of fineness but minted without attention to the precise weight of the individual coins. The sums weighed out would correspond to a multiple of a *dīnār* or *dirham* standard, but the number of actual coins in any particular batch would be of no importance. One consideration that had seemed to stand in the way of such a suggestion was that the highest denominations of coin weight in the later periods were taken to be double-*dirhams* and double-*dīnārs*. Bates provides two solutions to the difficulty. Firstly, he points to the existence of the occasionally mentioned but until recently rather neglected groups of multiple *dīnār* and *dirham* weights made of metal. These, he suggests, provide the larger denominations and the glass disks the smaller ones in progressive sets of weights, like ordinary sets of kitchen weights by which varying quantities of a commodity can be weighed out. Secondly, he suggests that in any case quantities of coin could have been weighed against the appropriate quantity of glass weights. The thesis is for the most part convincing but Bates does not deal with the earlier glass coin weights. To what extent does it apply to, or receive support from, the evidence of the earlier period? The answers seem to differ according to whether one is considering the coin weights within the main official Egyptian series or one group that appears to be outside it, the weights for *dirhams kayl*. In the case of the latter the surviving evidence does attest the existence of sets of progressive weights. The weights of this group are difficult to date but some of them can hardly be later than the ninth century AD, indicating that the weighing of coins in bulk was normal by then. As is stated in more detail below, the writer is also of the opinion that there are in fact glass weights of the Fatimid period and probably later which have previously been misclassified but which should be regarded as multiple *dirham* and *dīnār* weights. With the types within the official series, as will become apparent, there are in many cases problems when one tries to work out precisely what was weighed with them but, in spite of these, the fact that not a single multiple type is known for any of the different series argues for their having been used as standard weights (French *étalon*) designed to check the accuracy of individual coins. Given the extreme elaborateness of the officially controlled system of weights and measures in eighth-century Egypt, if multiples existed in any material it is extraordinary that none has yet been recorded. Nor does the number of surviving pieces, which is much less than that of the Fatimid ones, or their distribution in collections, make it likely that low-denomination weights of these categories were used in large quantities for weighing large sums; if they were we would expect by now to have come across discernible traces of hoards of pieces of one type among the material in the collections.

The coin weights of the official Egyptian series were almost without exception issued in the eighth century AD, and it was only towards the end of the period that precious metals began to be coined in Egypt itself. Miles (1964b, 83) gives 172/788-9 as the date of the first *dirham* known to him from the mint of Miṣr (Fusṭāṭ, Egypt). This might be thought to explain the widespread use of *dīnār* and *dirham* weights in the country: all the gold and silver coin in use was imported and there was no local mint for precious metals, the products of which could serve as a reliable standard subject to local controls and checks. However, copper currency was produced in Egypt, as were the great variety of *fals* weights which *prima facie* seem designed to check it.

Dīnār-system weights

The earliest *dīnār* weights in the official series are, if No. 1 has not been misattributed, of the Umayyad prince ʿAbdallāh b. ʿAbd al-Malik b. Marwān, which lack a denomination. Under his successor, Qurra b. Sharīk, half- and third-*dīnār* weights also appear and the denomination is nearly always given. All three denominations correspond to real coins. A slight puzzle is that the fractional weights continued to be issued long after the fractional coins, which appear to have always been scarce, had ceased to be produced. Even during the Umayyad period fractional *dīnārs* were only minted in the west of the Empire, in Spain and North Africa, and even there they went out of production in the first decade of the second century AH (Walker, p. lviii: cf. Miles 1964b, 82, where this point is made). No corresponding fractional gold coins are recorded for the early Abbasid period. The Umayyad fractional coins would no doubt have continued to circulate for a time but it seems unlikely that the ordinary shopkeeper would have needed to bother about them much in the latter part of the century. One wonders if in fact the issue of the fractional weights was continued out of sheer conservatism. In this connection there is a change in the later fractional weights which might be interpreted as a reaction to the fact that they had lost prestige because there were few if any coins to check with them. In the beginning all *dīnār*-system weights bore on the obverse the name of the highest-ranking of the people whose names were currently appearing on the stamps, i.e. the Caliph or the Finance Director. With regard to the *dīnār* weights this continued to be the normal practice until the Governorship of al-Ḥasan b. al-Baḥbāḥ (193-194/808-810), the last Finance Director of Egypt who is known to have issued *dīnār*-system weights of any sort and after whom they were presumably abandoned, or at any rate not made of glass. The half and third denominations, however, began to be issued with anonymous obverses combined with reverses with the names of executives, reverses which are also used on the contemporary *dīnār* weights. (The die links of the reverses are of course the means of precisely dating the fractional types.)

The change can be dated closely: fractional types were produced in the name of the Caliph al-Mahdī for most of his reign and in the name of Mūsā b. al-Muṣʿab, who was Governor and Finance Director in 167-168/784-785, near the end of it (see Balog 1976, 578-80). Under Mūsā's successor, al-Faḍl b. Ṣāliḥ, *dīnār* weights bore al-Faḍl's name on the obverse, which was combined with a reverse of ʿĀṣim b. Ḥafṣ that also occurs in combination with anonymous half-*dīnār* obverses (see Nos 327, 338). The corresponding third-*dīnār* weight, which probably existed, has yet to be recorded, but from this time on half- and third-*dīnār* weights with anonymous obverses and reverses of executives are the rule up to the time of al-Ḥasan b. al-Baḥbāḥ (see Balog 1976, 643-5, reading the executive's father's name as ʿUthmān). There are occasional variations from this standard pattern in the last period; for instance, some *dīnār* weights are described as lacking reverses. However, the only fractional piece known to the writer with a possible Finance Director's name on it is the half-*dīnār* weight of Ḥuwayy b. Ḥuwayy in the present collection (No. 337).

The remarkable consistency of the official coin weights of all sorts has long attracted attention and the *dīnār*-system weights are even more consistent than the others. They provide the best evidence there is, and excellent evidence, for the weight standard of the *dīnār* introduced by the Caliph ʿAbd al-Malik in the great currency reform which established the pattern of Islamic coinage for centuries. The various figures put forward for the *dīnār* on the basis of the glass weights since the nineteenth century naturally differ little, but it is still worth presenting the evidence of the British Museum's large collection on the point. Excluding damaged pieces, ones without denominations (except No. 257) and one freak (No. 196), as well as all those outside the official Egyptian series, there are 24 *dīnār* weights, 25 halves and 17 thirds, with weights as follows:

Dīnār	4.17	4.19	4.20	4.21	4.22	4.23	4.24	4.25	4.27g
	1	1	2	1	3	8	6	1	1
Half	2.08	2.10	2.11	2.12	2.13	2.14g			
	2	4	9	8	1	1			
Third	1.27	1.37	1.38	1.39	1.40	1.41	1.43g		
	1	1	1	1	5	7	1		

It will be seen that there are very marked frequency peaks for the three denominations: 4.23-4.24g. for the *dīnār*, 2.11-2.12 for the half and 1.40-1.41 for the third. These figures are slightly higher than those given by Balog from his even larger collection (1976, pp. 23, 25) but are almost exactly the same as those obtained by Miles (1964b, 81-2) in the most extensive examination of the metrology of glass weights that has yet been carried out. Miles (1961a, 214-6) has previously compared the data on the *dīnār* weights (not the fractions) with the weights of actual Umayyad and early Abbasid *dīnārs*. For the coins he found a marked frequency peak at 4.14-4.20g. To reconcile the two figures completely he gave a higher allowance for wear for the coins than for the harder glass and suggested a standard of 4.25g, a figure which had previously been arrived at by Bergmann. To make some allowance for wear in the case of the coins seems acceptable; whether any should be made for the glass when many pieces are in 'mint' condition is open to question and, as Miles himself pointed out, Bergmann's figure is derived directly from a rather small number of coins and glass weights. However, 4.25g is a convenient figure for calculation and has been used as such throughout the catalogue. If the standard was a centigram or two lighter it makes little difference.

Besides the official Egyptian series which we have hitherto been discussing there are two other now definible groups of early *dīnār*-system weights, firstly those of the Aghlabid dynasty of western North Africa (see No. 373) and, secondly, a larger group with anonymous religious legends, probably Egyptian, but otherwise difficult to place (see, e.g. Nos 512-21). In addition, there are occasional pieces with names which may not belong to the main series, such as No. 393, and anonymous ones which resemble each other in having denominations, though differences in the scripts employed on them make it unlikely that they all belong to one historical series (e.g. No. 411; Petrie, 202).

Dirham-system weights

It might be expected that, like *dīnār*-system weights, *dirham* weights would correspond to actual coins, but it is now clear that at least three *dirham* standards are represented among the glass weights and that two of them are distinct from the generally accepted standard of the post-reform silver *dirham*, 2.97g. The situation was first clearly described quite recently by Balog (1976, pp. 25-6). In accordance with Balog's terminology the series are here called weights for *dirhams* of two-thirds, weights for *dirhams* of 13 *kharrūba* and weights for *dirhams kayl*. The first two groups are well attested in the main official Egyptian series of weights and measures. On the other hand there appear to be no specimens of the third group which can be unhesitatingly attributed to the official series.

Dirham *weights of two-thirds*

Within the Egyptian series are a number of types which have the denomination *dirham*, in all but one case without further qualification, other than the standard 'full-weight' (*wāf*). Most bear the names of well-known officials; one is issued in the name of the 'House of Muḥammad' and one in the name of the Caliph al-Manṣūr. The legends are generally similar to those of the *dīnār*-system weights, but when in the early Abbasid period it became the custom for reverses to be used with *dīnār*-system weights, the reverses of *dirham* weights usually remained unstamped; the exception is the issue of al-Manṣūr, which has a reverse of ʿAbd al-Malik b. Yazīd and Chael. The earliest of the issues, as at present known, is one of al-Qāsim b. ʿUbaydullāh and Dāʾūd b. al-Murr dated 123/740-1 (Petrie, 117; Fahmī 1957, 52), the latest is of Muḥammad b. Saʿīd (Miles 1958a, 164). *Dirham* weights of this kind are much scarcer than *dīnār*-system weights: there are only two in the present collection (Nos 140, 244). If it could be securely established that they were for weighing silver coins their comparative scarcity would not be unnatural, for, as is well known, in the western, mostly once Byzantine, provinces of the early Islamic empire, including Egypt, gold was the basic currency.

In his study of the metrology of glass coin weights Miles (1964b, 82) found a frequency peak at 2.84-2.85g among 16 specimens. Thinking, it is evident, in terms of a single *dirham* standard of 2.97g, he was reluctant to accept a lower standard and was reduced to suggesting that the pieces he knew of might all happen to be badly worn. The consistency of the weights of other categories of glass shows that this is an unacceptable solution. Since his presentation of the data was summary and his definition of the group not entirely clear a table of the weights of 22 pieces belonging to it is presented here, mostly on the basis of published material. The pieces all indisputably belong to the main official series and are not described as in any way damaged, though whether the weights given are as accurate as might be wished is, as always, somewhat doubtful.

2.71	2.76	2.77	2.78	2.79	2.80	2.81	2.82	2.83	2.84	2.85	2.88	2.90	2.92g
1	1	1	1	1	1	2	0	3	5	3	1	1	1

The frequency peak occurs at 2.83-2.85g, agreeing well with Miles's figure and in itself indicating a weight standard close to the peak. Epigraphic confirmation of the existence of such a standard is provided by the type of Yazīd b. Ḥātim, on which the word *dirham* is followed by *thulthayn*, 'two-thirds' (see No. 244). The reading was first proposed by Rogers who pointed out in support of it that the weight of the piece he was describing corresponded to two-thirds of a *dīnār*. The same conclusion has since been reached by others, but it was left to Balog (1976, pp. 25-6) to note that the otherwise similar types which lack the crucial word in the legend seem to be on the same standard. Taking the *dīnār* at 4.25g, two-thirds comes to 2.833g, within the frequency peak of the actual weights. The existence of the two-thirds standard appears incontrovertible, though, to introduce a note of caution, it is not impossible that more than one standard is represented in the group as it is here defined: the two highest weights in the table above would be quite acceptable for weights on the *dirham-kayl* standard of 2.97g and both are of al-Manṣūr (Fahmī 1957, 102; Launois 1969, 11). On the other hand, the two other pieces from the same pair of dies are recorded as weighing 2.78 and 2.83g (Casanova 1893, 36; Balog 1976, 357).

The existence of the weights on the two-thirds-*dīnār* standard immediately raises the question of what kind of *dirhams* they were intended to weigh. It is well known that a number of Arabic sources relate that the weight standard of the *dirham* introduced in ʿAbd al-Malik's reform was seven-tenths of the *dīnār*, i.e. 2.97g. That the standard is no figment of the imagination is demonstrated not only by figures based on the weights of the actual coins but also by the existence of weights in glass and other materials which conform to the standard, that here called the *dirham-kayl* standard (see, for the coins, Miles 1960a, 212-4). No satisfactory answer has yet been proposed. One conceivable line of argument is that the two-thirds-*dirham* weights were not intended for weighing coins at all. Besides being used for silver coins, the word *dirham* is sometimes found as the name of a sub-unit in a *raṭl*-system series of progressive weights, for instance a twelfth of a *wuqiyya* (see, e.g. Hinz, 29). The weights of two-thirds could, on this theory, have been used to weigh out small quantities of precious substances, the rare drugs and spices perhaps which, in spite of received theory, are not represented on the vessel stamps. But in that case we would expect larger denominations to exist as well and the 2.833g *dirham* does not belong to the Umayyad *raṭl* system in use at the time or to any other such system yet firmly attested on glass. Furthermore, the fact that the standard is derived from the *dīnār* strongly suggests a connection with coinage. Alternatively, some category or categories of *dirham* might have been struck at this period to the two-thirds standard. If so they remain to be detected among those which represent the 2.97g standard.

At this point mention should be made of an unusual and hitherto unpublished type in the collection which may be related to the weights of two-thirds, No. 188 (*q.v.*). the piece is of Muḥammad b. Shuraḥbīl, and thus datable to the period when the other series was being issued; its obverse legend states that it is a weight of two thirds of a *dīnār* less a *shaʿīra*, or barleycorn. The *shaʿīra*, as a unit of weight, may be either a seventy-secondth or a ninety-sixth of the *dīnār* - the difference between the two is of course minute. It seems likely that the standard represented by the piece is a slight variation on the two-thirds-*dīnār* one and that it is a *dirham* standard rather than being connected with gold coinage (the *dīnār*). However, as with the two-thirds standard, precisely what kind of *dirham* is meant remains a mystery.

Dirham *weights of 13*-kharrūba

The second class of *dirham* weights are those with legends declaring them to be weights for *dirhams* of 13 *kharrūba*. They were issued during a period of about ten years, the first type being one of the 'House of Muḥammad', produced shortly after the Abbasid conquest of Egypt in 133/750, the latest belonging to the beginning of the governorship of Muḥammad b. al-Ashʿath, 141-3/759-60 (Balog 1976, 388). The number of types is therefore small, but a good proportion of them are relatively common compared with the *dirham* weights of two-thirds, which were issued over a longer period. The known corpus of each group is about the same size.

The sub-unit of the legends, the *kharrūba*, is familiar from *fals* weights and is discussed under that heading below. As a general figure for calculation 0.195g has been adopted for the *kharrūba* in this catalogue. However, among the *fals* weights there are occasional, perhaps unimportant, but noticeable variations between the *kharrūba* standard used for certain particular issues and that derived from analysis of the material as a whole. The same is true of this class of *dirham* weights: the weights of pieces of the first issue, that of the 'House of Muḥammad' (e.g. Nos 163-4) are mostly over 2.60g, implying a 'heavy' *kharrūba* of just over 0.2g, while the other issues come at the lower end of the expected weight range and give a *kharrūba* of about 0.19g.

The question of function, so far unsolved for the *dirham* weights of two-thirds, is equally or even more baffling in the case of those of 13 *kharrūba*. Both, it should be noted, were for a time in simultaneous production. There appears to be no silver coinage of the period, Islamic or other, produced on a standard of c. 2.6g. That of Ṭabaristān is of the right date but, on a standard of c. 2.0g, is far too light. Balog, attributing the view to Miles, has gone so far as to say that the group should be considered to be *fals* weights. (Balog 1976, p. 26, seemingly relying on Miles 1964b, 84. Miles does there say that there is no difference between the *dirham* weights and 13-*kharrūba fals* weights, but from the passage as a whole appears to be referring only to their actual weights and suspending judgement on their function.) Against this suggestion it may be noted that, besides the fact that the carefully executed legends plainly state them to be *dirham* weights, there are *fals* weights with normal legends issued during the same period and that the use of reverses on several issues of the 13-*kharrūba dirham* weights also distinguishes them from the *fals* weights of the period.

Weights for dirhams kayl

The first weights on the *dirham-kayl* standard were published long ago, but the clear distinction that needs to be made between this standard and that of 'two-thirds' was only in fact made recently by Balog (1976, pp. 25-6). It has been explained already that the standard is that of the post-reform silver *dirham*, that it is seven-tenths of that of the post-reform *dīnār* and that it is equivalent to 2.97g. On a number of the weights in this group the denomination is followed by the word *kayl*, which serves as a useful means of providing the standard with a distinguishing name. It is obscure why *kayl*, which normally means 'measuring by volume' and is particularly applied to the use of dry measures, should appear on coin weights and it should be noted that in the sources for, and modern literature on, Arabic metrology the term *dirham kayl* is at times used for other *dirham* standards.

The corpus of published pieces with legible denominations in this group is so small as to allow an attempt to be made to list them all; the British Museum's five specimens form the largest body yet published together. It has been mentioned at the beginning of this section on coin weights that the glass *dirham-kayl* weights differ from the other series in the fact that they belonged to progressive sets of weights and that this shows that they must have been used for weighing out coins in quantity, not checking their weights individually. As evidence of this we have pieces of five denominations which, with their theoretical weights in grammes, are as follows: ½ (1.485g), 1 (2.97g), 2 (5.94g), 10 (29.7g), 20 (59.4g), 50 (148.5g). A 5-*dirham* denomination seems to be required to fill the gap between the 2 and 10-*dirham* pieces; none is known among the types here classified as early, but the denomination is well attested among the later *dirham-kayl* weights discussed briefly below.

The only half-*dirham* weight with a clear denomination is No. 392 of ʿAbd al-ʿAzīz b. Ḥumayd. The legend includes the word *kayl* but the actual weight of the piece is very low. (However, c.f. Launois 1958, 35, weighing 1.47g.) A very clearly inscribed *dirham* type with a reverse of one Yaḥyā is known from two specimens (see No. 407) and an anonymous type, also with a reasonably clear legend from two more (Miles 1948, 132 - broken; Balog 1976, 834 - 2.95g). A third type is of an Amir called Aḥmad b. Dīnār (No. 381) and a fourth is of another Amir whose name can be read Ītākh (Balog 1976, 680 - 2.95g). The only double-*dirham* type is Balog 1976, 752a, weighing 5.89g, in the name of yet another unknown Amir whose name is read, with reservations, as al-Ḥasan b. Muʿādh. The higher denominations have not to the writer's knowledge previously been described as such by others. No. 351, here attributed, with little conviction, to Ītākh, is the first 10-*dirham* piece with a denomination to be published. No intact 20-*dirham* piece has yet been listed, but Balog 1976, 126 appears to be a damaged specimen, for the legend ends *ʿishrīn wāf* ('twenty, full-weight') corresponding to the 'ten, full-weight' of the Museum's 10-*dirham* piece. (The stamp differs greatly from those of Ḥafṣ b. al-Walīd, to whom Balog attributes it, and is plainly later; the Amir named on it may be the Aḥmad b. Dīnār of the British Museum's Nos 381-2.) The only 50-*dirham* weights so far described are No. 412 and a similar piece in the Fitzwilliam Museum, Cambridge.

The only weights of the group that have been associated with a person who is known otherwise are the two attributed to Ītākh. The very fact that they are on the *dirham-kayl* standard, added to the differences between their style and wording of their legends and that of the only undoubtedly official stamp with Ītākh's name, makes the attribution dubious. For the rest, and probably for these two pieces as well, the only dating criteria are the fabric of the pieces, which is of limited help, and more importantly, the style of the script. In some cases the legends are well executed and on the whole not dissimilar to those of the official stamps; in others the engraving is shallow and the letters irregularly spaced and weakly formed. The script of this second group is still to be characterized as Kufic but it does not appear to be closely related either to the script of the official stamps of the early period or to that of the official Fatimid glass disks. One variant letter form that occurs sometimes (e.g. on Nos 381-2) is a simplified form of *dāl*, differentiated from *kāf*. On the whole the script of this group seems to justify assigning them to the early period or, to be more cautious, since a conservative script could have remained in use for particular purposes, at least justifies provisionally including them in the present catalogue. In addition to the pieces already mentioned a disk-weight with a largely illegible inscription in this kind of feeble Kufic is also included and classified as a 10-*dirham* weight (No. 535).

With the exception of the two 'Ītākh' pieces and the two of Aḥmad b. Dīnār there is little reason to assume that the early *dirham-kayl* weights so far known were produced at the same time or even necessarily at the same place. The information on their provenance is, as usual, unsatisfactory; all that can really be said is that most of them come from collections formed in Egypt and were probably made there. This does not mean that others might not have been produced elsewhere. The small body of material at present available may only be a sample from a considerable variety of sets of *dirham* weights probably dating from before AD 900 and possibly produced in a number of places. In this connection it is appropriate to discuss a set of metal *dirham-kayl* weights from Egypt which, though the evidence is tantalizingly incomplete, seem likely to belong to the early period. In about 1880 a wooden box containing weights was found (precisely how is not clear) in the Fayyūm by E.T. Rogers Bey. Rogers sent a description of the find to Henri Sauvaire who published a brief note on it in his 'Contributions' (II, 44-5). The box was divided into two compartments. One contained glass weights for single *dīnārs* and fractions of *dīnārs* and is here only of interest as providing what dating evidence there is; the other held six *dirham*-system weights made not of glass but, it is said, of steel (*acier*), one half-*dirham* three 5-*dirhams* and two 20-*dirhams*. The set is evidently incomplete, since there is nothing to bridge the gap between the half and 5-*dirham* denominations. The actual weights of the pieces were very close to the *dirham-kayl* standard. On three of the larger ones the denomination was given as the appropriate number, followed by a phrase given in translation as *poids de sept* ('weight of seven', *wazn sabʿa*?). As Sauvaire noted, this must refer to the *dirham-kayl* standard, which is based on the ratio of 10 *dirhams* to 7 *dīnārs*. The only evidence of the box's date that is given is that the latest of the glass *dīnār*-system weights was a half-*dīnār* type of al-Muqtadir (r. 295-320/908-932). As Casanova (1893, p. 350) pointed out, this is obviously a misreading for al-Mahdī. The mistake was an easy one to make at the time: Rogers had made it before (1878, 18) as had Castiglioni (7) before him. Allowing for the emendation of the name the legend is exactly that of al-Mahdī's commonest half-*dīnār*-weight obverse (see, e.g., Nos 294-6). Since the piece was not of al-Muqtadir, of whom no glass weights are known, it becomes questionable whether it was in fact the latest of the group, but they must presumably have been official issues of the eighth century AD since Rogers was able to date them. Strictly speaking, of course, the datable pieces do not necessarily date the contents of the box as a whole at all closely; the glass weights could have been used long after they were issued. Nevertheless, an early date for the box is likely and it can probably be taken as providing some confirmation of the evidence of the glass pieces and as indicating that sets of *dirham-kayl* weights were in use in early Islamic Egypt. Mention may also be made of a barrel-shaped bronze 10-*dirham* weight with a denomination which has been assigned to the Abbasid period on stylistic grounds by Balog (1970, 1).

Although there thus seems to be sufficient reason to accept that sets of *dirham-kayl* weights were in use in Egypt in the early period the question arises why few or none of them were made in the workshop that so efficiently produced the undeniably official glass weights and measures. The stylistic features and the unknown names that appear on them are such as to rule out the possibility that they were in nearly all cases. The answer is not clear. All that can be said at present is that they were made elsewhere, apparently outside the immediate control of the main office of weights and measures, perhaps because they were used for a slightly different function from that of the ordinary official weights.

It has been said above that glass weights of multiple *dirham-kayl* and *dīnār* denominations were also produced in later periods, notably under the Fatimids, and, in view of the uncertainty which still remains about the dating and official status of the *dirham-kayl* weights here classed as early, some brief description of the later types is called for, even if it is beyond the proper chronological limit of the present work. Double-*dirham* and *dīnār* weights have long been recognized among the small glass disks of both Fatimid and Mamluk times, but larger denominations, of disk-weight form, exist and though some have been published they have, in the writer's opinion, been classified incorrectly. The British Museum's collections include a handful of such pieces, omitted from this catalogue, but it is simpler to refer here to some of the published examples. The interpretation of these types has been made difficult because, while many of them are impressed with stamps, the impressions are usually either illegible or lacked legends in the first place. Dating depends in many cases on the fabric of the pieces, i.e. the nature of the glass and the shape of the weights and stamps; classification into denominations depends solely on the actual weights of the pieces. The major publication is Jungfleisch's article (1929a) on polychrome Fatimid glass weights. The author divides the material into three groups distinguished by fabric. The first group are of transparent white glass with spots of blue glass, sometimes touched with grey, on the surface, the second of translucent yellow-green glass, with spots of opaque orange, grey or Prussian blue, the third of dark opaque glass with spots as on the second group and sometimes pistachio green ones. Two pieces of the third group are stamped with the name of the Fatimid Imām al-Ẓāhir (r. 411-27/1021-36). This is the evidence for the date of the third group. Perhaps the second can be associated with it on the grounds that the opaque spots on both groups are similar. The first group may be later, for some of the small disks of the Mamluk period are also of white glass with superficial blue inclusions (e.g. Petrie, 677 etc.). The metrological evidence is least satisfactory for the first group. No. 0, at 7.525g does not easily fit into a coin standard unless we resort to the dubious expedient of regarding it as a 2½-*dirham-kayl* weight. 0 *bis* and 0 *ter*, weighing 8.21 and 42.06g, would appear to be 2 and 10-*dīnār* weights. 0 *quarto*, at 58.62g, could easily be a 20-*dirham* weight, though Jungfleisch says the weight has been adjusted by chipping the back. The second group offers no problem: the five pieces weigh between 14.18 and 14.85g and may be classified as 5-*dirham* weights. Five pieces in the third group, some of which, as has been said, are evidently official Fatimid issues, fall between 14.59 and 15.32g. Two are over 15g and may appear rather heavy, but their weights are still within the range of fluctuation of the Fatimid *dirham* standard as calculated by Petrie (p. 10 and pl. XXIV) on the basis of the small disks. All may, therefore, be regarded as 5-*dirham* weights. The sixth, weighing 29.58g, is close to the theoretical value of a 10-*dirham* weight.

Jungfleisch argued that all the pieces, including those here suggested to be on the *dīnār* standard, were assorted denominations on a *raṭl* system, and was therefore obliged to postulate two unlikely denominations, the quarter-*wuqiyya* and the 1½-*wuqiyya*. The *wuqiyya* as derived from the weights of the individual pieces under his scheme also differs considerably, from 28.04 to 32.84g, in itself a suspicious circumstance, though it is always difficult to tell what allowance should be made for wear and slight damage. In fact Balog (1959) has since demonstrated, on the basis of actual examples which are made of lead, that the Fatimids used a *raṭl* system that was significantly heavier, the *wuqiyya* coming to slightly over 36g. Admittedly it is not unlikely that more than one *raṭl* system was in use for weighing different commodities at the same period but, as Balog points out, the issue of official *raṭl*-system weights made of lead in the Fatimid empire was noted in a famous passage by Muqaddasī (240), who was writing not long after the Fatimid conquest of Egypt. Also well known in the study of glass weights is the same author's statement (*loc. cit.*) that Fatimid coin weights (*sinaj*) were of glass. The reference has often been quoted in connection with the small disks of the Fatimid and other periods but in view of the prevalence of the custom of weighing coins in quantity which, as has been mentioned previously, has recently been amply demonstrated for Fatimid Egypt by Bates (1981) it is evident that Muqaddasī need not be referring to small denominations alone; larger multiples would also have been needed. Elsewhere (398) Muqaddasī does imply that *sinaj* were used for larger quantities, for discussing those of the region of Jibāl in Persia he says that they were of the type used in Khurāsān, but that those of Rayy were heavier by a *dirham* and a quarter in every hundred (*dirhams*). His evidence together with the existence of pieces apparently produced on *dirham* and *dīnār* standards in the the corpus published by Jungfleisch supports the case for taking the anonymous glass disk weights of the later periods as being, for the most part at least, multiple coin weights. Further examples of what are probably multiple weights on the *dirham-kayl* standard can be detected by their weights in the sections on illegible or unassignable pieces in a number of the catalogues (e.g. Miles 1958a, 239, 241-2, 247-50). They often show features like those of the groups defined by Jungfleish and are usually misclassified as *raṭl*-system weights.

Fals weights

The earliest datable *fals* weight is of Qurra b. Sharīk (Launois 1959, 2); the latest appears to be of Aḥmad b. Ṭūlūn (Fahmī 1958). The latter, however, is the only one so far known from the ninth century AD and may represent a brief revival of their use. Otherwise they all appear to belong to the eighth century and to have gone out of use towards the end of it: the latest of the datable eighth-century issues are either those of ʿĀṣim b. Ḥafṣ or, more probably, those of Ṣāliḥ b. Muslim. Besides those bearing known names there are a considerable number of anonymous types and also ones with unidentified names. Nearly all of these two last groups can be said for mainly stylistic reasons to belong to the eighth century and the main official series. Though they can to some extent be dated more precisely by the script and other features of their legends it is difficult to place them exactly in the succession of types with known officials' names. *Fals* weights evidently carried less prestige than the other main categories of glass stamps: the Caliph was never named on them and, though on the named Umayyad issues the Finance Director appears, a number of the anonymous types are certainly Umayyad. Under the Abbasids anonymous types were numerous and on issues which bore a name at all it came increasingly to be that of an executive alone.

The legend on most *fals* weights not only specifies that the piece is a *fals* weight but also defines the particular weight standard to which it belongs in terms of *kharrūba* or *qīrāṭ*. The two words are synonyms for the seed of the carob tree (*Ceratonia siliqua* L.). The carob seed had been used as a unit of weight since before the Islamic period: *qīrāṭ* is connected with Greek *kerátion* and the Latin equivalent is *siliqua*, which may also mean the tree itself. As so frequently happens with denominations of weight, there is more than one standard named after the carob seed but, allowing for slight fluctuations, only one was employed for the glass weights. The earliest *fals* weights with such denominations have it in *qīrāṭ*, but before the end of the Umayyad period *qīrāṭ* had gone out of use for this purpose, having been replaced by *kharrūba*. Miles (1964b, 85) has shown that there is no significant difference between the weights of pieces marked in *kharrūba* and *qīrāṭ* with the same denominations and that both terms refer to the same unit. It is often convenient to refer simply to the *kharrūba* when both groups are discussed together. On a small number of issues the denomination in *kharrūbas* is expressed in Coptic figures, which are in fact letters of the Coptic alphabet to each of which a numerical value is assigned, as in the Arabic *abjad* system. The earliest datable types with such figures are of the executive Salama and belong to the middle of the second century of the Hijra, the late 760s AD. The figures continued to be used on later issues though the earlier practice of writing out the number in words survived as well. (For examples of Coptic figures see Nos 249-53, 278-80, 328, 388, 390-1, 403, 436.)

The largest *fals* weights are of 36 *kharrūba*; the smallest type is of 9 *qīrāṭ*, but is marked as a half-*fals* issue. The smallest non-fractional types are of 10 *kharrūba*. Almost every possible number between 9 and 36 is represented by one or more issues. Balog (1976, p. 26) has declared his conviction that the *fals* was 'a well-determined weight unit of fixed value' and that that value was 36 *kharrūba*. This is somewhat surprising when the legends of so many issues of less than 36 *kharrūba* declare them to be *fals* weights. Three points are brought forward to support the theory. First there is the fact that no denominations higher than 36 are recorded. Though we still cannot be quite sure that larger types will not turn up, the fact may have some significance, but it need not be more than that 36 *kharrūba* was regarded as a suitable upper limit for *fals* weights. Secondly, Balog points out that the smaller denominations are all fractions of the supposed fixed standard, e.g. a 35-*kharrūba* weight is 35/36 of the 'complete *fals* unit'. Here it seems to have been overlooked that the same will be true whatever number is taken to represent the standard, provided it is more than 35. Suppose, at random, a 43-*kharrūba* unit; 35 *kharrūba* will be 35/43 of the standard and so on. The third point is that an 18-*qīrāṭ* type is known with a legend stating it to be a half-*fals* weight (Balog 1976, 825). This does indeed imply a corresponding *fals* of 36 *kharrūba*, but not necessarily that there was an invariable standard at that figure. Balog notes the point that there are other half-*fals* types of lower values, 17, 15 and 9 *kharrūba*, and to maintain his theory has to suggest that the *niṣf* ('half') of their legends is an error for 'part'. He takes the latter to be the meaning of *shaṭr* which appears on a fractional issue of 12 *kharrūba* which can, however, be shown to be another half-*fals* type (see Nos 33-5, 41). That the legends of the smaller half-*fals* issues are not incorrect can be shown in most cases by the fact that they are paired with non-fractional types with double the numer of *kharrūba*. For instance, 'Ubaydallāh b. al-Ḥabḥāb's 17-*qīrāṭ* half-*fals* weight shares a number of features with the same official's 34-*qīrāṭ* weight, which is obviously the corresponding whole denomination (see Nos 36, 42). Not only, then, are there many types of less than 36 *kharrūba* with legends proclaiming them to be *fals* weights but in a handful of cases we possess half denominations whose legends imply even more clearly that the whole denominations are in fact whole units. There is therefore no reason to suppose a fixed *fals* standard. On the contrary, it is clear that the *fals* weights were issued on different standards at different times - a matter that will be discussed further in connection with their function.

The *kharrūba*, on the other hand, was a unit of weight and did not, in the early period, denote a coin. Its weight has been calculated many times from the actual weights; the most extensive corpus, 423 pieces, was assembled by Miles (1964b, 84-5) and gave an average *kharrūba* of 0.1947g; 0.195g has been adopted here as the theoretical figure for calculation. On this basis the smallest denomination, 9 *kharrūba*, comes to 1.755g and the largest, 36 *kharrūba*, to 7.02g. In the present age there is no need to give the values of all the denominations, but if a calculator is not at hand, dividing the number of *kharrūbas* by 5 gives slightly over the theoretical figure in grammes. Miles detected the presence of a slightly higher standard in addition to the usual one among the issues of 20 and 25 *kharrūba* and also of a third, lower, one among the former. In the present work it is noted which issues produce a figure for the *kharrūba* of more than 0.20g. They are not in fact confined to the 20 and 25-*kharrūba* denominations and seem to occur sporadically throughout the series. As has been said, there is also a heavy issue of *dirham* weights of 13 *kharrūba*. A group of stylistically related heavy types is found among the anonymous Abbasid issues (see Nos 4, 37-9, 416-17, 419-21, 428, 431-4, 438). It is difficult to say that these slight fluctuations have any great significance. Very possibly they represent nothing more than an unintentional variation which could occur when the standard for particular issues was being set, perhaps by means of actual carob seeds.

With regard to the way in which *fals* weights were used, underlying many of the divergent views that have been put forward is an understandable reluctance to accept that it would have been tolerable, or even possible, to check the weights of copper coins individually. It has generally been assumed that early Islamic copper coins were not struck to a precise weight standard and that the convenience of having small change would outweigh trivial discrepancies in intrinsic value between one copper coin and another. An argument that has therefore been found appealing and used to support various theories is to say that *fals* need not mean a copper coin but can mean money in general. *Fals*, and more particularly its plural *fulūs*, are known to have had this meaning but no evidence has been brought forward to show that it is anything but a relatively recent one. Even if the idiom was current in the early period it is inappropriate as a reading for the weights; it is evidently a slang usage, comparable to English 'dough' or, rather more appropriately, northern English 'brass', while the legends of certain of the weights require at least the meaning 'piece of money'. It is extremely unlikely in any case that *fals* would appear in any such meaning in an early official context; it is found in the legends of many early Islamic copper coins and there means 'a copper coin', which is exactly what would be expected from its derivation from the Byzantine *follis*. For the copper, it clearly corresponds to *dīnār* and *dirham* for gold and silver. There is thus no need to discuss the theory of Petrie (p. 10) or an early one of Miles (1948, pp. 7-8) who both proposed that *fals* weights were used in connection with precious metal coinage, except to note that there are other serious objections to both theories.

Accepting then that *fals* weights are connected with copper coinage, there are still two possibilities, that they were used for weighing it out in quantity, or to check the pieces one by one. The former is essentially the view taken by Lane-Poole (pp. xiii-xv), though expressed in a complicated way. However, as has already been said, the absence of multiple denominations or evidence of the use of the early glass weights in quantity make such an interpretation extremely unlikely.

One point that has often been neglected is the distribution of the issues of *fals* weights in time. Lane-Poole, for example, assumed that all the denominations were in use at once. When few pieces were known such a view was not unreasonable but, even before Lane-Poole, Rogers (1878, pp. 103-4) had taken another line, arguing that the different issues might represent different standards for *falses* produced at different times (cf. Petrie, pp. 9-10). As the corpus has grown it has become more and more evident that all the denominations were not issued together and that they basically represent a chronological series. Many officials only issued one denomination, very few more than two or three. The relative profusion of types belonging to the two obvious exceptions, ʿUbaydallāh b. al-Ḥabḥāb and his son al-Qāsim, can be explained as due to their exceptionally long tenure of office; to some extent their issues can be dated within their finance directorships. Occasionally, as has been said, half and whole denominations were produced together and at times there may have been fractional issues without explicit legends. It is also possible that some of the uncommon and stylistically unusual issues were produced and used elsewhere than at Fusṭāṭ. However, with these slight reservations, the natural way to understand the series is as representing a *fals* standard which could be, and frequently was, altered by official decision.

The actual copper coinage of eighth-century Egypt provides some evidence, both epigraphic and metrological, for a connection between the series of glass weights and that of *fals* issues. Nothing like a definitive description of the copper has appeared but a substantial corpus is made available by the works of Walker, Miles (1958b), Fahmī (1965) and Bacharach and Awad, in which the types referred to can easily be found. The epigraphic evidence is provided by two issues. The second in date is one of the Finance Director Maṭar (157-9/774-6) and was first described by Fahmī. The marginal legend of the obverse ends '*mithqāl fals*' ('weight of a *fals*') and the central legend, which may be a continuation from the margin, is read as *kharrūba*. (Fahmī, 2894, the only illustrated specimen, is not very clear. Could a Coptic figure for *kharrūba* appear somewhere?) That these pieces are not in fact weights is evident from the reverse legend which includes the phrase '*ḍuriba hādhā al-fals*' ('this *fals* was struck'). The other type to be noted here is an anonymous one recently published by Bacharach and Awad (188) with the following legend: *Fals Miṣr wāf; wazn thamaniya ʿashar qīraṭ* ('*Fals* of Miṣr, full-weight; weight eighteen *qīrāṭ*'). The script and the use of *wazn* and *qīrāṭ* in the legend leave no doubt that this is an Umayyad issue of before about 116/734. The metrology of these types is discussed below but the legends themselves show that the *kharrūba*-weight system did have some application to the coinage and that the idea of a weight standard for particular issues had some validity.

In general descriptions of early Islamic copper coinage, those of Walker (p. xcv) and Udovitch (*E.I.*², *s.v. fals*) for instance, it is usually said to be a token currency, though Walker at least envisages that its intrinsic value was not completely overlooked. Certainly, although ʿAbd al-Malik's currency reform affected copper to the extent that designs came to be almost entirely epigraphic, no single weight standard was imposed for the *fals* in the way that happened with gold and silver. It is also apparent that the copper was not subject to central control to the same extent. However, the question of what variations in weight there might be between particular issues and, if they exist, what they might mean, does not appear to have been investigated. As is demonstrated below, different issues are often metrologically distinguishable, which, together with the occasional weight denominations on copper issues, suggests that the idea of token copper currency needs at least to be questioned.

There are difficulties in the way of comparing the Egyptian series of weights and coins on a large scale. Firstly, of course, there is the comparative susceptibility of copper to corrosion and hence alteration in weight. None of the numismatic works used here attempt, except occasionally, the difficult task of assessing the condition of the pieces described. Then there is the question of which weights correspond to which coins. While a high proportion of the weights are closely datable it is impossible to tell where precisely the undatable issues fit into the series. With the coinage the situation is worse: many issues are undated and name no official. The main thing that can be done therefore is to look at the few cases where we have coins and weights of the same official. To summarize some general conclusions in advance may make the picture a little clearer, since special qualifications must frequently be made. Individual weights vary widely within each issue of coin. Nevertheless, when the weights are tabulated, marked, if coarse, frequency peaks are revealed. (An interval of 0.5g was used for the tabulation.) These peaks, representing a weight standard of some kind, are usually higher than, or roughly in the same range as, the glass weights produced at the same period.

The earliest case to discuss is that of al-Qāsim b. ʻUbaydallāh. Of his four denominations of weights, two, of 15 and 33 *kharrūba* with theoretical weights of 2.925 and 6.435g, are only known from single and stylistically unusual specimens. The bulk of his output consists of an early issue of 24 *kharrūba* (4.68g) followed by successive ones of 30 (5.85g) (see Nos 73-84). His copper coins all have the same legend. In a corpus of 115 pieces weights range from 2.90 to 8.52g, but 61 (53 per cent) fall between 6.00 and 6.99g, and 92 (80 per cent) are over 6g and thus considerably heavier than the 30-*kharrūba* weights with which they are likely to be most closely associated. Of ʻAbd al-Malik b. Marwān we have weights on which three executives are named which are likely to cover his whole governorship; all are of 30 *kharrūba* (5.85g) (see Nos 148-9). The coinage is less simple since four different mints are known. Coins of three of them are, however, very rare, and here only those of Fusṭāṭ itself are considered. Excluding, for the moment, three very light pieces, weights of 11 specimens are between 5.66 and over 7g, 7 (64 per cent) are between 6.00 and 6.99g and 8 (73 per cent) are over 6g. Thus far the profile is similar to that of al-Qāsim's coins. However, there are three pieces, the fabric and low weight of which are commented on in the literature, ranging from 1.16 to 1.61g. Could these be fractional types? Or a kind of make-weight used to bring an underweight *fals* up to the 30-*kharrūba* standard?

ʻAbd al-Malik b. Yazīd is the first Abbasid official in whose name we have both coins and *fals* weights. Of the latter two denominations are known, of 23 and 24 *kharrūba* (4.485, 4.68g) (see Nos 178-80). Where they are to be placed within his two governorships is unknown: anonymous *fals* weights may have been issued under him as well. There are also two types of coin, the more common of which is dated 133 and belongs to his first period of office: 106 specimens of this type range between 2.63 and 6.16g; 33 (31 per cent) are between 4.00 and 4.49g, 84 (79 per cent) between 3.50 and 4.99g and only 12 (11 per cent) under 3.5g. The notable point here is that the underlying standard is quite different from that of the Umayyad issues discussed above. The peak of weights is not heavier than the standard of the glass weights but it is not far from them. ʻAbd al-Malik's other copper issue is undated; only 8 weights are available and they produce a profile similar to that of the dated issue. Coming, after a considerable interval, to Maṭar, the only weights are of 36 *kharrūba* (theoretically 7.02g, though the known specimens, Balog 1976, 533-4, point to a standard of c. 6.90g). There are two issues of coin which appear to be on different standards. The most common is ornamented with a spray like the one on the reverse of Maṭar's *dīnār* weights (see No. 284). The main peak, 13 out of 25 specimens (52 per cent) is between 7.50 and 8.49g, though there is a subsidiary one (6 pieces, 24 per cent) at 6.50-6.99g. Only 3 are under 6.50g; 16 (64 per cent) are over 7.00g. Here again the majority are heavier than the weights; if some are a little worn the effect would originally have been even more striking. Maṭar's other issue is the one with *mithqāl* in the legend mentioned previously. Fourteen weights fall between 5.54 and 7.39g. The profile is rather flat but would seem to indicate a standard considerably below that of the other issue. For Ibrāhīm b. Ṣāliḥ we have two issues of weights, of 36 and 30 *kharrūba* (7.02, 5.85g) which may belong to either of his governorships (see Nos 318-19. The only coins are 7 specimens dated 167, the beginning of the first governorship. The weights are so widely scattered between 5.24 and 8.95g that one can only say that the issue was fairly heavy, comparable perhaps to Maṭar's heavier one. The last of the named glass weights to consider are those of Ṣāliḥ b. Muslim. It is not clear how the four denominations were distributed within his long period of activity but all are very small: 14, 12, 11 and 10 *kharrūba* (2.73, 2.34, 2.145, 1.95g) (see No. 333). Ṣāliḥ b. Muslim acted as executive in connection with glass stamps under Maḥfūẓ b. Sulaymān and certain of Maḥfūẓ's copper issues also bear the name of an 'executive' called Ṣāliḥ, who may reasonably be presumed to be Ṣāliḥ b. Muslim. There are differences in the weights of the three issues of these coins, of which we have an adequate number for investigation but Miles's types 17 and 18 are similar in weight and are here considered together. Among 29 specimens the lowest weight is 1.15g, the highest 3.46g: 11 (38 per cent) are between 2.50 and 2.99g, 25 (86 per cent) over 2g. Miles's type 20 is distinctly lighter, ranging from 1.20 to 2.44g, but the 10 weights do not reveal a pronounced peak. For the present discussion, what emerges is that the coins of Maḥfūẓ are far smaller than the earlier issues discussed here and that this is parallelled by the low denominations of the *fals* weights of about the same period.

Finally, there is the anonymous Umayyad issue marked 18 *qīrāt*. Only 8 weights are published but, for what it is worth, they are curiously bunched; 3 are between 2.65 and 2.80g, 3 between 4.54 and 4.62g and the remaining two are of 3.3 (*sic*) and 4.13g. None are therefore very close to 18 *qīrāt* - 3.51g - and half are conspicuously lighter. Conceivably in this case the lower weights represent a half denomination, for the centre of the reverse bears a hexagram inscribed in a circle, a device which also appears on an anonymous issue of 9-*qīrāt* half-*fals* weights of similar date (see Nos 413-4).

The metrological picture is far from tidy but does appear to indicate some kind of correlation between the two series, glass and copper. That the copper was actually struck to a very precise weight standard seems most unlikely. However, *fulūs* could still have been checked individually against weights if the precise weight of each coin was not important but it was required to be equal to or higher than the corresponding glass weight. Perhaps it was also acceptable to use more than one piece to make up a '*fals*-worth'. This admittedly seems a laborious and complicated procedure but in the absence of any other explanation for the *fals* weights, and given the evidence that the *kharrūba* system was applied to coins, a theory that links the two seems necessary.

Other small disks

In addition to the categories discussed above, which are all weights of one sort or another, there are a number of types of small glass disks which are shown not to be weights by the fact that the weights of different specimens from the same die vary greatly and seemingly, within certain limits, at random. These have, of course, no denomination; most of them are either anonymous or bear the names of unidentified persons. Within the same two classes there are also many types where there is insufficient data to tell whether they are weights or not; the weight of a single piece of an isolated type is of very little value as evidence on the point; even if it is near to a well-known standard, that of the *dīnār* for instance, the possibility of coincidence always exists.

What function the non-metrological disks served is an open question but they may be conveniently referred to as tokens. It should be emphasized at the same time that to call them tokens need not imply that they were used as token money, though that is a possibility that can not be dismissed. In a wider sense tokens might include such objects as entry passes, gambling chips or receipts for deposits, say of clothes at a bath-house. The whole group need not have been produced for the same purpose and other kinds of use are quite possible; some could, for instance, have been gaming pieces, or jetons like the medieval European ones used for financial calculations. All this, however, is entirely speculative and merely put forward to indicate the range of possibilities.

As an example, the common disks of Abu 'l-Ḥazan (?) may be mentioned. The seven specimens in the British Museum weigh from 4.11 to 7.98g and within that range there is no obvious grouping (Nos 374-80). The related type of Ḥazan (?) is represented by two pieces weighing 3.91 and 4.43g (Nos 385-6). Other such types are those of the pairs of brothers, Idrīs and Mūsā and Zakariyy and ʿĪsā (see Nos 383, 387) and the anonymous type represented by Nos 510-1, even though the legend includes the word *wafā* ('honest dealing'), which often occurs on weights and measures. Even within the official series there is one issue of disks which are evidently not weights, that on which the legend consists simply of the name ʿUbaydallāh b. al-Ḥabḥāb. The weights of the six known specimens range from 3.38 to 4.52g (see the commentary on No. 50 and Balog 1976, 87-8, where the pieces are listed). Similar disks without denominations are known for other early Umayyad officials but in such small numbers that it is premature to judge whether they are weights or not. The earliest, of Qurra, weighs 4.43g (Balog 1976, 3). The others are of Usāma b. Zayd and Yazīd b. Abi Yazīd (see commentary on No. 111).

3. *RAṬL*-SYSTEM WEIGHTS

The second major category of early stamped glass objects consists of the larger weights on *raṭl* standards. At times it is convenient to refer to these, together with the multiple coin weights discussed previously, as heavy weights. The word *raṭl* itself is connected with the Greek *litra*. *Raṭls* of widely different weight were employed in the Islamic world but, though a number of *raṭl* standards are represented on the glass, the variation among most of them is, though distinct, not enormous, the *raṭl* and its fractions supplying the kind of weights required for ordinary retail transactions. In this sense the *raṭl* corresponds to the pound. The ounce is similarly represented by the *wuqïyya*, the two words being in fact of common origin. The literary sources mention occasional exceptions but generally there were twelve *wuqiyyas* to the *raṭl*. For the *raṭl* systems represented by glass weights, where there is evidence for both denominations, this customary ratio obtains.

Almost without exception the *raṭl*-system weights can be classified as being of one of two formal types for which Miles proposed the useful names disk weight and ring weight. The typical disk weight is a quite thick circle of glass with a flat, if not necessarily smooth, bottom and a circular stamp impressed in the centre of the top. The pressure of the stamp usually causes the rest of the top to bulge upwards and outwards, giving, viewed from above, rather the effect of an inflated tyre round a flat central hub. The proportion of the top occupied by the stamp varies; it is usually smaller on the large pieces. Varieties occur with rectangular stamps and with more than one stamp. When a second smaller stamp is applied on the rim the disk becomes distorted. When, as was the usual practice in the later second century AH, several stamps were employed side by side, variations on the basic disk were produced. The resulting ellipses, lozenges and quatrefoils can hardly be called disks but it is convenient to classify pieces of such shapes as disk weights.

The salient feature of the ring weight is that it has quite a large hole through it. The typical shape may be taken to be roughly rectangular, the length and height being about equal, or not far from it, and the width about half or two-thirds of that figure. The hole goes through the middle of the sides. It may, as has been suggested, have been used to suspend the weights from cords though, in any case, the ring weight form has the advantage of providing the user with a much better grip than the disk weight. Sometimes the pressure of the stamps has made the weight more squat and in the early period the top was often a little shorter than the bottom, giving a trapezoid profile. There are other perceptible changes of style at different periods. On later weights of both shapes tool marks, of various types, are sometimes found impressed round the stamps.

The metrology of the *raṭl*-system weights

The question of the *raṭl* standard or standards represented by the glass pieces has long been discussed. For a long time the number of intact pieces known was very small and since, as it is now possible to tell, a number of different standards were represented it is not surprising that no coherent picture emerged. There was an obvious approach, to attempt to match the actual weights with literary evidence for the *raṭl* and *wuqiyya*, but it has so far been productive of confusion rather than anything else. The literary data, the main collection of which is still Sauvaire's great nineteenth-century compilation, is copious but of diverse origins and quality and mostly much later than the glass weights. There is very little from before the tenth century AD, nothing, certainly, that would lead one to suspect the complex story of the issue of *raṭls* of different standards in eighth and ninth century Egypt which has recently been revealed from the study of the actual pieces by Balog. A bewildering variety of *raṭls* are recorded as having been used in the Islamic world and it is usually possible to find one which, give or take a certain amount, will accommodate any given weight over a wide range, but what has been lacking is proof of, or even plausible argument for, any historical connection between the actual weights which survive and the literary data. That such a connection exists in some cases is very probable but, in the present state of the study of the *raṭl*, to say that a piece may be on the standard recorded in a much later work seems to lead nowhere. Though the literary sources, which provide important information on other units of weight for which the evidence is less complicated, cannot in the end be left out of account, the literary approach has been deliberately ignored in this catalogue, as far as *raṭls* and *wuqiyyas* are concerned.

In the present century some slow progress was made in a different way, by assembling groups of pieces with related weights. Petrie (p. 13 and pl. xxvi), for example, classified together, for the most part correctly, a number of pieces of various denominations which he realized represented a *raṭl* system. He had in fact spotted what is now called the Abbasid system. Similarly, a group of three pieces with non-Egyptian provenances were seen by Ettinghausen to belong on one standard, which Balog has since called the Syrian Umayyad standard. However, the great leap forward, as it were, on this line of approach was taken only recently by Balog in the introduction to the catalogue of his collection (1976, pp. 10-23). His large and splendid collection itself includes a remarkable number of intact weights and with their evidence Balog was able to demonstrate the existence of three different *raṭl* standards employed in eighth and ninth century Egypt and associated with particular periods and particular series of officials. The existence of the standards, named by Balog the Umayyad, *raṭl-kabīr* and Abbasid standards, is incontrovertible; further confirmation is provided by pieces in the British Museum's collection. Nevertheless, it is possible to criticize Balog's data and to some extent expand on his presentation. In particular, his misattribution of two pieces on the Abbasid standard (discussed below) has obscured the fact that the three systems were each in use at a different period. They do not overlap. We cannot of course be certain that glass weights were not issued on more than one *raṭl* standard at the same time. It is possible, certainly, that the Umayyad commodity weights, also discussed below, were not on the 'Umayyad' *raṭl* standard. However, with the three ordinary *raṭl* systems, if they may be called that, for which the body of evidence is considerable, the lack of mutual overlap is conspicuous. As in the case of the *fals* weights, we are faced with a chronological series: evidently from time to time, for reasons that remain unknown, the Egyptian bureaucracy chose to change the *raṭl* standard.

In addition to the three Egyptian standards identified by Balog there is in fact evidence for the official use of several others. A fourth one was employed, briefly it would seem, in AH 226, and in the last quarter of the second century, in the quite long period between attested use of the *raṭl-kabīr* and Abbasid systems, several other standards were employed. Before going through the particular standards in detail it may be pointed out that the complexity of the picture is not without its wider implications: any attempt to use a quantitative approach to the history of early Islamic Egypt using literary or documentary references to *raṭls tout court* without taking the changes in the standard into account is likely to be hopelessly misleading.

The Umayyad raṭl *system of Egypt*

The evidence for the earliest of the *raṭl* systems represented on the Egyptian glass weights, Balog's Umayyad system, is particularly clear. The earliest intact piece published so far is a *wuqiyya* of Ḥayyān b. Shurayḥ (Balog 1976, 36) but there is little doubt that the system was employed under Usāma b. Zayd and it was probably already in use under Qurra b. Sharīk, with whose appointment as Governor in 90/709 the issue of glass stamps may be said to have got seriously under way. No change was made at the time of the Abbasid conquest and the Umayyad system remained in use for more than thirty years after the arrival of the new dynasty: there is an almost complete *raṭl* of Yaḥyā b. Dā'ūd in the Balog collection and it is reasonably certain from damaged pieces such as No. 316 that it survived through the finance directorship of Ismā'īl b. Ibrāhīm (164/780-1), to be replaced by the *raṭl-kabīr* system during the first governorship of Ibrāhīm b. Ṣāliḥ.

The majority of the surviving heavy weights of the period, as of all periods, are broken but, thanks to the relatively consistent method of production, the durable glass and the informative inscriptions, one can be reasonably certain that most of the damaged pieces, with the possible exception of the commodity weights discussed below, are on the Umayyad standard. There are almost no puzzles.

The common denominations were the *raṭl*, half-*raṭl*, quarter-*raṭl* and *wuqiyya*. A single double-*raṭl* has been described (Balog 1976, 137) and for a time under the Abbasids sixth-*wuqiyyas* were also issued. Of these last, the earliest known are of 'Abd al-Raḥmān b. Yazīd, the latest of Wāḍiḥ (see No. 227). With one or two exceptions the ordinary *raṭl*-system weights up to the time of the last Umayyad Governor, 'Abd al-Malik b. Marwān, are disk weights. From then on the ring-weight form was generally, though not exclusively, preferred for the *raṭl*; half-*raṭl* ring weights were occasionally produced, but otherwise the lower denominations are disk weights. The sixth-*wuqiyya* pieces must of course be classified with the 'heavy' weights but they weigh less than the largest *fals* weights and resemble coin weights in appearance. Of course, coins weights are in fact small disk weights.

As for the weight of the Umayyad *raṭl*, Balog has listed three intact and two almost intact *raṭls*, the lightest weighing 431.87g, the heaviest 441g. The average is 435.767g. Curiously, two of the best preserved pieces are the lightest. Allowing for the damaged pieces these data point to a *raṭl* of c. 440g. No intact halves or quarters have been described and the largest group of undamaged pieces is of *wuqiyyas*. Ten intact and unchipped ones are known, including three in the present collection. They range in weight from 36.50 to 37.90g. The average is 37.165g, which implies a *raṭl* of 445.98g. A slightly higher figure is produced by the four intact sixth-*wuqiyyas*, which vary from 6.21 to 6.26g and give an average of 6.2375g, on the basis of which the *wuqiyya* should come to 37.425 and the *raṭl* to 449.1g. It is noticeable that, as seems to be the case with pieces on the later Abbasid system, there is a small but distinct discrepancy between high and low denominations. Either the high ones are usually slightly underweight or the low ones slightly overweight. Evening out the difference, reasonably close figures for the standard would be: *raṭl* 444g, *wuqiyya* 37g, sixth-*wuqiyya* 6.166g.

Commodity weights
Two other series of weights were issued during the Umayyad period to be used for particular commodities. All the known specimens are ring weights; the form was probably preferred because it distinguished the commodity weights from the ordinary *raṭl* weights, which at that period were nearly all disk weights.

The commonest of the two series is that for meat (Ar. *laḥm*) of which specimens are known of officials from Qurra to ʿAbd al-Malik b. Marwān. The denominations appear to be confined to the half-*raṭl*, *raṭl* and double-*raṭl*. In the absence of any intact or nearly intact examples it remains uncertain whether the *raṭl* by which meat was sold was the same as the ordinary *raṭl* of the time or not. However, to judge from the proportions of damaged specimens, if it was different, it is likely to have been a little lighter.

The commodity named on the second series (*ʿBB/ʿBAB*, discused at length under No. 90) has not been satisfactorily identified. The only known denomination is the *raṭl* and no intact specimen has yet been described.

The raṭl-kabīr *system*
As is discussed in detail under Nos 321-2, it appears that the Umayyad *raṭl* was replaced by a *raṭl kabīr*, or great *raṭl*, during the first governorship of Ibrāhīm b. Ṣāliḥ, that is between AH 165 and 167 (AD 781-4). On pieces belonging to the great-*raṭl* system the denomination is followed by the word *kabīr* ('great'). There is evidence that the system remained in use for something over ten years but after that, though weights with *kabīr* after the denomination are known, some at least of them belong to different *raṭl* systems. The evidence concerning such types is discussed below; for the present we are only concerned with the system introduced under Ibrāhīm b. Ṣāliḥ.

On this system the *raṭls* are ring weights, the half-*raṭls* ring weights or disk weights and the lower denominations disk weights. *Wuqiyyas* exist die-linked to the larger denominations but they are all broken. A quarter-*raṭl kabīr* of Mūsā b. ʿĪsā, probably from his first governorship in 171-2/787-8, weighs 123.35g (Balog 1976, 589). A half-*raṭl* of Ibrāhīm b. Ṣāliḥ in the present collection (No. 320) comes to 249g. Two *raṭls* of the same official weigh 492.6 and 493.63g (Miles 1963 II, 33; Balog 1976, 572). The pieces of Ibrāhīm all belong to his first governorship. Together with the quarter-*raṭl* they point to a *raṭl* of 490-500g. A *raṭl* from Ibrāhīm's second governorship, with an actual weight of 508g and an estimated 5-10g lost through chipping, is a puzzle (No. 325, *q.v.*).

The late second century AH
The period after the latest date for which the *raṭl-kabīr* system is attested, roughly equivalent to the last quarter of the second century AH, presents a considerable problem. The scanty evidence shows that weights continued to be issued. On some the denomination is qualified by *kabīr* while on others it is not. The few surviving intact pieces point to the existence of several different standards but a full sorting out of the problem depends on the production of further evidence. However, three cases in which there seems to be a little firm ground to begin to build on seem worth mentioning here:

1. Casanova 1893, 1 is a small oblong disk weight of Isḥāq b. Sulaymān, who was Governor and Finance Director in 177-8/793-4. That it is not an isolated freak is shown by the existence of another example from the same die which, though damaged, is of similar dimensions (Balog 1976, 619). The intact piece is clearly marked *wuqiyya* (*pace* Casanova *et al.*) and weighs 12.2g, which would normally be expected to imply the existence of a very small *raṭl* of c. 146.4g.

2. No. 344 below is of Mālik b. Dalham (Governor and Finance Director 192-3/

808). It is marked *wuqiyya kabīr* and weighs 44.6g. Though it is not chipped almost the entire surface has decayed away; the consequent loss of weight is difficult to estimate; 46g for the original weight is probably a low guess. Somewhat similar is a disk weight of Ḥātim b. Harthama b. A'yan who was Governor and Finance Director in 194-5/810-1, shortly after Mālik (Launois 1969, 18 = Balog 1976, 689a). This piece has an impression of a second small round stamp which may have born the denomination but lacks a legible legend. Otherwise it is in good condition; its weight has been given as 46.7 and 47.67g. These two pieces point to a *wuqiyya* standard of c. 47g and a *raṭl* of c. 564g. They are too heavy for the earlier *raṭl-kabīr* standard of Ibrāhīm b. Ṣāliḥ, the *wuqiyya* of which, taking 500g for the *raṭl*, should weigh about 41.666g. Balog has classified the piece of Ḥātim and a second one of Ṣāliḥ b. Muslim (which may indeed be relevant) as 1½-*wuqiyya* weights on the Abbasid standard. This seems very unlikely since the denomination is otherwise unknown, the piece of Mālik is marked *wuqiyya kabīr*, and there is no evidence that the Abbasid standard was introduced so early. The *raṭl* of this standard may perhaps be represented by No. 538 in the present collection. Although its stamps are largely illegible there are grounds for assigning it to about the relevant date and when intact it would have weighed something close to 560g.

3. There is a common type of anonymous ring weight with the denomination marked as *wuqiyya kabīr* (e.g. Nos 460-3, *qq.v.*). They are datable to the end of the second century but are far too heavy to belong in the *raṭl-kabīr* series or to be classified with the *wuqiyyas* discussed under 2 above. Seven intact or nearly intact specimens range from 59.6 to 66.7g. The average is 63.33g. Balog has suggested that they are in fact double-*wuqiyyas* on the Abbasid standard. Their weights are consistent with such an assumption but it cannot be accepted in view of the relative abundance of the type and the fact that such a denomination would be unnecessary. Furthermore it is unlikely that the Abbasid *raṭl* system was in use at the time they were produced.

The Abbasid raṭl *system*

Balog, who named and first convincingly identified the Abbasid *raṭl* system, placed its introduction in the early Abbasid period, in the Caliphate of al-Manṣūr. However, it seems that this is much too early. What would be the earliest example, if it was in fact of Muḥammad b. al-Ash'ath (Balog 1976, 385), is, as explained in the commentary to No. 352, of the third century AH. The only other supposedly early piece (Balog 1976, 400) attributed to Nawfal b. Furāt is not illustrated, presumably because it is in poor condition, but the legend as transcribed differs from Nawfal's standard types - notably in giving him the title Amir - which, together with the very fact that the weight does appear to be on the Abbasid standard, seems to justify the rejection of this attribution too.

When these two pieces are thus disposed of it can be seen that the Abbasid *raṭl* was introduced much later, in the third century AH (ninth AD). Intact pieces are known of 'Īsā b. Manṣūr, who was Governor of Egypt for the first time in 216/831-2, but for the most part, or entirely, they are likely to belong to the latter part of his second governorship which lasted from 229-33/844-7. The reason for thinking so is that the small die used on most, perhaps all, of his own pieces is the natural pair to a larger rectangular die on which his name follows that of Ītākh, who became Overlord of Egypt after the death of Ashinās in 230/844-5. The earliest certain date for the Abbasid *raṭl*, then, is the governorship of Mālik b. Kaydur, 224-6/839-1. The standard remained in use until at least the time of Aḥmad b. Ṭūlūn, though it appears to have been briefly set aside for the standard of Muḥammad b. Bastām in 226 (see below).

Weights which are certainly on the Abbasid system fall into two groups, those with the names of identified officials, which do not bear denominations, and anonymous ones with denominations. Intact specimens of the latter group are all *wuqiyyas* or half-*wuqiyyas*; it is not in fact certain that anonymous types of the larger denominations were issued. As is demonstrated below, the weights of the two groups do not differ significantly: both are on the same standard. Thus it is possible to assign denominations to the pieces without them.

The anonymous pieces are quite well made, which, together with the fact that the dies are known from a number of specimens, suggests that they are official issues. Their dating depends on their association with the datable ones and on their very short legends. These are in a larger and bolder Kufic than that of the datable group in general and, though the evidence is admittedly slim, they are perhaps to be placed before the datable ones, at the beginning of the series, where there otherwise appears to be something of a gap in the issue of official heavy weights.

In calculating the weight of the Abbasid *raṭl*, Balog included in his data a number of dubious pieces, particularly for the higher denominations. In recalculating the figures it seems preferable to rely entirely on the known, here defined as the two groups which have already been mentioned: pieces of known officials and pieces with correct denominations, though in the latter case an exception has been made for half-*wuqiyyas* stamped from *wuqiyya* dies such as No. 456. Excluded therefore are all illegible pieces, all pieces of unknown persons, all pieces, with the exception just mentioned, with denominations that have to be assumed to be wrong in order to fit them into the system and some others which are damaged or of dubious attribution. Most of the data used here in working out the various denominations are those given by Balog, after the rejection of his uncertain material. To them is added the evidence of a few other published pieces, the relevant unpublished pieces in the British Museum and an anonymous half-*wuqiyya* in the Fitzwilliam Museum. The results, it may be noted in advance, are more consistent than Balog's both within and between the different denominations and give a rather lower figure for the *raṭl* than his 395g.

The denominations issued on the Abbasid standard are the double-*raṭl*, *raṭl*, half-*raṭl*, quarter-*raṭl*, *wuqiyya* and, first attested in this series, the half-*wuqiyya*. (There is no evidence, on the criteria used here, for the other, abnormal, denominations listed by Balog.) The ring-weight form is invariably used from the quarter-*raṭl* upwards, and on occasions for the smaller denominations, though *wuqiyya* and half-*wuqiyya* disk weights are more common. All the anonymous *wuqiyyas* and half-*wuqiyyas* are disk weights. Owing to the use of less durable glass the majority of the pieces have suffered some surface devitrification. The actual weights of the pieces, however, seem to show that superficially extensive decay of this kind often involves very little loss of weight, less, certainly in most cases, than the tolerance the craftsmen were working to.

Coming to the actual weights, three double-*raṭls* qualify to be considered. The best is the British Museum's No. 371, perfect but for devitrification, which weighs 753g. Balog 1976, 724 (p. 262) with an actual weight of 753.53g is slightly chipped and was originally a few grammes heavier. Petrie, 238, said to be badly worn, is lighter, at 737.71g. The average of the figures given is 748.08g, but evidently the true figure for the double-*raṭl* should be taken to be a little higher. For the *raṭl*, the best preserved example is the British Museum's No. 370, with surface devitrification, which weighs 377g. No. 352, which is slightly chipped, weighs 361g.

The evidence becomes more plentiful for the smaller denominations. For the half-*raṭl* it is remarkably consistent. The five acceptable specimens range from 188.60 to 191.83g, giving an average of 190.11g. Eight quarter-*raṭls* vary from 91.0 to 94.08g; the average is 92.527g. For the smaller denominations the data for the datable and anonymous groups can be compared. Eight *wuqiyyas* of the first category weigh from 30.90 to 33.22g, five anonymous ones from 30.45 to 31.92g. The averages are, respectively, 31.706 and 31.322g, the overall average being 31.558g. The corresponding figures for the half-*wuqiyya* are as follows: nineteen datable pieces from 15.51 to 16.52g; average 15.835g; five anonymous pieces from 15.00 to 15.74g; average 15.460g; overall average 15.757g.

More evidence is obviously required for the highest denominations, but it is possible that the series is distorted in the same way as the Umayyad one, i.e. that the weights of the highest denominations may have tended to be slightly light in comparison with the lower ones. As a working compromise the following may be suggested as, approximately, the standard of each denomination: double-*raṭl* 760g; *raṭl* 380g; half-*raṭl* 190g; quarter-*raṭl* 95g; *wuqiyya* 31.666g; half-*wuqiyya* 15.833g.

The* raṭl *system of Muḥammad b. Basṭām

The *raṭl* standard which it is convenient to call after the obscure official asociated with it is represented by only two pieces, an intact half-*wuqiyya* disk weight (No. 345, *q.v.*) and a slightly damaged half-*raṭl* ring weight. Both pieces have denominations and are dated, almost certainly, 226. Muḥammad b. Basṭām's name follows that of Ashinās, who was Overlord of Egypt at that date. The half-*wuqiyya* weighs 33.96g, implying a *wuqiyya* of 68 and a *raṭl* of 816g. The present weight of the half-*raṭl* is 398.53g. This standard thus comes to a little over double the Abbasid standard. The latter is known to have been in use just before and just after the issue of Muḥammad b. Basṭām's series and it appears that his heavier standard was only employed for a short time.

The fringe

As with most other categories of the early stamps, there are a number of the heavy weights which, for metrological and stylistic reasons, it is difficult or impossible to fit into the main official series, even though they seem to belong to the period covered by the present catalogue. They differ from the opaque glass weights of the Fatimid period identified by Jungfleisch (1929a) and also from the small macaroon-shaped disk weights which may be even later. A few examples will give an indication of the extensive metrological *terra incognita* which the fringe types reveal.

1. No. 382, a quarter-*raṭl* of the unidentified Aḥmad b. Dīnār, weighs 74.1g, giving a *wuqiyya* of nearly 25g and a rather small *raṭl* of just under 300g.

2. No. 397, of ʻAlī b. Muḥammad, has no denomination and weighs 346g. The script and legend date it reasonably securely to the middle of the second century AH, but it does not belong on the Umayyad standard in use at that time, though it could just be a *raṭl* on the standard known to have been in use in Syria during the Umayyad period.

3. Two intact or nearly intact ring weights issued in the name of one Yaḥyā bear the denomination quarter-*raṭl* (Petrie, 174; Balog 1976, 791). Though the dies are different the legends are very similar. The weights are 233.46 and 237.02g, giving nearly 950g for the *raṭl*, a considerably heavier figure than any of the established official standards. Balog has classified these pieces as half-*raṭls* on the *raṭl-kabīr* system but, in addition to the fact that *rubʻ raṭl* is written on them, they are too light for half-*raṭls kabīr*.

4. Petrie, 175, anonymous, also bears the denomination quarter-*raṭl* but weighs 188g, implying a *raṭl* of c. 750g. That its weight is not incorrect is to some extent confirmed by the weights of the British Museum's specimens from the same die (Nos 465-6) which, though much damaged, are obviously too large to belong on the Umayyad, *raṭl-kabīr* or Abbasid standards. This *raṭl* would appear to be about double the Abbasid *raṭl*.

4. VESSEL STAMPS

The vessel stamps were formed by placing a lump of molten glass on a vessel, usually at the rim, and stamping it with an iron die. The lump was flattened into roughly circular shape and became fused to the vessel. Occasionally stamps were placed lower down the wall of the vessel and probably sometimes on handles. The edges of the molten glass naturally cooled faster and the pressure of the die was relieved in the centre, which remained hot longer and bulged out at the back, together with the wall of the vessel at that point. As a result, nearly all the vessel stamps have a characteristic bubble-like bulge, usually elongated in the vertical direction, on the back.

The use of such appliqué vessel stamps as a decorative technique was of course familiar to glass-makers of many times and places, among them, as is well known, those of Hellenistic Egypt. However, it does not seem to have been pointed out in the context of the Islamic stamps that the use of vessel stamps to certify the correctness of official measures, like the use of glass coin weights, has precedents in the Egypt of the Byzantine period. A number of small vessel stamps have been published which bear monograms or Greek legends similar to those on the Byzantine exagia or coin weights (e.g. Fremersdorf, 703-5). The Department of Oriental Antiquities itself has two such pieces (OA + 4142, 5221), one of which bears the name Anastasiou, written out in full. Though they do not bear denominations, the similarity of these vessel stamps to the exagia, which evidently did serve an official metrological function, indicates that the stamps were used on official measures. The practice continued, or at any rate was revived, after the Muslim conquest, though under Islam the official use of vessel stamps, like that of glass weights, was elaborated and the legends made much more informative.

The actual information given varied and, in general, became more limited as time passed. At times more than one stamp was used on a single vessel. This practice was parallelled on the heavy weights and the various combinations and permutations found on both groups are for the most part discussed under dies and die-links. The remainder of this section is mainly concerned with the types of measures that were issued and with the two minor categories of anonymous counterstamps and decorative vessel stamps.

Qisṭ-system stamps

The word *qisṭ*, derived from the Greek *xestes*, may mean 'measuring', a measure in a general sense, or a defined measure of capacity. As with many units of weight and measure, *qisṭs* of different values are recorded in the Arabic metrological literature. An intact measure with an anonymous *qisṭ* stamp which, though otherwise unrecorded, is of convincingly early appearance, has been published by Day, but its capacity of 50cc is so small that it is unlikely to represent the ordinary *qisṭ* or *qisṭs* of the eighth and ninth centuries, especially since half and quarter-*qisṭ* measures were also issued. As we shall see there is some reason to believe that the same *qisṭ* did not remain in use throughout the eighth and ninth centuries, but the fragile nature of the glass measures imposes a certain limit to their size and it can probably be taken that the various ordinary *qisṭs* were of the order of the pint or the litre.

The main series begins with Qurra b. Sharīk. Over a long time most Finance Directors issued measures for all three denominations, *qisṭ*, half and quarter. It seems likely that at the beginning the ordinary *qisṭ*-system series to some extent dovetailed with another one for the same denominations but specified to be for olive oil; this point is discussed below. Otherwise the *qisṭ* series is well documented until the time of Ismāʻīl b. Ibrāhīm (164/780-1). As has been mentioned, under Ibrāhīm b. Ṣāliḥ, who controlled finance after Ismāʻīl, the Umayyad *raṭl* was replaced by the *raṭl kabīr* and it seems that a *qisṭ kabīr* was also introduced at the same time. The main evidence consists of anonymous stamps on a *qisṭ-kabīr* system (Balog 1976, 919-21). Only the *qisṭ* denomination has been illustrated but it is strikingly similar in appearance to the denomination stamps used for the *raṭl-kabīr*-system weights. Vessel stamps with the names of the Finance Directors of the *raṭl-kabīr* period and of the executives associated with them are known and a use can be found for them if we assume that the system of stamps applied on measures was the same as that on weights, i.e. that an anonymous denomination stamp was used in combination with the Finance Director's command stamp and an executive stamp.

A few vessel stamps are known from the end of the second century but in this respect, as in others, the evidence is too fragmentary and it is once again in connection with a well-established series of weights, those of the Abbasid *raṭl* system, that the traces of a corresponding system of measures can be detected. As has been said, the stamps used on the datable Abbasid heavy weights do not have denominations. The common pattern was for each official or set of officials to employ two stamps, one large and one small; for some time a large stamp with the Caliph's name was also in use. On the weights the small stamp was used on the smallest denominations, the larger one alone on the middle-sized ones while on the *raṭl* and double-*raṭl* either the official's large stamp was used beside the Caliph's one or, when the Caliph's stamp was not in use, the official's large stamp was impressed twice. Since the dies had no denominations they could equally well be used on vessel stamps. Vessel stamps of all three categories occur and most of them can by now be die-linked to impressions on weights. Evidently, therefore, there was a system of measures with the different denominations distinguished by the size and number of the stamps on them, for example with the small stamps on the lowest denominations. It is surely safe to deduce that this is a *qisṭ* system and not unlikely that the *qisṭ* itself is a new one, introduced at the same time as the Abbasid *raṭl*.

Qisṭs of wine and olive oil

There are two series of vessel stamps on which the denominations *qisṭ*, half and quarter are accompanied by the name of a commodity. The series for wine (*ṭilā*, commented on under No. 24) was short-lived. It is possible that a *qisṭ* of different capacity was used for wine, but the existence of special wine measures may just as easily be explained by assuming that wine was sold in special places for which the measures were produced.

The distribution of the series for olive oil calls for a more complicated explanation. They were only issued in the Umayyad period, the last official to produce them being al-Qāsim b. ʻUbaydallāh and he only in the early part of his term of office (see No. 103). The olive oil stamps of earlier Finance Directors are numerous, while anonymous ones are limited to a few types, on most of which the word *qisṭ* does not appear. None are known for fractions of the *qisṭ*. Whatever the explanation of the anonymous types it is clear that the full series of *qisṭ*-system stamps for olive oil was abandoned in the time of al-Qāsim. A problem arises when the output of the olive oil series by the early Finance Directors is compared with their output of ordinary *qisṭ*-system types. Two of them, Ḥayyān b. Shurayḥ and Yazīd b. Abī Yazīd, though issuing olive oil stamps in quantity, have no ordinary *qisṭ*-system stamps at all. (Such a categorical statement may appear rash but, while new stamps will continue to turn up, the evidence of die identities shows that common ones should by now by represented. One stamp of Ḥayyān has at times been identified as a quarter-*qisṭ* but the reading is unsatisfactory.) For Qurra, on the other hand, the complete *qisṭ* series is attested but no stamps for olive oil. A possible explanation for the failure of some officials to issue ordinary *qisṭ*-system measures is, obviously, that there was no need for them because olive oil stamps were functionally the same thing, that is that ordinary *qisṭ*-system stamps were in practice used exclusively, or nearly so, for measuring out olive oil. This would presumably also apply to the period after the special olive oil series ceased to be issued. For some of the early officials, Usāma b. Zayd, ʿUbaydallāh b. al-Ḥabḥāb and of course his son al-Qāsim, both series are represented but there are some indications, mainly from variations in the legends, that the two series may not have been produced at the same time and that one series could have replaced the other in the course of a particular tenure of the finance directorship.

Commodity stamps

Besides those for wine and olive oil already discussed, there are numerous vessel stamps for a variety of other commodities. Several different denominations of capacity are found on them. Clarified butter (*samn*) and honey (*ʿasal*) were sold by the *qisṭ*, though stamps for both are rare and no fractional ones are known. Fat (*duhn*) was sold by measure, but with denominations on the *raṭl* system: *raṭl*, half-*raṭl* and *wuqiyya*. There are a few anonymous stamps for other commodities with *raṭl*-system denominations. An unusual measure of Ḥayyān b. Shurayḥ for millet beer (*usqurqa*) is marked *qadaḥ*, or 'cup' (Miles 1956). However, most commodity stamps have the designation *mikyala*, meaning 'measure of capacity' or, less commonly, its synonym *mikyāl*. *Mikyalas* for many commodities were sometimes marked with a price, nearly always one *fals*. The case for saying so is made later, but the fact that *mikyalas* for commodities that may be presumed to have different values bear the same price shows that the word was not being used for a single specific measure of capacity and that there were *mikyalas* of different size for different commodities. The *mikyāl al-kabīr*, or great *mikyāl*, in use for a short time in the early Abbasid period, was presumably exceptional and had a definite capacity (see Nos 166-7).

The pharmaceutical theory

For several decades a particular explanation of the function of commodity stamps has held the field. What may be called the pharmaceutical theory can be summed up in the words of Miles, as he first put it forward in 1951 (b, p. 50): 'they [the commodity stamps] were attached to the cups and bowls in which druggists measured and doubtless sold their pharmaceuticals ... These containers were, in fact, the 8th century equivalent of the jars and bottles in which we buy proprietary products or receive our doctors' prescriptions from the pharmacy today.' Miles restated the theory on more than one occasion (esp. 1960b) and it was accepted by the other major figure in the recent study of the glass stamps, Balog. Their combined authority and the glamour of the idea of oriental drugs have given the theory wide currency; it is remarkable how often people with a slight acquaintance with glass stamps in general have firmly grasped the point that the commodities are supposed to be drugs. Mild demurrals may on occasion have been expressed (Launois 1958b, 232-3) but no sustained criticism of the pharmaceutical theory ever seems to have been put forward. The question is long overdue for re-examination, for when the evidence for the theory and its inherent plausibility are seriously considered there turns out to be very little of either.

It will have been noticed from the quotations that Miles's theory, as first put forward, is a double one: the measures served both to measure out the pharmacist's wares and as containers for the customers to take them away in. In later statements of the theory their use as containers is usually given greater emphasis. This aspect of the theory is influenced by a well-known literary reference, first quoted in connection with glass stamps by Casanova (1891, 95; 1893, p. 342) and mentioned by Miles himself (1948, p. 21) before he evolved the pharmaceutical theory. The Iranian traveller Nāṣir-i Khusraw (68), in his description of Cairo, mentions that the grocers, druggists and pedlars (*baqqāl*, *ʿaṭṭār*, *pīlawar*) provided receptacles for the goods they sold, whether of glass, pottery or paper; and so the customer had no need to bring his own. However, there are a number of objections to assuming that this really sheds any light on the commodity stamps. Firstly, Nāṣir-i Khusraw was writing in the middle of the eleventh century AD, while the commodity stamps had ceased to be issued over two and a half centuries earlier. Secondly, he does not say the containers were controlled by the government but rather implies the opposite: it is the retailers who supply them themselves (*az khud bidihand*). Thirdly, though his statement is positive enough, as part of an enthusiastic description of Fatimid Egypt appropriate to an Isma'īlī convert, it needs to be taken with a pinch of salt. Packaging may have been in relatively plentiful supply in Cairo bazaar but to assume that a glass container was thrown in with every purchase of an ounce of fat or copper's worth of chick peas is ridiculous even by twentieth-century standards of packaging.

At his first attempt to deal with the commodity stamps Miles (1948, pp. 21f) was aware of the last problem and rejected the idea that government containers were used in this way by grocers. To avoid assuming the existence of vast numbers of containers he, somewhat diffidently, proposed the theory that '... the use of many, if not all, of the vessels with official stamps may have been restricted to official, specifically Treasury, transactions'. He envisaged the tax collectors raising the taxes in minute quantities from the individual tax-payers and using the measures to check taxes paid in kind. The source of this idea is the statement of Balādhurī (214-5) that the taxes imposed by 'Amr b. al'Āṣ after the conquest of Egypt included, from each landowner, two *qisṭs* of olive oil and the same amount of honey and vinegar. Such taxes in kind did continue to be levied but it is known that, though assessed individually, they were collected for the government by local communities as a whole. An elaborate system of checking the small individual contributions would not have been necessary (see Dennett, pp. 114-5).

Putting forward the pharmaceutical theory, Miles dismissed his earlier one as mistaken without comment but still appears to have been concerned with the difficulty of the great quantity of containers needed if Nāṣir-i Khusraw's remarks were taken to be applicable to the vessels with commodity stamps. One attraction of the new theory was therefore that if the use of the stamped vessels was confined to pharmacists to the exclusion of other retailers there would not be a need for quite so many of them. Another minor argument brought forward was that ordinary groceries would not be sold in such small quantities as the quarter-*qisṭ*. This is plainly false. Even today olive oil is obtainable in the shops in quantities that are probably not much larger and the buying of small quantities is typical of the hand-to-mouth purchases of a poor society.

However, the main plank on which the pharmaceutical theory has survived so long is another argument. The commodities appearing on the stamps, in Miles's words again, '... had in mediaeval and ancient times medicinal and pharmaceutical uses'. There is a considerable element of truth in this statement. As Miles first made apparent, many of the substances named on the glass can be found listed in classical, medieval Arabic and even modern compilations of materia medica. In the literature of glass stamps a distinct type of commentary on the commodities has become current in which much emphasis is laid on their real or supposed medicinal properties. Many of these essays are interesting but the appearance of scholarly support they provide for the pharmaceutical theory is entirely specious, being based on the unwarranted assumption that substances that may be beneficial to the health are necessarily sold by pharmacists. As we have seen, Miles was attracted to the theory partly because it seemed unreasonable to suppose that ordinary groceries were sold in stamped containers; but it seems to have gone unnoticed that the theory demands that an equally unreasonable distinction is drawn between identical substances, depending on whether they were used medically or not, and that for the former purpose their sale was monopolized by pharmacists. Thus a patient prescribed lentils by his doctor, in accordance with the theory that they bind the bowels and calm the blood (Miles 1951b, 42, quoting Rāzī) would have lentils provided for him at the pharmacy in a standard glass container but if, on recovery, he felt like a dish of the same common vegetable he would presumably be able to buy them loose at the grocer's. This is absurd in any society, let alone that of eighth-century Egypt. To put it simply, the basic fallacy of the pharmaceutical theory is that it supposes that anything mentioned in a pharmacopoeia as having some medicinal virtue or property is *ipso facto* a drug that will be sold at pharmacies: in fact, most of the commodities concerned are certainly not substances that would normally be thought of as drugs and none of them certainly are drugs.

Even now, when medicine has a wide range of powerful drugs at its disposal, medical dictionaries do not overlook the fact that other substances may be medically useful and even the more narrowly defined modern pharmacopoeias include entries for things which are not drugs. From the fact that the *Pharmaceutical Codex* (11th edn, 1979) has entries for olive and sesame oil it would not be concluded that either was primarily a drug. Still less should similar assumptions be made about entries in medieval Arabic pharmacopoeias. Arabic medicine, as is well known, derived from the Greek and accepted the theory of the four elements and their combination in the four humours in the human body. The equilibrium of the humours in the body, equivalent to good health, was what the doctors tried to preserve or, if necessary, restore. The body's intake of food, itself composed of the four elements, would naturally alter the balance of the humours and physicians needed to know the qualities of ordinary foods as well as drugs proper. Ibn al-Bayṭār's great medical compendium has served as a major quarry for those searching for material on the medical properties of the commodities named on the stamps but it has been overlooked that the title of the work gives the clue to the unsoundness of the whole approach: it is called *The compendium of simple drugs and foods (al-Jāmiʿ li-mufradāt al-adwiya wal-aghdhiya)*.

Before coming to the actual commodities there is one minor consequence of the pharmaceutical theory that needs to be dealt with. Since they were taken to be drugs it followed that if a particular name was difficult to read the most likely place to find a clue to it would be in the pharmacopoeias. These works list hundreds - in the case of Ibn al-Bayṭār, thousands - of different substances and since the legends on stamps are written in undotted and sometimes badly formed Kufic there can be more than one possible reading. The proportion of uncertain types is in fact now quite small but at times what are, by other criteria, highly unlikely readings have been proposed because they can be supported by entries in the pharmacopoeia and even botanical works. Balog has provided a number of such suggestions but perhaps the best example is given by Miles, who rejected the previously accepted *julubbān* ('vetch') for *jullanār*, ('pomegranate flower'). Both in fact are listed by Ibn al-Bayṭār, but while the former is attested as a major item of coarse food in Egypt the latter has more attractively medical virtues. In this case there are also epigraphic reasons for preferring *julubbān* (see No. 56).

The commodities

Leaving aside the quite small proportion of types with dubious readings the stamps cover over thirty distinct commodities. Many of them are attested throughout the period the stamps were issued; as we would expect, the same ones occur under each different official. In a few cases, like those of wine and olive oil, special stamped measures were, or may have been, only issued for a short period. In the present collection, one new commodity, milk (*laban*), is found on a stamp for the first time (No. 499) and *samn*, clarified butter, is proposed as a new reading, though a stamp bearing the word has been published before (see No. 63). The list that follows includes all the identifications which can be regarded as certain and very few others; it represents the vast majority of the actual individual stamps. The commodities can be roughly divided into categories as follows:

Oils, fats and dairy products: olive oil (*zayt*), fat (*duhn*), clarified butter (*samn*), milk (*laban*), *mishsh* (see No. 64).
Pulses: lentils (*ʿadas*), chick peas (*ḥimmas*), chickling vetch (*julubbān*), beans (*fūl*), peas (*bisilla*).
Herbs and other seeds: cumin (*kammūn*), coriander (*ḥabb al-kusbur*), fennel (*shamār*), fenugreek (*ḥulba*), mustard (*ṣināb*), cress (*tuffā*, *ḥurf*), lupin (*turmus*), sesame (*juljulān*).
Sweet things: honey (*ʿasal*), jujubes (*nabq*), peaches or plums (*khūkh*), the fruit of the doum palm (*dawm*) or, more probably, some preparation from it.
Cooked foods: *ṭabīkh*, cooked noodles (*iṭriya maṭbūkha*).
Alchoholic drinks: wine (*ṭilāʾ*), beer (*mizr*), millet beer (*usqurqa*).
Cosmetics: henna (*ḥinnāʾ*, of two kinds), woad (*wasma*), *katam* (see No. 157).

A number of the commodities sometimes appear with various qualifications. Pulses are often described as skinned (*muqashshar*), for instance. There are stamps for dried and for roasted chick peas, as well as simply chick peas. Lentils may be red or black, sesame red or white, cumin black or white. In some cases the variants do tend to fall into parallel series, showing that well-distinguished varieties of the commodities were in use or, as possibly in the case of cumin, that essentially different substances were intended; in others the qualifications are found sporadically and may only mean that the same thing was more precisely described at one time than another.

It hardly needs to be pointed out that the list of commodities is unconvincing as a list of drugs or pharmaceutical preparations. Most of them are ordinary items of food and drink, though some of the oils and fats were no doubt used for lighting as well. The herbs are common seasonings. Some of the cosmetics might seem a little strange in Egypt today, and with the cosmetics one does get a little closer to the drugstore, but there is sufficient evidence of their use in early Islam. There is no need to go into further detail here; commodities represented in the British Museum's collection, which includes the majority of those listed, are commented on the first time they occur. No very thorough treatment of them is intended there, but an effort has been made in most cases to provide evidence of the often obvious fact of their widespread use. For this purpose use has been made of the administrative and agricultural material of much later Egyptian writers, Ibn Mammātī and Makhzūmī (the latter as studied by Cahen) of the Ayyubid period and the even later Maqrīzī, as well as the thirteenth-century Spanish writer on agriculture, Ibn al-ʿAwwām and later European descriptions of Egypt. Müller-Wodarg's study of Egyptian agriculture in the Abbasid period has also been useful, as has Wensinck's concordance of *Ḥadīth*, the latter particularly for the cosmetics. The pharmacopeias have also been consulted: though they can be misleading as to the ordinary uses of substances and though the names of still unidentified ones on glass stamps should be sought for in the circumstances of daily life rather than in lists of materia medica, they do contain interesting information.

Prices

It has been mentioned more than once that some of the commodity stamps have prices on them. A price has once tentatively been read on a stamp but the suggestion is not a part of current opinion and needs explanation. On a number of stamps the name of the commodity is followed by a word that has been read in several ways, though only one of the earlier readings, *nafīs*, need concern us. *Nafīs* was in fact the first reading of the word ever put forward, by Casanova (1893, 50), but did not reappear in the literature until it was suggested by Jungfleisch to Miles (1951b, pp. 47-8). *Nafīs* means precious, costly, priceless; it is a word to apply to jewels, sumptuous vestments and the like. Casanova translated it correctly, and queried the reading, but Miles, presumably half realizing that it is an odd word to apply to such things as olive oil and chick peas, suggested the more subdued meaning 'excellent, fine, of the first quality'. Later (1958, 109 etc.) he adopted the translation 'pure' which has since been widely accepted. One imagines that 'pure' was felt to be more appropriate when supposed pharmaceuticals were in question. However, *nafīs* is an emphatic word, giving the idea of great price and, even if the ideas of purity and high value may sometimes be correlated, *nafīs* does not mean pure.

Another solution is evidently required. A clue to it is to be found in a reading tentatively suggested by Launois (1957, 321) in the case of a stamp for shelled vetch issued by Salama, which is *li-fals*, for a *fals* or copper coin. On this type the first letter is rather elongated but the correct reading is nevertheless almost certainly *bi-fals*. In other cases where the word appears the first letter is usually an ordinary 'tooth' and to read it as *lām* not possible. *Bi-*, rather than *li-*, is the standard preposition used in Arabic when talking about a price. Of course in undotted Arabic *nafīs* and *bi-fals* are the same except for the third letter. In most scripts the 'tooth' of the *yāʾ* of *nafīs* would be easily distinguishable from the taller *lām* of *fals*, but in Kufic a 'tooth' standing next to the three 'teeth' of *sīn*, as in *nafīs*, may be elongated to avoid confusion. However, on the glass the elongation is not invariable: in *bismillāh*, which is a common beginning to the legends, the *bāʾ* is sometimes elongated and sometimes not. On the word on the commodity stamps the elongation is invariable and so, besides giving better sense, *lām* is in any case the preferable reading. (For a clear example of the word see No. 496.)

Confirmation that *bi-fals* is correct is provided by a unique type with a different price, of which No. 64 is the first reasonably intact specimen to be published. It is for a *mikyala* of *mishsh* priced at half a *fals* (*bi-niṣf fals*) and, appropriately, it was issued by ʿUbaydallāh b. al-Ḥabḥāb, the only official in whose name we possess half-*fals* weights, which show that he also issued half-*fals* coins.

Most of the measures with prices are *mikyalas*. Since many different substances, in some cases obviously of different values, are represented, it is clear that the word *mikyala* was not being used as a single measure of capacity with a defined size. Each commodity would have had its own *mikyala*. The same point can be deduced from the rare *mikyalas* noted below on which the price is accompanied by a weight, for the weights of a *fals*-worth of different commodities do differ. Intact measures with prices would provide valuable information on the cost of living in Egypt but are unlikely to be discovered in any quantity. One, an anonymous *mikyala* for a *fals*-worth of olive oil with a capacity of 60cc, has been published (Miles 1951b, p. 53). There are also, incidentally, small anonymous stamps for *qisṭs* of olive oil priced at a *fals* (e.g. Balog 1976, 874-5); clearly, though the price of olive oil may have varied, these *qisṭs* are likely to be about the same size as the *mikyala* and much smaller than the *qisṭs* for olive oil in the names of Umayyad officials. Some further information is given by the types with both weights and prices. Yet another small anonymous type for olive oil defines the *fals*-worth as 1½ *wuqiyya* (Balog 1976, 878-80). Like nearly all the anonymous commodity stamps it probably belongs to the period when the Umayyad *raṭl* was in use and, if the *wuqiyya* intended is the Umayyad *wuqiyya*, the price works out at 55·5g to the *fals*. Other commodities were less expensive. A *fals*-worth *mikyala* of *mishsh* contained half a *raṭl* (Balog 1976, 897), one of cooked noodles 2 *raṭls* (Miles 1971, 58, *cf*. 62), and one of an unidentified substance 2½ *raṭls* (Balog 1976, 866, for pickled gherkins?).

The function of commodity stamps

From the foregoing two sections it will have become clear that the commodity measures were not containers for drugs, and that the commonsensical idea that they were measures used mainly in shops, which has occasionally been put forward (e.g. Launois 1959, p. 2) has a number of points to recommend it. The goods themselves are not exotic drugs but prosaic items of mass consumption. The appearance of prices on some of the measures shows that they were designed for trade, the lowness of the prices that they were meant for the everyday transactions of retail trade. The world they reflect is that of the corner grocery, the cook-shop, the tavern, the street pedlar and the average consumer. The only concession that needs to be made to the pharmaceutical theory is to say that if certain drugs were in wide use it would not be surprising to find them sold by similar measures. As Balog (1976, p. 10) has suggested, it is likely that the users of the measures (and weights) had to pay for them. It is possible that their issue was a way of imposing a minor tax. Presumably steps were taken to enforce their use so they can also be regarded as a means of licensing and controlling retail trade.

In these respects, though nothing so elaborate is known later, the control of measures is essentially no different from that described as a customary and necessary part of urban Muslim life in the later literature on the duties of the *muḥtasib*, but the priced measures imply something more unusual. It should first be pointed out that though only a small proportion of the *mikyalas* have prices it is probable that many of the others were in fact intended for a fixed value of a commodity: since the value on the priced ones is, with the one exception, the same, i.e. a *fals*-worth, it would not have been necessary to specify it. In any case the priced measures themselves indicate that at times the Egyptian government was operating a system of retail price control.

This leads to a further conclusion about the nature of the commodities: they are unlikely to be ones subject to violent seasonal fluctuations in price. In many cases this is already obvious: olive oil can be kept without deterioration; the qualifications given to the pulses show that dried ones are meant; beers are made throughout the year from dried grains; dairy products either keep or are available for long periods. In other cases, the realization that only products of reasonably stable value can be meant helps to define precisely what they are: the herbs must be dried and presumably it is usually the seeds that are meant; the fruits must be dried or otherwise preserved.

Anonymous commodity stamps

Anonymous commodity stamps are quite plentiful and, from their appearance, all or nearly all of them are official issues of the Umayyad and early Abbasid periods, close in time to the ones with the names of officials. The series with names begins with Qurra b. Sharīk, though only one commodity, fat, is recorded for Qurra and the system only reached its full extent under Usāma b. Zayd. The named series continues without apparent interruption until the end of Umayyad rule and into the early Abbasid period. There may then be a slight gap but the series picks up with the stamps issued for a short period in the name of Caliph al-Manṣūr and those of Muḥammad b. al-Ash'ath and the executive associated with him, 'Abdallāh b. Rāshid. Thenceforth commodity stamps in the names of Finance Directors are unknown; the only later named ones are isolated types of the executive Salama (e.g. Balog 1976, 467-8).

Such evidence as we have for dating anonymous commodity stamps more precisely consists of a few fragments of measures on which an anonymous commodity stamp survives beside an executive stamp of a known executive. On two examples, one of them No. 335, a stamp for a *wuqiyya* of fat is accompanied by one of Ṣāliḥ b. Muslim. The die of the commodity stamp has no parallel and seems to represent the final stage of the use of commodity stamps, after it had already been greatly reduced and just before it was abandoned.

Three similar attached pairs attest an earlier phase, probably the last when a wide range of the measures was in use. Balog 1976, 549 has an executive stamp of al-Muhājir paired with one for a *mikyala* of skinned vetch (see Nos 306, 486), a similar one with a stamp of Salama and one for a *mikyala* of *khūkh* (peaches or plums) was excavated at Fusṭāṭ by Scanlon (see Nos 254-6) and one described by Casanova had one for a *mikyala* of lupins for a *fals* with what may be suggested to be an executive stamp of Qutayba b. Ziyād (see No. 288). Of the three commodity stamps only Balog's has been illustrated: it is from a quite common die and similar in appearance to a large group of anonymous stamps for other commodities. They are written in a bold clear Kufic found on other types of the period of al-Muhajir and the other two executives; they have simple legends consisting of the word *mikyala*, occupying the first line, the name of the commodity, occupying the second, and occasionally a price on a third line; and the *kāf* of *mikyala* is noticeably elongated. After this last feature it is proposed to call them the 'long-*kāf*' group. The group evidently forms a set, very similar in its range to that represented by the stamps of each of the Finance Directors and it plainly fulfilled much the same function at a different period. Since command stamps, that is stamps with the Finance Director's name alone, are not known for the 'long-*kāf*' period it is evident that on the commodity measures of the period only two stamps, the commodity stamp and the executive stamp, were employed. A number of the pieces in the present collection can be assigned with varying degrees of certainty to the 'long-*kāf*' group: Nos 482-6, 493-5, 497-8, 500-1.

To put this phase of the use of commodity measures into more precise chronological perspective then, after Muḥammad b. al-Ash'ath commodity measures appear to have fallen out of use for a while, for the evidence gives no reason to believe that the immediately subsequent Finance Directors or the executives associated with them issued such things. The few named commodity stamps of Salama are probably to be dated to the end of Yazīd b. Ḥātim's long governorship (144-52/762-9) for on one group of Yazīd's *raṭl*-system weights and *qisṭ*-system stamps Salama's name follows that of Yazīd and precedes the denomination on the same stamp (e.g. No. 245). Salama is also attested as executive under Muḥammad b. Sa'īd, who followed Yazīd in control of finance from 152-7/769-74, and presumably was active at the beginning of Muḥammad b. Sa'īd's period of office. However, on *raṭl*-system weights of Muḥammad b. Sa'īd, Salama's name appears on a separate counterstamp, stamped with the same die used for the vessel stamps, among them that on the rim with two stamps excavated at Fusṭāṭ. Thus the 'long-*kāf*' commodity stamps would appear to have come into use early in Muḥammad b. Sa'īd's Finance Directorship. The commodity stamps, being anonymous, would not need to be changed at the appointment of a new executive and would for the most part have remained in use until the time of al-Muḥājir, who was executive under Muḥammad b. Sulaymān (159-61/775-8). Executive vessel stamps of a number of the executives of the intervening period are known and though some of them would have been employed in combination with *qisṭ*-system stamps of Finance Directors, as on No. 288, others would have been used beside the anonymous commodity stamps on commodity measures. It is possible that this system remained in use a little later then al-Muhājir's time but it cannot have been for long because the small number of executive stamps known for most later executives indicates that they were only used beside *qisṭ*-system stamps. It is noticeable that the use of a wide variety of commodity measures thus appears to come to an end shortly before the Umayyad *raṭl* system was replaced by the *raṭl-kabīr* system. The only later evidence for commodity measures consists of the isolated fat measures associated with Ṣāliḥ b. Muslim.

Anonymous counterstamps

All the larger collections include small vessel stamps with the brief legend *al-wafā' lillāh*, 'honesty for God' or 'honesty is God's' (e.g. Nos 502-6, 508, *qq.v.*). The dies used to produce them were also employed on heavy weights, in combination with stamps of Finance Directors. A number of such weights have been published but no comment appears to have been made about the function of the small stamps on them nor, owing in part, no doubt, to the usual lack of attention to die identities, to their implications for the similar vessel stamps. When classified by die, the impressions on both weights and vessel stamps fall into a small number of groups each produced by a single die and, thanks to the fact that nearly all the dies are known from dateable weights, it can be seen that they form a single chronological series, beginning, on the present evidence, in the time of Usāma b. Zayd and ending in the early part of the finance directorship of al-Qāsim b. 'Ubaydallāh.

The use of the same dies on vessel stamps and weights is parallelled precisely by that of the dies with the executives' names which came in in the later Umayyad period. From the distribution of the stamps themselves and from a few pieces which preserve two vessel stamps joined together it is plain that vessel stamps were often used in combination. The first executive who has his own executive stamps with his name on was Yazīd b. Abi Yazīd and his stamps, like those of many later executives, are found in exactly the same way as the group with *al-wafā' lillāh*: on heavy weights beside the Finance Director's stamp and as a separate vessel stamp, which itself, on the original measure, would have been paired with a stamp with the Finance Director's name and the denomination. The obvious suggestion for the anonymous stamps is that they are, in function, executive stamps, representing the earliest stage of the system of having the weights and measures certified by more than one official. Since they bear no name, of course they would not have needed to be changed every time the executive was replaced.

There are a few other anonymous types. A stamp without a legend, but with the design of a pentagram, is known from a weight of al-Qāsim b. ʿUbaydallāh as well as separate vessel stamps (e.g. No. 507, *q.v.*). It follows the latest of the *al-wafā' lillāh* types and presumably had the same function, that is, served as an executive stamp. Two small stamps with legends that consist solely of dates are only known from weights and were probably not executive stamps (see No. 49). Finally, a slightly later stamp, on which *al-wafā' lillāh* is followed by a prohibition against the giving of short measure, is used in the same way as the early anonymous counterstamps, occurring on vessel stamps and on a half-*raṭl* of al-Manṣūr (see commentary to No. 199). It would seem to represent a brief revival of the earlier use of anonymous executive stamps.

Decorative vessel stamps

There are not a great number of vessel stamps that cannot be found a place in the main official series and most of them can be classified as decorative (e.g. Nos 551-6). The classic example of their use is on the Pegasus cup, now in Berlin and fully described by Erdmann, which fortunately makes it plain that such stamps did not have a metrological function. The piece is a bowl-like cup 11cm in diameter, with eight vessel stamps disposed in two registers round the outside, all stamped from a die bearing the figure of a winged horse and a brief Arabic legend. Most of the stamps in the decorative group are similar, having figures of animals, birds, mythological beasts and occasionally human figures, and legends such as *bismillāh*. To be associated with the figural types are some on which the decoration is solely epigraphic and consists of good wishes or blessings upon the maker or owner of the vessel or the person who drinks from it (e.g. Miles 1963 II, 63; Balog 1973, 44, from the same die; Balog 1976, 784, 913). Many of the animal figures come from the Sasanian decorative repertoire and what appear to be Sasanian vessel stamps do exist (see, in particular, Balog 1974, 1), though the possibility of other influences from the eastern provinces of the Byzantine Empire need not be excluded.

The script on the Islamic stamps points to an Umayyad date. Nearly all of them are of pale brown or yellow glass, quite different from the green or blue-green glass almost always used for the official Egyptian stamps. Obviously they were not made in the workshop of the office of weights and measures. Many of the known specimens were found in Egypt but others are recorded as being of Syrian or Iraqi provenance. No. 553, for instance, was excavated in Northern Iraq. Though the published corpus is not large the proportion of die duplicates is comparable to that found for the official stamps, indicating that total production was quite small. The number of workshops producing such wares is also likely to have been small. Since luxurious glassware was no doubt traded between the provinces of the early Islamic empire it is at present difficult to say in which ones the decorative vessel stamps were produced, but certainly Egypt need not have been the main centre.

5. DIES AND DIE LINKS

All the stamps were produced in the same way, by impressing the hot glass with, or in the case of reverses on to, an iron die. As Matson, in his excellent study of the technical aspects of the production of the stamps (39-40) has noted, this is shown by the occurrence of traces of iron scale on or just below the surface of the impressions. The weights were stamped on an iron plate, sometimes itself engraved with a reverse die, which was evidently more prone to corrosion than the upper dies, for larger deposits of scale are often visible on their undersides. Since the process of stamping with dies is similar to the striking of coins, the stamps offer the opportunity to apply the numismatic technique of die study. The technique rests on the hypothesis that hand-made dies differ sufficiently to be distinguishable by eye, and experience has shown that coins of the same type, that is with the same design or legend, can often be further classified by distinguishing the individual dies with which they are impressed. The same applies to the glass stamps, with the proviso that special allowance has to be made for the nature of glass: sometimes it was sufficiently hot to run after the impression was made, which caused blurred and distorted impressions of a kind not found on metal, and when two impressions were made beside each other distortion was also liable to occur. However, in practice such impressions can usually be identified with those on other specimens.

The study of dies requres that the impressions, or accurate reproductions of them, be compared side by side, so widespread use of the technique was only possible when it became easy and relatively cheap to reproduce coins by photography. The turning point can be placed in the early years of this century. Islamic numismatists were rather slow to take the idea up: other, more immediate, tasks called for attention and, since so many Muslim coins state clearly when and where they were made, there are less of the basic problems of attribution which die study has helped to solve in other series. However, in the Egyptologist Sir W.M. Flinders Petrie the study of glass stamps produced the pioneer student of dies in any Islamic field. Petrie pointed out that the technique could be applied to glass stamps in an article in the *Numismatic Chronicle* for 1918 and used it systematically in his catalogue of the collection he gathered for University College, London, noting the identities of the dies used on pieces in the collection both with others in it and with ones elsewhere which had been photographically illustrated. With the small body of material available he did not draw any conclusions from the die identities of the stamps of the early period.

Since Petrie's time the matter of the die identities of Islamic glass stamps of all periods has been almost completely neglected. Later writers, when describing particular pieces, naturally did not fail to refer to previously published ones that were similar, but no one since Petrie has pointed out that die duplicates are very common in the corpus and, except occasionally in the work of Launois and Balog, there are almost no positive declarations that a certain piece is from the same die as another. Admittedly, there is a semantic problem in describing degrees of similarity, as of assessing what is meant by other people's attempts to describe them. The literature abounds with statements that one piece is the same as, similar to or identical with another and since, in the majority of cases, only one die was used per issue, the relationship described is often that of two impressions from one die. It is nevertheless evident that the scholars concerned were using a definition of type which, though never made explicit, mainly depended on the legend and its arrangement with some attention to style and ornament, and that they often tended to rely on the written descriptions of their predecessors even when illustrations were available. There are not uncommon cases, for instance, where variant readings are mentioned as implying the existence of variant types when the photographs show that it is a question of die duplicates (e.g. Miles 1963 I, 22 on Fahmī 1957, 73; Balog 1976, 18 on Miles 1958a, 6). Where there are two dies so similar that they may be said to belong to one issue they have almost never been distinguished (see, for examples, Nos 278-80, 431-4) and in the rare cases where dies were altered, even when the variants were noted, it has almost never been said that the die is the same (see Nos 13, 30, 32, 41, 427). Though many dies were used on both heavy weights and vessel stamps the fact has seldom, if ever, been clearly pointed out.

Classification by die provides a more precise and firmly based typology. In the case of fragile glass it is particularly useful in making it possible to identify damaged specimens with certainty; a small piece of a stamp can often be securely placed on the evidence of the die. The dies and their associations or links, now that the corpus has grown to a certain size, can also provide information about the total output of stamps and the organization of the workshop, matters which are discussed briefly below. In the present catalogue a classification by dies has been adopted. In most cases the description of each piece is followed by a list of other impressions of the same die, established on the basis of published photographs and the, on the whole uncommon, unequivocal statements confirming die identities in the literature. Then comes a list of apparently similar but unillustrated pieces for comparison; in most cases the latter group are probably from the same die but one can not be certain. With dies used on weights of different denominations or on both weights and vessel stamps, only the pieces of the same denomination or functional type are given in the lists and discussion of the other uses of the die is left to the commentary. The readings given for the legends are intended to represent those of the original dies rather than the impressions on the British Museum's specimens; once the complete reading of a die is known it is rarely of importance how much of it is legible on any particular impression. The readings, therefore, are often composite and include the evidence of all illustrated specimens available, as well as of those in the collection. Parts of the legends marked as restored are not legible on the British Museum's specimens or any other illustrated one. The reader is unlikely to be greatly puzzled except in the few cases where the Museum has a badly damaged specimen but the complete reading can be established from elsewhere.

Output and organization

Much attention is nowadays paid to the question of estimating the output of currency of mints from the number of dies used at them over a known period. When a sufficiently large corpus of the coinage is available and the ratio of coins to dies reaches a certain point it can be taken that all, or very nearly all, of the dies that were used are known. The number of dies itself gives an indication of the scale of activity at the mint but to derive actual figures for output requires estimating the output of the average die. A number of variables, such as the quality of the dies, the way they are employed, when they are considered too worn for further use etc., will have affected the real average output per die to such an extent that estimates are not likely to be reliable (see the remarks on the subject by Grierson, 155-7). Nevertheless, estimates of die output for coins continue to be made and the same approach could be applied to glass stamps. The dies used for glass were certainly gradually worn by use: the evidence survives on the stamps in the form of the traces of iron already alluded to. However, whether an average figure for output for dies used on glass would be similar to one for coin dies remains an open question. In any case, though for the later Fatimid glass disks where, according to Petrie (p. 10), worn dies are commonly represented and dies were also recut, such an estimate could be made, in the case of the early stamps it can not because the dies were not normally, if ever, used until they wore out and estimates of the type mentioned are only valid at all if the dies continue to be employed until unfit for use. In the case of the early glass series dies were replaced for other reasons, most commonly the replacement of officials, long before wearing out. This can be stated in general terms because the majority of impressions are clear and exhibit no signs of wear to the dies; when impressions are not clear it is usually obvious that this is due to the running of the glass or, particularly on later issues, to the decay of the surface of the glass itself. We can also point to certain dies which were in use for a long time. For example, the Caliph al-Mahdī's most common *dīnār*-weight obverse was in use from the finance directorship of Muḥammad b. Sulaymān to the first governorship of Ibrāhīm b. Ṣāliḥ, c. 159-165. Though it received a severe knock on the edge at an early stage, for the rest the latest impressions from it are not noticeably less crisp than the earliest (see No. 298). The corresponding half and third-*dīnār* types lasted as long (see Nos 290-1, 294). Similarly, the first *raṭl-kabīr* denomination stamp is known to have been used under four, possibly five, Finance Directors but shows no obvious signs of wear (see Nos 321-2).

The evidence points, therefore, to a fairly small output of glass weights and measures in the early period. To go further is to speculate but perhaps it would not be far wrong to say that the total production of a particular type is likely to have been no more than a few thousands and may even have been in the hundreds in some cases. The majority of issues are only represented by one die or set of dies. What, though, of the few cases where two or occasionally even three very similar dies are known to have existed? It seems improbable that demand for any kind of weight or measure was so large as to make it necessary to have more than one die in use to increase the rate of production; if so we would expect signs of wear. However, a series of dies produced by relatively simple metallurgical techniques is likely to include occasional ones which are flawed in manufacture and break quite soon. Probably the pairs and trios of similar dies are mostly due to this circumstance.

It is generally, and for the most part certainly correctly, accepted that the glass weights and measures of the official Egyptian series were produced in a single workshop, which undoubtedly at the beginning must have been located at Fusṭāṭ. It is still worth pointing out, however, that the use of common dies links the three main groups of stamps together physically.

Almost throughout, the appropriate dies, those for executive stamps and at times 'command' stamps with Finance Directors' names but no denomination, were used on both heavy weights and measures. The link between heavy weights and coin weights is provided by the common reverses of *dīnār*-system weights and sixth-*wuqiyyas* (see Nos 227, 272). Casanova (1893, p. 341) suggested that the official stamps were produced in the Dār al-ʿIyār, or Office of Standards. Whether there was an institution known by that precise name in the early period is questionable; it is first mentioned under that name by Ibn Mammātī (333-4) centuries later but, Dār al-ʿIyār or not, the stamps were obviously issued by the corresponding office.

The information given on the stamps and the way they are arranged on the three main series varied from time to time. These alterations may sometimes reflect changes in the control of the institution responsible for them but we are unlikely ever to know how far that was so. A knowledge of the combinations and permutations of the dies is often of importance in classifying the material but discussion of these patterns is left to the body of the catalogue.

6. EPIGRAPHY

The legends on the stamps are in the Kufic script, that normally used for epigraphic purposes in the early Islamic period. The general term Kufic covers many sub-varieties, often of very different appearance; the main distinguishing features are the level script-line formed by the bases of letters and the ductus joining letters, the angular junctures between ductus and letters and a relatively high proportion of angular letter forms. In general, and allowing for individual peculiarities, the script of the official stamps develops like that of contemporary coinage. The earliest legends are very like those on post-reform Umayyad coins and other official Umayyad inscriptions. For the next half-century the script remains recognizably 'Umayyad', though less close to the coinage; from the second half of the century there is a tendency towards less bulky letters and the greater use of elongation, both of the ductus and of certain letters. These features also occur on contemporary Abbasid coinage.

Peculiarities of the language of the legends are for the most part noted under individual entries; an exhaustive treatment of them is not intended. However, there are two points which can be more conveniently dealt with here.

Ommission of *alif*

There are certain Arabic spellings in which, to judge by the normal orthographic rules, an *alif*, representing 'ā', is omitted. Such forms are found in the Qurʾan and a few of them, most notably the word God (*Allah*) are still accepted as the correct ones, owing to their occurrence in the sacred book. Their use can be regarded as a survival of a convention of the script in use in the very early days of Islam which did not require that 'ā' should always be explicitly recorded. Spellings of this type are occasionally found in early papyri (Grohmann 1956, 101) and, besides *Allah* and other standard ones such as *hadhā* ('this') and *dhalika* ('that') a number are met on the stamps, particularly in the first half-century of their production. *Dīnār* is almost always spelt without *alif* on glass, as it was on coins for several centuries. In other cases forms with and without the *alif* are both in common use, for example *mīzan* and *mīzān* ('weight'), *qīraṭ* and *qīrāṭ* ('carat-weight'), *thalath* and *thalāth* ('three'). In the case of *mithqāl*, also meaning weight, the fuller spelling is usual but *mithqal* is also found. Certain names, often, though not always, those for which such spellings are attested in the Qurʾan, are regularly spelt thus 'defectively', among them Ibrāhīm, Isḥāq, Ismāʿīl, Sulaimān, Ṣāliḥ, Muʿāwiya, Marwān and Mālik.

In the catalogue the original spellings are retained in the Arabic texts and indicated in the translations of the texts by the omissions of the macron over the 'a', but otherwise such forms are not noted except in special cases.

Ṭabʿa/ṣanʿa

The legends of a considerable number of official stamps of all categories include a word which, undotted and by itself, can be read in several ways. It is found in two formulae and it is possible that the correct reading in each of the formulae is in fact different. Among the possible readings are *ṭabʿa* ('stamping') and *ṣanʿa* ('making'); the others are alternative forms from the same two Arabic roots. The word first appears under ʿUbaydallāh

b. al-Habhāb and its latest occurrences in the official series are in the early part of the Caliphate of al-Mahdī. In most varieties of Arabic script the first letter would make it clear which root was involved, the rising stroke of *ṭā'* normally being distinctly longer than that of *ṣād*, but in the script of the early stamps the two are not clearly distinguished. Thus the actual appearance of the word as written on the stamps is unlikely to provide a conclusive answer to the question. There are specimens on which the upstroke of an undoubted *ṭā'* seems longer and others on which it is noticeably set at an angle backwards; I have observed no example of *ṭab'a/ṣan'a* which definitely exhibits either peculiarity. This would appear to be in favour of reading *ṣan'a*. However, a small number of types with unusual legends, discussed below, provide support for the reading *ṭab'a* which has been adopted throughout the catalogue. The most significant of these types in the present context came to light for the first time in the Balog collection.

The first and most common of the formulae in which the word occurs goes as follows: 'Ordered so-and-so (Caliph or Finance Director, with appropriate titles) *bi-ṭab'a/bi-ṣan'a* of such-and-such a weight or measure'. (There are some variations, mostly in the order of the words.) An extremely close parallel is found on two weights of Ḥayyān b. Shurayḥ (Balog 1976, 35-6) which read 'Ordered Ḥayyan b. Shurayḥ *bi-khatm* of such-and-such a weight'. Here the reading offers no problem: *khatm* means 'sealing' or, as here, 'stamping'. Though *ṭaba'a* has come to be used in particular for 'to print', before the invention of the printing press it and *khatama* were to a large extent synonymous; *Khātim* and *ṭābi'* both mean a seal. The root *khatama* is used in different forms in other legends: on the executive stamps of Ṣāliḥ b. Qusṭanṭīn we find the formula *khutima 'alā yaday*, 'There was stamped at the hands of ...' (see Nos 225-6) and on Ibrāhīm b. Ṣāliḥ's 36-*kharrūba fals* weights the words *khātim fulūs*, 'stamp of *fulūs*' (see Nos 318-9). Finally, No. 409, a *fals* weight which, though it cannot be assigned to a precise place in the official series, is of eighth-century appearance, provides evidence of the use of the root *ṭaba'a*; its legend includes the phrase *ṭābi' fals*, 'stamp of a *fals*'. These examples show that the idea of the actual stamping of the glass pieces was in the minds of those responsible for their issue; it seems likely that from the official point of view the important moment in the process of manufacture was that of the application of the stamps, for it was that which officially validated the pieces. This would nicely parallel the early Islamic coin legends which usually refer to the actual striking (*ḍarb* - a few examples of *ṭaba'a* occur on coins). That *ṭaba'a* could be considered appropriate for weights is also demonstrated by certain Fatimid lead *raṭl*-system weights on which it appears, sometimes even when *ḍaraba* ('to strike') is used on the opposite face of the weight (see Balog 1959, 1963b).

Alternative readings which have been adopted in this formula are *ṭab'ihi* and *ṣan'ihi* or *ṣun'ihi* ('the stamping of it', 'the making of it'). However they break the legend into syntactically unconnected parts. This in itself may not be out of the question but is unlikely and is not to be accepted when there is no difficulty about reading the legend as a continuous whole.

The second formula in which the word is found appears in the centre of the reverses of the coin weights and the sixth-*wuqiyya* weights of the early Abbasid period (e.g. Nos 171-2, 227). *Ṭab'a/ṣan'a* is followed by the name of an 'artisan' ('Stamping (or making) of so-and-so'). If the people who have been classified as artisans were really workmen the reading 'making' would be appropriate enough but since all that is known of them is that their names occur in this formula, to read *ṣan'a* because we have chosen to call them artisans is to rely on a circular argument. 'Stamping' seems preferrable in this case, too, for the same reasons as in the first. Here, however, a verbal form is equally possible: *ṭaba'ahu*, 'there stamped it ...' (or, less probably, *ṣana'ahu*, 'there made it ...'). For simplicity's sake the noun *ṭab'a* has been preferred in the catalogue.

1. UMAYYAD

ʻABDALLĀH B. ʻABD AL-MALIK B. MARWĀN

Governor and Finance Director AH 86-90/AD 705-9

1 (*Dīnār* weight)

بسم الله
لعبد الله
الامير

In the name of God.
Of ʻAbdallah
the Amir.

93 11-11 12. Olive green. 2.7cm; stamp 2.1cm; 4.14g. (*Plate 1*)

From the same die Miles 1948, 219 (information from Michael Bates); Launois 1960 II, 21.

This type has not previously been attributed to a particular person. If the attribution proposed here is correct it is the earliest known type of glass weight of a Muslim official in Egypt. Miles's reading of the last two lines was *yaʻbudu allāh al-amīr*, '... worships Allāh, the Amir', which seems unparalleled and, more importantly, fails to do justice to the first letter, which is taller than the ordinary 'tooth letter' and without very good reason for thinking otherwise can only be taken as *lām* (*li-*, 'of'). Launois translated the same lines '*L'émir, pour le serviteur de Dieu (le calife) (?).*', giving the same text as is offered here, but suggesting that *ʻabd allāh*, 'the slave of God', might be used as a title rather than a personal name. *ʻAbd allāh* is, of course, one of the standard titles of the Caliphs, being attested in a wide variety of epigraphic and other contexts from as early as the time of the first Umayyad Caliph, Muʻāwiya (r. 41-60/661-80). However, numerous examples show that the standard practice was to use the title, not by itself, but in combination, immediately preceding the Caliph's personal name. It seems very unlikely indeed that *ʻabd allāh* by itself would have been understood to refer to the Caliph; it would always have been liable to confusion with the common personal name ʻAbdallāh.

It is suggested that in this case the two words are to be taken as a personal name and that, although the name is a very common one, other features of the stamp suggest that it must be dated to a particular period in which only one suitable ʻAbdallāh can be found. The most important of these features is simply the placing of the title *al-amīr*, after the personal name rather than, as is usual, before it. There are two, possibly three, examples of the usage on glass; the writer knows of two in other contexts. The name of the Umayyad Prince al-Walīd (b. ʻAbd al-Malik, later the Caliph al-Walīd I) is followed by *al-amīr* on the heavy glass weight found in Jordan which also bears his father's name as Caliph (Abdel-Kader 1935, 1). Abdel-Kader, finding the placing of the title '*bizarre*', argued that placed thus it was a special one used by al-Walīd as heir apparent. However, the second example is on a glass disk of the well-known Governor of Egypt, Qurra b. Sharīk (90-6/709-14) who was not even a member of the Umayyad family (Balog 1976, 3). The third is on a vessel stamp from a four-sided flask described, but not illustrated, by Casanova (1893, p. 375, No. 6) on which he read 'ʻAbd al-ʻAzīz *al-amīr*', suggesting the name might be that of the Caliph ʻAbd al-Malik's brother, who was Governor and Finance Director of Egypt from 65-86/685-705. It would certainly be desirable to recheck the last piece before accepting it as the earliest datable glass stamp of any sort from Muslim Egypt, but if the title does follow the name Casanova's attribution is not to be dismissed out of hand. ʻAbd al-ʻAzīz b. Marwān's name certainly does appear with the postponed *al-amīr* in an inscription dated AH 69 on a bridge near Fusṭāṭ, the text of which is preserved by Egyptian historians (e.g. Maqrīzī II, 146). The final example of the usage is from a bronze weight of a third son of Marwān, named Bishr, who died in about AH 75 (Miles 1962). (It should be noted that no father's name appears on the glass examples but that in both the others Marwān is named and *al-amīr* follows his name rather than that of his sons, to whom, however, in these cases the title certainly applies.) It is clear that the postposition of *al-amīr* was acceptable, perhaps normal, in the latter part of the first century of the Hijra. There appears to be no evidence that the usage survived later.

Another rather uncommon feature of the legend of the type under discussion is the introductory *li-*, used in its common possessive sense to mean 'of'. This certainly is found later. Launois refers, apropos the Paris specimen, to its occurrence on lead sealings. These sealings, the main publication for which is by Casanova (1894), are mostly of the third and fourth centuries AH and from Iraq and Western Persia. However, there is a small group of examples of the use of introductory *li-* on glass stamps and coinage from the same early period when the postposition of *al-amīr* was accepted usage. In all the examples in the group the *li-* introduces a Caliph's name and titles, and stands directly before *ʻabd allāh* used as a title, making them seem at first sight more similar to the type with ʻAbdallāh as a name than is really the case. Such a use of *li-* is found on two, perhaps all three, of the published examples of the small glass disks in the name of ʻAbd al-Malik b. Marwān (Abdel-Kader 1939, 1; Launois 1959, 1; 1969, 1: all from different dies). Exactly the same legend occurs on certain categories of ʻAbd al-Malik's Syrian copper coinage (Walker, pp. 34ff, 207). The legend of the probable *dīnār* weight attributed by Petrie (129) to al-Walīd II (r. 125-6/743-4) but which would fit as well, probably better, into the longer reign of al-Walīd I (86-96/705-15) makes use of the same formula, and is even closer to the type of ʻAbdallāh in that the first line consists of *bismillāh.* The script of the type under discussion is also consistent with an early date.

The next point to consider is who at that period was entitled to be called *al-amīr.* In the early Islamic period, in contrast to the later practice with which we are familiar, the title was a grand one, restricted to very few people, not including the Caliphs themselves, who used the parallel, but superior, title *Amīr al-mu'minīn,* 'Commander of the Faithful'. An anecdote preserved by Kindī (62) makes plain that at the time of Qurra the only person in the Egyptian official hierarchy entitled to be called Amir was the Governor himself. The evidence of the glass stamps confirms that the Governors did use the title and that for some time the Finance Directors did not. The first of the latter to use it, and then only for a short while it would seem, was al-Qāsim b. ʻUbaydallāh (see No. 88). In the earliest period of the issue of glass stamps there is only one official with the name ʻAbdallah who otherwise fits the required picture, being both Governor, and therefore possessor of the title *al-amīr,* and Finance Director, and therefore, to judge by slightly later practice, in control of the issue of glass stamps. Son of the instigator of the Umayyad coinage reform, ʻAbdallāh b. ʻAbd al-Malik b. Marwān was appointed to Egypt with powers over both 'prayer' and finances in the last few months of his father's life and remained in office until replaced by Qurra at the beginning of AH 90. Kindī (58), it seems worth mentioning, records that during his governorship another step was taken in the gradual process of replacing pre-Islamic practice with more Muslim equivalents: he ordered that the registers (*dawānīn*) which had been kept in Coptic should thenceforth be written in Arabic.

The weight of the British Museum's piece is a little low for a *dīnār.* The Paris specimen, however, weighs 4.22g. and that of the American Numismatic Society, which is slightly damaged, the same (information from Michael Bates and N.M. Lowick). They can probably safely be assumed to be *dīnar* weights in spite of the lack of a denomination. Finally, it should be noted that the British Museum's specimen is recorded in the accessions register as coming from Egypt.

QURRA B. SHARĪK
Governor and Finance Director 90-6/709-14

2 *Dīnār* weight

امر الا
مير قرة
بميزن دينر
واف

Ordered the A
mīr Qurra
a weight of a *dīnar,*
full-weight.

Beaded border.

OA + 4158. Green. 2.8cm; stamp 2.2cm; 4.19g. (*Plate 1*)

From the same die Launois 1957, 2 = Fahmī 1957, 1; Balog 1976, 4.

A second *dīnār*-weight die of Qurra, has a different legend with *mithqāl* for *mīzān* (Miles 1964a, 1). For an anonymous *fals* weight probably to be attributed to about the period of Qurra, see No. 435.

USĀMA B. ZAYD
Finance Director 96-9/714-17 and c. 102/720-1

3 Half-*dīnār* weight

امر اسا
مة بن زيد
بميزن نصف
دينر واف

Ordered Usā-
ma b. Zayd
a weight of a half-
dīnar, full-weight.

Dotted border.

(Coins and Medals) 80 6-3 70. Lane-Poole, 2. Pale bluish green. 2.1cm; stamp 1.7cm; 2.12g. (*Plate 1*)

From the same die Fahmī 1957, 4-5. Cf. Launois 1957, 11; Balog, 1976, 15.

On a second half-*dīnār*-weight die of Usāma the legend ends /*mīzān niṣf*/*wāf.* (Miles 1958a, 4; 1963 I, 2. Cf. Miles 1958a, 5.)

4 *Fals* weight of 10 *qīrāṭ*

امر ا
سامة بن ز
يد ميزان ا
لفلوس عشر
قراريط

Ordered U-
sāma b. Z-
ayd a weight for
fulūs of ten
qīrāṭs

OA + 4221. Green. 2.2cm; stamp 1.7cm; 2.01g. (*Plate 1*)

A piece in the Cabinet des Médailles in Paris has the same legend arranged in the same lines but comes from a different die (Launois 1960 II, 2. *A*/*l-fulūs* can be read on the photograph). Another in the Benaki Museum, which has not been illustrated, is likely to be from one or other of these two dies, perhaps the same one as the piece in the Cabinet des Médailles, since the reading of the third line caused similar difficulty (Miles 1963, 3). The use of the plural, *fulūs,* instead of *fals,* is unusual, though grammatically and semantically acceptable. The other examples seem to be three: 36-*kharrūba fals* weights of Ibrāhīm b. Ṣāliḥ which are considerably later (Nos 318-9), an anonymous type which may be early (Fahmī 1957, 392) and another anonymous type of 30 *kharrūba* with the legend in reverse (Nos 439-41).

Ten *qīrāṭ* or *kharrūba* is the smallest denomination of *fals* weight attested; besides Usāma, the only official so far known to have issued them, is Ṣāliḥ b. Muslim (Launois 1957, 241 = Fahmī 1957, 228). A well-known type of 9 *qīrat* does exist, buts its legend designates it a half-*fals* (Nos 413-4).

Like the other published specimens of Usāma's 10-*qīrāṭ fals* weight, the British Museum's piece is slightly heavier than is to be expected, given an average weight for the *qīrāt* of c. 0.195g, and the standard of accuracy which the coin weights usually maintain. Miles noted that, at 2.03g, the piece in the Benaki Museum was heavy; the one in the Cabinet des Médailles, though slightly chipped, weighs 2.02g. This would appear to be one of those cases of slight fluctuation in the standard, perhaps usually to be explained as due to imprecision in making the standard weight against which the pieces were checked. Usāma's other denomination of *fals* weight, that of 14 *qīrāṭ*, is closer to the average standard. All published specimens of the 14-*qīrāṭ* weight are from the same die (Casanova 1893, 20; Fahmī 1957, 7; Miles 1958a, 6; Balog 1976, 18).

5 Disk-weight: quarter-*raṭl*

امر اس[ا]
مة بن [زيد بر]
بع ر[طل و]
اف

Ordered Usā
ma b. Zayd a qua-
rter-*raṭl*, full-
measure.

Counterstamp above

الوفاء
لل[ه]

Honesty
for God

There may be a central dot on the counterstamp.

OA + 4419. The right hand half only. Green. Length 8.4cm; diameter of counterstamp 1.9cm; 58g. (*Plate 1*)

The piece appears to be the earliest published quarter-*raṭl*, as well as the earliest example of a counterstamp surviving paired with another stamp. The counterstamp itself is the earliest yet known with the legend *al-wafā' lillāh*. Among the vessel stamps with that legend there is no illustrated example from this die and it still therefore has to be proved that such secondary stamps were used on vessels as well as weights before the period of Ḥayyān b. Shurayḥ (see Introduction, pp.38f). For other *raṭl*-system weights of Usāma see Miles 1958a, 7 and Balog 1976, 14.

6 Quarter-*qisṭ*

امر ا
سامة بن ز
يد ربع قسط
واف

Ordered U-
sāma b. Z-
ayd a quarter-*qisṭ*,
full-measure.

Six-pointed star at end of legend.

OA + 4001. Green. Width 3.7cm. (*Plate 1*)

From the same die Petrie, 91; Balog 1973, 2; 1976, 23. Cf. Casanova 1893, 98; Miles 1958a, 10, 11.

7-10 Half-*qisṭ*

امر ا
سامة بن ز
يد نصف
قسط واف

Ordered U-
sāma b. Z-
ayd a half-
qisṭ, full-measure.

Six-pointed star at end of third line.

OA + 4000. Green. Width 4.2cm. Damaged at bottom right. (*Plate 1*)
OA + 4330. Green. Width 4.0cm. Chipped at bottom left. (*Plate 1*)
OA + 4331. Green. Width 3.8cm. (*Plate 1*)
93 2-5 87. Green. Width 4.1cm. (*Plate 1*)

From the same die Petrie, 89, 90; Launois 1957, 3; Miles 1958a, 8. Dudzus 1961, 2; Balog 1976, 21. Cf. Launois 1957, 4; Miles 1958a, 9; 1963 II, 1; 1971, 1.

We illustrate all four of the British Museum's pieces, as examples of the production of a single die. All Usāma's half-*qisṭ* stamps of which photographs have been published are from the same one.

11 *Wuqiyya* of fat (*duhn*)

امر اسا
مة بن زيد
[و]قية دهن

Ordered Usā-
ma b. Zayd
a *wuqiyya* of fat.

OA + 4284. Green. Width 2.1cm. (*Plate 1*)

This, and No. 12 below, are the first stamps for *duhn* of Usāma to appear but, although stamps for the commodity are not among the commonest, they are known from the governorship of Qurra until approximately the time when the use of commodity stamps was abandoned. There are, however, considerable gaps in the series. Measures for *duhn*, unlike those for any other commodity, are always given denominations on the *raṭl* system: *raṭl*, half-*raṭl* and *wuqiyya*.

When qualified by another word, *duhn* is used to describe a great number of extracts and preparations of drugs, perfumes and other substances, of which a long list is given by Ibn al-Bayṭār. On the stamps, where it stands by itself it is to be taken to mean rendered animal fat, the American 'grease'. This is the basic modern meaning of the word and was presumably the classical one, though it appears to be normally passed over as not requiring explicit definition by the Arabic lexicographers. The dictionaries do mention the use of *duhn* to grease the hair and in the early Islamic Ḥadīth literature, where it is mentioned, it is as hair grease (Wensinck, *s.v. duhn*). Since cosmetics, for instance henna and woad, do appear on vessel stamps it is not entirely impossible that *duhn* too was sold in the measures as a cosmetic, but it seems more likely that it was mainly used for cooking.

Wuqiyya stamps for *duhn*, like the present one, are noticeably small. We cannot at present be certain which *raṭl* system of weight the measures for *duhn* conformed to but if, as is most likely, it was the Umayyad system documented on the contemporary heavy weights, a *wuqiyya* of fat would have come to about 37g, a little under $1\frac{1}{3}$ ounces, the kind of quantity needed by somebody wanting the wherewithal to cook the next meal. Whatever their precise capacity, the small size of these stamps helps to confirm that the market in which the stamped measures were used was the pettiest area of retail trade.

12 Half-*raṭl* of fat (*duhn*)

امر اسا
مة بن زيد
نصف رطل
الدهن

Ordered Usā
ma b. Zayd
a half-*raṭl*
of fat.

OA + 4002. Green. Width 3.1 cm. (*Plate 1*)

13 Half-*qisṭ* of *ṭilā'* (wine)

امر اسا
مة بن زيد
نصف قسط
للطلاء

Ordered Usā-
ma b. Zayd
a half-*qisṭ*
for *ṭilā'*.

Faint dotted border.

OA + 4332. Pale blue. Width 3.6 cm. (*Plate 1*)

From the same die in the same (first) state Miles 1971, 2; Balog 1976, 27. *From the same die in the second state* Balog 1976, 28.

This is the first specimen in the present catalogue from a die which is known in two states. In the second state the word *wāf*, 'full-measure', has been inserted in small, rather cramped script below the original legend. Why the addition was thought necessary is not clear but the cramped appearance of the word *wāf* on a number of other types, such as No. 16 below, suggests that it may have been added as an afterthought on them too. The meaning of *ṭilā'*, and the historical implications of the stamps for it, are discussed under No. 24. Usāma also issued stamps for the complete *qisṭ* of *ṭilā'* (Balog 1976, 25) and for the quarter-*qisṭ* of the same substance (Miles 1948, 7; Balog 1976, 30, from the same die. Cf. Viré, 1; Balog 1976, 29).

14 *Qisṭ* of honey (*'asal*)

امر اسا
مة بن زي[د]
بقسط عسل
واف

Ordered Usā-
ma b. Zayd
a *qisṭ* of honey,
full-measure.

Six-pointed star at end of legend.

OA + 4003. Green. Width 5.0cm. (*Plat. 1*)

The only other type of stamp for honey that has been published is the *qisṭ* of Ḥayyān b. Shurayḥ, represented by two specimens from the same die (Miles 1958a, 13; 1971, 5).

15 *Mikyala* of *mizr* (beer)

امر اسامة
بن زيد مكيلة
المزر

Ordered Usāma
b. Zayd a measure
of *mizr*.

OA + 4004. Green. Width 5.2cm. (*Plate 1*)

From the same die Miles 1958a, 8.

The specimen published by Miles lacked much of the last line and the commodity remained unidentified. *Mizr* was first suggested as a reading for a different, anonymous, type by Balog (1963, 4 = 1976, 896). It means a sort of beer, normally made from grains of various kinds and sometimes from other substances. The early Islamic Ḥadīth literature defines it variously as being made from wheat, barley or honey. A definition quoted by Ibn al-Bayṭār mentions wheat, barley and millet. In modern Egypt, one is told, it refers principally to rice beer (Wensinck, Ibn al-Baytar, *s.v. mizr*).

As an intoxicant, *mizr*, whatever its ingredients, is forbidden by Islamic law. The historians of later periods mention episodes when the government of the time tried to suppress it, and others when it was content to tax it, or even attempt to monopolize its sale (e.g. Maqrīzī I, 104-5). The question of official toleration of the sale of alcoholic drink in eighth-century Egypt is discussed in some detail under No. 24 and, in connection with that discussion, it is useful to note the other published stamps for *mizr*, two at the most, and their probable dates. The anonymous type published by Balog does look early. Miles 1971, 62, also anonymous, seems to be for *mizr*, though the reading is obscure immediately after the commodity. It is one of very few stamps which have both a denomination in *raṭls* (2 *raṭls*?) and a price (1 *fals*). The script indicates a date in the middle of the eighth century.

16 *Mikyala* of woad (*wasma*)

امر اسا
مة بن زيد
مكيلة ا
لوسمة
واف

Ordered Usā-
ma b. Zayd
a measure
of woad,
full-measure.

Dotted border.

OA + 4333. Greenish blue. Chipped at bottom. Width 3.7cm. (*Plate 1*)

From the same die Balog 1976, 33, on which a faint dotted border seems to be visible.

As has been mentioned in the commentary to No. 13, the cramped *wāf* of the last line looks as if it might be an addition but, if so, no specimen from the die in its first state is known.

Stamps for *wasma* are quite common and exist in all the larger collections, but for a long time were not correctly read. The reading and the identification with woad were finally suggested by Miles (1951b, 5) in the case of a stamp of ʿUbaydāllāh b. al-Ḥabḥāb. The translation 'indigo' put forward by Launois (e.g. 1959 II, 1) is based at least in part on a misunderstanding of Miles's remarks. The word *wasma* is discussed in detail by Meyerhof and Sobhy in their edition of Ghāfiqī (276). It was at times used to refer to indigo as well as woad; the blue dying agent produced by both plants is chemically the same. However, *wasma* properly so called, as Ghāfiqī puts it, which he states was used with henna for dying the hair, is certainly woad. According to the editors, his botanical description probably refers to a variety of wild woad, but no doubt the word would also have been used for the ordinary cultivated species, *Isatis tinctoria L* well known in the ancient world as a source of blue dye for cloth. In Egypt itself woad was at some stage completely superseded as a dye for cloth by indigo which, under the name *nīla*, is listed among the crops for Egypt by the late medieval writers (Ibn Mammātī, 268–9; Cahen, 147; Müller-Wodarg, 43–4). The measures for woad, like the other glass ones, must have been used for retail sales and there can be no question of woad being supplied in them for an industrial purpose, that is for dying cloth. It must, on the contrary, like henna and *katam*, which also appear on stamps, have been intended for use as a cosmetic. Even after it was ousted for industrial use by the more productive indigo, and when that happened seems to be uncertain, woad may have remained in vogue for a while as a hair dye, but long before modern times this use of it seems to have been abandoned as well. The actual substance sold in the measures was presumably the powdered dye prepared from the leaves rather than, as has been commonly accepted in the literature of glass stamps, the leaves themselves. The production of the dye from the ground leaves is described by Forbes (110–1).

ḤAYYĀN B. SHURAYḤ

Finance Director c. 99–101/717–20

17 *Dīnār*-weight

امر حيان
بن شريح
ميزان دينر
واف

Ordered Ḥayyān
b. Shurayḥ
a weight of a *dīnar*,
full-weight.

Beaded border; six-pointed star above.

(Coins and Medals) 53 4–6 1000. Pietraszewski, 371; Sawaskiewicz, 9; Castiglioni, 2; Lane-Poole, 1; see also Rogers 1878, pp. 100–1 and, for a list of pieces of Ḥayyān, Miles, 1956. Green 2.8cm; stamp 2.2cm; 4.20g. (*Plate 1*)

This much-published piece, acquired by the British Museum with Ignatius Pietraszewski's collection of Islamic coins, is still the only known *dīnār* weight of Ḥayyān. Several half-*dīnār* weights have been published but no third. Lane-Poole's erroneous reading of *mithqāl*, 'weight', for its synonym *mīzān* is no more than a slip, perhaps influenced by Pietraszewski's original attempt at a reading, *mithmān*, which Castiglioni and Rogers had already emended.

18–19 Quarter-*qisṭ* of olive oil

امر حيان بن
شريح ربع
قسط للزيت
وافى

Ordered Ḥayyān b.
Shurayḥ a quarter-
qisṭ for olive oil,
full-measure.

OA + 4335. Pale blue. Width 3.3cm.
91 6–13 23. Green. Width 3.3cm. (*Plate 1*)

From the same die Petrie, 92; Miles 1963 II, 5; Balog 1976, 49, 51. Cf. Rogers 1878, 2; Viré, 3; Balog 1976, 46–8, 50.

The penultimate letter of the name of the commodity is malformed, which has given rise to various interpretations. It certainly looks like *ḥā'* or its equivalents, leading Balog to identify the substance as *rakham*, which he translates 'sour milk'. However, when the last letter is clear it can be seen to be an ordinary 'tooth-letter'. Miles and Viré's reading, *zayt*, is undoubtedly correct. In the series of *qisṭ*-system stamps for olive oil the quarter-*qisṭ* denomination is normally much the most common, and for Ḥayyān.b. Shurayḥ one is required to accompany the half-*qisṭ* and *qisṭ* types described next. Miles 1948, 10, identified as a quarter-*qisṭ* of olive oil, is certainly not that, though a convincing reading of the type has yet to be proposed. (Other specimens from the die are Miles 1958a, 17 and Balog 1976, 59–60. Cf. Casanova 1893, 100–1?) Miles 1958a, 15 is a quarter-*qisṭ*, and possibly for olive oil, but seems to be unique.

This type and most of Ḥayyān's other vessel stamps, for example Nos 22–5, have a feature which has occasionally attracted attention but never been closely examined. On such pieces the round head of *fā'* in the last word of the legend is attached to what may be described as a retroflex tail. Miles (1958a, 17) described this as the turned-back tail of the *fā'* itself. Launois (1957, 17), on the other hand, said that the *fā'* was written in reverse. However, as the second explanation imples, the tail of the final *fā'* in early Kufic points forward, as can be seen in the very numerous occurrences of *wāf* on glass stamps of all sorts. The solution would appear to be to interpret the tail as a *yā'* and, as Viré alone does, read *wāfiy* for *wāf*. The form of the *yā'* presents no problem; retroflex varieties are common on the glass, and on early coinage. Grammatically, *wāfiy* is strictly speaking incorrect, being the definite form of the word, properly used when it occurs with the definite article or in an equivalent construction. Where the word is indefinite, as it is on the stamps, the correct form in the nominative and genitive is *wāf* (with vocalization of the ending: *wāfin* for **wāfiyun* or **wāfiyin*). However the legends of the earlier stamps are full or expressions which, by the accepted usages of classical Arabic, are grave solecisms. Adjectives fail to agree in gender as in the common phrase *mikyala wāf*, indefinite nouns are accompanied by definite adjectives (e.g. *'adas al-muqashshar*), and so on. A systematic study of such peculiarities is beyond the scope of this catalogue, but in such a context *wāfiy* for *wāf* need cause no surprise.

20–21 Half-*qisṭ* of olive oil

امر حيان
بن شريح
نصف قسط
للزيت وا
ف

Ordered Ḥayyān
b. Shurayḥ
a half-*qisṭ*
for olive oil, full-
measure.

OA + 4007. Green. Width 3.2cm. Chipped at top.
OA + 4334. Blue green. Width 3.1cm. (*Plate 1*)

From the same die Miles 1948, 9; Dudzus, 1961, 3b. Cf. Miles 1958a, 14; Balog 1976, 52.

On this die, exceptionally under Ḥayyān, the otherwise standard form *wāf* is used instead of *wāfī*.

22–23 *Qisṭ* of olive oil

امر حيان
بن شريح
بقسط للز
يت وافى

Ordered Ḥayyān
b. Shurayḥ
a *qisṭ* for olive
oil, full measure.

Six-pointed star at end of legend.

OA + 4005. Green. Width 3.4cm. (*Plate 2*)
OA + 4006. Green. Width 3.2cm.

From the same die Miles 1958a, 12; 1963 II, 4; Dudzus 1961, 3a; Balog 1976, 41-2. Cf. Balog 1976, 40, 43.

Faced with a specimen of this type, on which the end of the name of the substance was not apparent, Miles read *tīn* (figs), and held to the reading thereafter. It was also accepted by Balog. The fig has its well-known pharmaceutical virtue as a laxative, but, fresh or dried, would be an unsuitable commodity to sell by measure. No other fig stamps have ever been identified and it is most unlikely that there should have been a short-lived policy to enforce such a method of selling figs – which from the number of pieces of this type would have had to have been in enormous demand. In fact, on a number of specimens, including the one illustrated here, the end of the commodity is clear on the next line, leaving no doubt that Dudzus was right to read *lil-zayt*.

24 *Qisṭ* of *ṭilā'* (wine)

امر حيان
بن شريح
قسط للطلاء
وافى

Ordered Ḥayyān
b. Shurayḥ
a *qisṭ* for *ṭilā'*,
full-measure.

1978 11-15 1. Green. Width 3.0cm. (*Plate 2*)

From the same die Balog 1976, 54.

The only other person who issued stamps for *ṭilā'* was Usāma b. Zayd (see No. 13 above). No anonymous types are known. Like Usāma, Ḥayyān has a set of three denominations for it: quarter-*qisṭ* (Miles 1958a, 16; Dudzus 1961, 3c. Cf. Miles 1964a, 3; Balog 1976, 58) and half-*qisṭ* (Launois 1957, 17; Balog 1976, 56. Cf. 55, 57), as well as the *qisṭ*. The illustrated examples of each denomination are from a single die. The classical Arabic dictionaries, such as that of Lane, give a number of definitions of *ṭilā'*. As a substance, its basic meaning appears to be tar, whence it is applied by extension to any tarry or thick liquid and in particular to ointment, especially one used on camels, and to a heavy syrup produced by boiling down grape juice. In the literature of glass stamps, ointment is the meaning that has been generally preferred, though occasionally wine syrup or wine have been mentioned as possibilities. For the proponents of the pharmaceutical theory of the function of commodity stamps ointment naturally seemed quite appropriate. As has been stated in the Introduction (p. 34), however, the evidence shows that the stamps were used for items of everyday consumption. Thus it appears more likely that on the stamps *ṭilā'* means some kind of popular beverage.

Rather remarkably there is literary evidence of the consumption of *ṭilā'* in Umayyad Egypt which indicates clearly that it was a beverage, gives some idea of its nature and explains why the series of stamps for it comes to an end with Ḥayyān b. Shurayḥ. The relevant passages are in a work called the *Sīrat 'Umār b. 'Abd al-'Azīz*, a biography of the Caliph 'Umar II (r. 99-101/717-20) by 'Abdallāh b. 'Abd al-Ḥakam. The author, who died in AH 214, was not contemporary with his subject but includes in his book the texts of several of 'Umar's own decrees. One of them, addressed to Ayyūb b. Shuraḥbīl, Governor of Egypt, and the Muslim community of that country, is wholly concerned with the prohibition of drink to the Muslims. The three passages in the Quran concerned with the subject, which show a progressive hardening in the attitude taken to wine, are quoted and explained. Criticism, rather in the style of a Victorian temperance tract, is then directed at people who persist in drinking alcohol. Indulgence in it leads to all other kinds of sin. The only excuse such people offer, we are told, is that there is no harm in drinking *ṭilā'*. As is made clearer by the passage from a second decree cited below, the prohibition against alcohol was being circumvented by the pretence that it only applied to wine in a very narrow sense. In the Quranic passages themselves the only word used is *khamr*, the ordinary word for wine made of grapes. The first decree continues by pointing to the role the Christians played in supplying the Muslims with drink and stating that God has provided abundant, non-intoxicating, alternatives. It goes on to forbid in particular, on the basis of a Ḥadīth of the Prophet Muḥammad, drinks prepared in skins or jars treated with resin. Drinkers of *ṭilā'* are said to have known that it could only be properly made in such vessels. On the strength of Muḥammad's complete ban on intoxicants, as reported in a Ḥadīth, the drinker is threatened with severe punishment in this world. If he is not discovered God will deal with him in the next ('Abdallāh b. 'Abd al-Ḥakam, 100-3).

In banning all intoxicants the decree is in agreement with the position taken by later Muslim lawyers, but as far as *ṭilā'* itself is concerned it takes a less standard position, though one due perhaps to no more than a variant definition of *ṭilā'*. The definition accepted by the majority of jurists and supported, as usual, by Ḥadīth, has reached the dictionaries but not, it is interesting to note, the pharmacopoeias which appear to ignore *ṭilā'* completely. By this definition *ṭilā'* is grape juice reduced by cooking to one third of its original bulk. Most jurists accepted that it was lawful. Obviously the concentration of sugar in the thickened liquid would prevent it from fermenting and if the juice happened to have begun to ferment the alcohol would be driven off in the cooking (Wensinck, *s.v. ṭilā'*; E.I.[1,2] *art. khamr*). *Ṭilā'* of this kind therefore differs from that banned by 'Umar II which was normally intoxicating. A passage in another of his decrees, addressed to tax officials in general, is particularly concerned with *ṭilā'*. A well-known story is quoted in it which offers an explanation of how the word got this meaning and justifies the use of *ṭilā'* by the precedent of 'Umar I (r. 13-23/634-44). Some people came to 'Umar with a drink (*sharāb*) which had been cooked until it became thick. He asked if it was *ṭilā'*, meaning, it is explained, *ṭilā'* for camels, i.e. a kind of ointment used on them. On tasting the drink he said there was no harm in it and people drank it. The decree carefully points out that the pious Muslims who drank it did so before it became intoxicating but nevertheless goes on to ban it to the Muslims completely. Clearly, even for 'Umar II, *ṭilā'* was not always necessarily intoxicating. However, the word had come to be used for alcoholic beverages to get round the letter of the law. This is apparent from the sarcastic definition given in the second decree, evidently a popular one, for it is also found in the poetic citations for the word quoted in Lane's dictionary. In the words of the decree: '... as for *ṭilā'*, there is no good in it for the Muslims; it is only wine (*khamr*) nicknamed *ṭilā'*' ('Abdallāh b. 'Abd al-Ḥakam, 97-8). Exactly how the intoxicating *ṭilā'* was made we do not know.

The Governor to whom 'Umar's first decree was addressed was Ayyūb b. Shuraḥbīl, who was in charge of 'prayer' in Egypt from 99-101/717-20, when the finances were in the control of Ḥayyān b. Shurayḥ. The disappearance of *ṭilā'* from the list of commodities sold by the stamped measures after Ḥayyān shows that the Caliph's policy of banning drink did have some effect. In connection with it, it is appropriate to examine the evidence the stamps provide for other alcoholic drinks. Two are so far represented, *mizr*, 'beer', and *usqurqa* or *suqurqa*, which Balog has convincingly proposed to identify with what dictionaries and pharmacopoeias call *suqurqa'* and describe as a beer made from millet. Few stamps for either are known. The only one for *mizr* with an official's name is the type of Usāma b. Zayd represented in the British Museum's collection by No. 15. As noted in the commentary to that piece, two anonymous types for *mizr* have been published, one of which, judging by the script, may be early; the other seems to belong to the Abbasid period. As for *usqurqa*, the earliest known type is a *mikyala* of Ḥayyān b. Shurayḥ, presumably issued during the Caliphate of 'Umar II (Balog 1976, 39). Ḥayyān's name also appears, subordinate to that of the Caliph Yazīd II, on an unusual piece for a *qadaḥ*, or cup, of the same commodity (Miles 1956 = 1960b, fig. 4. The reading *usqurqa* is due to Balog). This was, of course, issued after the death of 'Umar, whom Yazīd succeeded. The only other published type is even later, a *mikyala* of al-Qāsim b. 'Ubaydallāh (Balog 1976, 173. Cf. Rogers 1878, 3). Thus, although it is reasonably certain that the sale of *ṭilā'* in officially approved measures came to an end as a consequence of 'Umar II's temperance policy, the same is not entirely true for other alcoholic beverages. However, in general, stamps for such drinks tend to be early.

Whether it was even intended that Egypt should become completely 'dry' is in any case uncertain. It is noticeable that 'Umar's decrees firmly forbid intoxicants to the Muslims but say nothing about preventing the protected communities from drinking. In Egypt at the time the vast majority of the population was Christian and accustomed to make use of wine and other such drinks. Later it was certainly accepted that the Muslim, and hence the Muslim government, could not participate in or profit by the manufacture and sale of intoxicants and perhaps the disappearance of *ṭilā'* from the stamps was due to the acceptance of that point of view.

25 *Mikyala* of an unidentified substance

امر حيان
بن شريح
مكيلة --
- وافى

Ordered Ḥayyān
b. Shurayḥ
a measure of -
-, full-measure.

OA + 4008. Green. Width 4.1cm (*Plate 2*)

The name of the commodity appears to begin with three 'tooth-letters' or *sīn*, followed by *dāl* or *kāf*. The letter visible on the next line could be *rā'* or *nūn* or the end of *sīn*. None of the possibilities suggests a reading that can be happily accepted.

YAZĪD II
Caliph 101-5/720-4

26 Quarter-*qisṭ*, with Usāma b. Zayd

[ام]ر عبد ا
[لل]ه يزيد امير ا
[ل]مؤمنين اصلح[ه]
[ا]لله بربع قسط
[و]اف على يد[ى]
[ا]سامة بن
[زيد]

Ordered the slave of G-
od Yazīd, Commander of
the faithful, may God keep him
righteous, a quarter-*qisṭ*,
full-measure, at the hands of
of Usāma b.
Zayd.

OA + 4285. Green. Width 4.1cm (*Plate 2*)

Stamps of Yazīd II together with Ḥayyān b. Shurayḥ, such as the next item, are well known and have long been correctly identified, but there is no parallel to the present piece on which Yazīd is joined by Usāma. Only part of the name survives and that of the father is missing, but the restoration seems certain and confirms those literary sources which say that Usāma was appointed Finance Director of Egypt a second time in the Caliphate of Yazīd. A number of writers state that Usāma's cruelty and injustice made him particularly offensive to the pious 'Umar b. 'Abd al-'Azīz, Yazīd's predecessor (r. 99-101/717-20). Immediately on his accession, before the former Caliph Sulaymān was buried, 'Umar sent orders for Usāma to be imprisoned. The Coptic historian, Severus (III, 67), relying on an early source, says that Usāma died at this time while being brought from Alexandria to Fusṭāṭ. Other writers, however, have him surviving later. Ṭabarī (II, 1436) briefly mentions Usāma once, as *'āmil*, i.e. Finance Director, of Egypt in AH 102. A similar tradition appears in the relatively early biography of 'Umar b. 'Abd al-'Azīz which, giving as an example of Usāma's cruelty his brutal habit of mutilating horses and throwing them to the crocodiles, relates that 'Umar ordered that Usāma should be kept fettered except at prayer-time and imprisoned for a year in each military district (*jund*). He had spent a year in prison in Egypt and a year in Palestine when 'Umar died. Yazīd placed him over Egypt again ('Abdallāh b. 'Abd al-Ḥakam, 34). Usāma's second appointment did not happen immediately upon Yazīd's accession, since the stamps of Yazīd with Ḥayyān, a few of which are dated 101, show that Ḥayyān was not replaced at once. Nor is it likely that Usāma remained long in office. (See also Jahshiyārī, 47-8; Grohmann 1924, 98; Miles 1948, p. 73.)

27 Quarter-*qisṭ* of olive oil, with Ḥayyān b. Shurayḥ

امر عبد الله
يزيد امير المؤ
منين ربع قسط
لزيت واف على
[يـ]ـدى حيان بن
[شريح]

Ordered the slave of God
Yazīd, Commander of the Faithful, a quarter-*qisṭ*
for olive oil, full-measure, at the
hands of Ḥayyān b.
Shurayḥ

OA + 4010. Green. Width 3.9cm. (*Plate 2*)

From the same die Petrie, 86; Miles 1951b, 7; 1958a, 20. Cf. Miles 1958a, 19, 21-2; Balog 1976, 62.

The half-*qisṭ* denomination for olive oil in the series of Yazīd and Ḥayyān is represented by a piece in the Museo Sacro of the Vatican (Fremersdorf, 892).

28 *Qisṭ* of olive oil, with Ḥayyān b. Shurayḥ (?)

امر عبد ا
لله يزيد امير
[ا]لمؤمنين اصلحـ[ـه]
[ا]لله بقسط للز[ا]
[يـ]ـت واف على
يدى - - -
[- - - -]

Ordered the slave of G-
od Yazīd, Commander
of the Faithful, may God keep him
righteous, a *qisṭ* for olive
oil, full-measure, at the
hands of - - -
- - - -

OA + 4009. Green. Width 3.9cm. (*Plate 2*)

From the same die Casanova 1893 I, 95.

The piece in the Fouquet Collection was the first stamp of Yazīd II to be published and it was some time before the original attribution to the Caliph Yazīd I (r. 60-4/680-4) was discarded. The name of the second official is not visible on either specimen. Since, on nearly all of Yazīd's stamps, where a second name is visible, it is that of Ḥayyān, it is most likely that the die of this type also bore the same name. However, the discovery of No. 26 above, on which Yazīd II is associated with Usāma b. Zayd means that the possibility that this type bore the name of Usāma cannot be entirely ruled out.

'UBAYDALLĀH B. AL-ḤABḤĀB
Finance Director 107-16/725-34

For the date of 'Ubaydallāh's appointment see Azdī (27) and p. 72 below.

29 Third-*dīnār* weight

مما امر
به عبيد ا
لله ابن الحبحا
ب مثقال ثلث
واف

Of what ordered
'Ubayda-
llah b. al-Ḥabḥā-
b. A weight of a third,
full-weight.

OA + 4161 (S. 330). Lane-Poole, 3G. Green. 2.1cm; stamp 1.5cm; 1.41g. (*Plate 2*)

From the same die Miles 1948, 11; Launois 1959, 6; Balog 1976, 73. Cf. Miles 1963 I, 6; Balog 1976, 71-2.

This is the commonest of 'Ubaydallāh's third-*dīnār* weights. Some specimens, including the British Museum's one, appear to have been produced when the die had become blurred, probably owing to rust. The two other known dies both have a legend beginning with *bismillāh* and with *mīzān* in place of *mithqāl* but the arrangement of the lines differs (Petrie, 103; Fahmī 1957, 14).

30 **Half-*dīnār* weight**

بسم الله
مما امر به عبيد
الله بن الحبحا
ب ميزان نصف
واف

In the name of God.
Of what ordered ʻUbayd-
allah b. al-Ḥabḥā-
b. A weight of a half,
full-weight.

(Coins and Medals) 1978 5-3 1. Green. 2.2cm; stamp 1.6cm; 2.11g. (*Plate 2*)

Other specimens from the die are known but all of them represent it in a later state, with a six-pointed star added over the end of *wāf* (Miles 1958a, 23; Balog 1976, 69. Cf. Miles 1964b, 5. Two other dies of ʻUbaydallāh are known to have had a similar star added, one a *dīnār*-weight type with legends corresponding to those of the present piece (see No. 32) and the other for *fals* weights of 24 *kharrūba* (see No. 41).

A second type of half-*dīnār* weight of ʻUbaydallāh is known with the legend beginning *mimmā amara bihi* and with *mithqāl* instead of *mīzān* for 'weight' (Balog 1976, 70. Cf. Castiglioni, 6; Fahmī 1957, 13).

31 ***Dīnār* weight**

مما امر به
عبيد الله ا
بن الحبحاب
مثقال د
ينر واف

Of what ordered
ʻUbaydallah
b. al-Ḥabḥāb.
A weight of a d-
īnar, full-weight.

OA + 4159. Green. 2.9cm; stamp 2.3cm; 4.23g. (*Plate 2*)

From the same die Launois 1959, 5; Balog 1976, 67. Cf. Miles 1951b, 3.

Five dies are known of the *dīnār* denomination under ʻUbaydallāh b. al-Ḥabḥāb, all easily distinguishable by differences in the legend or its disposition. Besides the one described immediately below there are two dated types of AH 114 (Fahmī 1957, 9) and 115 (Miles 1948, 10a described on p. 79. Cf. Miles 1964a, 4) and a fifth type represented by a single defective piece (Balog 1976, 68). On this last there would seem to be room on the missing lower part for a date.

On the present piece, note the curious division of the word *i/bn* between the second and third lines.

32 ***Dīnār* weight**

بسم الله
مما امر به عبيد
الله بن الحبحاب
ميزان دينر
واف

In the name of God.
Of what ordered ʻUbayd-
allah b. al-Ḥabḥāb.
A weight of a *dīnār*
full-weight.

Six-pointed star over the last letter of the legend.

OA + 4160. Green. 2.9cm; stamp 2.2cm; 4.21g. (*Plate 2*)

From the same die in the same (second) state Petrie, 99; Launois 1957, 51, = Fahmī 1957, 11. *From the same die in the first state* Fahmī 1957, 10; Launois 1959, 4.

The die was altered by the addition of the star (Cf. Nos 30, 41).

33-35 ***Shaṭr* (half-*fals*) weight of 12 *kharrūba***

بسم الله
امر عبيد الله
بن الحبحاب مثقال
شطر اثنى عشر
ة خروبة و
اف

In the name of God.
Ordered ʻUbaydallah
b. al-Ḥabḥāb a weight
of a *shaṭr* of twelve
kharrūba, full-
weight.

Border, seemingly beaded in parts.

OA + 4166. Green. 2.3cm; stamp 1.8cm; 2.32g.
OA + 4167. Olive green. 2.5cm; stamp 1.8cm; 2.33g. (*Plate 2*)
OA + 4222. Green. 2.3cm; stamp 1.8cm; 2.10g.

From the same die Petrie, 102; Miles 1948, 16; Launois 1957, 58; Fahmī 1957,36-7; Miles 1958a, 31; Balog 1976, 86. Cf. Miles 1948, 15; Launois 1957, 59; Fahmī 1957, 38-40.

This is the only common type of weight on which the word *shaṭr* occurs in the legend. A second die for the same denomination, lacking the border and the last line of the legend, is known from a single specimen (Launois 1960, 4). Elsewhere *shaṭr* is found on two different anonymous weights of 18 *kharrūba* (Launois 1969, 24; Balog 1976, 828) and Miles (1964b, p. 84) has mentioned its occurrence on an anonymous type of 22 *kharrūba* (?). The word is not known from any other numismatic context but, as Launois was the first to recognize, the dictionary meaning of *shaṭr*, 'half', makes excellent sense. Balog, committed to the hypothesis that there was an unvarying standard of 36 *kharrūba* for the *fals*, was naturally unable to accept that a 12-*kharrūba shaṭr* could be half a *fals* and preferred the translation 'part', but, as has been argued in the Introduction (pp. 21-2), there is little to recommend the hypothesis. Dictionaries do give 'part' as one of the meanings of *shaṭr* but on the whole the lexicographic tradition on *shaṭr* and its cognates supports the meaning 'half'. *Shaṭr*, for instance, may mean a hemistich of verse.

Although *fals* and *shaṭr* do not occur together in the same legend, the actual weights of *shaṭr* types have nothing to do with the *dīnār* or the *dirham*, and they evidently belong to the *fals* system. Confirmation of this point and of the fact that the *shaṭr* pieces are half denominations comes from the existence of a type of 24-*kharrūba fals* weight in the name of ʻUbaydallāh, the legends of which show considerable similarities to those of the 12-*kharrūba shaṭr* weights (e.g. No. 41 below). Evidently this type provides the corresponding whole denomination. ʻUbaydallāh is the only official in whose name half denominations were issued. The other half denominations which have *niṣf fals* (half a *fals*) in the legend are discussed under the next item.

36 Half-*fals* weight of 17 *qīrāṭ*

بسم الله
امر عبيد الله
بن الحبحاب
بمثقال نصف
فلس سبعة
عشر قيرط
واف

In the name of God.
Ordered ʻUbaydallah
b. al-Ḥabḥāb
a weight of a half (*niṣf*)
fals of seven-
teen qīraṭ,
full-weight.

OA + 4165. Green. 2.8cm; 3.24g. (*Plate 2*)

From the same die Miles 1948, 13; Fahmī 1957, 32; Balog 1976, 84. Cf. Fahmī 1957, 33.

ʻUbaydallāh b. al-Ḥabḥāb is the only official known to have issued half-*fals* weights with his name on them. As well as the 17-*qīrāṭ* variety he issued one of 15 *qīrāṭ* (Miles 1948, 14; Fahmī 1957, 34-5; Balog 1976, 85, all from one die. Cf. Launois 1957, 57; Miles 1958a, 30). Anonymous types with *niṣf fals* in the legend are the common one of 9 *qīrāṭ* described below (Nos 413-4) and another of 18 *qīrāṭ* (Balog 1976, 825). As has been argued in the commentary to Nos 33-5 pieces with the denomination *shaṭr* also appear to be half-*fals* weights. In most cases *shaṭr* and *niṣf-fals* types can easily be paired with *fals* weights containing double the number of *kharrūba* or *qīrāṭ* and with marked similarities of legend and script. These pairs are obviously the whole and half denominations in use at a particular time. Thus the 17-*qīrāṭ* half-*fals* weight of ʻUbaydallāh is the half denomination of his 34-*kharrūba fals* weight (see No. 42) and his 15-*qīrāṭ* half-*fals* weight the half of his 30-*qīrāṭ fals* weight (Petrie, 98, from the same die as Launois 1957, 58 = Fahmī 1957, 16. Cf. Casanova 1893, 21).

37-39 *Fals* weight of 18 *kharrūba*

مما امر
عبيد الله ابن ا
لحبحاب مثقال فلس
ثمنية اعشر
خروبة

Of what ordered
ʻUbaydallah b. a-
l-Ḥabḥāb. A weight of a *fals*
of eighteen
kharrūba.

Semicircle pointing downwards with dot inside below the legend.

OA + 4164. Green. 2.7cm; stamp 1.9cm; 3.64g.
OA + 4319. Green. 2.6cm; stamp 1.9cm; 3.67g. (*Plate 2*)
(Coins and Medals) 1910 6-9 12. Green. Chipped at bottom. 2.6cm; stamp 2.0cm; 3.37g.

From the same die Petrie, 100-1; Launois 1957, 54; Fahmī 1957, 26; Miles 1958a, 29; 1963 I, 8; Balog, 1976, 81. Cf. Launois 1957, 55-6; Miles 1964a, 8.

The spelling of the ʻ*ashar* of 'eighteen' with an initial *alif* is abnormal. As Miles (1958a, referring to Grohmann 1955, p. 105) has pointed out, the *alif* sometimes occurs in numbers in the teens on early papyri, while according to Fahmī it resembles the modern colloquial pronunciation of Upper Egypt. Both comments point to its being a dialect form rather than simply a misspelling.

The same orthographic peculiarity occurs on a second 18-*kharrūba*-weight die of ʻUbaydallāh, not represented in the present collection, which has the same legend, slightly differently arranged and a semicircle pointing upwards at the top (Launois 1957, 52; Fahmī 1957, 25; Balog 1976, 79. Cf. Launois 1957, 53; Balog 1976, 80. Fahmī 1957, 27-31 are compared to this type but, to judge from the pieces in the same collection published by Launois, must include at least two from the die with the semicircle below).

A high proportion of pieces of both types, like the British Museum's two intact specimens, weigh around 3.65g, rather heavier than is to be expected and implying a *kharrūba* of just over 2.0g.

40 *Fals* weight of 20 *kharrūba*

مما امر به
عبيد الله بن ا
لحبحاب مثقا
ل فلس عشرين
خروبة واف

Of what ordered
ʻUbaydallah b. a-
l-Ḥabḥāb. A weigh-
t of a *fals* of twenty
kharrūba, full-weight.

Eight-pointed star with semicircle pointing left behind the legend.

(Coins and Medals) 91 10-3 27. Bluish green. 2.9cm; stamp 2.4cm; 4.01g. (*Plate 2*)

From the same die Fahmī 1957, 22; Balog 1973, 5; 1976,

77. Cf. Castiglioni, 15; Fahmī 1957, 23-4; Miles 1964a, 7.

There appears to be only the one known 20-*kharrūba* die of ʻUbaydallāh. On the other hand there are three different dies recorded for his 20-*qīrāṭ* weights, all with different legends (1. Launois 1957, 49 = Fahmī 1957, 21; Miles 1958a, 26; Launois 1960 II, 2; Cf. Miles 1964a, 6; 2. Miles 1948, 12; Balog 1976, 78; 3. Miles 1958a, 27).

41 *Fals* **weight of 24** *kharrūba*

بسم الله
امر عبيد ا
لله بن الحبحاب
بمثقال فلس
اربعة وعشرين
خروبة وا
ف

In the name of God.
Ordered ʻUbayda-
llah b. al-Ḥabḥāb
a weight of a *fals*
of four and twenty
kharrūba, full-
weight.

Six-pointed star above end of fourth line.

OA + 4163. Green. 3.0cm; 4.58g. (*Plate 2*)

From the same die in the same (second) state Launois 1957, 45; Fahmī 1957, 17; Balog 1976, 76. Cf. Launois 1957, 46-7; Fahmī 1957, 18-20. *From the same die in the first state* Miles 1958a, 25; 1963 II, 7 (distorted); Launois 1960 I, 5. Cf. Miles 1971, 7-8.

The star is an addition on the die (cf. Nos 30, 32). As pointed out above under Nos 33-5 the 12-*kharrūba shaṭr* weights provide the half denomination of this type.

42 *Fals* **weight of 34** *qīrāṭ*

بسم الله
امر عبيد الله
بن الحبحاب
بمثقال فلس فيه
اربعة وثلثين
قيراط وا
ف

In the name of God.
Ordered ʻUbaydallah
b. al-Ḥabḥāb
a weight of a *fals* in which are
four and thirty
qīrāṭ, full-
weight.

Six-pointed star at end of third and seventh lines.

OA + 4162. Right edge distorted by a bubble and very slightly chipped. Green. 3.5cm; 6.47g. (*Plate 2*)

From the same die Fahmī 1957, 15; Miles 1958a, 24; Launois 1959, 7; Balog 1976, 75.

The construction of the end of the legend as a descriptive clause introduced by *fīhī* ('in it') does not seem to be found on any other weight and has caused some of the commentators difficulty. The legend on one type of anonymous vessel stamp is somewhat similar, reading, in its entirety, '*fihā wuqiyya wa niṣf zayt bi-fals*', meaning 'in it (is) an ounce and a half of olive oil for a *fals*' (Balog 1976, 878-8). As has already been suggested, it appears that ʻUbaydallāh's half-*fals* weight of 17 *qīrāṭ*, described under No. 36 above, is the half denomination of the present type.

43 *Fals* **weight**

(ب)سم الله
هذا ما (ا)مر به
[-]د الله بن الحبحاب
فلب سه عد --
خروبة مثق[--]
-- عر [--]

In the name of God.
This is what ordered
- - b. al-Ḥabḥāb
- - - -
kharrūba - -
- - - -

OA + 4180. Green. 2.8cm; 3.96g. (*Plate 2*)

The script is crude and the readings suggested tentative. However it is clear that the text resembles that of a *fals* weight and refers to ʻUbaydallāh, whose father's unusual name is reasonably plain. Its weight is perfect for 20 *kharrūbas* but one wonders whether it was an official issue. A few types with similar garbled legends are known for other governors, for instance what appears to be a comparable *fals* weight of Ḥayyān b. Shurayḥ, with the legend partly in reverse, was published by Casanova (1893 V, 30) and a rather more legible type of al-Qāsim b. ʻUbaydallāh is represented in the British Museum's collection (No. 77). This latter, though incompetently written, is clearly copied from al-Qāsim's ordinary *fals-al-kabīr* weights (e.g. Nos 74-6). There is no obvious model for the present piece which has little in common with ʻUbaydallāh's 20-*kharrūba* weights, such as No. 40. In general the types with garbled legends do not share any great family resemblance.

44 Disk weight: *raṭl*

[مم]ا امر
[به عب]يد الله
[ابن الحبحا]ب
[----]

Of what ordered
ʻUbaydallah
b. al-Ḥabḥāb
- - - -

OA + 4422. Most of the top right half, missing a large chip from the top and chipped elsewhere. Green. Length

10.8cm; stamp c. 4.5cm; 188g. (*Plate 2*)

From its size the piece is a *raṭl* and the legend may well have ended '*raṭl wāf*'. No ordinary *raṭl* weight of ʿUbaydallāh appears to have been published and, indeed, his weights on the ordinary *raṭl* system are remarkably rare in comparison with his meat weights. Only four seem to have been described, three rather badly damaged half-*raṭls* (Miles 1951b, p. 7; 1963 I, 23; Balog 1976, 66) and a single *wuqiyya* (Miles 1958a, 32).

45 Ring weight: half-*raṭl* of meat (*laḥm*)

بسم الله
امر عبيد الله
بن الحبحاب
بطبعة نصف ر
طل لحم واف

In the name of God.
Ordered ʿUbaydallah
b. al-Ḥabḥāb
the stamping of a half-*r-*
aṭl of meat, full-weight.

Counterstamp to left

الوفاء
لله

Honesty
for God.

OA + 4401. Green. Large pieces missing at bottom and on both sides. 5.2 x 6.0cm; main stamp 2.9cm; counter-stamp 1.5cm; 146g. (*Plate 3*)

No half-*raṭl* meat weight of ʿUbaydallāh has previously been published. The form of the legend, beginning *bismillāh*, and the associations of the counterstamp show that this type belonged to ʿUbaydallāh's later series of stamps, some of which are combined on weights with the anonymous stamp bearing the date 114 which occurs on No. 49.

The present counterstamp has been found on some of ʿUbaydallāh's other weights in association with stamps with legends beginning *bismillāh*, the *raṭl* of meat (e.g. No. 48) and the *raṭl* of ʿBB (Balog 1973, 3; for the substance see No. 90). It is also found together with the stamp dated 114 beside a damaged denomination stamp which presumably bore ʿUbaydallāh's name (Miles 1963 I, 23). It occurs once even later, in the time of al-Qāsim b. ʿUbaydallāh, on a double-*raṭl* meat weight (Miles 1948, 32). The writer knows of no example of the use of this counterstamp as a vessel stamp.

46–47 Ring weights: *raṭl* of meat

مما امر به
عبيد الله ابن
الحبحاب ر
طل لحم و
اف

Of what ordered
ʿUbaydallah b.
al-Habhāb. A *r-*
aṭl of meat, full-
weight.

95 3-12 2. The upper half, chipped around the stamp and elsewhere. Green. 6.6 x 4.1cm; top 5.6cm; stamp 3.0cm; 180g. (*Plate 3*)

95 12-20 4. Fragment of the top; stamp chipped at top. Green. Length 6.2cm; stamp 3.0cm; 99g.

Balog 1976, 64 has a very distorted impression but appears to be from the same die.

The word *laḥm* appears to begin with a *mīm*, and what is here taken to be the *lām*, above the *ḥā'*, is vestigial. Perhaps the engraver began the word absentmindedly, forgetting to work in reverse and them attempted to emend. On the other hand, the 2-*raṭl* piece of this issue (Miles 1948, 17) has a loop below the line which reads naturally as part of the *hā'* and the *mīm* on the *raṭl* may be a botched version of a similar loop.

No. 45 and Balog's specimen, which have largely intact tops, show that a counterstamp was not always, if ever, used with this type. A second die for a *raṭl* of meat, that of No. 48, is found on another piece (Balog 1976, 65) accompanied by the same counterstamp dated 114 as appears on No. 49. This shows that the stamp of Nos 46–7 was in use before the one associated with the stamp of 114, a year nearly at the end of ʿUbaydallāh's exceptionally long period of office. Our knowledge of his weight stamps is far from complete but most of them can be placed in two categories. One has legends beginning *mimmā amara bihi* ('Of what ordered'), the other legends beginning *bismillāh* ('In the name of God'). No stamp of the first category has yet been found with a counterstamp. Several of those of the second are known in combination with counterstamps of the end of ʿUbaydallāh's Finance Directorship, either the one dated 114 (see No. 49) or the one inscribed *al-wafā' lillāh* which is itself associated on occasion with the 114 stamp and which remained in use after al-Qāsim became Finance Director (see No. 45). One stamp occurs with both counterstamps together, but the beginning of the legend is missing (Miles 1963 I, 23).

As far as weights are concerned it is evident that the series of stamps with *mimmā amara bihi* precedes that with *bismillāh*. On vessel stamps of the *qisṭ* system a rather similar pattern can be discerned; stamps with *mimmā amara bihi* can be taken to precede a series with legends beginning *bismillāh*, which are dated 111 and also give the name of the executive, Junāda b. Maysara (see Nos 51–4). With coin weights and other vessel stamps the picture is more complicated but the same two categories of legend are found and the succession of types was probably to some extent similar.

48 Ring weight: *raṭl* of meat

بسم الله
امر عبيد ا
لله بن الحبحا
ب رطل لحم
واف

In the name of God.
Ordered ʻUbayda-
llah b. al-Ḥabḥā-
b a *raṭl* of meat,
full-weight.

Counterstamp to right Same die as counterstamp of No. 45.

OA + **4357**. Fragment. Part of the top, lacking the bottom of the large stamp and most of the right of the counterstamp. Green. Length 5.7cm; 86g. (*Plate 3*)

From the die of the main stamp Petrie, 96; Dudzus 1959, 1a; Balog 1976, 65.

The Berlin piece published by Dudzus has the same counterstamp placed to the right of the main stamp. Balog's has to the left the counterstamp dated 114 which appears on No. 49. As is argued under Nos 46-7, this type is the later of the *raṭl*-denomination meat-weight stamps of ʻUbaydallāh. The counterstamp has been discussed under No. 45.

49 Ring weight: 2 *raṭls* of meat

بسم الله
امر عبيد الله
بن الحبحاب
بطبعة رطلين
لحم واف

In the name of god.
Ordered ʻUbaydallah
b. al-Ḥabḥāb
the stamping of two *raṭls*
of meat, full-weight.

Counterstamp to left

سنة ا
ربع
عشرة
و مائة

Year f-
our-
teen
and a hundred.

OA + **4379**. Fragment. The right side and most of the top, missing part of the left hand stamp. Green 6.3 x 7.8cm; main stamp c. 3.0cm; counterstamp c. 2.2cm; 398g. (*Plate 3*)

The large stamp does not appear to have been published. One example is known of another 2-*raṭl* meat-weight stamp of ʻUbaydallāh (Miles 1948, 17). Its legend begins *mimmā amara bihi* and it belongs to the earlier series used without counterstamps (see Nos 46-7).
The counterstamp is naturally of importance for dating ʻUbaydallāh's weight stamps and has been mentioned in this context under the four preceding items. It has been illustrated on a *raṭl* meat weight (Balog 1976, 65) and on a presumed half-*raṭl* on which it is associated with the counterstamp of Nos 45 and 48 (Miles 1963 I, 23, where the date is misread). Not illustrated, but probably from the same die, is the counterstamp of Miles 1948, 24, on which the main stamp was largely illegible. The stamp of 114 is not known from vessel stamps and may not have been used on them. It seems that the only other stamp with a legend consisting solely of a date is one of 135, used on a weight of Muḥammad b. Shuraḥbīl (Balog 1976, 332).

50 Vessel stamp with name only

عبيد ا
لله بن
الحبحاب

ʻUbayda-
llah b.
al-Ḥabḥāb

OA + **4011**. Green, the surface partly iridescent. 3.8 x 2.5cm. Cf. Miles 1958a, 45 (*Plate 3*)

The completion of the reading is based on a specimen from the same die in the Fitzwilliam Museum, Cambridge. Miles did not illustrate the one in the American Numismatic Society's collection but mentions the 'exceptionally large and crude' script. This type is not to be confused with the small disks with the same legend in smaller script (e.g. Balog 1976, 87-8). The latter tend to show signs of smoothing on the bottom, but one cannot accept Balog's theory that they are vessel stamps that have been ground down by antique dealers. Occasional pieces, for example No. 262 below, are found which have been so treated to improve their appearance but the odds against all, or even many, specimens of a particular type suffering the same treatment must be astronomical. The smoothing of the backs of these disks of ʻUbaydallāh must therefore be assumed to be original and since their weights vary a lot they must be placed in the category of tokens without metrological function.
The function of the vessel stamps with ʻUbaydallāh's name but no denomination is also obscure. It appears unlikely that they were used by themselves. Later, of course, the use of two or more stamps, one of them with the denomination, is common but it is difficult to see which of the anonymous or unassigned stamps with denominations would make suitable partners for this type.

51-53 Quarter-*qisṭ*

مما امر
به عبيد الله
ابن الحبحاب ربع
قسط وا
ف

Of what ordered
ʻUbaydallah
b. al-Ḥabḥāb. A quarter-
qisṭ, full-
measure.

OA + **4013**. Green. Width 3.4cm.
OA + **4134**. Green. Width 3.7cm. (*Plate 3*)
OA + **4336**. Greenish blue. Width 3.6cm.

From the same die Petrie, 105-6; Launois 1957, 20; Miles 1958a, 38; Dudzus 1961, 4b (2 specimens); Balog 1976, 91, 94. Cf. Casanova 1893, 106-7; Miles 1948, 20; Launois 1957, 21-7; Viré, 11; Miles 1958a, 39-41; 1963, 8; 1971, 11; Balog 1976, 90, 92-3, 95-6.

This very common die appears to be the only quarter-*qisṭ* which has the name of ʻUbaydallāh b. al-Ḥabḥāb alone.

On his second type, represented here by No. 54, the name of a subordinate official, Junāda b. Maysara, also appears. The second type is dated AH 111 and presumably the type with ʻUbaydallāh alone was in use in the earlier part of his governorship - another case, like that of the heavy weights discussed above, which gives reason to think that under ʻUbaydallāh, in many cases, legends beginning *mimmā amara bihi* are earlier than those beginning *bismillāh*.

54 Quarter-*qisṭ*, with Junāda b. Maysara and dated 111/729-30

بسم الله
امر عبيد الله
بن الحبحاب ربع
قسط على يدى جنا
[د]ة بن ميسرة سنة
[ا]حدى عشرة
[و] مئة

In the name of God.
Ordered ʻUbaydallah
b. al-Ḥabḥāb a quarter-
qisṭ at the hands of Junāda b. Maysara in the year
eleven
and a hundred.

OA + 4019. Rogers 1878, 1; Lane-Poole, p. 108, No. 392. Green. Width 4.5cm. (*Plate 3*)

From the same die Miles 1948, 19; Dudzus 1959, 1d; Balog 1976, 118. Cf. Castiglioni 23; Launois 1957, 43; Dudzus 1961, 4e; Miles 1963 II, 10; 1964a, 10; Balog 1976, 117, 119-23.

Junāda is the first official lower than Finance Director whose name appears on stamps, although, as has been stated in the introduction, the anonymous counterstamps show that from the time of Usāma b. Zayd the delegation of responsibility for weights and measures was to some extent reflected by the use of counterstamps.

Junāda's name is not fully visible on any specimen of this denomination but is clear on the corresponding half-*qisṭ* (Miles 1958a, 37; Balog 1976, 115; both from one die. Neither is correctly identified; read *bi-niṣf* at the end of line 3). Balog has completed the set by publishing the *qisṭ* (1976, 116). Otherwise the only published type with Junāda's name is a measure of white cumin, also dated 111 (Miles 1958a, 44).

55 Half-*qisṭ*

مما امر به
عبيد الله ا
[بن] الحبحاب
[ن]صف قسط
[و]اف

Of what ordered
ʻUbaydallah
b. al-Ḥabḥāb.
A half-*qisṭ*,
full-measure.

OA + 4012. Green. Width 3.3 cm. Chipped at top left. (*Plate 3*)

From the same die Dudzus 1961, 4a. Cf. Casanova 1893, 104-5; Miles 1948, 18; 1958a, 36; possibly Launois 1957, 28-30.

56 *Mikyala* **of skinned chickling vetch (*julubbān muqashshar*)**

بسم الله
[ا]مر عبيد الله
بن الحبحاب
بط(ب)عة مكيلة
جلبان مقشر
وافية

In the name of God.
Ordered ʻUbaydallah
b. al-Ḥabḥāb
the stamping of a measure
of skinned vetch,
full-measure.

OA + 4020. Section of hollow rim attached. Green. Width 4.6cm (*Plate 3*)

Bā' of *ṭabʻa* is omitted.

The actual reading of the commodity which is named on this stamp, and on many others, was first suggested by Casanova (1891, 95; 1893, 72); his translation of the word as *pois chiche* ('chick peas') was, however, incorrect. The Arabic for chick peas is *ḥimmaṣ*, now familiar in English as hoummous, which also occurs on vessel stamps. Both kinds of pulse were grown in Egypt from pre-Islamic times and they could hardly have been confused. Among the commentators on glass stamps Miles (1958a, 269) was the first to identify *julubbān* or *julbān* correctly with the chickling vetch (*Lathyrus sativus L*) only to reject it as a reading on the stamps in favour of *jullanār*. He took the latter to mean the pomegranate; more precisely it means the wild pomegranate and particularly its flower, to which medical properties are ascribed in the pharmacopoeias (Maimonides, 75; al-Ghāfiqī, 194; Ibn al-Bayṭār, *s.v. jullanār*). His reason for rejecting *julubbān* was that he doubted that 'this seed or blossom was sold by the druggists'. We would entirely agree, but are not particularly expecting to find drugs named on the vessel stamps. According to Miles *julubbān* and *jullanār* are identical in Kufic script. This is true except, in a proportion of cases, for the last letter. In the script of the commodity stamps *rā'* and final *nūn* are very similar and at times indistinguishable; faced with an uncertain reading it is wise to try both possibilities. However, in many cases the final *nūn* is curved back further than *rā'* and *nūn* is ofter considerably larger, sometimes larger than any form of *rā'*. Examination of the stamps for this commodity reveals that *nūn* is certainly the preferable reading on many of them.

As Miles noted, the consumption of chickling vetch has a tendency to cause a kind of paralysis known, after the plant, as lathyrism. Despite the danger it has long been one of the standard crops of Egypt and was, and is, widely grown in other parts of the world. Its low status is indicated by Ibn al-Bayṭār who describes it as one of the foods of the peasants and fellahin. It is mentioned in Arabic papyri and listed in the administrative manuals which tell us the seasons in which it was sown and reaped, how much increase it gave and what tax was paid on it (Ibn Mammātī, esp. 260; Cahen, 144; Müller-Wodarg, 26).

Ibn Mammātī (359-60) also includes it among the crops for which there were set exchange rates at which one could be substituted for another when taxes were calculated. An ardebb of vetch was equivalent to two-thirds of an ardebb of wheat, one and a half of barley, one of beans (*fūl*) and so on.

A final point requiring comment is the word *muqashshar* which is also found on vessel stamps describing lentils and peas (*bisillah*) (e.g. Balog, 1976, 840-1). There is no doubt that *muqashshar*, from the same root as *qishr* meaning bark, shell, rind or skin, refers to the removal of some kind of integument from the leguminous seeds involved, but it may be suggested that it does not here refer to the removal of the outer shell or pod as has been generally accepted. Vetch, chick-peas and peas do, of course, grow in pods but these would have been removed in the usual way by threshing. Dried legumes may also be, and often are, subjected to a further process of decortication which is likely to be what is meant here, that is the removal, by milling, of the thin skin that covers the individual seeds. Examples of such products with and without the skins can be found in any grocery. Lentils, for instance, are nowadays most commonly sold with the skins removed. Explicit early evidence of the milling of legumes is, not surprisingly, difficult to find, but an account of the removal of the skins of lentils is given in the *Description de l'Égypte* (Histoire Naturelle II, 23) in the following words: '*On les monde quelquefois de leur écorce, en les broyant sous des meules à bras, afin de les rendre plus délicates lorsqu' on les fait cuire*'. As was pointed out by Miles (1948, 37) a group called *muqashshirīn* are mentioned in a list of tradesmen and craftsmen in a papyrus (Grohmann 1934, 228) and their occupation was presumably the milling of legumes to remove their skins.

57-58 Quarter-*qisṭ* of olive oil

بسم الله
[ا]مر عبيد ا
[ل]له بن الحبحاب
[ر]بع قسط
زيت و
اف

In the name of god.
Ordered ʻUbayda-
llah b. al-Ḥabḥāb
a quarter-*qisṭ*
of olive oil, full-
measure.

OA + 4018. Green. Width 3.5cm. Chipped at top and bottom. (*Plate 3*)

OA + 4286. Green. Width 3.4cm.

From the same die Dudzus 1959, 1e; Fremersdorf, 894; Balog 1976, 100, 104.

There is a second remarkably similar die of this denomination with the legend arranged in the same way. Specimens are most easily distinguished by the *ʻayn* of *ʻUbayd* and *qāf* of *qisṭ*. Examples of the second type are: Casanova 1893, 111; Petrie, 108; Viré, 10; Launois 1957, 31; Miles 1963 II, 9; Balog 1973, 4. A large number of specimens have not been illustrated and may belong to either type or, conceivably, others: Casanova 1893 I, 109-10, 112-19; Miles 1948, 21; 1951b, 4; Viré, 8-9; Launois 1957, 32-8; Miles 1958a, 42-3; Dudzus 1961, 4f; Miles 1964a, 11; 1971, 10-12; Balog 1976, 99, 101-3, 105.

59-60 Half-*qisṭ* of olive oil

بسم الله
امر عبيد [ا]
لله بن الحبحاب
[ن]صف قسط
[ز]يت واف

In the name of God.
Ordered ʻUbayda-
llah b. al-Ḥabḥāb
a half-*qisṭ*
of olive oil, full-measure.

OA + 4016. Green. Width 3.4cm.

OA + 4017. Olive green. Width 3.5cm. (*Plate 3*)

Cf. Viré, 6.

ʻUbaydallāh's half-*qisṭ* for olive oil is scarce compared with the *qisṭ* and quarter-*qisṭ*, as seems to be the case for other officials as well.

61-62 *Qisṭ* of olive oil

بسم الله
امر عبيد الله [بن]
الحبحاب قسط
زيت وا
ف

In the name of God.
Ordered ʻUbaydallah b.
al-Ḥabḥāb a *qisṭ*
of olive oil, full-
measure.

OA + 4014. Green. width 3.7cm. (*Plate 3*)

OA + 4015. Green. Width 3.5cm.

From the same die Petrie, 107; Viré, 4.

As in the case of the quarter-*qisṭ* denomination (see Nos 57-8) there is a second die very similar to the one represented in the present collection. The two can be distinguished by the final *bā'* of al-Ḥabḥāb and other letters. The illustrated examples are Miles 1958a, 35 and Balog 1976, 98. The specimens that have not been illustrated may be from either die. (Casanova 1893, 108; Viré, 5; Launois 1957, 40.)

63 *Qisṭ* of clarified butter (*samn*)

بسم الله ا
مر عبيد الله
بن الحبحاب
بقسط سمن
واف

In the name of God. Or-
dered ʻUbaydallah
b. al-Ḥabḥāb
a *qisṭ* of *samn*,
full-measure.

OA + 4022. Green. Width 4.7cm; stamp 3.3cm. (*Plate 3*)

The only close published parallel is a vessel stamp of Yazīd b. Abī Yazīd for a *qisṭ* of the same substance (Balog 1963, 10 = 1976, 236). After discussing other remoter possibilities Balog preferred to read the commodity as *shamar*, said to be one of several alternative forms for the normal *shamār*, with the *alif*, meaning fennel. Two other stamps, one of them No. 493 below (*q.v.*), bear the name of a commodity which may indeed be read *shamār*, with the *alif*, and are presumably designed for fennel, but it is unlikely that the present piece and the similar one of Yazīd b. Abī Yazīd are in fact for the same thing. In the first place, the denomination, *qisṭ*, is unprecedented for a herb or seed the *shamār* stamps are both for the *mikyala*. In the second, on the stamp of Yazīd b. Abī Yazīd the last letter of the commodity is of the large size in proportion to the rest of the script which is characteristic of final *nūn* rather than *ra'*. In early Kufic the forms are often very similar: on the British Museum's stamp the last letter is exactly like *rā'*. However, in a good proportion of cases *nūn* is quite easily distinguishable on account mainly of its greater size (see for example the Kufic alphabets illustrated by Abbott, Pl. V.).

Clarified butter, *samn*, the Indian ghee, is a popular cooking fat in Egypt to the present day. As is usual with animal products, the more systematic sources, original and secondary, give almost no information about its production in the medieval period. A few rather random references will suffice to show that it was in common use. It is mentioned several times in the extended version of the calendar of the year's events and activities found in one of the later manuscripts of the *Qawānīn al-Dawānīn*: as with many foods, there are certain seasons when it is said to be advisable to eat it and others when it is better avoided (Ibn Mammātī, 238, 240, 245). 2,996 skins of clarified butter is one of the items in a list of arrears of taxes remitted by the Fatimid Vazir al-Ma'mūn al-Baṭā'ihī in 515/1121-2 (Maqrīzī I, 84). Its price is occasionally noted by the Mamluk historians (Ashtor, 320).

64 *Mikyala* of *mishsh* for half a *fals*

امر عبيد
الله بن الحبحا
ب مكيلة ا
لمش بنصف
فلس واف

Ordered ʻUbayd-
allah b. al-Ḥabḥā-
b a measure of
mishsh, for half
a *fals*, full-measure.

OA + 4021. Green. Width 3.2cm. Chipped at top. (*Plate 3*)

From the same die Miles 1963 II, 12. Cf. Casanova 1893, 122.

The beginning of the last two lines is missing on the specimen in the Ruthven Collection published by Miles, ensuring that the most unusual feature of the type could not be appreciated. On the British Museum's one the words *bi-nisf fals* are clear and show that the measures from which the stamps came were designed for selling *mishsh* by the half-*fals*-worth. No other stamps with that price on them are known and, as noted in the Introduction (p. 36), the present type provides valuable confirmation that a word which occurs in a variety of stamps and which has been variously interpreted should be taken as a price and read *bi-fals*, 'for a *fals*'. It is significant that the half-*fals*-worth stamps were issued by ʻUbaydallāh b. al-Ḥabḥāb, the only official who is known to have issued glass weights for the half-*fals* denomination (e.g. Nos 33-6 above) and who presumably therefore also issued half-*fals* coins.

There may have been a particular reason for the specification of the price in this case. Described next is another stamp of ʻUbaydallāh, probably for *mishsh*, with similar legends except that no price is stated. It may be suggested that on the half-*fals* type the price was needed to distinguish it from the other, which would have been for a whole *fals*-worth of *mishsh*. If the *fals* was the standard price for a *mikyala* of a commodity, as in many, though not all, cases it may well have been, the specification of the price on the standard *mikyalas* would not have been strictly necessary, since everybody would have known what the price was in any case.

The commodity *mishsh* is one of the commoner ones on vessel stamps but it was a long while before it was correctly read by Miles (1958a, 85). The word appears to be unknown to the classical Arabic lexicographic, and medical, traditions but is nowadays used for a peculiarly Egyptian dairy product, still widely consumed, which fits well into the range of everyday products represented on the stamps and which may be presumed, in spite of the lack of other contemporary evidence, to have been available in the early Islamic period. The making of *mishsh* has been described by Balog (1963, 226; 1976, 377-9): white buffalo-milk cheese is placed in salted milk with a natural lactic ferment and the whole allowed to mature for several months; the cheese is then removed and the pungent semi-liquid that remains is the *mishsh*. From this description it is clear that the common translation of *mishsh* as 'whey' does not accurately describe *mishsh* produced in this way.

65 Mikyala of *mishsh* (?)

بسم ا
لله امر
عبيـ{ـد}ـد الله
بن الحبحاب
مكيلة المش
واف

In the name of
God. Ordered
ʻUbaydallah
b. al-Ḥabḥāb
a measure of *mishsh*,
full-measure.

Five-pointed star at end of legend.

OA + 4023. Most of the bottom two lines broken off. Green. Width 2.9cm. (*Plate 3*)

From the same die Balog 1976, 97.

The commodity's name is not fully visible on Balog's specimen and he read *al-ās*, myrtle, a plant to which the pharmacopoeias ascribe various medical properties, but which would not have been one of the items of mass consumption for which, by our hypothesis, stamped measures were used. *Mishsh*, discussed under No. 64 above, is well attested on the stamps. In either case the reading is not free from difficulty. For *al-ās* the form of *lām-alif* is very curious while for *al-mishsh* it has to be assumed that *mīm* is elongated until it does look like *lām*. Another error in the legend is the surplus 'tooth' in ʻUbayd.

AL-QĀSIM B. ʻUBAYDALLĀH
Finance Director 116-24/734-42

During the latter part of al-Qāsim b. ʻUbaydallāh's Finance Directorship the name of one of four executives appears after his own on almost all his stamps. Most of them are also dated, which enables us to place the executives in order as follows: Muslim b. al-ʻArrāf (AH 119, 121), Ẓaffār b. Shabba (122), Yazīd b. Abī Yazīd (122, 123) and Dā'ūd b. al-Murr (123). Some of the names of the executives and their fathers have been much discussed in the past, partly because they tend to be obscurely or incorrectly written on the more common small stamps, particularly the coin weights. Enough clear examples have been illustrated by now to establish the forms of all the names in undotted Kufic beyond doubt but in at least three cases it is still not certain how they should actually be read. Ẓaffār has been, and could equally well be, read Ṣaffār, or might be something else. Al-ʻArrāf and al-Murr are not implausible but their use as names elsewhere does not seem to have been substantiated by the commentators. Alternative readings are possible for both.

66 Third-*dīnar* weight, with Ẓaffār b. Shabba and dated 122/739-40

امر الله با
لوفاء و امر
بطبعة م(ث)قال ثلث
القاسم بن عبي[د]
الله على يدى ظف[ا]
ر بن شبة سن[ة]
ثنتين و [عشرين]
[و مائة]

God ordered hon-
esty; and ordered
the stamping of a weight of a third
al-Qāsim b. ʻUbayd-
allah at the hands of Ẓaffā-
r b. Shabba in the year
two and twenty
and a hundred.

Star (?) at end of second line.

OA + 4224. Green. 2.0cm; 1.41g. *(Plate 3)*

Cf. Miles 1964a, 13; Launois 1969, 4.

No specimen appears to have been illustrated. Both of those cited above are said to have a star at the end of the second line, specified in the case of the one published by Launois to be six-pointed. On the British Museum's piece, owing to the positioning of the die, only the blurred edge of the presumed star is visible. On the one in the Muntazah Palace collection Miles notes the omission of *thā*' in *mithqāl*, an error also found on the present piece.

67 Third-*dīnār* weight, with Yazīd b. Abī Yazīd

بسم الله
امر الله با
لوفاء و امر
بطبعة مثقال
ثلث دينر ا
لقاسم بن عبيد
الله على يدى ي[ز]
[يد بن ابى يزيد]

In the name of God.
God ordered hon-
esty; and ordered
the stamping of a weight
of a third-*dīnar* a-
l-Qāsim b. ʻUbayd-
allah at the hands of Yazīd b. Abī Yazīd.

93 11-11 11. Olive green. 2.0cm; 1.40g. *(Plate 3)*

The script of the last two lines is visible but minute and seemingly confused; the restoration of the executive's name depends to some extend on the fact that what can be seen does not fit with the names of the other three executives known to have been in office under al-Qāsim. A half-*dīnār* weight of al-Qāsim and Yazīd has been published (Fahmī 1957, 47).

68 **Half-*dīnar* weight**

بسم الله
امر القاسم
بن عبيد الله
بمث(ق)ال نصف
واف

In the name of God.
Ordered al-Qāsim
b. ʻUbaydallah
a weight of a half,
full-weight.

Beaded border.

OA + 4322. Pinkish brown. 2.4cm; stamp 1.7cm; 2.11g. *(Plate 4)*

From the same die Miles 1963 I, 10; Balog 1976, 146.

The colour is unusual and, as Miles noted, *mithqāl* is mis-spelt, with ʻ*ayn* or *ghayn* instead of *qāf*. Balog records a star at the top of his specimen which, however, looks as if it might be no more than a flaw. Balog 1976, 147, another half-*dīnar* weight, has a different legend ending *bi-ṭabʻat niṣf wāf*.

From the latter part of al-Qāsim's Finance Directorship there are numerous dated glass weights and vessel stamps of all types. Excepting a series of heavy weights dated 118 (see Nos 88, 91 below) and an isolated vessel stamp dated 122 (Balog 1976, 171), on the dated pieces al-Qāsim's name is accompanied by that of one of his four executives. The undated pieces must for the most part belong to the earliest of his years in office. The undated coin weights were no doubt superseded by the series issued by Muslim b. al-ʻArrāf in 119, (e.g. Nos 69-70, 72, 78-81).

69–70 Half-*dīnār* weight, with Muslim b. al-ʿArrāf and dated 119/737

بسم الله ا
مر الله بالو
فاء و امر بطبعة
مثقال نصف (د)
(ينـ)ر القاسم بن
عبيد الله على يدى
مسلم بن العر
اف سنة تسع
عشر (و) مئة

In the name of God. Or-
dered God hon-
esty; and ordered the stamping
of a weight of a half *d-*
īnar al-Qāsim b.
ʿUbaydallah at the hands
of Muslim b. al-ʿArr-
āf in the year nine-
teen and a hundred.

OA + **4169**. Green. 2.4cm; 2.10g.
OA + **4170**. Bluish green. 2.5cm; stamp 2.1cm; 2.10g. (*Plate 4*)

From the same die Miles 1948, 28; Launois 1957, 89; Fahmī 1957, 48-50; Balog 1976, 148. Cf. Launois 1957, 90-1; Miles 1964a, 12; Balog 1976, 149-50.

Attempts have been made to explain the word after *niṣf* ('half') in various ways but to make the correction to *dīnar*, as Fahmī did, seems much the most satisfactory solution, bringing the legend into conformity with other types. The initial *dāl* of *dīnar* has been written *wāw* and the next two letters run together into a *mīm*. It would appear that this is to be explained as a partial dittography of *wa amara* from line three, made easier because of the resemblance between that phrase and *dīnar* in Kufic script.

This is much the commonest of al-Qāsim's half-*dīnār*-weight dies. As is often the case with coin weights with long legends, the date is too cramped to be really legible. It is presumably meant to be 119, the only legible date found on Muslim's glass pieces except for a single type of *fals* weight dated 121 (e.g. No. 82 below).

71 *Dīnār* weight

بسم الله
امر القاسم
بن عبيد الله
بمثقال دينر
واف

In the name of God.
Ordered al-Qāsim
b. ʿUbaydallah
a weight of a *dīnar*,
full-weight.

Beaded border

OA + **4168**. Green. 2.9cm; stamp 2.2cm; 4.22g. (*Plate 4*)

From the same die Miles 1948, 27; Fahmī 1957, 45. Cf. Launois 1957, 87-8; Fahmī 1957, 46.

All the illustrated specimens of *dīnār* weights with al-Qāsim's name alone are from the same die. As has been pointed out under No. 68, pieces on which al-Qāsim appears without an executive are normally to be dated to the earlier part of his period of office. The present type was presumably replaced by that issued 'at the hands of' Muslim b. al-ʿArrāf in 119 which is described next.

72 *Dīnār* weight, with Muslim b. al-ʿArrāf and dated 119/737

بسم الله ا
مر الله بالوفاء
وامر بطبعة مثقا
ل دينر القاسم بن
عبيد الله على يدى
مسلم بن العرا
ف سنة تسع
عشرة و مئة

In the name of God. Or-
dered God honesty;
and ordered the stamping of a weigh-
t of a *dīnar* al-Qāsim b.
ʿUbaydallah at the hands
of Muslim b. al-ʿArrā-
f in the year nine-
teen and a hundred.

OA + **4171**. Green. 3.1cm; stamp 2.6cm; 4.23g. (*Plate 4*)

This is the first *dīnār* weight of al-Qāsim and Muslim to be published. The half and third denominations have long been known.

73 *Fals*-weight of 24 *kharrūba*

بسم الله
مما امر به ا
لقاسم بن
عبيد الله مثقا
ل فلس اربعة
و عشرين خرو
بة واف

In the name of God.
Of what ordered a-
l-Qāsim b.
ʿUbaydallah. A weigh-
t of a *fals* of four
and twenty *kharrū-*
ba, full-weight.

Beaded border. Semicircle pointing upwards at the end of the third line.

OA + **4177**. Green. 3.2cm; stamp 2.4cm, 4.65g. (*Plate 4*)

From the same die Petrie 115; Miles 1958a, 52.

The whole range of al-Qāsim's recorded *fals* weights is represented in the British Museum's collection with the exception of types of 15 *kharrūba* and 33 *qīrāṭ*, both known from unique pieces and with crude script (Miles 1948, 31; 1958a, 48). Of the remaining types, the dated issues of 119, 121 and 122 fill much of the latter part of his term of office and the 24-*kharrūba* and great-*fals* or *fals-al-kabīr* weights, on which no executive appears, belong earlier. As is mentioned in the commentary on the *fals-al-kabīr* weights, on which no executive appears, belong earlier. As is mentioned in the commentary on the *fals-al-kabīr* type, the word *kabīr* probably indicates nothing more that that the weights, and no doubt the coinage they went with, were preceded by a lighter issue: the 24-*kharrūba* weights and the coinage they accompanied would fit the bill nicely. The semicircular ornament of the 24-*kharrūba* weight may also support an early dating since it is similar to the ornament found on al-Qāsim's first issue of *qist*-system stamps and an anonymous counterstamp associated with his first issue of heavy weights (see Nos 85-7, 92, 101-2, 505-6).

It seems likely that the *fals-al-kabīr* weights themselves preceded the dated issues which are also of 30 *kharrūba*, and that all four 30-*kharrūba* types were used with a long-lasting issue of copper theoretically on that standard.

Al-Qāsim is the first Muslim official in Egypt whose name is found on the copper coinage (e.g. Walker, p. 294).

74–76 *'Fals-al-Kabīr'* or great-*fals* weight of 30 *kharrūba*

بسم الله
مما امر به ا
لقاسم بن عبيد
الله مثقال فل(س)
الكبير ثلثين خر
وبة (وا)
ف

In the name of God.
Of what ordered a-
l-Qāsim b. ʻUbayd-
allah. A weight of a *fals*
al-kabīr of thirty *kharr-*
ūba, full-
weight.

Beaded border.

OA + 4320. Green. 3.3cm; stamp 2.6cm; 5.87g. (*Plate 4*)
OA + 4321. Green. 3.5cm; stamp 2.6cm; 5.83g.
(Coins and Medals) 89 6-4 68. Lane-Poole, 5. Bluish green. 3.3cm; stamp 2.6cm; 5.84g.

From the same die Petrie, 112-4; Launois 1957, 96; Fahmī 1957, 53, 58, Launois 1960, 7; Balog 1976, 153. Cf. Rogers 1873, 37; Casanova 1893, 22; Miles 1951b, 8; Launois 1957, 97-8; Fahmī 1957, 54-7; Miles 1958a, 49-50; Launois 1969, 5; Balog 1976, 152, 154-5.

The pecularities of the legend have been discussed many times. The *sīn* of *fals* is written with two 'teeth' instead of three. Three seeming letters at the end may be described as *alif*, a semicircle pointing upwards and *fā'*, by itself on the bottom line. The semicircle has been described as a *nūn*, but like the similar marks on certain of al-Qāsim's vessel stamps (see No. 92), is not a form of *nūn* found on the early glass. It has become generally, and sensibly, accepted that the legend should have ended *wāf*.

The denomination, *fals al-kabīr*, of this die is otherwise only found on the crude type copied from it, which is described immediately below. Miles (1964b, p. 83) has shown, and the British Museum's pieces confirm, that the *kharrūbas* of the *fals al-kabīr* are of the usual standard. Probably *al-kabīr* means no more than that the type, and of course the copper coinage which it belongs to, were larger than the issues immediately preceding them (see No. 73).

77 *Fals-al-kabīr*, or great-*fals* weight, of 30 *kharrūba*

Legend a crude copy of the type of Nos 73-5. Plain border.

OA + 4226. Green. 3.4cm; 6.32g. (*Plate 4*)

From the same die Petrie, 116.

The script is very weak and loosely spaced. Some peculiarities of the ordinary *fals-al-kabīr* weight, such as the letters and semicircle at the end of the legend, are easily recognizable. At other points the letter-forms and ligatures of that type have obviously been misunderstood. The weight of the present piece is also badly astray, coming to well over 32 average *kharrūbas*. (Petrie's piece lacks a large segment). Probably this was some kind of unofficial issue and served no normal metrological function.

78–81 *Fals* weight of 30 *kharrūba*, with Muslim b. al-ʻArrāf and dated 119/737

بسم الله ا
مر الله بالوفاء
و امر بطبعة
مثقال فلس ثلثين
خروبة القاسم
بن عبيد الله على يدى
مسلم بن الع(ر)ا
ف سنة تسع
عشرة و ما
ئة

In the name of God. Or-
dered God honesty;
and ordered the stamping
of a weight of a *fals* of thirty
kharrūba al-Qāsim
b. ʻUbaydallah at the hands
of Muslim b. al-ʻArrā-
f in the year nine-
teen and a hund-
red.

OA + 4172. Green. 3.4cm; stamp 2.9cm; 5.83g. (*Plate 4*)
OA + 4173. Green. 3.3cm; 5.86g.
OA + 4174. Slightly over half, the lower part. Green. 3.5cm; 3.27g.

(Coins and Medals) 89 6-4 68. Lane-Poole, 4. 3.3cm; 5.84g.

From the same die Miles 1948, 30; Launois 1957, 95; Fahmī 1957, 59; Launois 1959, 8; Miles 1963 I, 12. Cf. Fahmī 1957, 60; Miles 1958a, 51; Miles 1963 I, 11; Balog 1976, 156-7.

The name of Muslim's father, al-'Arrāf, is spelt without the *rā'* on this die alone, an error which has long been recognized as such.

82 ***Fals* weight of 30 *kharrūba*,** with Muslim b. al-'Arrāf and dated 121/738-9

بسم الله ا
مر الله بالوفاء
و امر بطبعة مثقا
ل فلس ثلثين خروبة ا
لقاسم بن عبيد ا
لله على يدى مسلم (بن)
العراف سنة ا
حدى و عشرين
و مائة

In the name of God. Ordered God honesty;
and ordered the stamping of a weight of a *fals* of thirty *kharrūba* al-Qāsim b. 'Ubaydallah at the hands of Muslim (b.) al-'Arrāf in the year one and twenty and a hundred.

Six-pointed star at top.

OA + 4176. Something less than half the top. Green. Length 3.4cm; 2.89g. (*Plate 4*)

From the same die Launois 1957, 92; Fahmī 1957, 61. Cf. Launois 1957, 93; Fahmī 1957, 62.

Fahmī notes that *ibn* (son) is omitted between the names of Muslim and his father. The specimens of this type are the only stamps of Muslim so far known dated 121. On others, where the date is clear it is 119 and in most other cases certainly to be read 119.

83-84 ***Fals* weight of 30 *kharrūba*,** with Ẓaffār b. Shabba and dated 122/739-40

بسم الله
امر الله بالو
فاء و امر بطبعة
مثقال فلس ثلثين خرو
بة القاسم بن عبيد ا
لله على يدي ظفار بن
شبة سنة ثنتي{-}ن
و عشرين و
مائة

In the name of God. Ordered God Honesty; and ordered the stamping of a weight of a *fals* of thirty *kharrūba* al-Qāsim b. 'Ubaydallah at the hands of Ẓaffār b. Shabba in the year two and twenty and a hundred.

Crescent facing right at top.

OA + 4175. Green. 3.3cm; 5.88g. (*Plate 4*)
OA + 4178. Fragment from the lower part. Width 2.5cm; 2.61g.

From the same die Fahmī 1957, 63-4. Cf. 65-6; Launois 1957, 99-101.

The digit of the date is miswritten, with five 'teeth' followed by a final *nūn*, the fourth 'tooth' being noticeably taller. If the word were by itself the obvious reading would be *sittīn* (sixty), but in the context that is nonsense. It seems best to adopt Fahmī's tacit emendation and read *thintayn*, assuming that the extra 'tooth' is a mistake. On most of Ẓaffār's glass pieces the digit is plainly two (*thintayn* or *ithnayn*).

85-86 **Disk weight: *wuqiyya***

بسم الله
مما امر القاسم
[بن عبي]د الله
[----]
[----]

In the name of God.
Of what ordered al-Qāsim b. 'Ubaydallah
[- - - -]
[- - - -]

Counterstamp

الوفاء
لله

Honesty for God.

Semicircle pointing upwards below legend.

OA + 4292. The top half, with the upper part of the large stamp and part of the counterstamp to the left. Green. Length 5.8cm; 20.0g. (*Plate 4*)

OA + 4293. The top half, with the upper part of the large stamp and the edge of the counterstamp to right. Green. Length 6.0 cm; 19.6g.

The size and weight of these damaged pieces make it clear that they are *wuqiyya* weights, but the restoration of the legend must await other examples. The only other published *wuqiyya* of al-Qāsim is of a different type with Dā'ūd b. al-Murr, dated 123 (Petrie, 111).

Undated heavy weights with al-Qāsim's name alone must belong for the most part, probably entirely, to his first two years in office and have been succeeded by the series dated AH 118 (e.g. No. 88). They are the only weights of al-Qāsim on which anonymous counterstamps are found. The present *wuqiyyas*, and the quarter-*raṭl* below, enable us to date the counterstamp with *al-wafā' lillāh* and semicircle, which has long been known as a vessel stamp (see Nos 505-6 below). It is likely that it came into use after the counterstamp with *al-wafā' lillāh* used at the end of 'Ubaydallāh b. al-Ḥabḥāb's Finance Directorship and attested once under al-Qāsim (Miles 1948, 32 and see No. 45). The pentagram counterstamp described below (No. 507) probably in turn replaced it, since the pentagram occurs with an undated stamp on which al-Qāsim bears the title *al-amīr*, suggesting that it is to be associated with the series dated 118 on which he also has that title.

87 **Disk weight: quarter-*raṭl***

بسم الله
امر القاسم
بن عبيد الله
بطبعة ربع
[رطل --]
[----]

In the name of God.
Ordered al-Qāsim
b. 'Ubaydallah
the stamping of a quarter-
raṭl - - -
- - - -

OA + 4420. A little over half of the top; edge of counterstamp to left. Green. Length 7.7cm; large stamp 3.8cm; 60g. (*Plate 4*)

From the same die Balog 1976, 141 (Illustration incorrectly numbered 140).

On the counterstamp part of a semicircle is visible. Too little survives to establish the identity of the die but it is reasonably certain that the stamp is from the usual die with the legend *al-wafa' lillah* and the semicircle pointing upwards below (e.g. Nos 85-6, 505-6). On Balog's specimen also the large stamp is damaged and gives us exactly the same part of the legend. On it the counterstamp, on which nothing is legible, is to the right.

88 **Disk weight: quarter-*raṭl*,** dated 118/736-7

بسـ[ـم الله]
مما امـ[ـر به الا]
مير القا[سم بن عبيد]
الله سنة [ثمان عشر]
ة و مئة [-- ر]
بع رطل [--]
[--] -

In the name of God.
Of what ordered the A-
mir al-Qāsim b. 'Ubayd-
allah in the year eightee-
n and a hundred - - a qu-
arter-*raṭl* - -
- - -

Plain border.

OA + 4294. Fragment, with rather less than half of the legend, on the right-hand side. Green. Length 6.4cm; 35.46g. (*Plate 4*)

The digit of the date is entirely missing; its restoration appears justified by the similarities of the legend with those of the series of heavy weights dated 118 on which al-Qāsim is still without a subordinate executive. The other known pieces in the series are the *raṭl* (Balog 1976, 140, illustration numbered 139) and the *raṭl* of meat (e.g. No. 91 below). There is reason to think, incidentally, that the weights dated 118 did not always bear counterstamps. The weights dated 118 and a half-*raṭl* of meat which may be associated with them (Balog 1976, 135) are the only pieces known on which al-Qāsim takes the title *al-amīr*. They are the first examples of the use of that title by a Finance Director. The only other Umayyad Finance Director to use it was 'Īsā b. Abī 'Atā.

The remaining parts of the legend may have been similar to those of the *raṭl* of meat in the same series, with *al-wafā' lillāh* intervening between date and denomination and *wāf* at the end. The surviving remnant on the last line of the present piece might be the final *fā'* of *wāf*, with part of an annulet over the missing tail. On the *raṭl* of meat the tail of the *fā'* has two annulets over it.

89 **Disk weight: 3 *wuqiyya*,** with Ẓaffār b. Shabba and dated 122/739-40

[بسم الله]
[امر الله بالو]
[فاء و امر بطبعة]
[ثلاث وا -- القا]
[سـ]ـم بن عبيد
الله على يدى
ظفار بن شبة سنة
ثنتين و عشرين و مائه

In the name of God.
Ordered God hon-
esty; and ordered the stamping
of three - - al-Qā-
sim b. 'Ubayd-
allah at the hands
of Ẓaffār b. Shabba in the year
two and twenty and a hundred.

OA + 4421. Fragment. About a third, the bottom part. Olive green. Length 6.9cm; 38.36g. (*Plate 4*)

The restoration of the legend depends on two other fragments, Miles 1971, 13 and Balog 1976, 143 (illustration numbered 142). So far as they overlap the legends of all three are identical and the spacing of the words very similar but certain seeming variations in the forms of letters make it difficult to declare positively that they are produced from one die. Balog's specimen is the only one showing even part of the denomination. He read *thalāth* [*wuqiyyāt*], 3 *wuqiyya*, but the illustration plainly shows *thalāth wā* [...], and perhaps the second word should be restored *wāf*, 'full-weight'.

The denomination is an unusual one. It otherwise only occurs in the form *thalāth awāq*, on a fragment of a disk weight of ʿAbd al-Malik b. Marwān (Miles, 1952), where it is immediately followed by its equivalent, *rubʿ raṭl*, 'quarter-*raṭl*. As Miles commented, this was the earliest confirmation in Arabic of the traditional correspondence of 12 *wuqiyya* to the *raṭl*.

90 Ring weight. *raṭl* of an unidentified substance, with Dā'ūd b. al-Murr and dated 123/740-1

بسم الله ا
مر الله بالوفاء
وامر بطبعة رطل
العباب الق{ـ}اسم
بن عبيد الله على يد
ى داود بن المر
سنة ثلث و عشر
ين و مئة

In the name of God. Or-
dered God honesty;
and ordered the stamping of a *raṭl*
of – – al-Qāsim
b. ʿUbaydallah at the hand-
s of Dā'ūd b. al-Murr
in the year three and twenty and a hundred.

Ornament, probably a star, at the end of the legend. There is an extra tooth after the *alif* of al-Qāsim.

OA + 4353. Fragment, the top with a large chip off its bottom right. Length 6.5cm; width of stamp 3.5cm; 120.7g. (*Plate 4*)

From the same die Balog 1976, 138.Cf. 139.

This is the only weight for a commodity other than meat in the collection. Such pieces are less common than meat weights but a considerable series has by now appeared, starting, probably, from the time of Qurra b. Sharīk and ending in that of Yazīd b. Abī Yazīd. The only denomination of weight that occurs in this group is the complete *raṭl*. The readings that have been suggested for the commodity or commodities named on them are none of them entirely convincing; though satisfactory solutions are elusive it seems worthwhile to attempt a full statement of the problems.

On the weights of this group the name of the commodity takes one of two forms, distinguished only by the addition or omission of a single letter, *alif*. The two forms could stand for different things or be alternative spellings for one and the same thing. As will be shown there is some reason to believe that the latter explanation is correct. Most of the types are very clearly written. No doubt exists about the forms as they stand in undotted script.

The British Museum's piece belongs to the smaller of the two sub-groups, on which the name of the commodity is written *ʿayn* or *ghayn*, 'tooth', *alif*, 'final tooth' (*ʿBAB*). The only other types are one of al-Qāsim b. ʿUbaydallāh and Ẓaffār b. Shabba dated 122 (Petrie, 109-10) and possibly one of Qurra b. Sharīk. The legend on the one published specimen of the latter (Balog 1976, 1) is defective, but the last letter appears to be a final unattached 'tooth' rather than the *fā'* of *wāf* read by Balog and the inscription could therefore have ended [*ʿayn*, 'tooth', *alif*,] final 'tooth', i.e. *ʿBAB*. Petrie did not recognize the word as the name of a commodity. Balog's suggestion was *ʿunnāb*, meaning the fruit of the jujube tree, of which there are a number of species. As a reading of the letters this is sound and the jujube has been cultivated and its fruit consumed in Egypt from early times (Ibn al-Bayṭār, s.v. *ʿunnāb*; Maimonides, 291; Ibn Mammātī, 235; Müller-Wodarg 59). However, as an explanation of the word on the weights it can hardly be accepted. One would not be surprised to find vessel stamps for jujubes. The fruit is quite small and, particularly when dried, would be well suited to be sold by measure but that it was ever an important enough item of diet to be picked out, together with meat, from all others and have a special set of weights provided for it seems extremely unlikely.

On pieces belonging to the second sub-group, the form of the name of the commodity is the same as the longer one except that it lacks the *alif* (*ʿBB*). Specimens in the names of the following officials are known: Ḥayyān b. Shurayḥ (Miles 1956, p. 152 = Balog 1976, 35); ʿUbaydallāh b. al-Ḥabḥāb (1. Miles 1963 II, 7, with legend beginning *mimmā amara bihi*. Read *raṭl* for the editor's *ru[bʿ ra]ṭl*; 2. Balog 1973, 3, with legend beginning *bismillāh*); al-Qāsim b. ʿUbaydallāh (1. Dudzus 1959, 3d and cf. Miles 1948, 35, of al-Qāsim alone; 2. Balog 1976, 136, with Muslim b. al-ʿArrāf and dated 119); Yazīd b. Abī Yazīd (Balog 1976, 215-6). To these may probably be added a piece in the Louvre noted briefly and without mention of an official's name by Viré (p. 24) as a vessel stamp (*estampille*) but which appears likely to be a fragment of a weight.

Three readings have been suggested for the shorter form. That of Viré, *ʿubab*, meaning the winter cherry, the fruit of the alkekenji (*Physalis alkekengil L*) is open to the same objections made above with regard to the jujube. The small fruit of the alkekenji were no doubt eaten in early Islamic times as they were later but would not have been a very significant product (Maimonides, 201, 297). Balog (1976, 25) mentions having considered and rejected *ʿayn*. There is some doubt whether it means, as he states, 'precious metal, or unminted gold or silver' and in any case it is epigraphically unacceptable. With some reservation, he preferred the reading first suggested by Miles (1956, p. 5; 1963 II, 7), that is, *ʿinab*, meaning grapes. Grapes, it is true, are not suitable for sale by measure and would have been widely consumed. However, they must in fact have been so common that it is difficult to see why, if the weights of this sub-group were designed for them, the weights themselves are so scarce. Grapes too are a seasonal product, which the other commodities named on weights and vessel stamps appear not to be. (For grapes see Müller-Wodarg, 48-53.)

Considering both the sub-groups together it is noticeable that at any one time only one or the other is being issued, which makes it likely that they are not to be taken as forming two chronological series for two different commodities but as a single one on which the name of the commodity is written in two different ways. The two spellings might represent differently pronounced forms derived from the same root, or the shorter form might simply be the longer one with the *alif* omitted by so-called *scriptio defectiva*. In this case a further difficulty arises with the reading *'inab*, 'grapes', that no alternative form with the *alif* is recorded in the dictionaries. No obvious reading of any sort comes to mind. Finally, it may be remarked that, although the similarity of these types with the commodity stamps and above all the meat weights naturally suggests that the word qualifying *raṭl* is the name of a commodity, it is possible that it is something else. It might, for instance, designate the weights as a different kind of *raṭl* from the usual one. The use of different weight systems with similarly named denominations for different substances at the same period is of course a metrological commonplace, outside the Islamic world as well as within it. To give an example from Egypt itself, two different *raṭl* systems, the Miṣrī and the Jarawī, were in use simultaneously in the Ayyubid period (Ibn Mammātī, 361-2).

91 Ring weight: *raṭl* of meat (*laḥm*), dated 118/736-7

بسم الله
مما امر به الا
مير القاسم بن
عبيد الله سنة
ثمان عشرة و مئة
الوفاء لله رطل
لحم واف

In the name of God.
Of what ordered the A-
mir al-Qāsim b.
'Ubaydallah in the year
eighteen and a hundred.
Honesty for God. *Raṭl*
of meat, full-weight.

Pentagram above; two annulets over the end of the legend.

OA + 4354. The top, chipped at top right, and part of the lower side. Cloudy green. Length 6.0cm; rectangular stamp 3.8cm; 149.4g. (*Plate 4*)

From the same die Dudzus 1959, 3c.

It is possible that the pentagram on this die is in some way connected with the anonymous pentagram counterstamp used at about the same time. (See Nos 88, where the other weight stamps in the series dated 118 are also discussed, and 507.)

92 Quarter-*qisṭ*

بسم الله
امر القاسم بن
عبيد الله ربع
قسطا
اوف

In the name of God.
Ordered al-Qāsim b.
'Ubaydallah a quarter-
qisṭ,
full-measure.

OA + 4025. Slightly chipped at top. Green. 3.7cm. (*Plate 4*)

From the same die Casanova 1893, 126; Miles 1958a, 60; Dudzus 1961, 6e. Miles 1963 I, 14; Balog 1976, 164. Cf. Casanova 1893, 123-5, 127; Launois 1959, 60-64; Balog 1976, 162-3, 165-9.

This type and the similar *qisṭ* and half-*qisṭ* stamps (e.g. Nos 101-2) belong to the first part of al-Qāsim's Finance Directorship. He appears to have employed no other *qisṭ*-system dies before the dated issues with the names of his executives, which begin in 119/737. The last word of the legend is written *alif, wāw, fā'*, the letters of *wāf*, but written out of order.

On all three denominations of this series the *ṭā'* of *qisṭ* is followed by an *alif* which is accompanied by a semicircular mark pointing upwards. On the *qisṭ* and quarter-*qisṭ* stamps the semicircle follows immediately; on the half-*qisṭ* it is on the line below and *wāf* intervenes. There is a dot in the semicircle on *qisṭ* and half-*qisṭ*. Opinion has been divided over whether the mark is an ornament or a letter, *nūn* or *rā'*. Launois read *mustār* 'must, new wine'; Balog (1976, p. 30) has suggested that *qisṭān* or *qisṭār* is an otherwise unknown measure of capacity. Miles pointed out that *qisṭān* could be the dual form of *qisṭ*, meaning 2 *qisṭ*s, but preferred to take the semicircle as an ornament. Only the last of these suggestions seems likely. The pattern of issues before and after the series under discussion also suggests that they are in function ordinary *qisṭ*-system types.

Epigraphically as well it is difficult to read the mark as a letter. It has not been pointed out that it differs greatly from the form of final *nūn* in use in early Kufic, and also from *rā'*. In most later scripts the tail of final *nūn* does curve round to about the level of the head, but on the glass and early coinage final *nūn* is a downstroke with a relatively slight curve to the left in the lower part; at times it is indistinguishable from *rā'*. The dot inside the semicircle on the *qisṭ* and half-*qisṭ* is, of course, correct for *nūn* but there is no other example of the use of consonantal pointing on the glass weights. Finally, the position of the semicircle on the half-*qisṭ*, after *wāf*, also argues against its being a letter. Words can, under certain circumstances, be divided between lines in early Kufic, but the second part of a divided word is placed at the beginning of the next line. It should be noted that semicircles which are unmistakably ornamental occur on other stamps from the early part of al-Qāsim's period of office (e.g. Nos 73-6), as well as an anonymous counterstamp in use at the same time (e.g. Nos 85-7, 505-6).

The *alif* at the end of *qisṭ* still requires explanation; it could be an accusative, but, if so, is ungrammatical. Miles was probably right to suggest that it is a variant form of a loan-word. *Qīrāṭ* also a borrowing from Greek, occasionally occurs with a similar final *alif* (e.g. on No. 435).

93-96 Qarter-*qisṭ*, with Muslim b. al-ʻArrāf and dated 119/737

بسم الله ا
مر الله بالوفاء
و امر بطبعة ر
بع قسط القا
سم بن عبيد الله
على يدى مسلم
بن العراف سنة
(ت)سع عشرة و مئة

In the name of God. Or-
dered God honesty;
and ordered the stamping of a quarter *qisṭ* al-Qā-
sim b. ʻUbaydallah
at the hands of Muslim
b. al-ʻArrāf in the year
nineteen and a hundred.

OA + 4026. Olive green. Width 3.9cm.
OA + 4027. Olive green. Width 3.9cm. (*Plate 5*)
OA + 4028. Olive green. Width 3.9cm; stamp 3.1cm.
OA + 4029. Olive green. Width 4.1cm.

From the same die Petrie, 122; Miles 1951b, 11; Dudzus 1961, 6d; Miles 1963 II, 15; Balog 1976, 188. Cf. Launois 1957, 69-72; Miles 1958a, 61; 1971, 16; Balog 1976, 182-7, 189.

Once again the date is cramped: *tis*ʻ (nine) begins with three rather than four 'teeth'. A large portion of pieces with Muslim's name are olive-green rather than the more usual green or bluish green.

97 Quarter-*qisṭ*, with Ẓaffār b. Shabba and dated 122/739-740

بسم الله
امر الله با
لوفاء و امر
بطبعة ربع
[ا]لقاسم بن عبيد
الله على يدى ظف[ا]
ر بن شبة سنة ا
ثنين و عشرين و
مائة

In the name of God.
Ordered God hon-
esty; and ordered
the stamping of a quarter
al-Qāsim b. ʻUbayd-
allah at the hands of Ẓaffā-
r b. Shabba in the year t-
wo and twenty and
a hundred.

Six-pointed star above end of third line.

95 3-12 3. Green. Width 3.9cm. (*Plate 5*)

From the same die Petrie, 127; Miles 1948, 36; Launois 1959, 9; Balog 1976, 199. Cf. Launois 1957, 70-81; Miles 1958a, 62; Balog 1976, 200-2.

The denomination is simply written *rub*ʻ (quarter), instead of the usual *rub*ʻ *qisṭ*.

98 Quarter-*qisṭ*, with Yazīd b. Abī Yazīd and dated 122/739-40

بسم الله
امر الله بالو
فاء و امر بطبعة
[ر]بع قسط الق[ا]
سم بن عبيد ال[له]
[ع]لى يدى يزيد بن ابى
[يز]يد سنة اثنتين
و عشرين
و مئة

In the name of God.
Ordered God hon-
esty; and ordered the stamping
of a quarter-*qisṭ* al-Qāsim b. ʻUbaydallah
at the hands of Yazīd b. Abī
Yazīd in the year two
and twenty
and a hundred.

OA + 4338. About a third chipped off at top and sides. Green. Width 3.6cm. (*Plate 5*)

From the same die Casanova 1893, 128; Balog 1976, 208. Cf. Casanova 1893, 129; Grohmann 1925, 3.

99-100 Quarter-*qisṭ*, with Dā'ūd b. al-Murr and dated 12(3)/740-1

بسم الله ا
مر الله بالو(فاء) و ا
مر بطبعة ربع
قسط القاسم بن
عبيد الله على يدى دا
[ود بن]المر سنة
[ثلاث]و عشرين و
مئة

In the name of God. Or-
dered God honesty; and ordered the stamping of a quarter-
qisṭ al-Qāsim b.
ʻUbaydallah at the hands of Dā-
'ūd b. al-Murr in the year
three and twenty and
a hundred.

Six-pointed star at end of third line.

OA + 4030. Green. Width 4.3cm. (*Plate 5*)
OA + 4031. Green. Width 4.4cm.

In the second line *fā' alif* of *al-wafā'* has been omitted, doubtless by haplography since the *wāw alif* of *wa amara* that follows it looks very similar. The digit of the date is invisible but all Dā'ūd's pieces with legible dates are of the same year. Though a quarter-*qisṭ* in his name has not been published before the *qisṭ* and half-*qisṭ* are known (Launois 1957, 85; Balog 1976, 204).

101 Half-*qisṭ*

بسم الله
امر القاسم
بن عبيد الله
نصف قسطا
واف

In the name of God.
Ordered al-Qāsim
b. ʻUbaydallah
a half-*qisṭ*,
full-measure.

Semicircle with a dot in it pointing upwards at end of legend.

OA + 4032. Green. Width 3.7cm. (*Plate 5*)

From the same die Petrie, 124; Dudzus 1961, 6b; Balog 1976, 161. Cf. Balog 1976, 159-60.

For the spelling of *qisṭ* see No. 92.

102 *Qisṭ*

بسم الله
امر القاسم
بن عبيد الله
قسطا
واف

In the name of God.
Ordered al-Qāsim
b. ʻUbaydallah
a *qisṭ*,
full-measure.

Semicircle with a dot in it pointing upwards at the end of the fourth line.

OA + 4033. Green. Width 3.4cm. (*Plate 5*)

From the same die Miles 1958a, 55; Launois 1969, 6.

For the spelling of *qisṭ* see No. 92.

103 Quarter-*qisṭ* of olive oil

بسم الله
[ا]مر القاسم
[ب]ن عبيد الله
بطبعة ربع
قسط زيت
واف

In the name of God.
Ordered al-Qāsim
b. ʻUbaydallah
the stamping of a quarter-
qisṭ of olive oil,
full-measure.

OA + 4337. Green. Width 3.6cm. (*Plate 5*)

From the same die Petrie 123; Dudzus 1961, 6e; Balog 1976, 172. Cf. Launois 1957, 65; Miles 1964a, 15.

Considering how large a proportion of Umayyad vessel stamps in general are for olive oil, remarkably few of al-Qāsim have been published and none at all are known on which his name is accompanied by that of any of his four executives. One suspects that during the latter part of his Finance Directorship either the sale of olive oil was not controlled by measures or, more probably, that it was sold by the standard *qisṭ* and its subdivisions. As has been mentioned in the introduction, with al-Qāsim the series of *qisṭ*-standard stamps for olive oil comes to an end.

104 Half-*qisṭ* of olive oil

بسم الله
[ا]مر القاسم بن عبيد
[ا]لله بطبعة نصف
قسط زيت وا
ف

In the name of God.
Ordered al-Qāsim b. ʻUbaydallah the stamping of a half-
qisṭ of olive oil, full-
measure.

OA + 4034. Green. Width 3.9cm. (*Plate 5*)

105 *Mikyala* of a kind of henna (*ḥinnāʼ murr?*)

بسم الله
امر الله بالوفاء
وامر بطبعة مكيلة
حناء مر القاسم بن
عبيد الله على يدى
مسلم بن العراف
سنة تسع عشر
ة و مئة

In the name of God.
Ordered God honesty;
and ordered the stamping of a measure
of *ḥinnāʼ murr* al-Qāsim b.
ʻUbaydallah at the hands
of Muslim b. al-ʻArrāf
in the year ninetee-
n and a hundred.

OA + 4036. Olive green. Width 4.8cm. (*Plate 5*)

There are two parallel series of vessel stamps for what are apparently two different kinds of henna. One, not represented in the collection, is for *ḥinnāʼ al-raʼs*, 'henna for the head'. Since the practice of dying the hair with henna is long established, and particularly popular in the Muslim world, the accepted view that 'henna for the head' is the hair dye is obviously correct. The case of the second series is not so simple and it is first necessary to examine the forms of the word which qualifies henna on them; these vary somewhat, though not to the extent that it need be doubted that all designate one and the same substance. The word, or words, appear with or without the definite article. The British Museum's piece is the only one on which it certainly consists of only two letters, which are *mīm* and *rā'* (or *zā'*). On all but one of the other published examples the same two letters are certainly followed by a third. The exception is a *mikyala* of ʿUbaydallāh b. al-Habhab (Launois 1957, 42) on which *al-MR* is clear at the end of one line but it is not certain whether there is a third letter on the next. On a piece of Ḥayyān b. Shurayḥ (Balog 1976, 45) *MR* is followed by an unusual heavy downstroke with a slight reversed S-bend to it. The top of what might be a similar form, or possibly a *yā'*, is visible on another of Usāma b. Zayd (Balog 1973, 2. The reading *quraysh* is unjustified.). On one of al-Manṣūr (Miles 1963 I, 34) the third letter is in the form of a slightly open *dāl* or *kāf* and placed, with relation to the script line, as those letters should be. On the only other published type of al-Qāsim b. ʿUbaydallāh, on which the executive is Dā'ūd b. al-Murr, Miles (1964a, 16) read *al-MRA*. On one of Yazīd II and Ḥayyān the last letter is a clear retroflex *yā'* (Balog 1976, 63. *Ḥinnā'* is not fully visible but needs to be restored.). The name of the commodity, ending again in retroflex *yā'*, is visible, though the issuer's name is not, on a stamp of late Umayyad appearance illustrated by Hamarnah (p. 99, bottom row, third from left). The only reasonably simple way of reconciling the variants seems to be to assume that in all cases they are, or were meant to be, *yā's*. The reversed S-bend and *alif*-like forms, if not actually mistakes, can fairly easily be accepted as unusual varieties of *yā'* and the *dāl*-like one may be no more than the error of an engraver misled by the similarity of the non-retroflex forms of *yā'* with *dāl*. We may conclude then that the qualifying word on this series of henna-stamps is either *MR* or *MRY*.

Of possible readings of these none is very obviously superior. *Murr* and *murrī* are not wholly implausible; they might mean respectively 'of myrrh' and, as it were, 'myrrhy', but it needs to be confirmed that the words were in fact used in connection with henna. Approaching the question from another point of view, the only important uses of henna were as a dye for cloth and as a cosmetic. In the market for which the stamped measures were used cosmetics figured while dyes for industrial purposes did not. As a cosmetic henna was, and is, used in two ways, to dye the hair and to stain the skin, especially the hands and feet. Since *ḥinnā' al-ra's* must refer principally to the hair dye, it is possible that in early Islamic Egypt a somewhat different preparation of henna was used for staining the skin and known by a different name.

The dye henna is produced from the powdered leaves and twigs of the shrub of the same name (*Lawsonia alba Lam.*). Applied to the body it is often said to have a cooling effect (*Encyclopaedia Britannica* 1911). Some of its more strictly medical properties have been noted by Miles (1963 I, 34). Naturally the substance is noted in the Arabic pharmacopoeias (Maimonides, 149; Ibn al-Bayṭār, *s.v.*, *ḥinnā'*). It may be added that the dye is mentioned in Arabic papyri (Müller-Wodarg, 45), that its cultivation is described by the Spanish agriculturalist Ibn al-ʿAwwām (II, 121-5) and also occasionally mentioned in the long calendar found in one of the manuscripts of Ibn Mammātī (236, 250, 252). Henna may not have been one of the major agricultural products but must have been in constant retail demand.

106 *Mikyala* of white cumin (*kammūn abyaḍ*), with Dā'ūd b. al-Murr and dated 123/740-1

بسم الله
امر الله بالو
فاء و امر بطبعة
مكيلة الكمن الابيض
[ا]لقاسم بن عبيد ا
لله على يدى داود
بن المر سنة ثلث و
عشرين و مائة

In the name of God.
Ordered God hon-
esty; and ordered the stamping
of a measure of white cumin
al-Qāsim b. ʿUbayda-
llah at the hands of Dā'ūd
b. al-Murr in the year three and
twenty and a hundred.

OA + 4040. Green. Width 4.0cm. (*Plate 5*)

From the same die Miles 1948, 38; Balog 1976, 205.

It was Balog who suggested that the curiously written name of the commodity was meant to be *kammūn* and that the accompanying adjective was *abayḍ*, 'white', rather than *aswad*, 'black', as Miles had read it. *Abyaḍ* is certainly correct. As for *kammūn*, two other dies for white cumin are known to have been in use under al-Qāsim: on one he appears by himself (Launois 1957, 67; Balog 1976, 205. Cf. Launois 1957, 68); on the other Muslim b. al-ʿArrāf is also named (Miles 1971, 17). The present type fits admirably with these. No other stamps of a commodity qualfied as white have been published in the name of al-Qāsim. As for the spelling of *kammūn*, it would seem that the first letter has been taken for the similarly shaped *dāl* and therefore separated from the next letter, as *dāl* should be but *kāf* should not. At the end of the word, assuming we are not faced with an alternative form of it, final *nūn* is omitted and the *wāw* preceding it is written more like *rā'* or *nūn* or, alternatively, the *wāw* has been left out.

Miles (1951b, 16) has provided a lengthy discussion of cumin. The 'white' variety is to be identified with the ordinary cumin (*Cuminum cyminum L*). The herb, the pungent seeds of which are, of course, used for seasoning, was an important field crop. Ibn Mammātī, writing in the Ayyubid period lists cumin with caraway and beetroot among the standard crops. The tax on it had been reduced from 2 to 1 *dīnār* per feddan (Ibn Mammātī, 264; Cahen, 146; Müller-Wodarg, 43). As Miles has said, stamps for *kammūn* alone are presumably also for 'white' cumin. For 'black' cumin see the next item.

107 ***Mikyala* of black cumin (*kammūn aswad*),** with Muslim b. al'Arrāf and dated 119/737

بسم الله امر ا
لله بالوفاء و امر
بطبعة مكيلة الكمون
الاسود القاسم بن
عبيد الله على يدى مسلم
بن العراف سنة تسع
عشرة و مئة

In the name of God. Ordered G-
od honesty; and ordered
the stamping of a measure of cumin,
black, al-Qāsim b.
'Ubaydallah at the hands of Muslim
b. al-'Arrāf in the year nineteen and a hundred.

OA + 4037. Olive green. Width 5.5cm.; stamp 3.9cm. (*Plate 5*)

From the same die Miles 1963 II, 14.

The only other published stamp of al-Qāsim for 'black cumin' is one dated 122 with Ẓaffār b. Shabba (Launois 1957, 77). For the identification of the herb reference should once again be made to the discussion of cumin by Miles (1951b, 16). In the medieval literature, which dates of course from long after the period of the vessel stamps, and in more recent times, *kammūn aswad* is most often used for the herb *Nigella sativa L*; this in Arabic is also called *kammūn barrī* (wild cumin), and *shūnīz* and its seeds, like those of cumin, are used for seasoning. In English, too, it is known as black cumin, fennel-flower being one of the alternative names. Possibly this is what is meant on the stamps; if evidence of its widespread cultivation and use in the early Islamic and later medieval periods is lacking our information on such matters is far from complete. Nonetheless it seems worth pointing out that the name is not unsuitable for a seed which appears noticeably absent from the vessel stamps and which was, in the Ayyubid period certainly, grown by the field rather than in the kitchen garden, that is the caraway (Ar. *karāwiyā*). The suggestion that *kammūn aswad* on the stamps is caraway seed can only be speculative for the present but it may be noted that one of the Arabic names for caraway is *kammūn armanī*, 'Armenian cumin' (Ibn al-Bayṭār, *s.vv. kammūn*; Maimonides, 193, 195, 365: Ibn Mammātī, 264; Cahen, 146; Müller-Wodarg, 43).

108 ***Mikyala* of woad (*wasma*),** with Dā'ūd b. al-Murr and dated 123/740-1

بسم الله
امر الله بالو
فاء (و) امر بطبعة
مكيلة الوسمة
[ا]لقاسم بن عبيد
الله على يدى داو
[د] بن المر سنة
ثلث وعشرين
و مائة ·

In the name of God.
Ordered God hon-
esty; and ordered the stamping
of a measure of woad
al-Qāsim b. 'Ubayd-
allah at the hands of Dā'ū-
d b. al-Murr in the year
three and twenty
and a hundred.

OA + 4038. Green. Width 4.0cm. (*Plate 5*)

From the same die Dudzus 1961, 6g; Launois 1969, 9; Balog 1973, 7.

Wāw ('and') in the third line is miswritten, without its circular head, in fact in the form of a *rā'*. Stamps for woad of all four of al-Qasim's executives are known. The type with Yazīd b. Abī Yazīd is described below and the other two are represented in the Balog collection (Balog 1976, 193-5, 203 where further references are given).

109 ***Mikyala* of woad (*wasma*),** with Yazīd b. Abī Yazīd and dated 123/740-1

[بسم الله]
[امر الله با]
لو[فاء و] امر
[ب]طبعة مكيلة ال[و]
سمة القاسم [بن]
عبيد الله على يد[ى]
[ي]زيد بن ابى يزيد
سنة ثلاث و عشرين
و مئة

In the name of God.
Ordered God hon-
esty and ordered
the stamping of a measure of w-
oad al-Qāsim b.
'Ubaydallah at the hands
of Yazīd b. Abī Yazīd
in the year three and twenty
and a hundred.

OA + 4039. Nearly half missing at top and left. Green. Width 4.7cm. (*Plate 5*)

From the same die Petrie, 121.

110 **Half-*qisṭ* of an unidentified substance for a *fals*,** with Yazīd b. Abī Yazīd

بسم الله
امر القاسم
[ب]ن عبيد الله
[ب]طبعة نصف
قسط --
[ب]فلس على يد[ى]
يزيد بن ابى
يزيد

In the name of God.
Ordered al-Qāsim
b. ʿUbaydallah
the stamping of a half-
qisṭ of - -
for a *fals* at the hands
of Yazīd b. Abī
Yazīd.

OA + 4035. Green. Width 4.2cm. (*Plate 5*)

The first letter of the commodity looks like *fā'* or *qāf*, but the glass is flawed and it may be an ordinary 'tooth'. A 'tooth' follows and then *dāl*, *dhāl* or *kāf* which may or may not be the end of the word. *Fundu[q]* or *bundu[q]*, 'hazelnut' suggests itself as a possible reading. Hazelnuts have never yet been found on a vessel stamp but they would fit well enough into the range of commodities for which the stamps were used and could easily be sold by measure.

There does not appear to be any other example of a vessel stamp which has a denomination on the *qisṭ* system having a price as well. The first letter of the first word of the sixth line, here reads *bi-fals*, is off the edge of the impression and one would be tempted to read *muqashshar*, 'shelled', a suitable epithet for hazelnuts, instead, if the 'tooth' after the first visible letter was not markedly taller than those that follow it, a *lām* therefore rather than the first stroke of *shīn*.

YAZĪD B. ABĪ YAZĪD

Finance Director c. 103-7/721-6; later Executive under al-Qāsim b. ʿUbaydallāh, Ḥafṣ b. al-Walīd and ʿĪsā b. Abī ʿAṭā.

Yazīd b. Abī Yazīd is the first executive whose name appears on its own on glass stamps. Among his pieces are counterstamps used on the heavy weights of Ḥafs b. al-Walīd and ʿĪsā b. Abī ʿAṭa and also found on separate vessel stamps which must originally have been paired with stamps of the Finance Directors. These counterstamps are of a type that became very common, bearing the executive's name preceded by the phrase *ʿalā yaday* ('at the hands of'). The formula is also of course commonly used with the executive's name when it appears on the same stamp as that of the Finance Director. Yazīd's name occurs in this way together with that of al-Qāsim b. ʿUbaydallāh as well as with Ḥafs and ʿĪsā, but there is reason to think that Yazīd did not have any independent stamps under al-Qāsim.

However, most of Yazīd's considerable output of stamps have legends beginning *amara* ('ordered'), a most unusual formula for executives. The only other example appears to be an isolated commodity stamp of ʿAbdallāh b. Rāshid (Miles 1971, 31; Balog 1976, 452-6. Cf Casanova 1893, 170-1). It need not be assumed that 'ordering' in this context was always the prerogative of a particular rank but it is certainly true that two people of different ranks could not have both done the 'ordering' on a particular occasion. If the Finance Director was in command the executive would have to assume a subordinate role. At a higher level the stamps with names of Caliphs demonstrate the situation: on them the name of the Finance Director is preceded by the subordinate formula *ʿalā yaday*. Yazīd's use of *amara*, then, implies a freedom of action which an executive did not usually enjoy. It was for this reason that Miles (1948, p. 73) suggested that Yazīd might have been Interim Finance Director in the interval between ʿĪsā's two terms of office, that is during Ḥafṣ's third governorship.

However, when the text of this catalogue was all but complete the writer came across an item of literary evidence which provides the explanation for the seeming anomalies of Yazīd's output of stamps. Azdī's *History of Mosul*, an early and valuable chronicle, was published only relatively recently and has not been utilized for the study of the Egyptian officials whose names appear on glass stamps. The scope of the work is wider than its name might imply but in fact it has little to say about Egypt. Among the items of Egyptian interest it does preserve, however, are a number of references to ʿUbaydallāh b. al-Ḥabḥāb, a branch of whose descendants settled in Mosul. According to Azdī (27), in the year 107/725-6 the Caliph Hishām appointed ʿUbaydallāh over Egypt and dismissed Yazīd b. Abī Yazīd. The term used for appointed is simply *wallā*, meaning 'put in charge of', which could equally well be used for the appointment of a Governor, but we know from Kindī and elsewhere that ʿUbaydallāh was Finance Director and Yazīd must have been his predecessor in the same position.

On looking again at Yazīd's own stamps with a mind freed from the preconception that they ought to be close in date to those on which he appears as a subordinate, one immediately realizes that the ones with legends beginning *amara* fit perfectly into the series at the date which Azdī indicates and are exactly what might be expected of a Finance Director of that period. The script varies somewhat within the group but on most the lines are widely spread and the letters bulky in proportion to the ductus; the style closely resembles that of the stamps of Usāma b. Zayd, Ḥayyān b. Shurayḥ, Yazīd II and some of those of ʿUbaydallāh, presumably the earlier ones. By the time Yazīd reappears toward the end of al-Qāsim b. ʿUbaydallāh's Finance Directorship, the lines of the script in use on glass are closer together, the letters lower and the total effect more compact. The abrupt beginning of the legends, with *amara*, is also typical of the earlier period, being the standard opening from Qurra to Ḥayyan and on the stamps in the name of Yazīd II. With ʿUbaydallāh new formulae are used at the beginnings of legends. *Amara* by itself is not found again in the Umayyad period.

It can therefore be accepted that Yazīd preceded ʿUbaydallāh as Finance Director and that the bulk of his own stamps were issued during the period he held that office, which implies that in the arrangement of this catalogue he should come before ʿUbaydallāh. When he was appointed we do not know; it may have been after Usāma's second term of office, that is in about 103/721-2. Yazīd, incidentally becomes the first official on whose commodity stamps prices appear.

111 Disk, without denomination

ابى يزيد
يزيد ابن

Of Abī Yazīd.
Yazīd, son

OA + 4181. Pale blue green. 2.9cm; 4.24g. (*Plate 5*)
From the same die Balog 1976, 217.

The legend reads from the second line to the first, a familiar feature of later Arabic epigraphy but one which occurs on no other glass stamp of an identifiable Umayyad or Abbasid official. The weights of this type present a problem. The British Museum's piece is of an excellent weight for a *dīnār* weight but Balog's at 2.80g, conforms to that of the early *dirham* weights (see Introduction p. 17). But if the same die was used to produce weights on both standards the users would have had difficulty in telling them apart. Perhaps the weights of these two specimens conform to the different standards by coincidence and the pieces are tokens, like the disks of varying weights on which the legend consists of the name ʿUbaydallāh b. al-Ḥabḥāb (see under No. 50). One the other hand, two specimens of a type with only the name of Usāma b. Zayd weigh 2.86 and 2.83g. remarkably close to each other and well within the usual range for early *dirham* weights (Petrie, 88; Miles 1951, 26, 2). More material is required before it can be decided whether all these types are tokens or not.

112-113 Half-*dīnār* weight

امر يزيد بن
ابى يزيد مثقا
ل نصف واف

Ordered Yazīd b.
Abī Yazīd a weigh-
t of a half, full-weight.

Six-pointed star in the second line.

OA + 4225. Green. 2.1cm; stamp 1.5cm; 2.12g. (*Plate 5*)
(Coins and Medals) 82 8-3 100. Lane-Poole, 8; Small chip. Green. 2.1cm; stamp 1.5cm; 2.08g.

From the same die Fahmī 1957, 76.

Lane-Poole tentatively read *wazn* (weight) for *mithqāl* but the beginning of the word is clear and on the piece illustrated here the final *lām* is faintly visible at the beginning of the third line.

114-116 *Fals* weight of 20 *qīrāṭ*

امر يزيد
بن ابى يزيد
مثقال فلس
عشرين قير
ط

Ordered Yazīd
b. Abī Yazīd
a weight of a *fals*
of twenty *qīra-*
ṭ.

OA + 4182. Blue green. 2.7cm; 3.86g.
OA + 4323. Green. 2.6cm; 3.84g. (*Plate 5*)
(Coins and Medals) 81 7-6 58. Lane-Poole, 7. Green. 2.6cm; 3.66g.

From the same die Nies, 10 = Miles 1948, 43; Launois 1957, 130; Fahmī 1957, 80, 83; Launois 1959, 12 (illustration numbered 13); Balog 1976, 218, Cf. Virê, 13; Launois 1957, 131; Fahmī 1957, 81-2; Miles 1964a, 18; Balog 1876, 219.

This is much the most common of Yāzīd's *fals*-weight dies. A second variety of the same denomination has a similar legend except that *qīrāṭ* is written in full, with the *alif*, and with its final *tāʾ* reversed. There is also a star above the legend (Balog 1976, 220. Cf. Miles 1948, 44). A 20-*kharrūba* type is described next. A single specimen of a 14-*qīrāṭ* denomination is known (Launois 1957, 128 = Fahmī 1957, 84).

117 *Fals* weight of 20 *kharrūba*

بسم الله ا
مر يزيد بن ا
(بى) يزيد وزن
فلس عشر
ين خروبة

In the name of God. Or-
dered Yazīd b. A-
bī Yazīd a weight
of a *fals* of twen-
ty *kharrūba*.

(Coins and Medals) OR 3600. Olive Green. 2.6cm; 3.86g. (*Plate 5*)

From the same die Miles 1948, 45. Cf. 46.

The script is rather careless and *-bi* of Abī has been omitted.

118 Executive stamp

على يدى
يزيد بن ا
بى يزيد

At the hands
of Yazīd b. A-
bī Yazīd.

Six-pointed star below.

OA + 4042. Olive green. Width 2.7cm. (*Plate 5*)

Vessel stamps from the same die Petrie, 132; Launois 1957, 120; Balog 1976, 212. Cf. Miles 1948, 48; Launois 1957, 121-4; Miles 1964a, 20; Balog 1976, 213-4.

With Yazīd b. Abī Yazīd begins the long series of counterstamps with the names of executives and legends most commonly beginning *ʿalā yaday* ('at the hands of') (See Introduction, pp. 12f). Four dies for counterstamps of Yazīd have been described. Two are very similar to the present type. One, lacking the star beneath the legend, is described below. Another, with a slightly different arrangement (*/Abī* for *A/bī*) is known from one specimen (Miles 1948, 47). On the fourth, also represented by a single specimen, the legend begins *amara*, so it probably belongs to Yazīd's own Finance Directorship. (Balog 1976, 221, where the reference to Miles 1971, 18-19 is mistaken.)

Like the earlier anonymous ones, the counterstamps with executives' names were used on heavy weights as well as vessel stamps and are therefore found linked with the stamps of Finance Directors, which usually include the denomination. The present stamp was used on heavy weights of both Ḥafṣ b. al-Walīd and ʿĪsā b. Abī ʿAṭā. It came into use when Ḥafṣ became Finance Director, for it is found on half and quarter-*raṭls* of the series dated 124/741-2 (No. 131; Nies, 15 = Miles 1948, 25, on which the denomination is presumably to be read *ru[bʿ ra]ṭl.*). With stamps of ʿIsā it is known from half-*raṭls* (Petrie, 137-8. Cf. Balog 1976, 240) and from two different half-*raṭl* meat weights (Launois 1958a, 2; Petrie, 194, reading *li-lah*[*m*] at the end of the legend). It also occurs on a meat weight of uncertain denomination and probably on another damaged ring weight (Miles 1958a, 80, which seems more likely to be a double-*raṭl* than a half-*raṭl*; Miles 1951b, 13). Curiously, none of Yazīd's other counterstamps has yet been recorded on a weight.

119 Executive stamp

Legend as on No. 118, but without the star.

OA + 4340. Green. Piece of rim attached. Length 3.5cm.

From the same die Balog 1976, 210. Cf. Launois 1957, 125; Miles 1958a, 74-5; 1963 II, 17. Casanova 1893, 175-82 are briefly described and may be of more than one type.

The piece is too blurred to illustrate. As noted in the commentary to No. 118, this die appears only to have been recorded as used on vessel stamps.

120-123 Quarter-*qisṭ* of olive oil

امر يزيد
بن ابى يزيد ر
بع قسط ز
يت واف

Ordered Yazīd
b. Abī Yazīd a qu-
arter-*qisṭ* of ol-
ive oil,
full-measure.

OA + 4044. Green. Width 3.2cm; Small chip off top left.
OA + 4045. Green. Width 3.7cm. (*Plate 5*)
OA + 4046. Green. Width 3.4cm.
94 3-9 9. Green. Width 3.1cm. Large chip off top left.

From the same die Launois 1957, 116; Miles 1958a, 71-2; 1963, 20; Balog 1976, 227-8, Cf. Miles 1951b, 14; Launois 1957, 117-8; Miles 1958a, 73; Balog 1976, 229-32.

Yazīd b. Abī Yazīd issued quarter-*qisṭ*, half-*qisṭ* and *qisṭ* measures for olive oil. The legends all begin *amara* and all illustrated specimens of each denomination are from one die. The half-*qisṭ* is described below; specimens of the *qisṭ* are as follows: Petrie, 93; Miles 1958a, 68; Balog 1976, 222. Cf. Miles 1958a, 69; Balog 1976, 223.

124-125 Half-*qisṭ* of olive oil

امر يزيد
بن ابى يزيد نصف
قسط زيت
واف

Ordered Yazīd
b. Abī Yazīd a half-
qisṭ of olive oil,
full-measure.

Dot beneath *ṭā'* of *qisṭ*.

OA + 4043. Green. Width 3.5cm. (*Plate 6*)
OA + 4339. Blue-green. Width 4.0cm.

From the same die Miles 1958a, 70. Cf. Launois 1957, 119; Miles 1963 II, 16; Balog 1976, 224-6.

126 *Mikyala* of lentils (*'adas*) for a *fals*

امر يزيد بن
[ا]بى يزيد مكيلة
[ا]لعدس
بفلس

Ordered Yazīd b.
Abī Yazīd a measure
of lentils
for a *fals*.

OA + 4047. Green. Hollow rim. Width 4.2cm. (*Plate 6*)

Balog (1976, 233) has published a specimen of a different stamp of Yazīd's for a *fals*-worth of lentils on which the lentils are described as *muqashshar* (decorticated).

For botanical and medical references to *'adas*, the edible lentil (*Lens esculenta Moench.*) see Miles 1951b, 42. According to the Spanish agricultural writer Ibn al-'Awwām (II, 71-3), who incidentally gives a recipe for cooking lentils, the broad white kind (*al-abyaḍ al-'arīḍ*) is the best. As well as those on which the colour is not specified, stamps for red (*aḥmar*) and black (*aswad*) lentils are known, the latter being represented in the British Museum's collection by the anonymous No. 496. No doubt the coloured types were, as Miles suggested, the varieties of the common lentil which have differently coloured seeds. It may be noted that in the *Description de l'Egypte* it is more than once stated that Egyptian lentils were reddish. The Romans regarded the lentil as being particularly associated with Egypt and it has remained of course a major food crop since that time. The usual details concerning cultivation and taxation are given in the Ayyubid and Mamluk manuals. Lentils are also mentioned in papyri (Ibn Mammātī, esp. 260-1; Cahen, 145; Müller-Wodarg, 26-7; *Description*, Histoire Naturelle II, 23; Etat Moderne II (1), 527-8, 702-3).

127 *Mikyala* of woad (*wasma*) for a *fals*

امر يزيد بن
ابى يزيد
مكيلة الو
سمة واف
بفلس

Ordered Yazīd b.
Abī Yazīd
a measure of wo-
ad, full-measure,
for a *fals*.

OA + 4048. Green. Width 4.0cm. (*Plate 6*)

128 *Qisṭ* **of an unidentified substance**

امر يزيد
بن ابى يزيد
قسط - -
واف

Ordered Yazīd
b. Abī Yazīd
a *qisṭ* of – –,
Full-measure.

OA + 4049. Green. Width 5.0cm. (*Plate* 6)

The name of the commodity seems to begin with two *lāms*, most probably *li-* preceding the definite article. What follows may be *ʿayn* or a 'tooth-letter' followed by *jīm*. Another 'tooth' and then final *rāʾ* or *nūn* appear to follow.

ḤAFṢ B. AL-WALĪD

Ḥafṣ b. al-Walīd was first appointed Governor of Egypt in 108/727. The direction of finances was then in the control of ʿUbaydallāh b. al-Ḥabḥāb, who had succeeded in having the previous governor dismissed and dealt similarly with Ḥafṣ himself in the space of a few weeks. Ḥafṣ was appointed Governor again in early 124/742 but did not receive charge of finances until Shaʿbān of the same year (June 742). In Shawwāl 125/ August 742 ʿĪsā b. Abī ʿAṭā was made Finance Director, though Ḥafṣ remained Governor till the accession of Marwān II as Caliph in Ṣafar 127/November 744 when he resigned. The Arab forces in Egypt refused to submit to his successor Ḥassān b. Atāhiya who arrived in Fusṭāṭ in Jumādā II 127/April 745. Ḥassān's house was besieged and after sixteen days he was driven out, together with ʿĪsā b. Abī ʿAṭā. The army made Ḥafṣ Governor against his will. Marwān II was able to dismiss him at the beginning of 128/October 745 (Kindī, 74-5, 82-91; Grohmann 1924, 101; Miles 1948, p. 82).

Most of Ḥafṣ's rather limited output of glass stamps is to be placed in the period in 124-5 when he was Finance Director. All his known heavy weights are in fact dated 124. A few of his issues could belong to his last governorship when we have no information about who was in charge of finance.

129 **Half-*dīnār* weight,** with Yazīd b. Abī Yazīd

بسم الله
امر الله بالو
فاء و امر الامير
حفص بن الوليد
بطبعة مثقال
نصف دينر واف
على يدى يزيد بن
ابى يزيد

In the name of God.
Ordered God hon-
esty; and ordered the Amir
Ḥafṣ b. al-Walīd
the stamping of a weight
of half a *dīnar*, full-weight,
at the hands of Yazīd b.
Abī Yazīd.

Beaded border.

OA + 4223. Green. 2.2cm; stamp 1.7cm; 2.11g. (*Plate* 6)

From the same die Launois 1960 I, 9; Balog 1976, 130.

Yazīd's name accompanies that of Ḥafṣ on all but one of the latter's published coin weights, the exception being a third-*dīnār* weight in the Benaki Museum which has Ḥafṣ's name alone (Miles 1963 I, 16).

130 ***Dīnār* weight,** with Yazīd b. Abī Yazīd

بسم الله
امر الله بالو
فاء وامر الامير
حفص بن الوليد
بطبعة مثقال دينر
واف على يدى يز
يد بن ابى يز
يد

In the name of God.
Ordered God hon-
esty and order the Amir
Ḥafṣ b. al-Walīd
the stamping of a weight of a *dīnar*,
full-weight, at the hands of Yazīd b. Abī Yaz-
īd.

Beaded border.

OA + 4179. Green. 2.8cm; stamp 2.2cm. 4.22g. (*Plate* 6)

From the same die Balog 1976, 129; Cf. Rogers 1878, 14; Balog 1976, 127-8.

A second *dīnār*-weight die is represented by Fahmī 1957, 42 and a third one, crudely written, by Grohmann 1925, 5 and Launois 1960 I, 8.

131 **Disk weight: half-*raṭl*,** dated 124/741-2, with counterstamp of Yazīd b. Abī Yazīd

Main stamp

بسم الله
امر الامير حفص
بن الوليد بط(بع)ة
نصف رطل و
[اف سـ]نة اربع و
[عشر]ين و مئة

In the name of God.
Ordered the Amir Ḥafṣ
b. al-Walīd the stamping
of half a *raṭl*, full-
weight in the year four and
twenty and a hundred.

ʿAyn and *bāʾ* of *ṭabʿa* have been transposed.

Lower edge of counterstamp below; same die as No. 118.

OA + 4415. About half, the left side. Green. Length 9.7cm; 117g. (*Plate* 6)

From the same die Balog 1976, 125. Cf. 124.

Ḥafṣ's only known quarter-*raṭl* is also dated 124 and has the same counterstamp (Nies, 15 = Miles 1948, 25, reading *ru[b ʻra]ṭl*). On the only *raṭl* (Miles 1963 I, 17) the date is incomplete but the legend is similar and the piece probably belongs to the same series, which may have been Ḥafṣ's only issue of *raṭl*-system weights. Ḥafṣ is not known to have issued commodity weights.

132 Quarter-*qisṭ*

[بـ]سم الله
[ا]مر الامير
[حـ]فص بن الوليد
[بط]بعة ربع
[قسط] واف

In the name of God.
Ordered the Amir
Ḥafṣ b. al-Walīd
the stamping of a quarter-
qisṭ, full-measure.

OA + 4287. Green. Width 3.5cm. (*Plate 6*)

Cf. Launois 1957, 103; Miles 1958a, 46.

133–134 Half-*qisṭ*

[بـ]سم الله
[ا]مر الامير
[حـ]فص بن الوليد
[بـ]طبعة نصف
قسط واف

In the name of God.
Ordered the Amir
Ḥafṣ b. al-Walīd
the stamping of a half-
qisṭ, full-measure.

OA + 4024. Green. Width 4.7cm. Face chipped at top left and bottom right. (*Plate 6*)
OA + 4091. Green. Piece of vessel attached. Width 5.3cm.

The only previously published half-*qisṭ* stamp of Ḥafṣ appears to be Grohmann 1925, 121, which is from a different die, although the arrangement of the legend is the same.

135 *Wuqiyya* of fat (*duhn*)

امر حفص
بن الوليد
بوقية د
هن وا
ف

Ordered Ḥafṣ
b. al-Walīd
a *wuqiyya* of fa-
t, full-
measure.

OA + 11474. Green. Width 2.2cm. (*Plate 6*)

From the same die Casanova 1893, 133.

The beginning of the name Ḥafṣ is oddly written: the first two letters seem to be written one on top of the other. This type appears to be the only one of Ḥafṣ's stamps on which he does not bear the title *al-amīr* but that is probably due to nothing more than its small size. No larger denominations for *duhn* are yet known in his name.

ʻĪSĀ B. ABĪ ʻAṬĀ

Finance Director 125-7/743-5 and 128-31/745-9

136 Half-*dīnār* weight, with Yazīd b. Abī Yazīd

بسم الله
امر عيسى بن ابى
عطا بط(بـ)عة م(ثـ)قا(ا)
ل نصف دي(نـ)ر على
يدى يزيد بن
ابى يزيد

In the name of God.
Ordered ʻĪsa b. Abī
ʻ*Aṭā* the stamping of a weigh-
t of a half-*dīnar* at
the hands of Yazīd b.
Abī Yazīd.

(Coins and Medals) 90 8-4 22. Lane-Poole 6d. Green. 2.3cm; stamp 1.8cm; 2.11g. (*Plate 6*)

From the same die Launois 1957, 115; Fahmī 1957, 70; Launois 1959, 10; Balog 1976, 241. Cf. Fahmī 1957, 71.

As has been pointed out, there are several errors in the legends. At the end of the first line is a mark like an *alif*. Perhaps this can be explained by regarding the *alif* at the beginning of the second line as due to dittography. *Bā'* in *ṭab'a* is omitted and the *nūn* of *dīnār* is written like *mīm*. Quite what has happened with *mithqāl* is rather uncertain, but probably Balog was right to consider that *thā'* and *alif* were both omitted.

137 Half-*dīnār* weight, with Yazīd b. Abī Yazīd

بسم الله
ا(مر) عيسى بن (ا)بى
(عطا) بطبعة مثقا
ل نصف على
يدى يزيد بن ا
بى يزيد

In the name of God.
Ordered ʻĪsā b. Abī
ʻAṭā the stamping of a weigh-
t of a half at
the hands of Yazīd b. A-
bī Yazīd.

(Coins and Medals) 81 7-6 59. Lane-Poole, 9. Green. 2.1cm; stamp 1.7cm; 2.11g. (*Plate 6*)

From the same die Casanova 1893, 24; Miles 1948, 40; Fahmī 1957, 72; Miles 1963, 21. Cf. Miles 1958a, 76.

The errors on this second half-*dīnār* type of Yazīd are even more considerable than those of the first, to the extent that Lane-Poole read the second line *'amara allāh bil-wafā'*'. All other commentators have recognized the name of 'Īsā. Probably the best explanation is that put forward by Miles and Fahmī, that *mim rā'* of *amara*, *alif* of Abī and the whole of 'Aṭā have been omitted. The beginnings of the last two lines are also obscure, though there is no doubt what they ought to say.

138–139 *Dīnār* **weight,** with Yazīd b. Abī Yazīd

بسم الله ا
مر الله بالوفاء
وامر عيسى بن ابى
عطا بطبعة
مثقال دينر على
يدى يزيد بن
ابى يزيد

In the name of God. Or-
ordered God honesty;
and ordered 'Īsā b. Abī
'Aṭā the stamping
of a weight of a *dīnar* at
the hands of Yazīd b. Abī
Yazīd.

OA + 4183. Green. 2.8cm; stamp 2.2cm; 4.23g.
OA + 4227. Green. 2.1cm; stamp 2.2cm; 4.24g. (*Plate* 6)

From the same die Petrie, 134; Fahmī 1957, 68. Cf. Miles 1958a, 39; 1964a, 21.

The bottom line is hardly visible on these specimens or any of the photographs but, as Miles has said, there is no question that Yazīd b. Abī Yazīd is meant, and not Yazīd b. Tamīn, whose name is associated only with 'Abd al-Malik b. Marwān. There are two other published *dīnār*-weight dies of 'Īsā and Yazīd, with minor differences in the legend and its arrangement (Fahmī 1957, 67, 69).

140 *Dirham,* with Yazīd b. Abī Yazīd

بسم الله ا
مر الله بالوفاء و ا
مر عيسى بن ابى عطا
بطبعة مثقال درهم
على يدى يزيد بن ابى
يزيد

In the name of God. Or-
dered God honesty; and ordered 'Īsā b. Abī 'Aṭā
the stamping of a weight of a *dirham*
at the hands of Yazīd b. Abī
Yazīd.

(Coins and Medals) 76 11-5 6. Lane-Poole, 6. Green. 2.6cm; stamp 2.1cm; 2.85g. (*Plate* 6)

From the same die Petrie, 133; Miles 1958a, 78.

There is a vertical line, like an *alif*, but superfluous to the sense, after the end of the last line on all specimens of this type. Umayyad *dirham* weights are rather uncommon, with the exception of those of 'Īsā b. Abī 'Aṭā. Besides the present type two other dies have been recorded, both with Yazīd b. Abī Yazīd (Balog 1976, 243-5). For the different *dirham* standards represented by various types of glass weights see the Introduction (pp. 16-21).

141 Disk weight: ***wuqiyya***

بسم الله
امر الله بالو
[فـ]اء وامر الا[مير]
[عيـ]سى بن ا[بى عطا]
[----]
[----]

In the name of God.
Ordered God hon-
esty; and ordered the Amir
'Īsā b. Abī 'Aṭā
- - - -
- - - -

OA + 4299. Triangular fragment, from the top. Green. Length 3.9cm. 11.23g. (*Plate* 6)

The size shows that this is part of a *wuqiyya*. On the great majority of 'Īsā's weights, small and large, his name is accompanied by that of Yazīd b. Abī Yazīd and there appears to be room for the executive formula as well as the denomination on the missing part of this piece. A likely restoration of the end of the legend would be *bi-ṭab'a wuqiyya wāfiya* (or *wāf*) *'alā yaday Yazīd b. Abī Yazīd* ('the stamping of a full-weight *wuqiyya* at the hands of Yazīd b. Abī Yazīd').

142–143 Quarter-*qisṭ*

بسم الله
[ا]مر عيسى بن
[ا]بى عطا
بطبعة ربع
قسط واف

In the name of God.
Ordered 'Īsā b.
Abī 'Aṭā
the stamping of a quarter-
qisṭ, full-measure.

OA + 4050. Green. Piece of vessel attached. Length 5.0cm. (*Plate* 6)
OA + 4052. Green. Width 3.9cm. Bottom part broken off and chipped at top.

From the same die Balog 1976, 250. Cf. Launois 1957, 113; Balog 1976, 251.

Another stamp of the same denomination on which ʻĪsā bears the title *al-amīr* is much more common (Petrie, 135; Miles 1948, 42; Launois 1957, 106, 110; Dudzus 1959, 4a, b; Balog 1973, 13; 1976, 249. Cf. Casanova 1893, 134-5; Launois 1957, 107-9; Miles 1958a, 83).

144 Half-*qisṭ*

[بسـ]ـم ال[لـه]
[ا]مر الامير
[عيـ]ـسى بن ابى عطا
[بـ]ـطبعة نصف
قسط واف

In the name of God.
Ordered the Amir
ʻĪsā b. Abī ʻAṭā
the stamping of a half-
qisṭ, full-measure.

83 6-21 28. Lane-Poole, p. 109, No. 394. Olive green. Width 3.5cm; Chipped at top. (*Plate* 6)

From the same die Balog 1976, 248. Cf. Miles 1958a, 81-2.

Miles 1964a, 22 is of the same denomination but the legend is differently arranged and does not include the title *al-amīr*.

145 Half-*raṭl* of fat (*duhn*)

[بسـ]ـم الله
[امـ]ـر الامير
[عيـ]ـسى بن ابى عطا
[نصـ]ـف رطل
[د]هن

In the name of God.
Ordered the Amir
ʻĪsā b. Abī ʻAṭā
a half-*raṭl*
of fat.

OA + 4051. Green. Width 3.2cm. (*Plate* 6)

146 *Mikyala* of black cumin (*kammūn al-aswad*)

[بـ]ـسم ا
[لله] امر الاميـ[ـر]
عيسى (بن) ابى
عطا مكيلة
كمون الا
سود

In the name of G-
od. Ordered the Amir
ʻĪsā b. Abī
ʻAṭā a measure of
cumin, bla-
ck.

OA + 4092. Green. Width 3.4cm. (*Plate* 6)

From the same die Balog 1976, 253.

Balog noted the omission of *ibn* ('son of') between the names of ʻĪsā and his father. The piece of glass on which the British Museum's specimen was impressed is much thicker at the top than the bottom and evidently sagged forward after the impression was made, making the first two lines all but illegible.

147 *Mikyala* of woad (*wasma*)

بسم الله
[ا]مر الله بالوفاء
[و ا]مر الامير عيسى
[بن ا]بى عطا بطبعة
مكيلة وافية
[ل]لوسمة

In the name of God.
Ordered God honesty;
and ordered the Amir ʻĪsā
b. Abī ʻAṭā the stamping
of a measure, full-measure,
for woad.

89 8-6 2. Lane-Poole, p. 108, No. 393. Olive green. Width 3.4cm. (*Plate* 6)

From the same die Casanova 1893, 136; Launois 1957, 111.

It is most unusual for the name of a commodity to follow, rather than precede, the word *wāf* in the legends of vessel stamps. For this reason, and because on most specimens the word is only partly visible, *wasma* has not been recognized on this type before. However it is sufficiently clear on the specimen in the Fouquet Collection. Woad is one of the more common commodities on vessel stamps, which makes it unlikely that ʻĪsā did not issue stamps for it; no others have been described. Miles 1958a, 84, which is not illustrated but has the same legend without the last line, may well be a product of the same die (Cf. also Miles 1964a, 24).

ʻABD AL-MALIK B. MARWĀN
Finance Director, later Governor and Finance Director 131-3/749-50

148 *Fals* weight of 30 *kharrūba*, with Yazīd b. Tamīm

بسم الله امر
الامير عبد الملك
بن مرون اصلحه الله
بطبعة مثقال فلس
ثلثين خروبة واف
على يدى يزيد بن
تميم

In the name of God. Ordered
the Amir ʻAbd al-Malik
b. Marwan, may God make him righteous,
the stamping of a weight of a *fals*
of thirty *kharrūba*, full-weight,
at the hands of Yazīd b.
Tamīm.

OA + 4185. Green. Fragment. A little over a third, the right side. Length 3.0cm; 2.16g. (*Plate 7*)

From the same die Casanova 1893, 27; Petrie, 140; Launois 1957, 137; Fahmī 1957, 92-3; Miles 1958a, 90; Balog 1976, 262. Cf. Casanova 1893, 28; Miles 1948, 49, Launois 1957, 138-40; Fahmī 1957, 94-6; Scanlon 1968, p. 191; Balog 1976, 263-4.

This is the commonest of ʻAbd al-Malik's *fals*-weight dies, all of which are of 30 *kharrūbas*. Another type with Yazīd b. Tamīm, described below, is only known from the British Museum's fragmentary specimen. Two other dies have names of other executives, one Kaʻb b. ʻAlqama (Fahmī 1957, 97; Balog 1976, 260), the other a newly discovered name which Balog reads Mukhallad (1976, 261).

149 ***Fals* weight of 30 *kharrūba*,** with Yazīd b. Tamīm

ب[سم الله ا]
مر الامي[ر عبد ا]
لملك بن مر[ون اصلحه]
الله بطبعة [مثقال]
فلس ثلثين [خروبة]
واف على يدى [يز]
يد بن تميم

In the name of God. Or-
dered the Amir ʻAbd a-
l-Malik b. Marwan, may God
make him righteous, the stamping of a weight
of a *fals* of thirty *kharrūba*,
full-weight, at the hands of Yazīd b. Tamīm.

OA + 4184. Fragment. Nearly half, bottom and right side. Length 3.3cm; 3.0g. (*Plate 7*)

150 Disk weight: *raṭl*

[بسم الله ام]ر
[الله بالوفاء]و امر
[الامي]ر عبد الملك
بن مرون بطبعة
رطل واف

In the name of God. Ordered
God honesty; and ordered
the amir ʻAbd al-Malik
b. Marwan the stamping
of a *raṭl*, full-weight.

OA + 4423. Rather over half, bottom and right. Length 12.0cm; stamp 4.3cm; 256g. (*Plate 7*)

From the same die Balog 1976, 258.

On the top edge is the mark of a counterstamp, its surface chipped away and with no more than a trace of one obscure letter visible. Balog's specimen has part of the counterstamp of Mukhallad (?) b. Yaḥyā.

A second *raṭl* stamp of ʻAbd al-Malik b. Marwān is recorded on ring weights and not disk weights (Miles 1948, 50; Balog 1976, 256-7). Before his time the ring-weight form was used almost exclusively for weights for specific commodities. Weights of all denominations on the ordinary *raṭl* system were at that period nearly always disk weights (in fact, the only published exception appears to be Balog 1976, 137). No doubt the distinction was maintained to avoid confusion. ʻAbd al-Malik b. Marwān is the last person whose commodity weights we have, the British Museum's meat weights (Nos 151-2) being the only known examples. The Umayyad series of commodity weights is now quite extensive but no Abbasid one has yet appeared. In fact it is clear that glass commodity weights ceased to be issued. Probably the commodities in question were henceforth sold by the ordinary *raṭl*-system weights. The fact that the ring-weight form was used for ordinary *raṭls* under ʻAbd al-Malik b. Marwān may indicate that the use of commodity weights was abandoned in the course of his Finance Directorship, and that there was no longer any reason for not having ring-weight *raṭls*. In the Abbasid period ring weights and disk weights on the *raṭl* system are found of almost all denominations, though the ring weight tends to become more favoured for the larger ones.

151 Ring weight: half-*raṭl* of meat, with counterstamp of Yazīd b. Tamīm

[ب]سم الله [ا]
مر الله بالو[فاء]
و امر الامير
عبد الملك بن مر
ون بطبعة نصف
رطل للحم واف

In the name of God. Or-
dered God honesty;
and ordered the Amir
ʻAbd al-Malik b. Mar-
wan the stamping of a half-
raṭl for meat, full-weight.

Counterstamp to left Same die as Nos 159-61.

OA + 4356. Fragment of the top. Half the counterstamp missing. Green. Length 5.3cm; 45.7g. (*Plate 7*)

This piece and the next are the first meat weights of ʻAbd al-Malik b. Marwān to be published. No later ones are known and, as noted under No. 150, it is likely that the use of weights for specific commodities was abandoned at, or very shortly before, the fall of the Umayyads.

152 Ring-weight: 2 *raṭls* of meat, with the counterstamp of Kaʻb b. ʻAlqama

بسم الله ا
مر الله بالوفاء و
امر الامير عبد
الملك بن مرون
بط(ب)عة رطلين
للحم واف

In the name of God. Or-
dered God honesty; and
ordered the Amir ʿAbd
al-Malik b. Marwan
the stamping of two *raṭls*
for meat, full-weight.

Counterstamp to left

على يدى
كعب
بن علقمة

At the hands
of Kaʿb
b. ʿAlqama.

OA + 4355. Fragment. Most of the top, with the left end broken off. Green. Length 6.7cm; 200g. (*Plate 7*)

On the main stamp *bāʾ* has fallen out of *ṭabʿa*. On the counterstamp no more than the greater part of the first line and the edge of first letter of the second survive, but that is sufficient to establish that it is from the same die as a number of other impressions. It appears on two other weights, a *wuqiyya* and a large disk weight which lacks most of the main stamp (Dudzus 1959, 5a, b; Balog 1976, 275). Two examples are known of the use of the same die on vessel stamps (Launois 1957, 310; Balog 1976, 276). Kaʿb b. ʿAlqama also appears as the executive on some of ʿAbd al-Malik b. Marwān's coin weights (Fahmī 1957, 97; Miles 1971, 20; Balog 1976, 260).

153–154 Quarter-*qisṭ*

بسم الله امر
[ا]لله بالوفاء و امر
[ا]لامير عبد الملك
[بن]مرون بطبعة ربع
قسط واف

In the name of God. Ordered
God honesty; and ordered
the Amir ʿAbd al-Malik
b. Marwan the stamping of a quarter-
qisṭ, full-measure.

OA + 4053. Green. Width 3.5cm. (*Plate 7*)
OA + 4054. Green. The right half. Length 3.4cm.

From the same die Miles 1958a, 92; 1963 I, 25; Balog 1976, 266.

155 Half-*qisṭ*

[ب]سم الله
[ا]مر الله بالو
فاء و امر الام[ير]
عبد الملك بن م[رون]
بطبعة نصف
قسط و
اف

In the name of God.
Ordered God hon-
esty and ordered the Amir
ʿAbd al-Malik b. Marwan
the stamping of a half-
qisṭ, full-
measure.

80 6–14 23. Lane-Poole, p. 107, No. 391. Green. Width 4.4cm. (*Plate 7*)

From the same die Balog 1976, 265. Cf. Miles 1964a, 25.

156 *Mikyala* of skinned lentils (*ʿadas muqashshar*)

بسم الله ا
مر الله بالوفاء
و امر الامير عبد ا
لملك بن مرون بطبعة
مكيلة عد{ـ}س
مقشر وا
فية

In the name of God. Or-
dered God honesty;
and ordered the Amir ʿAbd a-
l-Malik b. Marwan the stamping
of a measure of lentils,
skinned, full-
measure.

OA + 4055. Green. Width 4.0cm. Chipped at top. (*Plate 7*)

From the same die Balog 1976, 269.

There is an extra 'tooth' to the *sīn* of *ʿadas* and the initial letter of the same word is mis-shapen.

157 *Mikyala* of *katam*

بسم الله امر
[ا]لله بالوفاء و امر
[ا]لامير عبد الملك
[بن] مرون بطبعة
مكيلة للكتم
وافية

In the name of God. Ordered
God honesty; and ordered
the Amir ʿAbd al-Malik
b. Marwan the stamping
of a measure of *katam*,
full-measure.

OA + 4056. Green. Width 4.0cm. (*Plate 7*)

From the same die Miles 1963 II, 18.

Stamps for *katam* are uncommon; besides the present type single examples are known of the Caliph Yazīd II, with Ḥayyān b. Shurayḥ, and of ʿUbaydallāh b. al-Ḥabḥāb (Miles 1971, 6; Balog 1976, 108). Miles (1963 II, 18) has also noted the existence of a specimen of an anonymous type in a private collection.

Katam is mentioned a number of times in the literature of Ḥadīth in connection with henna. The two substances were used together to dye the hair, a practice said to have been adopted by, among others, the Prophet Muḥammad himself (Wensinck, *s.v. katam*). Since henna also appears on stamps, most commonly as *ḥinnā' al-ra's* ('henna for the head' i.e. for the hair), there is no difficulty in accepting that the *katam* of the stamps is also a hair dye. It is said to have reinforced the effect of the henna. The dye was produced by the dried and ground leaves of a plant: this much we are informed of by both Ibn al-ʻAwwām and Ibn al-Bayṭār. The identity of the plant however still remains obscure. Banqueri, editor and translator of Ibn al'Awwām's book on agriculture, took it to be the dittany or fraxinella, but as Clément-Mullet, in his later French version of the same work, pointed out, Ibn al-ʻAwwām's descriptions of the three types of *katam* are of trees or shrubs; he even says that *katam* can be grafted on to laurel. One of Ibn al-Bayṭār's sources also describes *katam* as a tree. Dittany, then, is excluded, as are woad and indigo which some dictionaries identify with *katam*. Dozy, in his dictionary, argued that certain references to *katam* are to privet (Fr. *troëne*). He noted also that the eighteenth-century botanist Forskål gave a description of a plant called *katam* which he assigned to the Box family (*Buxus dioica*, Forsk.). It was presumably this entry that led Miles to suggest that the *katam* of the stamps might be privet and also to give the scientific name of privet as *Buxus dioica*. Privet of course belongs to an entirely different botanical family, the Oleaceae. Clément-Mullet also noted Forskål's description but pointed out that the types of *katam* described by Ibn al'Awwām have characteristics which are not those of box. Privet (*Ligustrum vulgare L.*) may be the real meaning of *katam* in some contexts but further investigation is needed before it can be regarded as reasonably certain that the *katam* of the stamps is not something else (Ibn al-Bayṭār, *s.v. katam*; Ibn al-ʻAwwām I, 425, 427, 431; II, 383-4; Clément-Mullet I, 398, 400, 403; II, 370-1.).

158 *Mikyala* **of** *mishsh*

بسم الله
امر الله بالو
[فـ]ـاء و امر الامير
[عـ]ـبد الملك بن مر
ون بطبعة م(كيـ)[ـلة]
[ا]لمش وافية

In the name of God.
Ordered God hon-
esty; and ordered the Amir
ʻAbd al-Malik b. Mar-
wan the stamping of a measure
of *mishsh*, full-measure.

OA + 4057. Green. Width 4.0cm. (*Plate 7*)

The word *mikyala* seems required by the context but what is visible of it is curiously written. The text given here is based on the assumption that *kāf* and *yā'* have been transposed.

YAZĪD B. TAMĪM
Executive under ʻAbd al-Malik b. Marwān

It has been suggested (Miles 1948, p. 96) that Yazīd b. Tamīm also served under ʻĪsā b. Abī ʻAṭā but the suggestion is based on a number of coin weights of ʻĪsā where the executive's name, even where it is not clear, must be Yazīd b. Abī Yazīd. Pieces with the name of Yazīd c. Tamīm are more plentiful than those of ʻAbd al-Malik's other two known executives, Kaʻb b. ʻAlqama (see No. 150) and Mukhallad (?) b. Yaḥyā (Balog 1976, 257-8, 261). Presumably Yazīd's term of office was much the longest.

159–161 Executive stamp

على يدى
يزيد بن
تميم

At the hands
of Yazīd b.
Tamīm.

OA + 4058. Green. Length 4.9cm, with attached piece of vessel. Stamp deformed.
OA + 4086. Green. Width 3.1cm; stamp 2.1cm. (*Plate 7*)
94 3-9 10. Green. Width 2.8cm. Stamp deformed.

All illustrated examples of Yazīd b. Tamīm's executive stamp are from the one die, which was used on both weights and vessel stamps. Its appearance on a half-*raṭl* meat weight has been recorded under No. 151, a damaged example on a *raṭl* has been illustrated by Miles (1948, 50) and one surviving alone on a fragment of a disk weight described by Balog (1976, 271). Vessel stamps are numerous. Originally, of course, they would have been used jointly with vessel stamps showing the denomination and with the name of ʻAbd al-Malik b. Marwān. The list is as follows: Casanova 1893, 190; Launois 1957, 141; Miles 1958a, 88; Balog 1976, 272. Cf. Launois 1957, 152; Miles 1971, 18-19; Balog 1976, 273-4.

2. ABBASID

THE HOUSE OF MUḤAMMAD (ĀL MUḤAMMAD)

The words Āl Muḥammad were first correctly read on glass stamps by Casanova (1893 I, 162-5; II, 44; see also pp. 347-8), who interpreted the political claim suggested by the phrase as indicating that they were issued by the Fatimid dynasty (297-567/909-1171; conquest of Egypt 358/969), which claimed descent from the Prophet Muḥammad. Later it was realized that the style of such pieces made it necessary to date them to the second century AH. It has been suggested that they are to be associated with one or other of the movements to replace Abbasid rule with that of the descendants of Muḥammad's daughter Fāṭima and son-in-law ʻAlī which took place in the second century (see e.g. Fahmī 1957, 245; Miles 1971, 45).

Launois (1957, 147), on the other hand, took a different line. She argued that the phrase *amara Āl Muḥammad bil wafā'* ('The House of Muḥammad ordered honesty'), which occurs on the vessel stamps of the group, was a development of the similar 'God ordered honesty' which first appeared on late Umayyad stamps, pointing out that the movement that led to the establishment of the Abbasid Caliphate made use of propaganda in favour of the rule of an unnamed Imam from the family of the Prophet. She therefore assigned the group to the late Umayyad period as products of Abbasid propagandists. Restating the argument later (1958b, 234; 1960 I, 10), she further pointed out that the name of Abū Muslim, the great organizer and general of the revolutionary movement, appears on coins with the title Amir of the House of Muḥammad. As Balog has since noted, the historians also mention the use of the phrase Āl Muḥammad in titles (e.g. Ṭabari III, 60. For the coins see Zambaur, 6-7; Miles 1938, pp. 15-21). There are, as we shall see, other reasons for dating the Āl Muḥammad stamps close to the period which Launois suggests which make it certain that in this context the phrase comes from the stock-in-trade of Abbasid propaganda, but it cannot be precisely correct to maintain that the stamps were made during the declining years of the Umayyads. In appearance they closely resemble the official output of both the late Umayyad and early Abbasid periods. The range of types so far known has some peculiarities, no heavy weights being recorded for example, but otherwise the classes and denominations are closely comparable only to those of the Finance Directors and the Caliph al-Manṣūr. The similarities are such that there can be no doubt that they too are official issues produced by the weights-and-measures office in Fusṭāṭ. The story of the Abbasid conquest of Egypt itself was not, of course, that of a local opposition movement gaining the political control needed before such matters as the issue of weights and measure could be thought of, but that of a rapid campaign by an invading army. Clearly the stamps must date from the time when the Abbasids had won control of Egypt but when there was still uncertainty about the nature of the legitimacy of the new dynasty and the slogans of the revolutionary period retained some of their appeal and utility.

The date suggested by this line of argument agrees with that recently put forward by Balog (1976, pp. 109-10) who places the Āl Muḥammad stamps in Ṣāliḥ b. ʻAlī's first governorship (133/750-1). Ṣāliḥ was himself a member of the Abbasid family and led the army that conquered Egypt. One of Balog's supporting arguments, that the script of the Āl Muḥammad vessel stamps is extremely close to that on vessel stamps of Ṣāliḥ b. ʻAlī, need not be given too much weight. Certainly one would not agree that they seem to have been engraved by the same hand. Another item of Balog's evidence is, however, of great importance, a quarter-*qisṭ* vessel stamp in his own collection on which Ṣāliḥ b. ʻAlī's name is preceded by a unique variation of the command for honesty. The beginning of the phrase has yet to be fully explained, but the name Hāshim appears in it and refers no doubt to Muḥammad's great grandfather, ancestor also of the Abbasids. It does seem clear that this case some person, or perhaps persons, from among the decendants of Hāshim 'commands (or command) honesty'. A satisfactory link is therefore provided between Ṣāliḥ b. ʻAlī and the deliberately vague propaganda of the early Abbasid movement.

Some confirmation for this dating is provided by certain of the types of stamp produced in the name of the House of Muḥammad. Among them for instance, is the enigmatic *dirham* weight of 13 *kharrūba* (e.g. Nos 163-4). These were otherwise only issued in the early Abbasid period when we have a complete run in the names of ʻAbd al-Malik b. Yazīd, from both his governorships, of Ṣāliḥ b. ʻAlī, from his second and of Muḥammad b. al-Ashʻath, i.e. from about 133-43 (see Nos 174-7; Balog 1976, 296-7, 388). The Āl Muḥammad type would fit in very well at the beginning of the series. Similarly, the Āl Muḥammad commodity stamps are only comparable to those with the names of Finance Directors or Caliphs, a series that comes to an end once again with Muḥammad b. al-Ashʻath.

The picture that we have of Ṣāliḥ b. ʻAlī's own issues is also consistent with this dating, since almost none of them can belong to his first governorship. On coin weights his name is only known to appear on reverses, most commonly paired with obverses of al-Manṣūr. Only the 13-*kharrūba dirham* weights have anonymous obverses, but the reverse dies used on them are elsewhere linked with obverses of al-Manṣūr who became Caliph in 136/754 and the single obverse die is one that can be shown to have been introduced in Ṣāliḥ's second governorship (see Nos 177, 193). With regard to the rest of his output the evidence is admittedly not decisive but, except in the case of the quarter-*qisṭ* where the unusual type discussed above is parallelled by a more common one with ordinary legends, in no case does it yet appear that more than one die was used for any one denomination. If stamps in Ṣāliḥ's name were issued in any quantity in both his governorships we would expect that by now obvious indications of the fact would have appeared in the form of stamps from corresponding pairs of dies for the different denominations.

In conclusion it may be said that a number of different arguments, of varying nature and force, support each other to confirm that Balog's dating of the Āl Muḥammad stamps to the first governorship of Ṣāliḥ b. ʿAlī is correct.

162 *Dīnār* weight

بسم الله
امر آل محمد
مثقال دينر
واف

In the name of God.
Ordered the House of Muḥammad
a weight of a *dīnar*,
full-weight.

Six-pointed star below.

OA + 4168. About a third broken off, at top and right. Green. 2.9cm; stamp 2.4cm; 2.64g. (*Plate 7*)

From the same die Fahmī 1957, 241; Miles 1958a, 211; Launois 1959, 12; Balog 1976, 277. Cf. Launois 1957, 145; Miles 1958a, 212.

A single specimen of another *dīnār*-weight die clearly of the House-of-Muḥammad-type has been published (Launois 1957, 144 = Fahmī 1957, 242) as well as a curious piece tentatively identified as of the same denomination from a third die (Miles 1964a, 56). Half- and third-*dīnar* weights in the series are known (Launois 1959 I, 10; Balog 1976, 279-81). Balog 1976, 278 is not of the House of Muḥammad and belongs to a class of tokens represented by Nos 510-511 in the British Museum's collection.

163-164 *Dīrham* weight of 13 *kharrūba*

بسم الله
امر آل محمد
مثقال درهم
ثلثة عشر خر
وبة واف

In the name of God.
Ordered the House of Muḥammad
a weight of a *dīrham*
of thirteen *kharr-*
ūba, full-weight.

Faint dot in centre above; a semicircular loop to its right; mark, perhaps a star, below. The first tooth of *shīn* in *ʿashar* is jammed up against the *ʿayn*.

OA + 4228. Green. 2.6cm; stamp 2.0cm; 2.62g (*Plate 7*)
(Coins and Medals) 74 7-8 34. Lane-Poole, 33. Green. 2.6cm; stamp 2.0cm; 2.64g.

From the same die Casanova 1893, 44; Petrie, 94; Fahmī 1957, 243; Miles 1971, 45. Cf. Launois 1957, 146; Fahmī 1957, 244.

This is the first type of the series of 13-*kharrūba dirham* weights. The standard on which this type was issued must have been a little heavy as almost all specimens weigh more than 2.60g. The later 13-*kharrūba dirham* weights approach closely to the normal average *kharrūba* standard (see introduction, p. 18). A single specimen is known of another type of *dirham* of the House of Muḥammad (Launois 1957, 147 = Fahmī 1957, 245). There is no mention of *kharrūbas* on it and the weight approaches that of the standard silver *dirham*, being given as 2.88g and 2.92g.

165 Quarter-*qisṭ*

بسم الله ا
مر آل محمـــد
بالوفاء ربع
قسط واف

In the name of God. Or-
dered the House of Muḥammad
honesty. Quarter
qisṭ, full-measure.

Double-loop ornament at end of third line.

OA + 4059. Green. Width 4.3cm. (*Plate 7*)

From the same die Casanova 1893, 162; Petrie, 95; Balog 1976, 285-6. Cf. Casanova 1893, 163-4; Launois 1957, 143; Balog 1976, 287.

166-167 Great measure (*mikyāl al-kabīr*)

بسم الله امر
آل محمد بالو
فاء مكيل الكبير
واف

In the name of God. Ordered
the House of Muḥammad honest-
y. *Mikyal al-kabīr*,
full-measure.

OA + 4093. The bottom half only. Green. Width 3.6cm.
OA + 4288. Green. Width 4.3cm. (*Plate 7*)

From the same die Launois 1958a, 3; Balog 1976, 288. Cf. Balog 1976, 289.

The end of *al-kabīr* was not clear on Launois' piece and she read *al-kusbur*, coriander, a substance which has been found on stamps in the form *habb al-kusbur*, coriander seed. Balog read *mikyāl al-kabīr*, pointing out that such a denomination is not known earlier. Nor, in fact, is it known later, nor has the possible synonym *mikyala al-kabīra* been found. Consideration of the very small number of commodity stamps with Āl Muḥammad on them suggests that Balog's reading is correct and that the introduction of the new measure can be explained. The rest of the corpus consists of one half *raṭl* of fat (*duhn*), two *mikyāls* of white cumin and one of woad (Casanova 1893, 163; Balog 1976, 290-2). On the other hand five specimens of the *mikyāl al-kabīr* are now known and all other common commodities are so far unrepresented. Some will no doubt eventually turn up, but probably not all for the absence of so many commodities is likely to be due to the fact that some of them were not then sold by their own individual measures but by the *mikyāl al-kabīr*. The introduction of the new measure would be a short-lived and presumably not very successful attempt to simplify the system. Commodities sold in rather larger quantities, lentils, chick-peas, vetch and the like, in all possibility, would have been sold by the new measure. It seems unlikely that identical measures of different commodities could have all been sold at one price and it would therefore seem that we cannot assume, just because prices are marked on some stamps, that the prices of measures were always fixed.

The word *mikyāl* is a synonym of *mikyala*, both meaning measure. It is occasionally found on anonymous stamps but otherwise its use is limited to Āl Muḥammad types, on which *mikyala* never occurs, and on which *mikyāl* is invariably written without the *alif*.

ṢĀLIḤ B. ʻALĪ

Governor 133/750-1; Governor and Finance Director 135-7/753-5

As stated in the discussion of the House of Muḥammad, the stamps of that series are to be assigned to Ṣāliḥ b. ʻAlī's first governorship. With the possible exception of the weight with the Hashimite legend already mentioned, it is likely that the stamps with his name belong to his second term of office.

168 Disk weight: half-*raṭl*

[مما ا]مر
[به الا]مير
[صلح ب]ن على ا
[صلحه ال]له
[بطبعة] نصف
[رطل] واف

Of what ordered
the amir
Ṣāliḥ b. ʻAlī, may
God keep him righteous,
the stamping of a half
raṭl, full-weight.

OA + 4424. The left hand half. Slight depression on the rim at the edge of the break below, perhaps caused by the application of a counterstamp further right. Green. Length 9.4cm; 108g. (*Plate 8*)

The restoration follows the formula found on the majority of Ṣāliḥ b. ʻAli's heavy weights and vessel stamps, for instance the quarter-*qisṭ* described next. The clumsy construction (*mimmā amara . . . bi-ṭabʻa*) appears to be standard under this governor. His other known heavy weights are the *wuqiyya* (Balog 1976, 295) and the *raṭl*, the specimens of which are all ring weights (Petrie, 150; Herz, 107c; Miles 1948, 61; Balog 1976, 294, all from one die. Cf. Balog 1976, 293).

169 Quarter-*qisṭ*

مما امر به
صلح بن على اص[ل]ح[ه]
الله بطبعة ربع
[ا]لقسط واف

Of what ordered
Ṣāliḥ b. ʻAlī, may God keep him
righteous, the stamping of a quarter
qisṭ, full-measure.

OA + 4077. Green. Width 3.9cm. (*Plate 8*)

From the same die Launois 1957, 158; Balog 1976, 299.
Casanova 1893, 141; Launois 1957, 159-60; Balog 1976, 300.

The *lām* of *aṣlaḥahu* is not clear on any specimen. It may have been missed out, as occurs on a number of Ṣāliḥ b. ʻAli's other pieces. If the reading given is complete this type is unique in having Ṣāliḥ b. ʻAli's name without the title *al-amīr* but it is possible that *al-amīr* was on the die at the end of the first line or perhaps at the beginning of the second. Casanova implies that the legend of Fouquet's specimen included the title.

ABBĀN B. IBRĀHĪM

Executive under Ṣāliḥ b. ʻAlī and the Caliph al-Manṣūr

170 Executive stamp

على يدى
ابان بن
ابرهيم

At the hands
of Abbān b.
Ibrahīm

OA + 4095. Green. Width 2.8 cm. (*Plate 8*)

From the same die Casanova 1893, 191; Miles 1948, 111; Launois 1957, 317; Miles 1971, 48; Balog 1976, 742a-747. Cf. Launois 1957, 318; Miles 1951b, 33; 1958a, 102.

The pieces listed above are all vessel stamps. The edge of the impression of what appears to be the same die can be seen on the edge of two weights in the Balog collection, a half-*raṭl* of al-Manṣūr and a *wuqiyya* of Ṣāliḥ b. ʻAlī. Balog (1976, 724a-7) has argued that Abbān may have been active towards the end of Al-Manṣūr's Caliphate and even in the early years of that of al-Mahdī, on the grounds that the script of the stamp is identical with those of al-Muhājir (*qv*). The resemblance, however, is hardly very striking and such a late date conflicts with Abbān's association with Ṣāliḥ b. ʻAli, which implies that he was active in the early part of al-Manṣūr's reign. There is reason to think that the few heavy weights issued in the name of that Caliph are to be dated to the earlier period (see Nos 198-199).

Castiglioni published an engraving of a curious *dirham* weight with an executive's name which it is tempting to read Abbān b. Abrāhīm (No. 9). The first two lines read *amara al-amīr/aṣlaḥahu allāh* ('ordered the Amir/may God keep him righteous'). The benediction is one used by a number of officials, among them Ṣāliḥ b. ʻAlī. It may be that he was the nameless Amir of the pieces, if indeed the name is not omitted in the printed engraving by error.

ʿABD AL-MALIK B. YAZĪD
Governor and Finance Director 133-6/751-3 and 137-41/755-8

171-172 Half-*dīnār* weight, with Muḥammad b. Shuraḥbīl and Chael

Obverse

بسم ا
لله امر عبد
الملك بن يز
يد بمثقال
نصف واف

In the name of G-
od. Ordered ʿAbd
al-Malik b. Yaz-
īd a weight
of a half, full-weight.

Reverse
Margin:

على يدى محمد بن شرحبيل

At the hands of Muḥammad b. Shuraḥbīl

Centre:

طبعة
كيل

Stamping
of Chael

For the script of the reverse, see Commentary.

OA + 4229. Green. 2.3cm; stamp 1.6cm; 2.11g. (*Plate 8*)
OA + 4282. Green. 2.3cm; stamp 1.6cm; 2.10g.

From the same pair of dies Petrie, 146; Miles 1948, 62-3 (information from N. M. Lowick); Fahmī 1957, 107; Balog 1976, 316. Cf. Balog 1976, 315.

The introduction of the practice of using a reverse die for coin weights can be dated to the first governorship of ʿAbd al-Malik b. Yazīd, the intention being perhaps to make it more difficult to tamper with the weights by grinding down their backs. The molten glass was still placed on an iron plate preparatory to being impressed with the die from above, only now the plate itself was engraved with a die.

One reverse die designed for use on *wuqiyya* disk weights is known (see Nos 181, 198, 214) and one type of *fals* weight is sometimes found with a reverse (see No. 388). Otherwise reverses have only been found on *dīnār*-system and *dirham* weights. The practice was to produce the whole series at any one time from a single reverse die, which was designed for the largest type, the *dīnār* weight, with the result that only part of it is ever visible on the other denominations. The reverse impression is almost invariably far less clear than the obverses, but it is usually possible to establish the identity of impressions of the same die.

The reverse of the present type always occurs on pieces with ʿAbd al-Malik b. Yazīd's name on the obverse, which enables us to assign them to his first governorship. A single example of a second reverse with a positive legend dating to the same period has been published by Rogers (1878, 10). Other reverses, with the name of ʿAbd al-Malik himself and Chael, are used with obverses which are either anonymous or in the name of the Caliph al-Manṣūr (see Nos 177, 197). These obverses are in turn linked with reverses of Ṣāliḥ b. ʿAli and Chael (see No. 193). Plainly all these types belong in the reign of al-Manṣūr, that is to the second governorships of both Ṣāliḥ b. ʿAlī and ʿAbd al-Malik b. Yazīd.

ʿAbd al-Malik's own *dīnār*-system weights are known from a single set of obverses. The *dīnār* weight is described next; the third-*dīnār* is at present represented by Fahmī 1957, 107. So far as can be told from the publications, the same reverse is found on all the known specimens. It is also found with two different obverses for *dirham* weights of 13 *kharrūba* (see Nos 174-176).

Castiglioni (3) was the first to publish what may be taken to be the same reverse, though reproduced by hand, and realized that the inscription itself was in reverse, i.e. that the engraver had failed to reverse it on the die. It has, however, occasionally been misunderstood since, for instance by Lane-Poole in his description of the British Museum's No. 173. Similar lapses by engravers are not unknown (see for example Nos 439-441, 451), but the particular explanation in this case may be that it was the first time the craftsman was instructed to produce a reverse die for glass and that he had the mistaken idea that the process of the transfer of the impression would be different below from above.

Chael is the first of a new class of people who appear on glass weights, and who, with the reservation expressed in the Introduction (p. 13), may be called artisans. The name strictly transcribed is *kayl*, which in Arabic would primarily mean measuring by capacity, and is used in other metrological contexts such as the term *dirham kayl* (see Nos 407,412). However the parallels demand that in this context the word should be a name and Grohmann's explanation that it is the common Coptic name Chael is generally accepted (see Grohmann 1924, 109, 113; Miles 1948, p. 106).

173 *Dīnār* weight, with Muḥammad b. **Shuraḥbīl** and Chael

Obverse

بسم الله
امر عبد ا
لملك بن يزيد
بمثقال دينر
واف

In the name of God.
Ordered ʿAbd a-
l-Malik b. Yazīd
a weight of a *dīnar*,
full-weight.

Reverse Same die as on Nos 171-172

(Coins and Medals) 88 7-2 9. Lane-Poole, 10. Green. 2.9cm; stamp 2.2cm; 4.23g. (*Plate 8*)

From the same pair of dies Petrie, 145; Launois 1957, 167-8 = Fahmī 1957, 105-6; Miles 1958a, 99; Balog 1976, 314. Cf. Castiglioni, 3.

174 ***Dirham*** **weight of 13** ***kharrūba,*** with Muḥammad b. Shuraḥbīl and Chael

Obverse

بسم الله ا
مر عبد الملك
بن يزيد بمثقا
ل درهم و
زن ثل(ث) عشرة
خروبة

In the name of God. Ordered ʻAbd al-Malik b. Yazīd a weight of a *dirham* of the weight of thirteen *kharrūba.*

Rectangular stamp.

Reverse From the same die as Nos 171–173.

OA + 4230. Green. 2.4cm; stamp 1.6 x 1.6cm; 2.51g. (*Plate 8*)

From the same pair of dies Miles 1958a, 101.

The third tooth of *thalath* (three) is written much like a *dāl*. It would be possible to read *aḥad* and take the type to be one of 11 *kharrūbas*, but the weights are correct for 13 *kharrūbas* and it must belong to the series of *dirham* weights of that denomination.

So far as can be judged from the engraving, the obverse of Rogers 1978, 10, is from the same die but the reverse is different, with a positive and not a reversed impression. *Ṭabʻat kayl* is visible in the centre; the margin may include the name of Muḥammad b. Shuraḥbīl. As has been mentioned under Nos 171–172, this seems to be the only published example of this second reverse die from ʻAbd al-Malik b. Yazīd's first governorship.

ʻAbd al-Malik b. Yazīd's other types of the same denomination are described immediately below.

175–176 ***Dirham*** **weight of 13** ***kharrūba,*** with Muḥammad b. Shuraḥbīl and Chael

Obverse

بسم الله ا
مر عبد الملك
بن يزيد بمثقا
ل در(هم) و
زن ثلثه عشرة
خروبة

In the name of God. Ordered ʻAbd al-Malik b. Yazīd a weight of a *dirham* of the weight of thirteen *kharrūba*

Rectangular stamp

Reverse From the same die as on Nos 171–174.

OA + 4187. Pale green. 2.4cm; stamp 1.5 x 1.6cm; 2.50g. (*Plate 8*)

(Coins and Medals) 89 6–4 71. Lane-Poole, 11. Green 2.3cm; 1.6 x 1.6cm; 2.51g.

The legend is very similar to that on No. 174 but, while *thalatha* is spelt correctly the last two letters of *dirham* are written to look more or less like *mīm*, 'tooth', *rā*'.

177 ***Dirham*** **weight of 13** ***kharrūba,*** with Chael

Obverse

بسم الله
مثقال درهم
وزن ثلث عشر
ة خروبة

In the name of God. Weight of a *dirham* of the weight of thirteen *kharrūba.*

Rectangular stamp.

Reverse

Marginal legend between two circles:

عبد الملك بن يزيد

ʻAbd al-Malik b. Yazīd

Centre:

طبعة
كيل

Stamping of Chael

OA + 4190. Green. 2.4cm; stamp 1.5 x 1.6cm; 2.50g. (*Plate 8*)

From the same pair of dies Launois 1957, 348 = Fahmī 1957, 109; Launois 1960, 3; Balog 1976, 322–3. Cf. Rogers 1873, 38 = Rogers 1878, fig 12; Launois 1960, 4–5; Miles 1964a, 26; Balog 1976, 324–5.

All the illustrated specimens share the same reverse die, but there are three different dies with the same legend and some of the pieces which are not illustrated may be from other dies. The same reverse is also found on *dīnār*-system weights with obverses of al-Manṣūr (see for example No. 197, where the other reverse varieties are also discussed).

As for the obverse, it was introduced in Ṣāliḥ b. ʻAlī's second governorship for it is found with two different reverses in the name of Ṣāliḥ b. ʻAlī and Chael (Fahmī 224–5; Balog 1976, 296, which is from the reverse die of No. 193. Cf. Balog 1976, 297). Since it had no name on it the obverse could continue in use when ʻAbd al-Malik replaced Ṣāliḥ as governor once again.

178–180 ***Fals*** **weight of 24** ***kharrūba***

بسم الله
امر الامير عبد
الملك بن يزيد
بمثقال فلس اربعة
و عشرين خر
وبة

In the name of God.
Ordered the Amir ʻAbd
al-Malik b. Yazīd
a weight of a *fals* of four
and twenty *kharr-*
ūba.

Faint star or cross at end of lègend.

OA + 4188. Blue green. 3.0cm; stamp 2.3cm; 4.65g. (*Plate 8*)
OA + 4189. Green. 3.0cm; stamp 2.3cm; 4.67g.
OA + 4324. Blue green. 3.0cm; stamp 2.3cm; 4.65g.

From the same die Casanova 1893, 29; Petrie, 144; Miles 1948, 64; Fahmī 1957, 110; Launois 1959, 14; Miles 1963 I, 27; Balog 1976, 318. Cf. Casanova 1893, 30-1; Launois 1957, 169-72; Fahmī 1957, 111-6; Miles 1958a, 100; Balog 1976, 317.

An extraordinary piece in the Islamic Museum in Cairo (Launois 1957, 173 = Fahmī 1957, 177) is also from the same die but has a projection with an executive counterstamp reading *ʻalā yaday* ('at the hands of') followed by a name that has yet to be deciphered. Its weight is given by Fahmī as 6.12g., hopelessly large for 24 *kharrūbas*. It may be some sport that somehow left the workshop.
ʻAbd al-Malik b. Yazīd's other type of *fals* weight, of 23 *kharrūba*, is not represented in the British Museum's collection (Miles 1948, 65; Launois 1957, 174; Fahmī 1957, 119; Balog 1976, 321, all from one die. Cf. Miles 1948, 66; Launois 1957, 175; Fahmī 1957, 118; Balog 1976, 319-20).

181 Disk weight: *wuqiyya*, with Muḥammad b. Shuraḥbīl

Obverse

بسم الله ا
مر عبد الملك بن
يزيد بطبعة و
قية واف على يدى
محمد بن
شرحبيل

In the name of God. Or-
dered ʻAbd al-Malik b.
Yazīd the stamping of a w-
uqiyya, full-weight, at the hands
of Muḥammad b.
Shuraḥbīl.

Reverse
Marginal legend written round a circle:

على يدى عبد الملك بن يزيد اصلحه الله

At the hands of ʻAbd al-Malik b. Yazīd, may God keep him righteous.

OA + 4296. A little over half, the right side. Green. Length 5.4cm; 19.75g. (*Plate 8*)

From the same pair of dies Balog 1976, 304-7. *Same obverse die* Miles 1963 I, 24 (reverse not illustrated). Cf. Casanova 1893, 4-5 (no reverse inscription mentioned); Balog 1976, 303, 308-14.

No other reverse die for a *wuqiyya* is known, but the present one is found paired with a different obverse on the only known *wuqiyya* of the Caliph al-Manṣūr (No. 198). Both before and after these issues *wuqiyyas* are often counterstamped on the obverses and perhaps the use of a reverse was an experiment which did not turn out very successfully, probably because a good impression of the reverse was rarely produced.
The present type is extremely unusual in having the name of the Governor twice, introduced by *amara* on the obverse and by the subordinate formula *ʻalā yạday* on the reverse. This very strange anomaly can be explained by assuming that the reverse was designed for use on *wuqiyyas* issued in the Caliph's name, on which the Governor's name would naturally take a subordinate place, and was carelessly retained in use after ʻAbd al-Malik began to issue *wuqiyyas* with his own name on the obverse and Muḥammad b. Shuraḥbīl as executive. Al-Manṣūr's *wuqiyyas* then belong to the early part of ʻAbd al-Malik's second governorship. There is some reason to think that most of al-Manṣūr's heavy weights were issued at about the same time.(see No. 199).
The reverse die continued in use in the governorship of Mūsā b. Kaʻb, where it is entirely out of place (see No. 214).

182–185 Quarter-*qisṭ*, with Muḥammad b. Shuraḥbīl

بسم الله امر
عبد الملك بن يزيد
بطبعة ربع قسط
واف على يد(ى) محمد
بن شرحب(ي)ل

In the name of God. Ordered
ʻAbd al-Malik b. Yazīd
the stamping of a quarter *qisṭ*
full-measure, at the hands of Muḥammad
b. Shuraḥbīl.

The name Shuraḥbīl is written with one tooth instead of two before the *lām*, and the final *yā'* of *yaday* has been omitted.

OA + 4062. Green. Width 4.2cm. (*Plate 8*)
OA + 4063. Green. Chipped at left. Width 3.7cm.
OA + 4064. Green. Inscription weak. Width 4.3cm.
OA + 4078. Green. Much chipped at left and bottom right. Width 4.2cm.

From the same die Petrie, 141; Miles 1963 I, 29; Balog 1973, 13; 1976, 330; Fremersdorf, 896, Cf. Miles 1948, 67; 1951, 20-1; Launois 1957, 163-6; Miles 1958a, 102-3; 1964a, 28; Balog 1976, 329, 331.

186–187 *Qisṭ*, with Muḥammad b. Shuraḥbīl

بسم الله امر
عبد الملك بن يزيد
بطبعة قسط و
اف على يدى محمد
بن شرحبيل

In the name of God. Ordered
ʻAbd al-Malik b. Yazīd
the stamping of a *qisṭ*, full-
measure, at the hands of Muḥammad
b. Shuraḥbīl.

OA + 4060. Green. Width 4.8cm. (*Plate 8*)
OA + 4061. Green. Faint, blurred impression. 4.7cm.

From the same die Petrie, 147; Balog 1976, 326. Cf. Castiglioni, 24; Launois 1957, 161-2; Balog 1976, 327-8.

A specimen of the half-*qisṭ* denomination in the series issued by ʻAbd al-Malik b. Yazīd and Muḥammad b. Shuraḥbīl has been published by Miles (1948, 51), who incorrectly attributed it to ʻAbd al-Malik b. Marwān. Miles has also described (1964a, 27) a *qisṭ* with the name of ʻAbd al-Malik b. Yazīd alone.

MUḤAMMAD B. SHURAḤBĪL
Executive under ʻAbd al-Malik b. Yazīd, during both his governorships, Mūsā b. Kaʻb, Ḥumayd b. Qaḥṭaba and Yazīd b. Ḥātim

188 Weight of two-thirds of a *dīnār* less a *shaʻīra*

Obverse

وزن ثلثن
دينر الا
شعيرة

Weight of two thirds
of a *dīnar* less
a *shaʻīra*.

Reverse

Marginal legend between two circles:

بسم الله على يدى محا[مد ب]ن شرحبيل

In the name of God. At the hands of Muḥammad b. Shuraḥbīl.

Centre:

طبعة
كامل

Stamping
of Kāmil.

OA + 4192. Almost opaque. Dark brown. 2.5cm; stamp 2.2cm; 2.767g. (*Plate 8*)

The colour of this most unusual piece might at first seem to suggest that it is to be associated with the group of dark-coloured coin weights produced during the second governorship of ʻAbd al-Malik b. Yazīd (e.g. No. 197). On the other hand, the artisan named on the reverse, Kāmil, is not known to have been active before the finance directorship of Nawfal b. Furāt (see Nos 221-222), making a slightly later dating more probable. The reverse is from a die of which no impressions have previously been illustrated but reverses of Muḥammad b. Shuraḥbīl and Kāmil with the same legends were in use under Ḥumayd b. Qaḥṭaba (e.g. Fahmī 1957, 139-40; Balog 1976, 411) and Yazīd b. Ḥātim (examples listed in the commentaries to Nos 236-243).

Although the legend is very clear, *thulthayn* ('two-thirds') is defectively written by normal standards: it would appear that the *yāʼ* of the oblique case-ending of the dual has been omitted. The weight leaves no doubt about the intended meaning, being a little under that of two-thirds of a *dīnār*, which, using the conventionally accepted figure of 4.25g to the *dīnār*, comes to 2.833g. As for the *shaʻīra*, it is synonymous with *ḥabba*; both mean barleycorn. As tends to be the case with denominations of weight, the *shaʻīra* or *ḥabba* had different values at different times and places. Several figures are quoted in modern sources (E.I. [1] & [2], *s.v. ḥabba*; Grohmann 1954, 146; Hinz, *s.vv. ḥabba, shaʻīra*). Grohmann also notes that in the papyri *ḥabba* is used as a fraction of both the *dīnār* and the *dirham*. In the case of the British Museum's weight it may presumably be taken that the *shaʻīra* is a simple fraction of the *dīnār*. In papyri fractions of the *dīnar* are often expressed in twenty-fourths, the term used being *qīrāṭ*, which, incidentally, would have been a little lighter than the *qīrāṭ* or *kharrūba* of the glass *fals* weights (Grohmann 1954, 158). The existence of a conventional division of the *dīnār* into twenty-fourths makes a fraction of that figure likely for the *shaʻīra* in the present context; of the figures quoted the seventy-secondth and the ninety-sixth are the possibilities. The list of fractions of the *dīnār* mentioned in papyri given by Grohmann (*loc. cit.*) includes both the third and the quarter of the *qīrāṭ*, that is the seventy-secondth and the ninety-sixth of the *dīnār*, which does not help us to choose between them. The weight of the British Museum's piece, 2.767g, seems to point to the seventy-secondth, which, calculating from the weight of the *dīnār*, comes to 0.059g, while the ninety-sixth would weigh 0.044g. Subtracting the actual weight from two-thirds of a *dīnār* (2.833g) gives 0.066g to represent the *shaʻīra*, which is obviously closer to the seventy-secondth. However, seeing how small the differences involved are, it is probably unwise to be dogmatic on the present evidence.

What, finally, could a weight for forty-seven seventy-secondths or sixty-three ninety-sixths of a *dīnār* be used for? No other weight for such a curious fraction is known. Half- and third-*dīnār* glass weights are common but they do correspond to coins that were once issued. The question has to be left open, although two points are worth making. First, there may be some link with the standard attested on the '*dirhams* of two thirds [of a *dīnār*]' of Yazīd b. Ḥātim which are almost, possibly absolutely, contemporary (e.g. No. 244). A standard of two-thirds less a *shaʻīra* could easily represent the reduction of the two-thirds standard by the smallest manageable sub-unit. Second, the fact that the Caliph's or Finance Director's name does not appear on it, though it was produced at a time when *dīnār*-system and *dirham* weights had one or both somewhere on them, seems to indicate that the piece was in some way of lower status and makes one wonder whether it had anything to do with gold or silver coinage at all.

189-190 Disk weight: *wuqiyya*

بسم الله
على يدى محمد
بن شرحبيل
وقية واف

In the name of God.
At the hands of Muḥammad
b. Shuraḥbīl
Wuqiyya, full-weight.

OA + 4297. Green. 5.4cm; stamp 3.5cm; 37.21g. (*Plate 9*)
OA + 4298. Green. 5.4cm; stamp 3.5cm; 37.90g.

From the same die Miles 1958a, 96; Balog 1976, 333. Cf. Balog 1976, 333.

Both specimens are intact and in excellent condition. Together with an intact piece of al-Manṣūr (No. 198) they provide a substantial addition to the number of intact *wuqiyyas* on what Balog has called the Umayyad *raṭl* standard of which he listed eight.

191 Quarter-*qisṭ*

بسم الله
على يدى محمد
بن {د}شرحبيـ{ـ}ل ربع
قسط واف

In the name of God.
At the hands of Muḥammad
b. Shuraḥbīl, quarter
qisṭ, full-measure.

OA + 4341. Green. Width 4.0cm. (*Plate 9*)

From the same die Petrie, 155; Launois 1957, 189 *bis*, 203 *bis*; Balog 1976, 337. Cf. Balog 1976, 336, 338.

The name Shuraḥbīl is written with two extra 'teeth', one at the beginning and one before the final *lām*.

Launois 189 is one of the rare pieces which has two surviving vessel stamps attached together. The second one is the command stamp of Yazīd b. Ḥātim (see Nos 246-247). It would seem that the practice of putting the denomination on the stamp with the executive's name was already in use under Yazīd b. Ḥātim's immediate predecessor, Ḥumayd b. Qaḥṭaba, whose only known type of vessel stamp is a command stamp similar to that of Yazīd. A similar pattern of usage can be observed on heavy weights (See No. 233). Another executive of the same period, ʿAbd al-Raḥmān b. Yazīd, has similar *qisṭ*-system stamps, using the formula *ʿalā yaday*, which would also have been paired with the command stamps of Ḥumayd and Yazīd (e.g. Nos 231-232). Muḥammad b. Shuraḥbīl's half-*qisṭ* stamp would have been employed in the same way (Casanova 1893, 183; Miles 1958a, 98; Balog 1976, 334, all from one die. Cf. Miles 1958a, 97; 1971, 21-2; Balog 1976, 335).

ʿABDALLĀH AL-MANṢŪR
Caliph, 136-58/754-75

192 Third-*dīnār* weight

مما امر به
عبد الله عبد الل[ه]
امير المؤمنين او
فوا الكيل ولا تكونوا
من المخسرين مثقال
ثلث واف

Of what ordered
the servant of God ʿAbdallah,
Commander of the Faithful. 'Give
full measure and be not
among the defrauders'. Weight
of a third, full-weight.

Loop above legend.

OA + 4232. Green. 2.1cm; stamp 1.8cm; 1.38g. (*Plate 9*)

The *dīnār*-system obverses of al-Manṣūr fall into three groups according to their legends. The present piece belongs to a small but well-defined series distinguished by the inclusion of the Quranic command for honest measurement (from Sūra XXVI, 181) and by the ornamental loop above the legend. The *dīnār* and half-*dīnār* denominations have been found, like the present third, without a reverse (Miles 1971, 23; Balog 1976, 354). A second specimen from the half-*dīnār* die has the same reverse of ʿAbd al-Malik b. Yazīd and Chael which occurs on Nos 177 and 197 (Miles 1948, 60). This enables the obverse series to be dated to the second governorship of ʿAbd al-Malik b. Yazīd and thereabouts.

193 Third-*dīnār* weight, with Ṣāliḥ b. ʿAlī and Chael

Obverse

بسم الله
عبد الله
عبد الله امير
المؤمنين
م(ثق)ال ثل(ث)
واف

In the name of God.
The servant of God
ʿAbdallah, Commander
of the Faithful.
Weight of a third,
full-weight.

Reverse

Marginal legend around a circle:

[مما امر به ا]لامير صلح بن على (ا) صلـ(ـحـ)ـه الله

Of what ordered the Amīr Ṣaliḥ b. ʿAlī, may God keep him righteous.

Centre:

طبعة
كيل

Stamping
of Chael.

Central dot.

OA + 4233. Green. 2.0cm; 1.40g. (*Plate 9*)

There are two errors in the fifth line of the obverse legend: in *mithqāl thā* and *qāf* are transposed and the final *thā'* of *thalath* is written like a *mīm*. Miles (1958a, 123), has described, but did not illustrate, a broken piece with similar defects in the legend which is probably from the same obverse die. The reverse had Chael's name in the centre; there are said to be only traces of the marginal legend but the colour of the piece, described as dark purple, inclines one to think the reverse must be of ʿAbd al-Malik b. Yazīd, since a number of pieces of al-Manṣūr with his reverses are of unusual dark colours (see No. 197).

The reverse of the British Museum's piece is also defectively written, *alif* and *ḥā'* being omitted in *aṣlaḥahu*. The die is distinguishable from two similar ones which do not have errors in the legend by the open-topped ʻ*ayn* of *ṭab'a* and the central dot. It also occurs on a *dirham* weight of 13 *kharrūba* (Balog 1976, 296). Of the other two dies, one is so far known from similar *dirham* weights and *dīnār* weights of al-Manṣūr (Fahmī 1957, 99, 101, 224-5), the other only from *dīnār* weights of al-Manṣūr (Fahmī 1957, 98, 100). Miles 1958, 122, is a half-*dīnār* type with a similar obverse legend. Though Miles tried to read part of ʻAbd al-Malik b. Yazīd's name on the reverse margin it appears in fact to be of Ṣāliḥ b. ʻAlī and probably from one of the two dies just mentioned.

The obverse legend is of the type which includes the Caliph's name, ʻAbdallāh, but lacks the Quranic quotation found on such types as No. 192. Weights for fractions of *dīnārs* in this group are remarkably rare. Only the one-third and one-half already referred to seem to have been published before. The *dīnār*-weight types are discussed under Nos 196-197.

194-195 Half-*dīnār* weight, with Muḥammad b. Saʻīd

Obverse

بسم الله
امر امير ا
لمؤمنين مثقال
نصف واف

In the name of God. Ordered the Commander of the Faithful a weight of a half, full-weight.

Reverse

Marginal legend within dotted circle and around a plain circle:

بسم الله على يدى محمد بن سعيد

In the name of God. At the hands of Muḥammad b. Saʻīd

Centre:

مصر

Miṣr

Star above, two dots (?) below.

93 11-11 13. Green. 2.2cm; stamp 1.6cm; 2.11g. (*Plate* 9, *obv.*)
(Coins and Medals) 88 7-2 11. Lane-Poole, 30. 2.1cm; stamp 1.5cm; 2.12g. (*Plate* 9, *rev.*)

From the same pair of dies Petrie, 199, Miles 1958a, 125. Cf. Balog 1976, 359.

On his third group of coin-weight dies al-Manṣūr is not referred to by name but simply by the title Amir al-Mu'minīn, Commander of the Faithful, used by all the Caliphs. Pieces in the series have occasionally been attributed to the succeeding Caliph al-Mahdī but, as Miles (1958a, 124) pointed out, since they are most often combined with the reverse of Muhammad b. Saʻīd they must belong to the reign of al-Manṣūr. Each denomination, *dīnār*, half and third, is represented by a single die. The series belongs to the later part of al-Mansūr's reign, from the finance directorship of Muḥammad b. Saʻīd, the last part of it presumably, and probably the first part of the governorship of Maṭar. For a long period in the middle of al-Manṣūr's reign, approximately from the finance directorship of Nawfal b. Furāt to the early part of that of Muḥammad b. Saʻīd *dīnār* and *dirham* weights were issued in the name of the Governor or Finance Director without mention of the Caliph. Thus Muḥammad b. Saʻīd has his own types of *dīnār*-system weights, which usually occur with reverses in the names of executives and artisans, and presumably they were in use earlier than the obverse types of al-Manṣūr with Muḥammad b. Saʻīd's name on the reverse.

Of the obverses, the illustrated specimens of the third-*dīnār* one all have the same reverse of Muḥammad b. Saʻīd, with Miṣr, 'Egypt' or possibly 'Fusṭāṭ', in the centre, as appears on the British Museum's half-*dīnār* pieces (Miles 1948, 88; Fahmī 1957, 164; Miles 1958a, 126; Balog 1976, 362-3. Cf. 361, 364). The *dīnār* obverse also appears to have been found exclusively in combination with this reverse (Launois 1957, 209 = Fahmī, 1957, 163; Miles 1958a, 124; Balog 1976, 358. Cf. Miles 1964a, 30). Two specimens of the half-*dīnār* die, however, have a different one (Miles 1948, 87; Balog 1976, 360). This second reverse die again has Miṣr in the centre but the marginal legend is of the executive Qutayba b. Ziyād. It is also found with a *dīnār* obverse of Maṭar, as on No. 284, where the problems it raises are discussed at greater length. Since Qutayba was active with Muḥammad b. Saʻīd as well as Maṭar it is not certain that the reverse was only in use under the latter.

Not all the illustrated specimens of Muḥammad b. Saʻīd's reverse are very clear. The star and dots, in particular, are invisible on many of the photographs, even in some cases where their presence is indicated by the commentators. However, so far as can be judged, only one die has been employed. No other reverse type of Muḥammad b. Saʻīd is known.

196 '*Dīnār* weight'

مما امر[ه]
عبد الله عب[د]
الله امير المؤ
منين مثقال د
ينر واف

Of what ordered the servant of God, ʻAbdallah, Commander of the faithful. Weight of a *dīnar*, full-weight.

(Coins and Medals) 81 7-6 57. Lane-Poole, 57. Green. 4.2cm; 14.09g. (*Plate* 9)

From the same die Balog, 1976, 353.

That the script lacks the crispness found on most of al-Manṣūr's glass stamps maybe of little demonstrable significance but the weight is certainly very wrong, coming to about three-and-a-third *dīnārs* and, furthermore, having no relevance to the Umayyad *raṭl* system. Balog's piece, on the other hand, at 4.16g. is a fairly respectable weight for a *dīnār*. Miles (1964a, 29) compared a piece in the Muntazah Palace collection to the British Museum's specimen.

No comparable fractional issues seem to be known. The type is evidently something of an oddity but the text of the legend is the same as the obverse of the one described next, with a different arrangement of the lines. The obverse of Miles 1948, 59, seemingly unique at the moment, has the same legend arranged in the same lines, but the script, a bold, firm Kufic, is very different.

197 ***Dīnār* weight,** with ʻAbd al-Malik b. Yazīd and Chael

Obverse

مما امر به
عبد الله عبد
الله امير المؤ
منين مثقال دينر
واف

Of what ordered
the servant of God, ʻAbd-
allah, Commander of the Faithful. Weight of a *dīnar*,
full-weight.

Reverse From the same die as No. 177.

OA + 4231. A slight iridescence and wear. Black, opaque. 2.8cm; stamp 2.2cm; 4.17g. (*Plate 9*)

From the same pair of dies Balog 1976, 356. Cf. Balog 1976, 355.

The obverse belongs to the group with the Caliph's name but without the quotation from the Qur'ān. The fractional types have been discussed under No. 193. The present piece has the most common obverse which is found with reverses of Ṣāliḥ b. ʻAlī and Chael (examples listed under No. 193) as well as ʻAbd al-Malik b. Yazīd and Chael. A second, poorly engraved die which occurs without a reverse has been described under No. 196 and a single specimen of a third die, which is combined with one of ʻAbd al-Malik's reverses, has been illustrated (Miles 1948, 59).

Turning to the reverse, three dies with the same legends have been illustrated. The die of the present type appears to be the most common. It has been found on *dīnārs* and on *dirham* weights of 13 *kharrūba* (see No. 177) and also with the half-*dīnār* die in the group with the Quranic quotation in the legend (Miles 1948, 60 and see No. 192). The second die is written in a larger script; it has been found with the obverse of the present piece (Miles 1958a, 120. Cf. 121), with the other well-executed *dīnār* die with the same legend (Miles 1948, 59) and with al-Manṣūr's *dirham*-weight obverse in the same series (Balog 1976, 357). The third die is known only from two *dirham* weights from the same obverse as the one just mentioned (Casanova 1893, 34; Fahmī 1957, 102).

The colour and opacity of the piece are very unusual in the general context of eighth-century glass stamps which are nearly all some shade of green or greenish blue. It is noticeable that a small number of al-Manṣūr's pieces, seemingly those with reverses of ʻAbd al-Malik b. Yazīd, are of some dark colour. They are not invariably quite opaque; some are translucent when held against a light. The actual colour also varies: such pieces have been described as deep claret and dark brown as well as black. The explanation is no doubt that for a while a batch of glass was being used which differed in composition from the usual formula. The phenomenon is helpful in suggesting a possible date for certain types of anonymous *fals* weight which share the same peculiarity (see Nos 429-430).

198 **Disk weight: *wuqiyya*,** with ʻAbd al-Malik b. Yazīd

Obverse

امر عبد
الله عبد الله
امير المؤمنين ا
صلحه الله بطبعة
وقية وا
ف

Ordered the servant
of God ʻAbdallah,
Commander of the Faithful, may
God keep him righteous, the stamping
of a *wuqiyya*, full-
weight.

Reverse
Marginal legend round a circle:

على يدى عبد الملك بن يزيد اصلحه الله

At the hands of ʻAbd al-Malik b. Yazīd may God keep him righteous.

OA + 4295. Olive green. 5.7cm; stamp 3.4cm; 36.86g. (*Plate 9*)

The reverse die is the same as that of No. 181. As is pointed out in the commentary to that piece, it seems that it must have been originally designed for use with the obverse of the present type, which is therefore to be dated to the earlier part of ʻAbd al-Malik's second governorship. For the curious continuation in use of the same reverse under Mūsā b. Kaʻb see No. 214.

199 **Ring weight: *raṭl***

مما امر به
عبد الله عبد الله
امير المؤمنين او
فوا الكيل ولا تكونو
ا من المخسرين ر
طل واف

Of what ordered
the servant of God ʻAbdallah,
Commander of the Faithful. 'Give
full measure and be not
among the defrauders'. *R-
aṭl*, full-weight.

OA + 4359. Fragment of the top, with part of the top and left of the stamp. Green. Length 4.7cm; 66.6g. (*Plate 9*)

From the same die Casanova 1893, I, Sup 5 and III, 54; Petrie, 151.

The first of the two specimens in the Fouquet collection was taken by Casanova to be from the flat bottom of a vessel and classified with the vessel stamps. It must, in fact, be a fragment of a weight, presumably a ring weight. No other *raṭl* die of al-Manṣūr has been illustrated or described. Three specimens of the corresponding half-*raṭl* are known (Miles 1948, 53, 129; Balog 1976, 352, all from one die) and single ones of the *wuqiyya*, quarter-*raṭl* and double-*raṭl* (No. 198; Miles 1948, 54; Balog 1976, 349). On all except the *wuqiyya* the legend includes the Quranic injunction against false measure.

The question of the precise dating of these heavy weights has already been referred to a number of times. All of al-Manṣūr's Finance Directors in Egypt issued weights on the *raṭl* system in their own names and so did some of the executives of the period. This fact, together with the small number of weights in the Caliph's name and the lack of variant dies, demonstrates that the issue can only have lasted a short time. A number of indications all point to about the same date for it. As has already been mentioned the *wuqiyya* (No. 198) which has ʿAbd al-Malik b. Yazīd's name on the reverse can be dated to the earlier part of ʿAbd al-Malik's governorship. Balog's specimen of the half-*raṭl* bears the edge of the counterstamp of Abbān b. Ibrāhīm who, as pointed out under No. 170, is confirmed by another die-link to have acted as executive under Ṣāliḥ b. ʿAlī. Finally the Quranic phrase in the legend is paralleled on one of al-Manṣūr's series of *dīnār*-system weight dies, of which one specimen is known paired with a reverse of ʿAbd al-Malik b. Yazīd (see No. 192). All these associations show that al-Manṣūr's own heavy weights were issued in a period beginning probably at the end of Ṣāliḥ b. ʿAlī's second governorship and ending in the earlier part of that of ʿAbd al-Malik, say about 137-9/754-8. The same may well be true of some of the Caliph's other series, notably his *qisṭ*-system stamps, which also have the Quranic injunction in the legends (e.g. Nos 200-205).

One of the specimens of al-Manṣūr's half-*raṭl* (Miles 1948, 129) is combined with a counterstamp with a legend consisting of another injunction, not from the Qur'ān, against false measure. The same die was also used on vessel stamps (Miles 1963 II, 50; Balog 1976, 910. Cf. Miles 1963 II, 51; Balog 1976, 909, 911-2). Very probably we here have a throwback to the early Umayyad use of anonymous counterstamps by executives. In any case the type presumably belongs to the early part of the reign of al-Manṣūr.

200-204 Quarter-*qisṭ*

مما امر به
عبد الله عبد ا
لله امير المؤمنين
[او]فوا الكيل و لا تكو
[ن]وا من المخسرين ربع
قسط واف

Of what ordered.
The servant of God ʿAbda-
llah, Commander of the Faithful.
'Give full measure and be no-
t among the defrauders'. Quarter
qisṭ, full-measure.

OA + 4065. Green. Width 3.9cm. (*Plate 9*)
OA + 4066. Green. Width 3.9cm.
OA + 4067. Green. Width 4.0cm.
OA + 4068. Green. Chipped at top and bottom right. Width 3.6cm.
OA + 4342. Green. Width 3.9cm.

From the same die Launois 1957, 151; Miles 1958a, 112, 114; Balog 1976, 368. Cf. Miles 1948, 57; Viré, 17; Launois 1957, 152-4; Miles 1958a, 113, 115; Miles 1958a, 113, 115; Balog 1976, 366-7, 369-70.

As with the heavy weights discussed immediately above, it is evident that the Caliph's issue of *qisṭ*-system stamps did not cover his entire reign. Only a single die is known for each denomination and many other series in the names of officials also belong to the Caliphate of al-Manṣūr. The similarity of the legends to those of nearly all the heavy weights suggests that the *qisṭ*-system stamps belong to about the same period.

205 *Qisṭ*

مما امر به
عبد الله عبد الل[ه]
[ا]مير المؤمنين [او]
فوا الكيل و لا تكو[نوا]
من المخسرين قسط
واف

Of what ordered
The servant of God, ʿAbdallah,
Commander of the Faithful. 'Give
full measure and be not
among the defrauders.' *Qisṭ*,
full-measure.

OA + 4069. Green. Width 4.1cm. (*Plate 9*)

From the same die Petrie, 152; Balog 1976, 365.

The only published specimens of the half-*qisṭ* of al-Manṣūr seem to be Miles 1948, 55 and Fremersdorf, 897.

206 *Mikyala* of skinned vetch (*julubbān al-muqashshar*)

امر عبد ا
لله عبد الله ا
مير الم{ـ}ؤمنين
بطبعة مكيلة
جلبان المقشر
واف

Ordered the servant of G-
od ʿAbdallah, Com-
mander of the Faithful,
the stamping of a measure
of skinned vetch,
full-measure.

OA + 4071. Green. Width 4.1cm; stamp 3.1cm. (*Plate 9*)

From the same die Launois 1957, 149; Miles 1963 I, 233. Cf. Miles 1964a, 31.

On this type and on a number of al-Manṣūr's other vessel stamps, among them Nos 208-210, there is an unwanted tooth after the first *mīm* of *al-mu'minīn*.

Al-Manṣūr has a wide range of commodity stamps but there are few, if any, variant types for particular commodities. From the script they would appear to belong to the earlier part of his Caliphate, like his heavy weights and *qisṭ*-system stamps (see Nos 198-205). However their legends lack the Quranic injunction against fraud found on those categories and begin amara instead of *mimmā amara bihi*, suggesting that the dies were not made at exactly the same time. They were probably in use during the governorships of Ṣāliḥ b. ʻAlī and ʻAbd al-Malik b. Yazīd, neither of whom appears to have issued any commodity stamps at all. In fact only one Finance Director, Muḥammad b. al-Ashʻath, is known to have produced them during al-Manṣūr's reign and after him they appear to have been issued in the names of executives. It seems possible, incidentally, that there were times during the early Abbasid period when commodity stamps were temporarily not in use, before they were finally given up.

207 *Mikyala* of white sesame seed (*juljulān al-abyaḍ*)

امر عبد الل[ه]
عبد الله امير
[ال]مؤمنين بطبعة
مكيلة الجلجلا[ن]
[ا]لابيض واف

Ordered the servant of God
ʻAbdallah, Commander
of the Faithful, the stamping
of a measure of sesame seed,
white, full-measure.

OA + 4072. Broken at left and bottom. Green. Width 4.0cm. (*Plate 9*)

The type does not appear to have been published before but it has been possible to supplement the reading and remove the doubt that would have existed about the name of the commodity from a specimen from the same die in the Victoria and Albert Museum.

Juljulān was first read on vessel stamps by Casanova who translated it as coriander. This is one of the meanings given by the dictionaries but, as Miles (1951b, 17) concluded, sesame seed is the more likely interpretation. There exist stamps for coriander seed under its ordinary name *ḥabb al-kusbur*. In the medieval pharmacopoeias *juljulān* is not identified with coriander but only with sesame (Ibn al-Bayṭār, *s.vv. juljulān, simsim*; Maimonides, 268). According to the dictionaries the word means sesame seed rather than the sesame plant (*Sesamum orientale L.*) and the seed is presumably what is meant on the stamps. Sesame oil, extracted from the seeds, was, and is, widely used and it is a slight puzzle that stamps for it are not known to exist. *Juljulān* has entered the English language as gingili and similar forms are found in most European languages.

On almost all stamps for *juljulān* the word is qualified by white, as here, or red (*aḥmar*). There are parallel series of vessel stamps for the two varieties. A specimen of al-Manṣūr's red *juljulān* stamp has been described by Miles (1951b, 17), who refers to a second one in a private collection. As Miles pointed out, there are varieties of the sesame plant with differently coloured seeds and it seems that the distinction made between red and white *juljulān* on the stamps is simply one between different varieties. The late medieval writers list sesame, which they refer to by its ordinary name, *simsim*, as one of the standard crops of Egypt and give the usual details of its cultivation (Ibn Mammātī, esp. 268; Cahen, 147; Müller-Wodarg, 40-1).

208-209 Half-*raṭl* of fat (*duhn*)

امر عبد ا
لله عبد الله ا
مير الم{ـ}ؤمنين
بطبعة نصف
رطل دهن
واف

Ordered the servant of G-
od ʻAbdallah, Com-
mander of the Faithful,
the stamping of a half
raṭl of fat,
full-measure.

Extra tooth after the first *mīm* of *al-mu'minīn*.

OA + 4070. Green. Legend blurred. Width 3.7cm.
94 3-9 5. Green. Width 3.9cm. (*Plate 10*)

From the same die Miles 1948, 56; Launois 1957, 150; Miles 1958a, 108; Launois 1969, 12; Balog 1976, 371. Cf. Miles 1958a, 109-10; 1971, 25.

On his specimen Balog read the commodity as *armāk* or *armāl*, assuming the omission of the *alif*. According to Ibn al-Bayṭār this means a kind of cinnamon. However *duhn* is clearly the correct reading.

210 *Mikyala* of skinned lentils (*ʻadas al-muqashshar*)

امر عبد الله
عبد الله امير
الم{ـ}ؤمنين
بطبعة مكيلة
عدس المقشا[ر]
واف

Ordered the servant of God
ʻAbdallah, Commander
of the Faithful,
the stamping of a measure
of skinned lentils,
full-measure.

Tall extra tooth after the first *mīm* of *al-mu'minīn*.

OA + 4073. Olive Green. Width 4.8cm. (*Plate 10*)

From the same die Balog 1976, 374.

211-212 *Mikyala* of black cumin (*kammūn al-aswad*)

امر عبد ا
لله عبد الله
[ا]مير المؤمنين
بط(ـ)عة مكيلة
كمون الاسو
د واف

Ordered the servant of G-
od ʻAbdallah,
Commander of the Faithful,
the stamping of a measure
of cumin, bla-
ck, full-measure.

OA + 4074. Green. Width 3.9cm.
OA + 4075. Green. Width 3.9cm. (*Plate 10*)

From the same die Miles 1958a, 116.

Miles noted that the *bā'* of *ṭabʻa* is omitted.

213 ***Mikyala* of *mishsh***

امر عبد ا
[ل]له عبد الله
[ا]مير المؤمنيا[ن]
[ب]طبعة مكيلة
المش و
اف

Ordered the servant of G-
od ʻAbdallah,
Commander of the Faithful
the stamping of a measure
of *mishsh*, full-
measure.

OA + 4343. Blue green. Small chip at the top. 3.9cm. (*Plate 10*)

From the same die Miles 1951b, 15; 1958a, 117; Balog 1973, 14; 1976, 377-8. Cf. Miles 1958a, 118-9; 1971, 27; Balog 1976, 379.

MŪSĀ B. KAʻB
Governor and Finance Director 141/758-9

214 **Disk weight: *wuqiyya*,** with Muḥammad b. Shuraḥbīl (and ʻAbd al-Malik b. Yazīd)

Obverse

ب[سم] الله ا
(مر) موسى بن
كعب بطبعة و
قية واف على يدى
محمد بن
شرح[بيل]

In the name of God. Or-
dered Mūsā b.
Kaʻb the stamping of a *wuqiyya*, full-weight, at the hands
of Muḥammad b.
Shuraḥbīl.

Reverse Same die as Nos 181, 198.

OA + 4300. Fragment, somewhat under half, top and left. Green. Length 4.0cm; 15.3g. (*Plate 10*)

From the same obverse die Miles 1948, 69.

Mūsā b. Kaʻb's governorship was brief and his known stamps are few. Other than the *wuqiyyas* the only heavy weight is a *raṭl* published by Balog (1976, 382). Otherwise the corpus consists of one *qisṭ* (Casanova 1893, 142), one half-*qisṭ* (Launois 1959, 15) and two quarter-*qisṭs* (Casanova 1893, 143; Miles 1958a, 127).

Miles noted the presence of a reverse legend on the American Numismatic Society's specimen of Mūsā's *wuqiyya*, but could only read, tentatively, *Allāh MN*. On the British Museum's piece enough of the reverse survives to establish its identity with the reverse used on the earlier *wuqiyyas* of al-Manṣūr and of ʻAbd al-Malik b. Yazīd himself (e.g. Nos 181, 198). What requires explanation is why ʻAbd al-Malik should appear on the present piece at all. One possibility is that Mūsā b. Kaʻb may have held the governorship of Egypt as in some way the dependent of ʻAbd al-Malik whose career continued after his final departure from Egypt in AH 141. Somewhat in favour of this view is the fact that Mūsā never uses the title *al-Amīr* on his stamps. By this period the title was sometimes used by Finance Directors but the Governor was still entitled to it and normally used it. On the other hand the historical account of ʻAbd al-Malik's departure and Mūsā's arrival (Kindī, 106-7) makes no mention of such an arrangement and describes Mūsā's appointment in perfectly normal terms. Secondly, if Mūsā was subordinate to ʻAbd al-Malik the legend is wrong, Mūsā, the subordinate, appearing in a role of command (*amara*) on the obverse, while ʻAbd al-Malik's name follows the executive formula *ʻalā yaday* on the reverse, seemingly duplicating the role played by Muḥammad b. Shuraḥbīl on the obverse. It has already been pointed out under No. 181 that a rather similar problem arises when this reverse is used with an obverse with ʻAbd al-Malik's name after *amara* and Muḥammad b. Shuraḥbīl's after *ʻalā yaday* and that the reverse must originally have been been designed for use with an obverse of al-Manṣūr, as on No. 198. It was suggested that the continued use of the reverse at that stage was a piece of carelessness. It is extremely probable that the further use of the reverse under Mūsā is, in fact, no more than carelessness carried to the point of utter negligence and that the implication that ʻAbd al-Malik and Mūsā had some particular association during the latter's governorship is entirely false.

MUḤAMMAD B. AL-ASHʻATH
Governor 141-3/759-60

Muḥammad b. al-Ashʻath had charge of the finances at the beginning of his governorship but at some point they were taken over by Nawfal b. Furāt (Kindī, 109).

215 **One third-*dīnār* weight,** with ʻAbdallāh b. Rāshid and Chael

Obverse

بسم الله امر
[ا]لامير محمد بن
الاشعث بطبعة
مثقال ثلث واف

In the name of God. Ordered
the Amīr Muḥammad b.
al-Ashʻath the stamping
of a weight of a third, full-weight.

Reverse

Marginal legend round a circle:

[على يدى عبد]الله بن راشد

At the hands of ʻAbdallah b. Rāshid.

Centre:

طبعة
كيل

Stamping
of Chael.

(Coins and Medals) Or. 3603. Green. 1.9cm; 1.40g. (*Plate 10*)

Very few *dīnār*-system weights of Muḥammad b. al-Ashʻath have been published. The present piece and the half-*dīnār* type that follows are the only representatives of one group. The reverse die used on both is also found on the only known example of a *dirham* weight of 13 *kharrūba* of the same official (Balog 1976, 388), which has a similar obverse legend.

What appears to be a second group has the legends arranged wholly or partly in the form of a square. The specimens are a single *dīnār* weight (Petrie, 156) and a single third-*dīnār* weight (Miles 1964a, 33. The weight given, 2.10g, is that of a half-*dīnār*.) The *dīnār* weight is said to have an obscure impression on the reverse. Miles 1958a, 31, a third-*dīnār* piece with the legend in lines in the usual way, is attributed to Muḥammad b. al-Ashʻath with some reservations.

216 Half-*dīnār* weight, with ʻAbdallāh b. Rāshid and Chael

Obverse

بسم الله
امر الامير محمد
بن الاشعث بطب(عة)
م(ث)قال نصف و
اف

In the name of God.
Ordered the Amīr Muḥammad
b. al-Ashʻath the stamping
of a weight of a half, full-
weight.

Reverse Same die as No. 215.

OA + 4193. Green. 2.2cm; stamp 1.6cm; 2.11g. (*Plate 10*)

The script of the obverse is very obscure towards the end. The last two letters of *ṭabʻa* are not present at all and *thāʼ* is missing from *mithqāl*.

217 *Fals* weight of 27 *kharrūba*, with ʻAbdallāh b. Rāshid

امر الامير
محمد بن الاشع[ث]
على يدى عبد الله
بن راشد بطبعة مثقا
ل فلا{ء}س سبعة و
عشرين خروبة

Ordered the Amīr
Muḥammad b. al-Ashʻath,
at the hands of ʻAbdallah
b. Rāshid, the stamping of a weigh-
t of a *fals* of seven and
twenty *kharrūba*.

OA + 4235. Green. 3.3cm; stamp 2.4cm; 5.28g. (*Plate 10*)

From the same die Nies, 11 = Miles 1948, 74; Fahmī 1957, 132; Balog, 387. Cf. Launois 1957, 181; Fahmī 1957, 133-4.

Fals has an extra 'tooth' at the end. *Mithqāl* is written very small and probably defectively though it seems unnecessary to read *hadhā* (this) as Balog does.

All of Muḥammad b. al-Ashʻath's known *fals* weights are of 27 *kharrūba*. Of the three dies, the two with ʻAbdallāh b. Rāshid as executive are represented in the British Museum's collection. Miles (1964a, 34) has described a specimen from a third die without an executive's name.

218 *Fals* weight of 27 *kharrūba*, with ʻAbdallāh b. Rāshid

امر الامير محمد
بن الاشعث على يدى
عبد الله بن راشد
بطبعة مثقال فلس
سبعة و عشرين
خروبة

Ordered the Amīr Muhammad
b. al-Ashʻath at the hands
of ʻAbdallah b. Rāshid
the stamping of a weight of a *fals*
of seven and twenty
kharrūba.

OA + 4234. Green. 3.3cm; stamp 2.4cm; 5.29g. (*Plate 10*)

From the same die Miles 1948, 73; Fahmī 1957, 136. Cf. Launois 1957, 180; Fahmī 1957, 135, 137; Launois 1960 I, 11.

219–220 ***Mikyala* of white cumin (*kammūn al-abyaḍ*)**

بسم الله
امر الامير محمد
بن الاشعث بطبعة
مكيلة كمون الا
بيض على يدى عبد
الله بن راشد

In the name of God.
Ordered the Amir Muḥammad
b. al-Ash'ath the stamping
of a measure of cumin, white, at the hands of 'Abdallah b. Rāshid.

OA + 4076. Green. Width 3.9cm. (*Plate 10*)
93 11-11 2. Green. Width 4.7cm, with attached piece of rim.

From the same die Miles 1951b, 23; Launois 1957, 176; Balog 1976, 393-4. Cf. Launois 1957, 177-8; Balog 1976, 395.

Muḥammad b. al-Ash'ath is the last Governor or Finance Director to issue commodity stamps in his own name. Six different substances are known on the published specimens.

NAWFAL B. FURĀT

Finance Director in the latter part of the governorship of Muḥammad b. al-Ash'ath (141-3/759-60).

221 Third-*dīnār* weight, with 'Abd al-Raḥmān b. Yazīd and Kāmil

Obverse

امر نوفل بن
فرات بطبعة
مثقال ثلث
واف

Ordered Nawfal b.
Furāt the stamping
of a weight of a third,
full-weight.

Reverse

Marginal legend round circle:

على يدى عبد [الرحم]ن بن يزيد

At the hands of 'Abd al-Raḥman b. Yazīd

Centre:

طبعة
كا(م)ل

Stamping
of Kāmil

OA + 4236. Pale greenish yellow. 1.9cm; stamp 1.5cm; 1.40g. (*Plate 10*)

Nawfal b. Furāt has two series of *dīnār*-system weight stamps. The present piece and the half-*dīnār* type described next belong to the series with legends beginning *amara*. One specimen of the corresponding *dīnār* weight has been published (Kmietowicz, 1). The reverse of the third-*dīnār* weight is of a type so far found only with the *amara* obverses of Nawfal. All the illustrated specimens with such obverses share the same reverse die with the exception of the half-*dīnār* weight, No. 222. The third letter of the artisan's name would certainly normally be taken for a *qāf* or *fā'* (implying a name such as Kāfil). However the name Kāmil does appear on several reverses of the same period and it it probable that, as Miles first suggested, Kāfil is an error for Kāmil. Other obverses of 'Abd al-Rahmān and, presumably, Kāmil were in use during the governorship of Yazīd b. Ḥātim (see No. 227).

Nawfal b. Furāt's other series of *dīnār*-system obverses has rectangular stamps with legends beginning *bismillāh*. Three specimens have been published, two half-*dīnār* types (Fahmī 1957, 128; Miles 1958a, 128) and one third (Fahmī 1957, 129). All have the same reverse with Miṣr (Egypt, Fusṭāṭ) in the centre, and, in the margin, the executive formula *'alā yaday*, followed by a name, of which only a small part is visible on the half-*dīnār* weights. Miles read '. . . ṣīr *'alā yaday* . . .' on his specimen and Fahmī '. . . *'alā yaday Yazīd* . . .' However, the two pieces show the same part of the margin and it is evident from the illustrations that Miles had recognized the executive formula while Fahmī had misplaced it. Miles's reading '. . . *ṣīr*' at the end of the name is sensible, but the recent publication by Balog of pieces which show that Nawfal b. Furāt had an executive called Salih b. Qusṭanṭin makes it clear that the letters should be read '-*ṭīn*' and the whole legend restored *'alā yaday* [*Ṣāliḥ* b. *Qusṭan*] *ṭīn*' (see Nos 225-226).

222 Half-*dīnār* weight, with 'Abd al-Raḥmān b. Yazīd (?) and Kāmil

Obverse

امر نوفل
بن فرات
بطبعة
مثقال نصف
دينر واف

Ordered Nawfal
b. Furāt
the stamping of
a weight of a half
dīnar, full-weight.

Reverse Marginal legend round circle:

[على يدى عبد الرحم]ن بن يزيد

At the hands of 'Abd al-Raḥman b. Yazīd

Centre:

طبعة
كا(م)ل

Stamping
of Kāmil

(Coins and Medals) 82 8-3 28. Lane-Poole, 13. Green. 2.2cm; stamp 1.7cm; 2.10g. (*Plate 10*)

From the same obverse die Miles 1948, 70; Balog 1976, 403.

The reverse is very similar to that of No. 221 and the name of the artisan is similarly written or, as argued above, miswritten. The die, however, is different; no other impression of this second one appears to be known.

223 *Fals* weight of 27 *kharrūba*

امر نوفل بن
فرات بطبعة
مثـ(قـ)ا(ل) فلـ{ـ}س
سبعة و عشر(ين)
خروبات

Ordered Nawfal b.
Furāt the stamping
of a weight of a *fals*
of seven and twenty
kharrūba

(Coins and Medals) 82 8-3 27. Lane-Poole, 12. Green. 3.4cm; 5.29g. (*Plate 10*)

From the same die Miles 1948, 71; Launois 1957, 184; Fahmī 1957, 130-1; Launois 1959, 16.

The errors in the legend of this type, apparently Nawfal b. Furāt's only type of *fals* weight, have of course been commented on in earlier publications. *Mithqāl* ends *wāw alif* instead of *-qāl*; there is an extra 'tooth' in *fals*; *kharrūba* is written exceptionally, and in the context ungrammatically, in the plural form *kharrūbāt* and finally the figure is clearly written 17 while the actual pieces are far heavier than 17 *kharrūba*. The weights of the five known specimens, including the British Museum's, range from 5.24g to 5.29g, which is precisely correct for 27 *kharrūba*. The correction of *ʿashara* (ten) to *ʿishrīn* (twenty), first explicitly made by Launois, is therefore evidently justified. Besides these metrological considerations, to have *wāw* between *tisʿa* and *ʿashara* for nineteen would be ungrammatical.

224 Disk weight: wuqiyya

[----]
[-- نوفل]
بن فرات
بطبعة و[قية]
واف

\- - - -
\- - Nawfal
b. Furāt
the stamping of a *wuqiyya*,
full-weight.

OA + 4301. Fragment, from the bottom. Green. Length 3.7cm; 10.02g. (*Plate 10*)

No *wuqiyya* of Nawfal b. Furāt has previously been published.

225 Disk weight: quarter-*raṭl*, with Ṣāliḥ b. Qusṭanṭīn

Rectangular stamp to left

بسم الله
ختم على يدى
[صلح بن قسطنطين]
[ربع رطل واف]

In the name of God.
Was sealed at the hands
of Ṣaliḥ b. Qusṭanṭīn
a quarter *raṭl*, full-weight.

Rectangular stamp to right

[بسم الله]
[امر نوفل بن فرات]
[اصلحه الله بالوفـ]ـاء
[والعـ]ـدل

In the name of God.
Ordered Nawfal b. Furāt,
may God keep him righteous, honesty
and justice.

OA + 4429. Less than half, the upper part. Green. Length 7.4cm; length of left hand stamp 2.9cm; 46g. (*Plate 10*)

In spite of the fact that so much of the legends is missing, and although it is impossible to establish the identity of either die with any published example, there are sufficient clues to make the restoration possible. The disk-weight form and the proportions of the fragment indicate that it is a quarter-*raṭl*. The rectangular shape and the script of the left-hand stamp are similar to those of Ṣāliḥ b. Qusṭanṭīn's few known stamps for *raṭl*-system weights. The actual wording of the first two lines of the legend on all of Ṣāliḥ's stamps, excluding reverse dies for coin weights, is exactly the same and the use of the verbal form *khutima*, meaning 'was sealed', is a feature peculiar to Ṣāliḥ's stamps alone, though *khatm* and *khātim* from the same root are occasionally found (see Introduction, p. 43).

Three other similar weight stamps of Ṣāliḥ have been illustrated by Balog (1976, 397,399,407. Cf. 398). On No. 399 the denomination *raṭl* is clear; on No. 397, which is from a different die, the denomination is missing and one wonders whether it is not a double-*raṭl* or half-*raṭl* rather than a *raṭl*. Balog's No. 407 is a *wuqiyya* of Ṣāliḥ alone. His only known vessel stamp is described next. His name also appears on the reverses of some of Nawfal's coin weights (see No. 221).

The few surviving letters on the right-hand stamp suggest that it completes the reading of a command stamp of Nawfal b. Furāt which appears paired with a stamp of Ṣāliḥ on one of the pieces in the Balog collection (Balog 1976, 397). There is no overlap between the surviving parts of the stamp on the British Museum's piece or Balog's so it cannot be established whether the die was the same, though that is quite probable. It should be noted that on Balog's piece the *ʿayn* of what is here read *ʿadl* appears to be written like a *mīm*. This legend of Nawfal b. Furāt, in which the official himself commands both honesty and justice, seems to be without an exact parallel though the slogan 'God commanded honesty and justice' is quite common on stamps of the third century of the Hijra.

ṢĀLIḤ B. QUSṬANṬĪN
Executive under Nawfal b. Furāt

226 Quarter-*qisṭ*

[بسم الله]
[خـ]تم على يد[ى]
صلح بن قسطنط[ين]
[ر]بع قسط واف

In the name of God.
Was sealed at the hands
of Ṣaliḥ b. Qusṭanṭīn
a quarter *qisṭ*, full-measure.

94 3-9 6. Chipped at top. Green. Width 3.7cm. (*Plate 10*)

This appears to be the only vessel stamp of Ṣāliḥ b. Qusṭanṭīn to have come to light so far. As on his weight stamps the legend, after the *basmala* begins *khutima*, meaning 'was sealed' or 'stamped'. Ṣāliḥ b. Qusṭanṭīn's other stamps have been noted under Nos 221 and 225.

ʻABD AL-RAḤMĀN B. YAZĪD
Executive under Nawfal b. Furāt and Yazīd b. Ḥātim

227 Sixth-*wuqiyya*

Obverse

سدس
وقية

A sixth
of a *wuqiyya*.

Reverse
Marginal legend between two circles:

[ع]لى يدى عبد الر(ح)من بن يزيد

At the hands of ʻAbd al-Raḥman b. Yazīd

Centre:

[ط]بعة
كمل

Stamping
of Kamil.

Dot below central legend.

83 6-21 30. Lane-Poole, 18. Green. 3.0cm; rectangular stamp 1.9 x 1.9cm; 6.21g. (*Plate 10*)

The reverse is from a die also used on *dīnār*-system weights with obverses of Yazīd b. Ḥātim. As has been mentioned under No. 221, reverses of the same executive and artisan were used under Nawfal b. Furāt. On the types of that period the third letter of the artisan's name appears to be miswritten. On the ones used under Yazīd the name is spelt *kāf, mim, lām*, without the *alif*; strictly speaking, indeed, since the first letter is not connected to what follows, it should be read *dāl* or *dhāl*. However, once again the reading Kāmil seems justified; it appears correctly written on the nearly contemporary reverses of Muḥammad b. Shuraḥbil.

Under Yazīd b. Ḥātim, ʻAbd al-Raḥmān and Kāmil have two reverses which are extremely similar. The one on the British Museum's sixth-*wuqiyya* weight is distinguishable by the miswriting of *ḥā'* in Raḥmān as *mīm* and by the smaller *hā'* in *ṭabʻa*. On *dīnār*-system weights the reverse has been illustrated on single specimens of the *dīnār* (Fahmī 1957, 143), half-*dīnār* (Miles 1948, 79) and third-*dīnār* (Balog 1976, 430). The second similar reverse appears in two states, on the later of which, as Petrie noted, a prominent dot is added beneath the central legend (see Nos 236-243).

As for the obverse of the sixth-*wuqiyya* it is known with several reverses. On Miles 1958a, 135, it is paired with the second reverse type of ʻAbd al-Raḥmān and Kāmil in its second state, as just described. On Miles 1963 I, 26, the reverse is of Muḥammad b. Shuraḥbīl and Kāmil and on the British Museum's No. 272, which is to be dated to the finance directorship of Muḥammad b. Saʻīd, of Saʻīd b. al-Musayyib and Severus. There is a single published example of another sixth-*wuqiyya* obverse with the same legend, but in use later, for the reverse is of Wāḍiḥ (Balog 1976, 564).

228 Disk weight: half-*raṭl*

[بسم ا]لله
[على يدى ع]بد
[الرحمن بن يز]يد
[نصف ر]طل
[وا]ف

In the name of God.
At the hands of ʻAbd
al-Raḥman b. Yazīd
a half *raṭl*,
full-weight.

OA + 4425. About half, the left side, Green. Length 8.9cm; 109g. (*Plate 11*)

Cf. Miles 1963 I, 37.

The piece in the Benaki Museum published by Miles bears a second stamp, the command stamp of Yazīd b. Ḥātim (see Nos 246-247). It is possible that the British Museum's piece originally had the same command stamp. On the other hand the corresponding *raṭl* stamp of ʻAbd al-Raḥmān, which is usually paired with Yazīd b. Ḥātim's command stamp, occurs on one intact piece by itself (Balog 1976, 440 and see No. 229).

229 Ring weight: *raṭl*

بسم الله
على يدى عبد
الرحمن بن يزيد
رطل واف

In the name of God.
At the hands of ʻAbd
al-Raḥman b. Yazīd
Raṭl, full-weight.

OA + 4416. Fragment. The right hand end of the top. Green. Width 4.5cm; 97g. Lower part of stamp pitted. (*Plate 11*)

From the same die Petrie, 159; Miles 1948, 81; Balog 1973, 17; 1976, 416, 440. Cf. Casanova 1893, 48-9; Balog 1976, 415.

One of the other pieces on which this stamp occurs is the intact disk weight described by both Jungfleisch (1927-8) and Balog (1976, 440). On it the stamp of ʿAbd al-Raḥmān b. Yazīd with the executive formula *ʿalā yaday* ('at the hands of') stands alone. All the other specimens listed above are, like the British Museum's piece, ring weights and on them ʿAbd al-Raḥmān's stamp is paired with the command stamp of Yazīd b. Ḥātim (see Nos 246-247). The position of the stamp on the present specimen, at one end of the top of the weight, shows that it was originally paired with another stamp, most probably Yazīd b. Ḥātim's command stamp.

230 Executive stamp

على يدى
عبد الرحمن
بن يزيد

At the hands
of ʿAbd al-Raḥman
b. Yazid.

OA + 4081. Green. Width 3.1cm. (*Plate 11*)

Cf. Miles 1964a, 35.

The die was in use during the finance directorship of Nawfal b. Furāt for it is found on two of his heavy weights, a *raṭl* (Petrie, 154) and a half-*raṭl* (Balog 1976, 402).

231 Quarter-*qisṭ*

بسم الله
على يدى
عبد الرحم[ن]
بن يزيد ربع
قسط واف

In the name of God.
At the hands
of ʿAbd al-Raḥman
b. Yazīd. A quarter
qisṭ, full-measure.

OA + 4094. Green. Width 3.9cm. (*Plate 11*)

From the same die Petrie, 187; Launois 1957, 320; 1959, 27; Balog 1976, 449-50. Cf. Miles 1951b, 22; 1958a, 137-9; 1971, 21; Balog 1976, 448, 451.

The half-*qisṭ* in this series is described next. A single specimen of the *qisṭ* has been published (Balog 1976, 445). This series would have been one of those used with Yazīd b. Ḥatim's command stamp, at least part of the time (see Nos 246-7).

232 Half-*qisṭ*

بسم الله
على يدى
عبد الرحمن
بن يزيد نصف
قسط واف

In the name of God.
At the hands
of ʿAbd al-Raḥman
b. Yazīd. A half
qisṭ, full-measure.

93 11-11 9. Inscription very blurred. Green. Width 3.9cm.

From the same die Miles 1958a, 136; Balog 1976, 447. Cf. Launois 1957, 319; Balog 1976, 446.

ḤUMAYD B. QAḤṬABA
Governor and Finance Director 143-4/760-2

233 Ring weight: *raṭl*, with Muḥammad b. Shuraḥbīl

Smaller stamp to left, the top half

بسم الله امر
(ا)لامير حميد
بن قحطبة ا
صلحه الله

In the name of God. Ordered
the Amir Ḥumayd
b. Qaḥṭaba, may
God keep him righteous.

Larger stamp to right

بسم الله
على يدى محمد
بن شرحبيل
رطل واف

In the name of God.
At the hands of Muḥammad
b. Shuraḥbīl.
Raṭl, full weight.

OA + 4358. Fragment. Part of the top and right side. Green. Length 6.7cm; large stamp 3.5cm; 215g. (*Plate 11*)

From the same two dies Launois 1959, 18; Balog 1976, 408. Cf. Balog 1976, 409.

The larger stamp survives alone on Miles 1948, 52, which obviously originally had a second stamp. It also probably appears, though much of the legend is missing and the impression is distorted, on Miles 1963 I, 38, where it is paired with the command stamp of the next Governor, Yazīd b. Ḥātim (see Nos 246-7).

As for Ḥumayd b. Qaḥṭaba's command stamp, which seems to have set a fashion for a while, it has appeared on other denominations of heavy weights as well as the *raṭls* listed above. It occurs on a *wuqiyya* on which the second stamp is largely missing (Balog 1976, 410) and probably, though the piece is not illustrated, on a possible quarter-*raṭl* on which the second stamp is of Mu'āwiya b. 'Abdallāh (Casanova 1893, 19 and see Nos 234-235). It was also used on vessel stamps which would originally have been paired with other stamps with the denomination and executive's name, like Yazīd b. Ḥātim's similar command stamp (Launois 1957, 185; Balog 1976, 413-4. Cf. Balog 1976, 412).

MU'ĀWIYA B. 'ABDALLĀH
Executive under Ḥumayd b. Qaḥṭaba

234 **Quarter-*qisṭ***

بسم الله
على يدى معو
ية بن عبد ال[له]
ربع قسط
واف

In the name of God.
At the hands of Mu'aw-
iya b. 'Abdallah
A quarter *qisṭ*,
full-measure.

OA + 4100. Green. Width 4.2cm. (*Plate 11*)

From the same die Miles 1971, 29.

Mu'āwiya's stamps are scarce, so he was presumably only in office a short time. His name appears on the reverse of a half-*dīnār* weight of Ḥumayd b. Qaḥṭaba (Fahmī 1957, 138), and his vessel stamps would have been used in combination with the command stamp of Ḥumayd, which has been discussed under the preceding entry. A half-*raṭl* stamp from a ring weight was published by Petrie (180) and a possible quarter-*raṭl* one on a disk weight by Casanova (1893, 19). There was a damaged second stamp on the latter piece on which Casanova read: *al-Amīr . . . b. Muḥammad*. It is likely that this is in fact Ḥumayd b. Qaḥṭaba's command stamp, on which the first letter of Qaḥṭaba is indistinguishable from a *mīm*.

On the stamps Mu'āwiya's name is always written without the *alif*.

235 *Qisṭ*

على يدى معو
ية بن عبد الله
قسط واف

At the hands of Mu'aw-
iya b. 'Abdallah.
A *qisṭ*, full-measure.

OA + 4099. Green. Width 4.2cm. Legend rather blurred. (*Plate 11*)

On all Mu'āwiya's other pieces the legend is introduced by *bismillāh*, but that does not appear to be the case here.

YAZĪD B. ḤĀTIM
Governor and Finance Director 144-52/762-9

236 **Third-*dīnār* weight,** with 'Abd al-Raḥmān b. Yazīd and Kāmil

Obverse

بسم الله
امر الامير
يزيد بن حاتم
مثقال ثلث
واف

In the name of God.
Ordered the Amir
Yazīd b. Ḥātim
a weight of a third,
full-weight.

Reverse
Marginal legend between two circles:

على يدى عبد الرحمن بن يزيد

At the hands of 'Abd al-Raḥman b. Yazīd

Centre:

طبعة
كمل

Stamping of
Kamil.

(Coins and Medals) 87 10-5 12. Lane-Poole, 17. Blue green. 1.9cm; 1.41g. (*Plate 11*)

The obverse appears to be the only third-*dīnār* type of Yazīd b. Ḥātim known. It is also found with reverses of both his other teams of executive and artisan, Muḥammad b. Shuraḥbil and Kāmil (Petrie, 168; Balog 1976, 429, with different reverses), and Salama and Severus (Petrie, 165-6; Launois 1957, 193; Balog 1976, 432-3). It also occurs with the other reverse which 'Abd al-Raḥmān and Kāmil used under Yazīd b. Ḥātim (Balog 1976, 430 and see No. 227). The present piece seems to be the only one of its denomination which has this reverse in its first state, lacking the dot beneath the central legend, but it has been found in the same state on the *dīnār* (see Nos 241-243) and the half-*dīnār* denominations (Balog 1976, 425-6). Described next are three specimens from the same dies but with the reverse in its second state.

237-239 **Third-*dīnār* weight,** with 'Abd al-Raḥmān b. Yazīd and Kāmil

Obverse From the same die as No. 236.

Reverse
Marginal legend:

على يدى عبد الرحمن بن يزيد

At the hands of 'Abd al-Raḥmān b. Yazīd.

Centre:

طبعة
كمل

Stamping
of Kamil

Dot below central legend.

OA + 4198. Green. 1.9cm; 1.40g. (*Plate 11*)
OA + 4238. Green. 1.9cm; 1.41g.
(Coins and Medals) 85 10-7 1. Lane-Poole, 16. Green. 1.9cm; 1.41g. (*Plate 11, rev.*)

From the same pair of dies Petrie, 167; Miles 1948, 80; Fahmī 1957, 146-7.

The reverse die is also the same as that of No. 236 but, as mentioned there, is in a later state distinguishable by the addition of a dot below the legend. In this state the die is used on the following other denominations: *dīnār* (Miles 1948, 77), half-*dīnār* (No. 240) and the sixth-*wuqiyya* (Miles 1958a, 135).

240 Half-*dīnār* weight, with ʿAbd al-Raḥmān b. Yazīd and Kāmil

Obverse

بسم الله
امر الامير
يزيد بن حاتم
مثقال نصف
واف

In the name of God.
Ordered the Amir,
Yazīd b. Ḥātim
a weight of a half,
full-weight.

Reverse Same die, in the same state, as Nos 237-239.

OA + 4194. Green 2.2cm; stamp 1.8cm; 2.08g. (*Plate 11*)

As with the third-*dīnār* type there appears to be only one half-*dīnār* die of Yazīd b. Ḥātim. It has been found with the same reverse in its first state (Petrie, 163; Balog 1976, 425-6) and also with the reverses of Muḥammad b. Shuraḥbīl and Kāmil (Casanova 1893, 33; Petrie, 164; Miles 1958a, 142; Balog 1976, 424, all with the same reverse) and Salama and Severus (Petrie, 162; Balog 1976, 427. Cf. 428).

241-243 *Dīnār* weight, with ʿAbd al-Raḥmān b. Yazīd and Kāmil

Obverse

بسم الله
امر الامير
يزيد بن حاتم
مثقال دينر

In the name of God.
Ordered the Amir
Yazīd b. Ḥātim
a weight of a *dīnar*.

Plain border.

Reverse Same die, in the same state, as No. 236.

OA + 4237. The left half. Green. Length 2.8cm; 2.27g. State of reverse die uncertain.
(Coins and Medals) 53 4-6 949. Rogers 1878, 16. Lane-Poole, 14. Green. 3.0cm; stamp 2.3cm; 4.24g. (*Plate 11*)
(Coins and Medals) 88 7-2 8. Lane-Poole, 15. Green. 2.9cm; stamp 2.3cm; 4.24g.

Yazīd b. Ḥātim has three known *dīnār*-weight dies of which the one on the present piece appears in three different states. One of the dies is used without an obverse (Miles 1948, 76; Launois 1957, 203; Fahmī 1957, 145; Balog 1976, 420. Cf. Fahmī 1957, 144) A second die, without a border and with *wāf* supplying a fifth line of the legend, is found paired with a reverse of Muḥammad b. Shuraḥbīl and Kāmil (Petrie, 161; Balog 1976, 421). The third die seems to be represented in its first state only by the British Museum's pieces. The second state is known only from a single specimen (Fahmī 1957, 142 = Launois 1957, 202 or 203). On it a crescent is added pointing upwards above the legend and a smaller crescent, pointing downwards, below. The reverse of this piece is of ʿAbd al-Raḥmān b. Yazīd and Kāmil, probably from the die of Nos 237-40, in the same state as on those pieces. In the third state of Yazīd's *dīnar*-weight obverse, what seems to be a final *fā'* is added to the left of the lower crescent - perhaps an attempt to make something looking a bit like *wāf*, 'full weight'. This obverse is found with the second state of the reverse die of ʿAbd al-Raḥmān and Kāmil, which has just been mentioned (Miles 1948, 77. Cf. Viré, 19; Miles 1958a, 140), with the other similar die of ʿAbd al-Raḥmān and Kāmil (Fahmī 1957, 143) and with the reverse of Salama and Severus (Balog 1976, 422. Cf. Miles 1951b, p. 25).

244 *Dirham* weight of two-thirds

بسم الله
امر الامير
يزيد بن حاتم
مثقل درهم
ثلثين واف

In the name of God.
Ordered the Amir
Yazīd b. Ḥātim
a weight of a *dīrham*
of two thirds, full-weight.

Mithqāl is spelt without the *alif*.

(Coins and Medals) Or. 3601. Green. 2.7cm; stamp 2.2cm; 2.83g. (*Plate 11*)

From the same die Fahmī 1957, 152; Balog 1976, 434; Rogers 1878, 12, now in the Ashmolean Museum, Oxford.

Rogers was the first to point out that the word after *dirham* should be read *thulthayn* rather than *thalathīn* (thirty). If the *alif* of *thalāthīn* is omitted, as it usually is on *fals* weights, the words are identical in unvowelled script. The same conclusion was reached idependently by Fahmī (1957, p. 34) and Balog. The weights of the known pieces are all close, with one exception extremely close, to the weight of two-thirds of a dinar, 2.833g, assuming a *dīnār* of 4.25g. The specimens listed above weigh 2.81g, 2.76g and 2.84g respectively.

A weight of 2.83g is, of course, considerably lighter than the normal standard of the silver *dirham* (see Introduction, pp. 16–17).

245 Disk weight: *wuqiyya*, with Salama

[امر الامير]
[يزيد بن حـ]ا
[تم على] يدى
[سلـ]مة وقية
واف

Ordered the Amir
Yazīd b. Ḥā-
tim at the hands
of Salama a *wuqiyya*,
full-weight.

Six-pointed star at end of third line.

OA + 4305. About half, bottom and left. Green. Length 5.3cm; 18.2g. (*Plate 11*)

Miles 1948, 82, is similar but since only the top and right part of it is preserved the identity of the die cannot be established. It appears that the only other denomination yet known in this series of Yazīd and Salama is the *raṭl* (Petrie, 160; Miles 1971, 32; Balog 1973, 19; 1976, 417, all from one die. Cf. Viré, 20; Balog 1976, 418–9).

246–247 Command stamp

بسم الله
امر الامير
يزيد بن حاتم
[ا]صلحه الله

In the name of God.
Ordered the Amir
Yazīd b. Ḥātim,
may God keep him righteous.

OA + 4079. Green. Width 3.1cm. (*Plate 12*)
OA + 4080. Green. Width 4.5cm, with attached piece of vessel. Legend very blurred.

From the same die Petrie, 169–70; Launois 1957, 189; Miles 1963 I, 39; Balog 1973, 16; 1976, 435, 437. Cf. Casanova 1893, 145; Miles 1948, 83; Launois 1957, 189–92; Miles 1958a, 144; Miles 1963 I, 39; Balog 1976, 436.

As noted under No. 191, this die appears on a vessel stamp in the Museum of Islamic Art in Cairo which is paired with a quarter-*qist* stamp of Muhammad b. Shuraḥbīl (Launois 1957, 189). It is found again on a ring weight where it is in combination with a denomination stamp, probably for a *raṭl*, of Muḥammad b. Shuraḥbīl (Miles 1963 I, 38 and see No. 233). On weights with denomination stamps of ʿAbd al-Raḥmān b. Yazīd it has been recorded on a half-*raṭl* (Miles 1963 I, 37 and see No. 228) and several *raṭls* (Petrie, 159; Miles 1948, 81; Balog 1973, 18; 1976, 416. Cf. Casanova 1893, 48–9; Balog 1976, 415). No doubt some of the vessel stamps were also paired with the *qisṭ*-system denomination stamps of ʿAbd al-Raḥmān, such as Nos 231–232.

SALAMA
Executive under Yazīd b. Ḥātim and Muḥammad b. Saʿīd

248 *Fals* weight of 24 *kharrūba*

سلمة
مثقال فلس
اربعة وعشر
ين خروبة

Salama.
Weight of a *fals*
of four and twen-
ty *kharrūba*.

Rectangular stamp. Six-pointed star at end of first line.

OA + 4240. Green. 2.9cm; stamp 1.9 x 2.0cm; 4.64g. (*Plate 12*)

From the same die Casanova 1893, 61; Petrie, 188; Fahmī 1957, 203; Miles 1958a, 151; Balog 1976, 460, 462. Cf. Fahmī 1957, 204–8; Miles 1958a, 152; 1963 II, 24; Balog 1976, 461.

Fahmī (1957, 202) has published a single specimen of a second die of the same denomination. Its stamp is rectangular and it has the same legend, but differently disposed and without the star. On the more common type the end of the word *fals* is curiously written; possibly the final *sīn* should be considered to lack a tooth.

The British Museum's collection lacks one of Salama's four known denominations of *fals* weight, that of 33 *kharrūba* (Casanova 1893, 60; Miles 1958a, 145, both from one die. Cf. Miles 1958a, 146; 1963 I, 40; 1971, 33).

249 *Fals* weight of 26 *kharrūba*

سلمة

Salama.
26.

Two semicircles pointing downward above. Groups of three dots to right and below. Annulet to left.

OA + 4239. Olive green. 3.0cm; stamp 2.4cm; 5.03g. (*Plate 12*)

From the same die Petrie, 190; Launois 1957, 381; Fahmī 1957, 199; Miles 1958a, 150; Launois 1960 II, 19; Balog 1976, 458. Cf. Fahmī 1957, 200–1; Miles 1963 I, 41; II, 24; Balog 1976, 459.

This is the first *fals* weight in the British Museum's collection on which the denomination in *kharrūbas* is expressed by a Coptic numeral (see Introduction p. 21).

250–253 *Fals* weight of 30 *kharrūba*

سلمة

Salama.
30.

Rectangular stamp, with dotted border.

OA + 4257. Olive green. 3.2cm; stamp 2.1 x 2.1cm; 5.82g.
OA + 4325. Olive green. 3.2cm; stamp 2.1 x 2.1cm; 5.81g. (*Plate 12*)
(Coins and Medals) 90 8-4 24. Olive green. 3.2cm; stamp 2.1 x 2.1cm; 5.82g.
(Coins and Medals) Or. 3606. Olive green. 3.1cm; stamp 2.1 x 2.1cm; 5.82g.

From the same die Casanova 1893, 72; Petrie, 189; Miles 1948, 99; Launois 1957, 372; Fahmī 1957, 198; Launois 1959, 32.

A single specimen from a second die of this denomination has been published by Fahmī (1957, 186). Its legend, arrangement, shape and ornamentation are the same and it is likely that there are other specimens from the second die among the considerable number of examples of the same denomination which have been described and not illustrated. The list is as follows: Miles 1948, 100; Launois 1957, 373-80; Fahmī 1957, 187-97; Miles 1958a, 147-9; 1963 I, 40; 1964a, 40-1; Launois 1969, 16; Miles 1971, 34; Balog 1976, 457.

254-256 Executive stamp

على يدى
سلمة

At the hands
of Salama.

OA + 4082. Green. Width 2.7cm.
OA + 4083. Olive green. Width 2.8cm. (*Plate 12*)
94 3-9 13. Green. Width 2.6cm.

From the same die Petrie, 226; Balog 1976, 464. Cf. Casanova 1893, 185; Miles 1948, 101; Launois 1957, 312-5; Miles 1958a, 153; Balog 1976, 463, 465-6.

Another vessel stamp from the same die was recovered from a rubbish pit in Fusṭāṭ in 1965 in the course of the excavations conducted by the American Research Center in Egypt (Scanlon, p. 191). It was attached to a rim from a vessel with a diameter of seven centimetres, on which a second stamp for a measure of *khūkh* (peaches, or more probably, plums) also survived. This and a very few other examples of an executive stamp paired with an anonymous commodity stamp, of which there is one in the British Museum's collection (No. 335) are valuable evidence for the organization of the system of commodity stamps in its last phase (see Introduction pp. 37-8). Salama himself also has commodity stamps on which his name appears as well as the commodity (e.g. Balog 1976, 467-8) and is the latest person to have such stamps.
The present executive stamp was also used as a counterstamp on weights of Muḥammad b. Sa'īd, for example No. 261, in the commentary to which a list of further specimens is given.

MUḤAMMAD B. SA'ĪD
Finance Director 152-7/769-74

257 (Third-*dīnār*) weight, with an unidentified person or persons

Obverse

امر الا
مير محمد
بن سعـ(ـيـ)ـد
مثقل

Ordered the A-
mir Muḥammad
b. Sa'īd
a weight.

Reverse Marginal legend round a circle, and a two-line central legend, both obscure.

(Coins and Medals) Or. 3602. Pale yellowish green. 1.9cm; 1.37g. (*Plate 12*)

The piece is unusual in lacking a denomination but its weight is close to the standard of third-*dinar* weights and it was presumably designed as such. On the obverse the *yā'* is omitted from Sa'īd and *mithqāl* is spelt without *alif*, or perhaps even without *lām*.
The reverse also does not appear elsewhere. Several letters are visible in the margin, which may be partly or wholly in reverse, but it does not seem worth attempting a reading. In the centre the top line seems to consist of a *mīm* followed by two 'teeth' and an *alif*, and the lower one of *mīm* followed by *dāl* or *kāf*, followed by a mark which may be another letter.
Balog (1976, 481) has published a specimen of a second third-*dīnār* obverse of Muḥammad b. Sa'id similar to the present type in lacking the denomination and with the same legend arranged in the same way but used without a reverse. What may be called his standard third-*dīnār* obverse is found with reverses of the executives Salama (Petrie, 186; Balog 1976, 485 - *sic*) and Sa'īd b. al-Musayyib (Casanova 1893, 49; Balog 1976, 484. Cf. 482-3 and see No. 259). Both executives are accompanied by the artisan Severus. Miles 1963 I, 44, is from the standard obverse and Miles noted that he might have overlooked a reverse.

258 Half-*dīnār* weight

امر الا
مير محمد
بن سعيد
مثقل نصف

Ordered the A-
mir Muḥammad
b. Sa'īd
a weight of a half.

OA + 4237. Pale olive green. 2.3cm; 2.11g. (*Plate 12*)

Mithqāl appears to be written without the alif.
Two other half-*dīnār* obverses of Muḥammad b. Sa'īd have been illustrated; all three have the same legend arranged in the same way. The die of Fahmī 1957, 158, is used, like the present one, without a reverse.

Compare Balog 1976, 479, which also lacks a reverse, but is not illustrated. The third die is the most common and like the corresponding *dīnār* and third-*dīnār* ones is found with two reverses, one of Salama and Severus (Launois 1957, 208 = Fahmī 1957, 157; Balog 1976, 480) and one of Sa'īd b. al-Musayyib and Severus (Miles 1958, 163).

259 ***Dīnār* weight,** with Sa'īd b. al-Musayyib and Severus

Obverse

بسم الله
امر الامير
محمد بن سعيد
مثقال دينر

In the name of God.
Ordered the Amir
Muḥammad b. Sa'īd
a weight of a *dīnar*.

Reverse

Marginal legend in double circle:

بسم الله على يدى سعيد بن المسيب

In the name of God. At the hands of Sa'īd b. al-Musayyib

Centre:

طبعة
سويروس

Stamping
of Severus.

(Coins and Medals) 82 8-3 29. Lane-Poole, 19. 2.8cm; stamp 2.2cm; 4.17g. (*Plate 12*)

From the same pair of dies Petrie, 185; Launois 1957, 207 = Fahmī 1957, 155; Miles 1963 II, 27; Balog 1976, 478. Cf. Launois 1959, 21, where there may be some confusion of obverse and reverse illustrations.

For a long time the name of the artisan on this and another reverse of Salama remained a puzzle. The suggestion made by Miles (1958a, 163) that it is a Coptic name, originally the Latin Severus, is eminently satisfactory and has been generally accepted.

Illustrated specimens of *dīnār* weights of Muḥammad b. Sa'īd are all from the one obverse die nor has any example been described as differing from them. It is apparently always used with a reverse, either that of Sa'īd and Severus as on the British Museum's example or that of Salama and Severus (Launois 1957, 207; Fahmī 1957, 153-4, 156; Miles 1958a, 162; Launois 1959, 20; 1960, 12; Miles 1963, 162; Balog 1976, 476-7).

260 **Disk weight: half-*raṭl***

بسم الله
امر الامير
محمد بن سعيد
نصف رطل وا
ف

In the name of God.
Ordered the Amir
Muḥammad b. Sa'īd
a half *raṭl*, full-weight.

Omega-like mark over *ṣād* of *niṣf* in the fourth line.

OA + 4426. Chipped on back and rim but largely intact. 9.0cm; stamp 3.9cm; 210g. (*Plate 12*)

From the same die Petrie, 181; Kmietowicz, 3; Miles 1963 I, 49; No. 261 below.

Except for No. 261, the other examples of the stamp are on ring weights. Except again for No. 261, none has a surviving executive stamp or even traces of one, but since none is intact they may originally have had counterstamps. To judge by the other denominations executive counterstamps were normally used on *raṭl*-system weights of Muḥammad b. Sa'īd (see, for example, Nos 261-264). However, on the present piece there is no doubt that the Finance Director's stamp stood alone.

The front of the weight is in perfect condition except for a small chip but the loss of a large flake at the back reduces its metrological value. Still, it is nearer to being intact than any other published half-*raṭl* on the 'Umayyad' standard, the correct weight for which would be a little over 220 grammes.

The omega-like mark appears on all of Muḥammad b. Sa'īd's *raṭl*-system stamps. H.W. Glidden (quoted under Miles 1963 I, 45-6) put forward the idea that it might be the initial *sīn* of the name of the executive Salama. The artisan Severus might be a better candidate than Salama whose name in any case sometimes appears on counterstamps beside stamps with the omega (see No. 261), but, as Miles pointed out, the use of Arabic initials is unknown to early Islamic numismatics and metrology. Furthermore, the mark always lacks the tail of an isolated *sīn*. Miles had earlier (1958, 165) noted the similarity of the mark to one found on certain anonymous disks which Jungfleisch (1952) had rather implausibly suggested was a date in the *abjad* alphabetical notation. Marks resembling Greek letters are occasionally found on other weights (e.g. Nos 341-2).

261 **Disk weight: half-*raṭl*,** with Salama

Large stamp Same die as No. 260.

Small stamp below Same die as Nos 254-6.

OA + 4427. Green. Length 9.5cm; small stamp 1.9cm; 91g. (*Plate 12*)

The counterstamp is also found on several of Muḥammad b. Sa'īd's *raṭl* weights (Casanova 1893, 50; Miles 1958a, 166; 1963 I, 47; Balog 1976, 470. Cf. Balog 1976, 471).

262–264 Ring weight: *raṭl*, with ʿUmar b. Yaḥyā

Large stamp

بسم الله
امر الامير
محمد بن سعيد
رطل واف

In the name of God.
Ordered the Amir
Muḥammad b. Saʿīd
a *raṭl*, full weight.

Vertical stroke over *mīm* of *amara* in second line. Six-pointed star at end of second line. Omega-like mark at end of legend.

Counterstamp From the same die as No. 281.

OA + 4360. The top. The back and sides have been ground smooth and shaped, presumably cosmetic work for the antique trade. Green. Length 6.4cm; 114g. (*Plate 12*)
OA + 4361. The top. Length 6.3cm; height of large stamp 3.5cm; 110g.
OA + 4362. The top, with only part of the executive stamp surviving. Length 5.5cm; height of large stamp 3.1cm; 116g.

From the same two dies Balog 1973, 20.

There appears to be only one *raṭl* die of Muḥammad b. Saʿīd. It is found together with stamps of three other executives as well as ʿUmar: Salama (Casanova 1893, 50; Miles 1958a, 166; 1963 I, 47; Balog 1976, 470. Cf. Balog 1976, 471), ʿAbd al-Wahhāb b. Tamīm (Petrie, 182; Balog 1976, 427) and Qutayba b. Ziyād (Petrie, 183; Miles 1948, 84). On a number of other specimens the main stamp appears alone though it is probable that in most such cases an original executive stamp has not survived (Petrie, 184; Miles 1963 I, 48. Cf. Casanova 1893, 51; Balog 1976, 473–4).
All illustrated specimens of the executive stamp of ʿUmar b. Yaḥyā are from the same die. It has also been found on *wuqiyyas* (Miles 1963 I, 45. Cf. 46) and vessel stamps (see No. 281).

265–270 Quarter-*qisṭ*

بسم الله
امر الامير
محمد بن (س)عيد
ربع قسط و
اف

In the name of God.
Ordered the Amir
Muḥammad b. Saʿīd
a quarter *qisṭ*, full-measure.

The *sīn* of *Saʿīd* is written with two 'teeth' instead of three.

OA + 4084. Olive green. Width 3.3cm.
OA + 4289. Dark green. Chipped at right. Width 3.2cm.
OA + 4344. Green. Chipped at top left. Width 4.4cm. (*Plate 12*)
OA + 4345. Green. Width 3.9cm.
93 2–5 86. Green. Width 3.7cm.
95 12–20 5. Green. Width 3.9cm.

From the same die Casanova 1893, 168; Launois 1957, 205; Miles 1958a, 171; Balog 1976, 493–4. Cf. Launois 1957, 206; Miles 1958a, 170; Balog 1973, 22; 1976, 488–92.

271 Half-*qisṭ*

بسم الله
امر الامير
محمد بن سع(ي)د
نصف قسط
واف

In the name of God.
Ordered the Amir
Muḥammad b. Saʿīd
a half *qisṭ*,
full-measure.

OA + 4085. Olive green. Width 4.2cm. (*Plate 12*)

From the same die Launois 1957, 204; Balog 1973, 21; 1976, 487. Cf. Miles 1958a, 167–9; 1964a; 46; 1971, 36.

Miles noted that the *yāʾ* of *Saʿīd* was omitted. A single specimen of the corresponding *qisṭ* denomination has been published by Balog (1976, 486).

SAʿĪD B. AL-MUSAYYIB
Executive under Muḥammad b. Saʿīd

272 Sixth-*wuqiyya*, with Severus

Obverse Same die as No. 227.

Reverse Same die as No. 259.

OA + 4302. Green. 3.1cm; rectangular stamp 1.9 x 2.0cm; 6.26g. (*Plate 13*)

The obverse has been discussed under No. 227. The reverse, from the only known die on which Saʿīd b. al-Musayyib's name appears, is also found on *dīnār*-system weights of Muḥammad b. Saʿīd, for example No. 259. The present piece is so far the only one with Saʿīd as the chief authority. No executive stamp of his has yet appeared and it may be that he did not use one or was not even involved in the issue of vessel stamps and the heavier weights.

ʿUMAR B. YAḤYĀ
Executive under Muḥammad b. Saʿīd

273 *Fals* weight of 30 *kharrūba*

عمر مثقال
فلس ثلثين
خروبة

ʿUmar. Weight
of a *fals* of thirty
kharrūba.

Beaded border. Trio of dots above, dot below.

OA + 4244. Green. 3.3cm; stamp 2.5cm; 5.82g (*Plate 13*)

From the same die Casanova 1893, 59; Petrie 215; Fahmī 1957, 291. Cf. Rogers 1878, 6.

Several examples from a second die of this denomination which has the same design have been published. It can be easily told from the other type by the placing of the dots above the legend. On the second die the dots are neatly arranged in a triangle with its base parallel to the lines of script. On the type represented in the British Museum the triangle is lopsided. Examples of the second type are the following: Lanois 1957, 362; Miles 1958a, 160; Balog 1976, 497. Specimens which have not been illustrated and may be from either die are: Casanova 1893, 58; Fahmī 1957, 292-4.

There are *fals* weights of three other denominations with a similar large script with the name ʻUmar which were evidently issued by the same person. Examples of the 32- and 33-*kharrūba* types are described below. Only one specimen has been described of a 24-*kharruba* type, which has the figure of the denomination in Coptic (Miles 1971, 39).

The generally accepted identification of the ʻUmar of the *fals* weights with the ʻUmar b. Yaḥyā who appears on an executive stamp and is associated with Muḥammad b. Saʻīd, as, for example, on Nos 262-4, was suggested by Miles (1958a, 161) chiefly on the grounds of the similarity of the *fals* weights of ʻUmar and those of the nearly contemporary Salama.

274-277 *Fals* weight of 32 *kharrūba*

عمر
اثنين وثلثين
خروبة

ʻUmar.
Two and thirty
kharrūba.

Rectangular stamp.

OA + 4242. Olive green. 3.2cm; stamp 2.1 x 2.2cm; 6.22g. (*Plate 13*)
OA + 4243. Green. 3.2cm; stamp 2.1 x 2.2cm; 6.19g.
(Coins and Medals) 88 7-2 10. Lane-Poole, 31. Green. 3.1cm; stamp 2.1 x 2.2cm; 6.20g.
(Coins and Medals) 83 5-10.1. Lane-Poole, 32 (illustration numbered 30). Green. 3.1cm; stamp 2.1cm; 6.20g.

From the same die Casanova 1893, 55; Launois 1957, 363; Fahmī 1957, 264; Miles 1958a, 158; Balog 1976, 496, Cf. Casanova 1893, 56-7; Miles 1948, 120-120a; Launois 1957, 364-7; Fahmī 1957, 265-79; Miles 1958a, 155-7, 159; Launois 1960 I, 17; Miles 1964a, 43-5; Launois 1969, 17; Miles 1971, 38.

278-280 *Fals* weight of 33 *kharrūba*

عمر

ʻUmar.
33.

Beaded border. Triangle of three dots pointing upwards above with a single dot at each side. Triangle of three dots below, apex downwards.

OA + 4195. Green. 3.3cm; stamp 2.5cm; 6.42g. (*Plate 13*)
OA + 4241. Green. 3.4cm; stamp 2.7cm; 6.43g.
(Coins and Medals) Or. 3605. 3.3cm; stamp 2.6cm; 6.40g.

From the same die Fahmī 1957, 280. Cf. Launois 1957, 370-1; Fahmī 1957, 281-90; Miles 1958a, 154; 1971, 37.

The figure 33 is written in Coptic numerals.

There is a second die of the same denomination, similar down to the ornamental detail, of which two specimens have been illustrated (Petrie, 192; Miles 1951b, 35). However, on it the triangle of dots above the legend has its apex downwards instead of upwards. On those specimens listed above as from the first die but not illustrated the apex is stated, directly or by implication, to point up, but one suspects some examples of the other type may be included. It is easy to make mistakes over such details. In the case of Miles 1951b, 35, for instance, the triangle was printed as it should be in the original description but this was 'corrected' on a later occasion (1958a, 154) presumably under the influence of a specimen from the other die.

281 Executive stamp

على يدى
عمر بن
يحيى

At the hands
of ʻUmar b.
Yaḥyā.

OA + 4090. Green. Width 2.6cm. (*Plate 13*)

From the same die Launois 1957, 309; Miles 1958a, 161; Launois 1960, 25, 25 *bis*; Balog 1976, 498. Cf. Casanova 1893, 186, 197; Miles 1963 II, 26; Balog 1976, 499-501.

For the use of the same die on weights of Muḥammad b. Saʻīd see Nos 262-264.

QUTAYBA B. ZIYĀD

Executive under Muḥammad b. Saʻīd and Maṭar

281-283 Executive stamp

على يدى
قتيبة

At the hands
of Qutayba.

OA + 4087. Olive green. Width 2.5cm.
93 11-11 4. Olive green. 2.6cm. (*Plate 13*)

Vessel stamps from the same die Miles 1948, 121; Balog 1976, 504.

This counterstamp is also used on weights, for example, No. 286. There is a second executive stamp of Qutayba with an inscription in three lines which includes his father's name and is used on weights and vessel stamps. No. 288 shows an example of it paired with a half-*qisṭ* stamp of Maṭar. The three-line stamp was in use earlier than the two-line one.

MAṬAR
Finance Director 157-9/774-6

284 ***Dīnār*** **weight,** with Qutayba b. Ziyād

Obverse

امر مطر مو
لى امير المؤ
منين اكرمه
الله مثقال
دينر واف

Ordered Maṭar, Maw-
lā of the Commander of the Faithful, may God show him
bounty, a weight
of a *dīnar*, full-weight.

Beaded border. Two dots below legend.

Reverse

Marginal legend between two circles:

على يدى قتيبة بن زياد

At the hands of Qutayba b. Ziyād.

Centre:

مصر

Miṣr
Five-leafed spray, with trios of dots on either side, below central legend.

OA + 4250. Green. 2.9cm; stamp 2.3cm; 4.25g. (*Plate 13*)

From the same obverse die Miles 1971, 24.

Miles was wrong to attribute the piece in the Corning Museum to the Caliph al-Manṣūr, though it is worth noting that the script of the obverse is very similar to that of al-Manṣūr's latest set of *dīnār*-system dies (see Nos 194-195). The reverse of the Corning specimen was not illustrated but may be the same as that of the British Museum's. Miles read Miṣr ('Egypt' or 'Fusṭāṭ') in the centre and the executive formula *'alā yaday* in the margin; his tentative restoration of the executive's name as Severus must be incorrect.

As already pointed out under Nos 194-195, the reverse die also occurs paired with a half-*dīnār* obverse of al-Manṣūr, which is also linked with the reverse of Muḥammad b. Sa'īd. On one of the two known specimens Miles (1948, 87) first read the word in the centre as Maṭar, but later (1958a, 124) corrected the reading to Miṣr. Balog (1976, 360) read Miṣr on the other specimen but assumed that the margin bore the name of Muḥammad b. Sa'īd. Miṣr and Maṭar are usually indistinguishable in early Kufic but, as Miles noted, if the word in the centre was a personal name we would expect it to be that of an artisan. Other reasons for not reading Maṭar are that it would mean that the Finance Director's name appeared on both sides of the weight which would be very unusual, though not quite without parallel, and, more significantly, that Maṭar's name would lack any titulature. Although he did not use the title Amir, on other stamps his name is always followed by *mawlā amīr al-mu'minīn* and usually by the benediction *akramahu allāh*. To read Miṣr, on the other hand, offers no problem; the appearance of the place of production on the reverse was a usage that had been introduced under Muḥammad b. Sa'īd.

The use of the reverse die of Qutayba b. Ziyād with Maṭar's *dīnār* obverse shows, of course, that it was in use during Maṭar's finance directorship, but since Qutayba is known to have acted as executive with Muḥammad b. Sa'īd as well it is not impossible that the half-*dīnār* weights of al-Manṣūr with the same reverse were issued during Muḥammad b. Sa'īd's governorship. However, since no weights of Maṭar for fractions of the *dīnār* have come to light it appears more likely that the half-*dīnār* obverse of al-Manṣūr remained in use beside Maṭar's *dīnār* obverse. Qutayba also appears as an executive on Maṭar's *fals* weights (Balog 1976, 533-4). The only published specimen of a second *dīnar* obverse of Maṭar lacks a reverse (Launois 1957, 221 = Fahmī 1957, 177).

285 Disk weight: ***wuqiyya***

بسم ا[لله امر]
مطر مو[لى امير]
المؤمنين اكرمه
الله وقية واف

In the name of God. Ordered
Maṭar, Mawlā of the Commander
of the faithful, may God show him
bounty, a *wuqiyya*, full-weight.

OA + 4414. Something less than a quarter is broken off at top and left. Green. 5.3cm; stamp 3.6cm; 29g. (*Plate 13*)

From the same die Miles 1963 II, 30.

286 Ring weight: ***raṭl*****,** with Qutayba b. Ziyād

Large stamp

بسم الله امر
مطر مولى امير
المؤمنين اكرمه
الله رطل واف

In the name of God. Ordered
Maṭar, Mawlā of the Commander
of the Faithful, may God show him
bounty, a *raṭl*, full-weight.

Counterstamp Same die as Nos 282-283.

95 12-20 3. Fragment. The top, with a large piece including half the counterstamp broken off the left end. Chipped at right. Olive green. Length c. 6cm; height of large stamp 3.4cm; 116g. (*Plate 13*)

From the same pair of dies Balog 1976, 530. Cf. 529.

The denomination stamp also occurs with Qutayba b. Ziyād's other executive stamp, the one with a three-line inscription which was in use earlier than the two-line one (Miles 1948, 94). It had also been found with the stamp of another executive 'Abd al-Raḥmān b. Tamīm (Balog 1976, 531) and by itself on a fragment which probably originally had an executive stamp (Balog 1973, 25). The executive stamp also occurs on a fragment of an uncertain disk weight (Miles 1963 I, 34).

287 **Quarter-*qisṭ***

[بسـ]م الله [امر]
[م]طر مولى ام[ير]
[الم]ؤمنين اكر[مه]
[الله] ربع قسط

In the name of God. Ordered
Maṭar, Mawlā of the Commander
of the faithful, may God show him
bounty, a quarter-*qisṭ*.

OA + 4089. Olive green. Width 3.3cm. (*Plate 13*)

288 **Half-*qisṭ*,** paired with executive stamp of Qutayba b. Ziyād

Large stamp

بسم الله ا[مر]
مطر مولى ام[ير]
المؤمنين اكرم[ه]
[ال]له نصف قسط
واف

In the name of God. Ordered
Maṭar, Mawlā of the Commander
of the Faithful, may God show him
bounty, a half-*qisṭ*
full-measure.

Rectangular counterstamp

على يدى
قتيبة
بن زياد

At the hands
of Qutayba
b. Ziyād.

OA + 4088. Two separate stamps attached to a section of rim. Green. Length 7.1cm. (*Plate 13*)

From the die of the large stamp Balog 1976, 535.

The executive stamp is also known from *raṭl* weights of Muḥammad b. Sa'īd (Petrie, 183; Miles 1948, 84) and Maṭar (Miles 1948, 94 and see No. 286). The rectangular outline of the stamp is clear on the weights. Perhaps the two paired vessel stamps on a seemingly anomalous piece in the Fouquet collection are another impression of the same die (Casanova 1893, I, p. 366, Pièces supplémentaires, 3, reading *Qutayba b. Ziyād* for *jubna barbariyya* and probably *bi-fals* for *malla* on the second stamp. See Nos 482-4.).

A second executive stamp of Qutayba, which has a two-line legend, has been discussed above (Nos 282-283). Since the type with the three-line legend occurs on pieces of both Muḥammad b. Sa'īd and Maṭar it must be earlier than the other which only occurs with stamps of Maṭar.

The piece of rim which joins the two pieces is slightly irregular in its curve, making it difficult to estimate the diameter of the original measure precisely from it, but it would seem to have been about six or seven centimetres. The wall of the vessel curves outward slightly below the rim.

THE CALIPH AL-MAHDĪ
158-69/775-85

289 **Third-*dīnār* weight**

بسم الله
امر المهدى
[ا]مير المؤمني[ن]
(م)ثقال ثلث
واف

In the name of God.
Ordered al-Mahdī,
Commander of the Faithful,
a weight of a third,
full-weight.

The first letter of *mithqāl*, 'weight', is written in the form of a *fā'*.

(Coins and Medals) 83 6-8 22. Lane-Poole, 22. Olive green. 1.9cm; 1.43g. (*Plate 13*)

According to Lane-Poole the reverse of this piece is obliterated. In fact there is no sign that a reverse was used at all. The majority of al-Mahdī's *dīnār*-system weights do have reverses and most of them come from a single set of obverse dies, the standard third-*dīnār* type being that of Nos 290-293. Three other third-*dīnār* weights are recorded as being used without a reverse. Casanova 1893, 35 and Balog 1976, 5, like the British Museum's piece, are each unique examples of a particular die. The third specimen is not illustrated (Miles 1948, 85).

290-291 **Third-*dīnār* weight,** with Muḥammad b. Sulaymān and al-Muhājir

Obverse

بسم الله
امر المهدى ا
مير المؤمنين
مثقال ثلث
واف

In the name of God.
Ordered al-Mahdī, Commander of the Faithful,
a weight of a third,
full-weight.

Reverse

Marginal legend between two circles:

على يدى محمد بن سليمن

At the hands of Muḥammad b. Sulayman.

Centre:

طبعة ا
لمهاجر

Stamping of Al-Muhājir.

Six-pointed star flanked by two dots below the central legend.

(Coins and Medals) 85 10-7 2. Lane-Poole, 21. Chipped. Green. 1.9cm; stamp 1.5cm; 1.39g.
(Coins and Medals) 91 10-3 29. Green. 1.9cm; stamp 1.5cm. 1.41g. (*Plate 13*)

From the same pair of dies Petrie, 200-1; Miles 1948, 89, Fahmī 1957, 167; Balog 1976, 512-3. Cf. Miles 1958a, 175; Launois 1959, 26; Miles 1971, 40.

The reverse die is the only known example of Muḥammad b. Sulaymān and al-Muhājir. It is also used with the corresponding half-*dīnār* and *dīnār* obverses of al-Mahdī (see Nos 294, 298).

The obverse is what may be called al-Mahdī's standard one, being used, as the corresponding half-*dīnār* and *dīnār* types are, with the reverses of a succession of Finance Directors from Muḥammad b. Sulaymān to Ibrāhīm b. Ṣāliḥ. The next in the chronological series of reverses is that of ʻIsā b. Luqmān (see No. 299) but it has yet to be found on a third-*dīnār* weight. Besides Muḥammad b. Sulaymān, there are weights of that denomination from the standard obverse die of the following Finance Directors: Wāḍiḥ, (see Nos 292-293), Ismāʻīl b. Ibrāhīm (Fahmī 1957, 173; Miles 1958a, 176; Launois 1959, 25; Balog 1976, 527. Cf. Miles 1951b, 26) and Ibrāhīm b. Ṣāliḥ (Fahmī 1957, 175; Balog 1976, 515)

Besides the obverses used without a reverse which have been discussed under No. 287, al-Mahdī has another third-*dīnār* type of which specimens have been published with a reverse of Ibrāhīm b. Ṣāliḥ and ʻĀsim b. Ḥafṣ (Fahmī 1957, 176; Balog 1976, 520. Cf. Balog 1976, 521). This last reverse is presumably later than the one which has Ibrāhīm b. Ṣāliḥ's name alone (e.g. No. 296).

Al-Muhājir is the only person whose name appears both on coin weight reverses after *ṭabʻa*, which normally introduces the name of the artisan, and on executive stamps after the excutive formula *ʻalā yaday*, as for example, on Nos 306-7. Both types of stamp belong to the finance directorship of Muḥammad b. Sulaymān. It need not be assumed, however, that al-Muhājir acted as both executive and artisan. The appearance of *ṭabʻa* on the coin weight reverse die is the latest known use of the formula in such a context and it is quite possible that it is used in an exceptional manner - to introduce the name of the executive.

292-293 Third-*dīnār* weight, with Wāḍiḥ

Obverse Same die as Nos 290-291.

Reverse
Marginal legend between two circles, the inner one beaded:

على يدى الامير واضح مولى امير

At the hands of the Amīr Wāḍiḥ Mawlā of the Commander

Centre:

المؤ
منين

of the Faith-
ful.

Central dot on reverse.

OA + 4249. Olive green. 1.9cm; stamp 1.4cm; 1.39g. (*Plate 13*)

93 11-11 14. Green. 2.0cm; stamp 1.5cm; 1.41g.

From the same pair of dies Balog 1976, 517-8. Cf. Balog 1976, 519.

The reverse of Wāḍiḥ also occurs with the corresponding obverses for the *dīnār* (see Nos 300-301) and half-*dīnār* (Petrie, 197; Miles 1948, 91; Launois 1957, 214 = Fahmī 1957, 170; Balog 1976, 516).

294 Half-*dīnār* weight, with Muḥammad b. Sulaymān and al-Muhājir

Obverse

بسم الله
المهدى امير
المؤمنين مثقا
ل نصف و
اف

In the name of God.
Al-Mahdī, Commander
of the Faithful. Weigh-
t of a half, full-
weight.

Reverse Same die as Nos 290-291.

(Coins and Medals) 82 8-3 30. Lane-Poole, 20. Green. 2.1cm; stamp 1.6cm; 2.12g. (*Plate 14*)

From the same pair of dies Launois 1957, 215 = Fahmī, 1957, 166; Miles 1958, 174; Balog 1976, 509-11.

The obverse is al-Mahdī's standard half-*dīnār* type and found with reverses of the usual later Finance Directors: ʻĪsā b. Luqmān (Balog 1976, 514), Wāḍiḥ (examples listed under Nos 292-293), Ismāʻīl b. Ibrāhīm (see No. 295) and Ibrāhīm b. Ṣāliḥ (see No. 296).

295 Half-*dīnār* weight, with Ismāʻīl b. Ibrāhīm

Obverse Same die as No. 294.

Reverse
Marginal legend between two circles:

بسم الله على يدى الامير اسمعيل

In the name of God. At the
hands of Ismaʻīl

Centre:

بن ابر
هيم

b. Ibrahīm.

Two dots below Ibrahīm.

OA + 4248. Green. 2.2cm; stamp 1.5cm; 2.12g. (*Plate 14*)

From the same pair of dies Petrie, 198; Fahmī 1957, 162, 172-3, Balog 1976, 525. Cf. Launois 1957, 212-3; Balog 1976, 524, 526.

The reverse is also used with the corresponding obverses for the *dīnār* (see Nos 302-303) and third-*dīnār* (examples listed under Nos 290-291).

296 Half-*dīnār* weight, with Ibrāhīm b. Ṣāliḥ

Obverse Same die as Nos 294-295.

Reverse

Marginal legend between two beaded circles:

[على يدى ا]لامير ابرهيم [بن]

At the hands of the Amir Ibrahīm b.

Centre:

صا
لح

Ṣā-
liḥ.

(Coins and Medals) 87 10-5 13. Lane-Poole, 25. Olive green. 2.2cm; stamp 1.5cm; 2.12g. (*Plate 14*)

From the same pair of dies Launois 1957, 216 = Fahmī 1957, 174.

As mentioned under Nos 300-301, the reverse also occurs with al-Mahdī's standard third-*dīnār* obverse. It has also been found on the corresponding *dīnār* denomination (Miles 1948, 92. Cf. 93).

297 Half-*dīnār* weight

Obverse

بسم الله
المهدى امير
المؤمنين مثقال
نصف و
اف

In the name of God.
Al-Mahdī, Commander
of the Faithful. Weight
of a half, full-
weight.

Reverse Crude legend or imitation of script in form of marginal legend and one-line central legend. Within a circle.

(Coins and Medals) 83 6-8 21. Lane-Poole, 34. Pale yellowish. 2.2cm; stamp 1.7cm; 2.13g. (*Plate 14*)

From the same obverse die Balog 1976, 505.

The obverse is well produced and the legend is that of al-Mahdī's standard half-*dīnār* type but the arrangement of the lines differs slightly. Balog's piece had no reverse. He compared it to Miles 1963 II, 28, which is said to have an illegible reverse but the legend of the obverse, as described by Miles, is arranged like that of the standard type.

The crude script of the reverse of the British Museum's piece is in sharp contrast to the obverse. Lane-Poole tentatively read Muḥammad in the centre and could be right. It should be noted that the actual impression is crisp – the illegibility of the script is due to the die, not to the process of striking.

Another non-standard half-*dīnār* die is known used with a reverse of ʿĀṣim b. Ḥafṣ, presumably at the end of al-Mahdī's caliphate (Launois 1957, 217 = Fahmī 1957, 161).

298 *Dīnār* weight, with Muḥammad b. Sulaymān and al-Muhājir

Obverse

بسم الله امر
المهدى محمد
امير المؤمنين
امتع الله به
مثقال دينر
واف

In the name of God. Ordered
al-Mahdī Muḥammad,
Commander of the Faithful,
may God give him joy,
a weight of a *dīnār*
full-weight.

Six-pointed star above.

Reverse Same die as Nos 290-291, 294.

OA + 4245. Cracked and glued together. Green. 3.0cm; stamp 2.4cm; 4.23g. (*Plate 14*)

From the same pair of dies Launois 1957, 211 = Fahmī 1957, 165; Miles 1958a, 172; Balog 1976, 507-8. Cf. Launois 1969, 13.

The obverse is the standard one of al-Mahdī. Four of the known reverses are represented in the British Museum's collection, including that of ʿĪsā b. Luqmān, which has not been found on the *dīnār* denomination before. The reverse of Ibrāhīm b. Ṣāliḥ used on No. 296 has also been found combined with the present obverse (Miles 1948, 92. Cf. 93). A piece in the Muntazah Palace collection (Miles 1964a, 48) may represent a sixth reverse used with the same obverse. Miles described the reverse as being of Yaḥyā, Mawla of the Caliph, referring for comparison to a piece in the American Numismatic Society collection on which he had previously (1958, 173) read the reverse in that way. The illustration of the American Numismatic Society piece however shows that the reverse is from the die with the name of Wāḍiḥ found on Nos 292-293 and 300-301. Nevertheless, since, in the catalogue of the Muntazah collection, Miles describes a *dīnār* weight with a reverse of Wāḍiḥ immediately before the one attributed to Yaḥyā his reading of the latter is not be dismissed out of hand. It is rather curious that no coin weight reverse of Yaḥyā b. Dāʿūd, who was Finance Director for a period between Wāḍiḥ and Ismāʿīl b. Ibrāhīm, has otherwise come to light. If coin weights with a reverse in his name were issued the obverses would naturally be al-Mahdī's standard ones, which were in use both before and after his term of office.

On most specimens stamped from this obverse die the *mīm* of *mithqāl* at the beginning of the fifth line is no more than a stroke or blob set at an angle. On the present piece and one other (Balog 1976, 508) the *mīm* is properly formed. Upon comparing the two varieties it can be seen that the deformation of the letter on the second variety is caused by an accident to the die. It must have received a sharp knock on the edge at about the 'five-o'clock' position which caused it to fold in slightly. The outer edge was brought a little forward and a small depression was formed behind it in which part of the *mīm* disappeared. The two specimens stamped with the undamaged die both have the reverse of Muḥammad b. Sulaymān under whom the standard series of obverses of al-Mahdī came into use. The other illustrated specimens with the same reverse show the obverse die after it had been damaged. The accident to the die, then, took place during his finance directorship.

299 ***Dīnār* weight,** with ʿĪsā b. Luqmān

Obverse Same die as No. 298.

Reverse
Marginal legend between two beaded circles:

على يدى الامير عيسى بن لقمان

At the hands of the Amir ʿĪsā b. Luqmān

Centre:

اصـ(لحـ)ه
الله

May God keep him
righteous.

Mark, perhaps intended as a star, at end of marginal legend. Central dot.

(Egyptian Antiquities) 87 4-2 64. Olive green. 2.9cm; stamp 2.4cm; 4.23g. (*Plate 14*)

In the top line of the centre of the reverse *ṣād* and *ḥā'* in *aṣlaḥahu* are transposed. The only published piece with this reverse is a specimen of the corresponding half-*dīnār* weight (Balog 1976, 514).

300-301 ***Dīnār* weight,** with Wāḍiḥ

Obverse Same die as Nos 298-299.

Reverse Same die as Nos 292-293.

OA + 4246. Olive green. 2.8cm; stamp 2.3cm; 4.24g. (*Plate 14*)
(Coins and Medals) Or. 3604. 2.9cm; stamp 2.3cm; 4.20g.

From the same pair of dies Miles 1948, 90; Launois 1957, 210; Fahmī 1957, 168-9; Miles 1958a, 173. Cf. Miles 1964a, 47.

302-303 ***Dīnār* weight,** with Ismāʿīl b. Ibrāhīm

Obverse Same die as Nos 298-301.

Reverse Same die as No. 295.

OA + 4247. Green. 2.9cm; stamp 2.4cm; 4.23g. (*Plate 14, obv.*)
(Coins and Medals) 70 5-4 12. Rogers 1878, 17; Lane-Poole, 23. Green. 2.9cm; stamp 2.4cm; 4.24g. (*Plate 14, rev.*)

From the same die Balog 1976, 523. Cf. 522.

304 ***Dīnār* weight,** with ʿĀṣim b. Ḥafṣ

Obverse Legend a rather crude copy of that of Nos 298-303, with the star above.

Reverse
Marginal legend between two circles:

على يد[ى عا]صم بن حفص

At the hands of ʿĀṣim b. Ḥafṣ

Star at beginning.

Centre: Illegible one- or two-line legend. The first letter of the second line *hā'* or *mīm*.

(Coins and Medals) 73 8-1 76. Lane-Poole, 24. 2.6cm; 4.23g. (*Plate 14*)

From the same obverse die Fahmī 1957, 160; No. 305 below.

The piece in Cairo published by Fahmī is not said to have a reverse. The reverse of the present piece is not recorded elsewhere though there are several other reverses with the name of ʿĀṣim, all rather faintly engraved, which are found in combination with non-standard obverses of al-Mahdī. One with ʿĀṣim b. Ḥafṣ's name in the centre and that of Ibrāhīm b. Ṣāliḥ in the margin is found on a number of third-*dīnār* weights (Launois 1957, 218 = Fahmī 1957, 176; Balog 1976, 520. Cf. 521). Another is known from a single half-*dīnār* weight (Launois 1957, 217 = Fahmī 1957, 161). A third is represented by Petrie, 196, the obverse of which is from another non-standard *dīnār*-weight die of al-Mahdī (Cf. Launois 1959, 24 from the same obverse die and said to have traces of a reverse legend). ʿĀṣim b. Ḥafṣ also has other reverses which evidently belong later (see Nos 327, 338).

305 ***Dīnār* weight**

Obverse Same die as No. 304.

Reverse
Centre:

[ا]لمؤ
[م]نين

The Faith-
ful.

Dot above central legend.

83 6-21 35. Lane-Poole, 24G. Green. 2.8cm; stamp 2.2cm; 4.27g. (*Plate 14*)

The puzzling reverse of this piece is also found on two half-*dīnār* weights which share the same anonymous obverse (Casanova 1893, 9 *bis*, to which the reverse illustrated as No. 25 clearly belongs; Launois 1969, 14). A third specimen from the same obverse die has a similar reverse, which has not been illustrated (Fahmī 1957, 240). Launois suggested, not unreasonably at first sight, that the reverse legend probably ended *mawlā amīr al-mu'minīn* ('client of the Commander of the Faithful'), and on the strength of its similarity to the reverse of Wāḍiḥ (e.g. Nos 292-293) attributed the anonymous half-*dīnar* to the reign of al-Mahdī. The association of the reverse with an obverse of al-Mahdī on the present piece supports the dating to al-Mahdī's caliphate but the appearance of the same obverse with a reverse of ʿĀṣim b. Ḥafṣ on No. 304, and the evidence that al-Mahdī's standard *dīnār*-weight obverse was in use from the time of Muḥammad b. Sulaymān to the earlier part of Ibrāhīm b. Ṣāliḥ's first governorship, shows that the obverse of Nos 304-305 and presumably that of the anonymous half-*dīnār* types must belong to the end of al-Mahdī's reign. This makes it difficult to see how the title *mawlā amīr al-mu'minīn* could have occurred in the legend. The Finance Directors who are known to have born the title under al-Mahdī, Maṭar, Wāḍiḥ and Yaḥyā b. Dā'ūd are too early and none of the governors of the end of the reign seems likely to have had the title which, though it could no doubt be a considerable honour, carried the implication of client status and was normally given only to non-Arabs. Ibrāhīm b. Ṣāliḥ himself and his brother al-Faḍl were members of the Abbasid royal family and for them the title would have been no honour. The Finance Director who came between them, Mūsā b. Muṣ'ab al-Khath'amī was an Arab who would probably not have qualified for the title either, and certainly did not use it on his few known glass stamps.

On the British Museum's piece the reverse is not properly centred. The visible part of the margin begins *fā'*, *ṣād* or the like, suggesting, in this context, [ʻĀṣim b. Ḥ]afṣ. Three or four indecipherable letters follow and then *lām-alif*, *mīm* seems fairly clear. The illustrations of other examples of the reverse show different parts of the margin but by themselves are of little help. It seems, however, that the legend is probably different from the usual types.

MUḤAMMAD B. SULAYMĀN
Finance Director 159-61/775-8

306 Disk-weight: half-*raṭl*, with al-Muhājir

Main stamp

[بسم الله ام]ر
[الامير محم]د بن
[سليمن اكرم]ه
[الله نصـ]ف رطل
[وا]ف

In the name of God. Ordered
the Amir Muḥammad b.
Sulayman, may God show him
bounty, a half-*raṭl*
full-weight.

Counterstamp below

على يدى
المهاجر

At the hands
of al-Muhājir

OA + 4428. Fragment. From the left side and bottom. Length 8.4cm; small stamp 1.6cm; 79g. (*Plate 14*)

The larger stamp appears not to have been published. The restoration of the largely defective legend is in accordance with those of Muḥammad b. Sulaymān's other stamps. That this one is his is confirmed by the counterstamp of al-Muhājir whose name appears on both *raṭl*-system and *dīnār*-system weights with that of Muḥammad b. Sulaymān but who is not associated with any other official (see Nos 290-291, 294, 298). Muḥammad b. Sulaymān's *raṭl* stamp is described below. A *wuqiyya* has also been published by Miles (1963 I, 50), and what is presumably the quarter-*raṭl* by Casanova (1893, 18).

Al-Muhājir's stamp is found in the usual way as a counterstamp on heavy weights such as the present piece and the next one, and as a separate vessel stamp (Casanova 1893, 192; Miles 1958a, 179; Launois 1960, II, 16; Balog 1976, 548). On Balog 1976, 549 al-Muhājir's stamp survives paired with a stamp for a *mikyala* of skinned vetch (*julubbān muqashshar*); the latter is from the die of No. 486 below and would seem to belong to the group of similar commodity stamps with the *kāf* in *mikyala* elongated which were in use at this period (see Introduction, p. 38).

A single specimen of another counterstamp has been published which reveals the name of al-Muhājir's father, Khālid (Balog 1973, 29). Although Balog had difficulty with the first name, the legend plainly reads: *ʻalā yaday/al-Muhājir/b. Khalid*. The script of this piece is similar to that of the stamps of the earlier Abbasid period, making it unlikely that a second person of the same name is referred to.

307 Ring weight: *raṭl*, with al-Muhājir

Main stamp

بسم الله ام[ر]
الامير محمد
بن سليمن اكرمه
الله رطل واف

In the name of God. Ordered
the Amir Muḥammad
b. Sulayman, may God show him
bounty, a *raṭl*, full-weight

Counterstamp Same die as counterstamp of No. 306.

OA + 4364. Fragment. The right end of the top. Green. Length 5.4cm; small stamp 1.7cm; 108.5g. (*Plate 14*)

From the same dies Petrie, 240-1; Scanlon 1966, 102. Cf. Casanova 1893, 57.

The large stamp has also been found with the counterstamp of a different executive, Abū Bakr b. Tamīm (Miles 1948, 97).

308 Quarter-*qisṭ*

بسم الله امر
الامير محمد بن
سليمن اكرمه
الله ربع قسط
واف

In the name of God. Ordered
the Amir Muḥammad b.
Sulayman, may God show him
bounty, a quarter-*qisṭ*
full-measure.

Six-pointed star below.

OA + 4098. Chipped at bottom right. Olive green. Width 4.1cm. (*Plate 14*)

From the same die Balog 1976, 546-7.

Several pieces are known from the corresponding half-*qisṭ* die (Launois 1957, 226; 1959 II, 8; Balog 1976, 545. Cf. Launois 1957, 225, 227).

'ĪSA B. LUQMĀN
Governor and Finance Director 161-2/778-9

309 Ring weight: *raṭl*, with 'Imrān b. 'Utba

Main stamp

بسم الله امر
الامير عيسى بن
[لق]مان اصلحه
[الله] رطل و
[ا]ف

In the name of God. Ordered
the Amir 'Īsā b.
Luqmān, may God keep him
righteous, a *raṭl*, full-
weight.

Counterstamp

على يدى
عمران
بن عتبة

At the hands
of 'Imrān
b. 'Utba

OA + 4399. Largely intact but chipped on the top and with large chips off two of the bottom corners. Green. 7.7 x 7.3cm; 390g. (*Plate 14*)

The large stamp does not appear to have been published before. The counterstamp is known from specimens of 'Īsā b. Luqmān's *wuqiyya* (Miles 1971, 42; Balog 1976, 554. Cf. 555). The die was also used on vessel stamps (Balog 1976, 560-1. Cf. 559, 562-3).

A second counterstamp of 'Imrān with the same arrangement of the legend occurs with a defective quarter-*raṭl* stamp which Balog was almost certainly right to attribute to 'Īsā b. Luqmān (Balog 1976, 556 - probably from the same die as 553, which lacks a counterstamp).

WĀḌIḤ
Governor and Finance Director Jumādā II - Ramaḍān 162/March - June 779.

310 Ring weight: *raṭl*. with Bakr b. Abī Bakr

Main stamp

بسم الله
امر الامير واضح
مولى امير المؤ
منين رطل و
اف

In the name of God.
Ordered the Amir Wāḍiḥ,
Mawlā of the Commander of the Faithful, a *raṭl*, full-
weight.

Counterstamp

على يدى
بكر بن
ابى بكر

At the hands
of Bakr b.
Abī Bakr

OA + 4395. Intact except for considerable chipping of the top and a chip off one of the lower corners. Green. 7.0 x 7.5cm; 421g. (*Plate 15*)

From the same dies Balog 1973, 24-5.

The only other *raṭl*-system weights of Wāḍiḥ yet published are a sixth-*wuqiyya* (Balog 1976, 564) and several *wuqiyyas*, none of which has a counterstamp (Casanova 1893, 2,2 *bis*, 3; Rice, 172 - which is intact).

Bakr b. Abī Bakr is not known to have had any other stamps. The same die also served for vessel stamps in the usual fashion (see Nos 312-313). Balog (1973, 24) suggested Badr as a possible alternative to Bakr for the first name but since the second letter is connected to the following one it must be *kāf*, and the name be read Bakr.

311 Quarter-*qisṭ*

[ب]سم الل[ه]
[ا]مر الامير و[ا]
ضح مولى ام[ير]
[ال]مؤمنين ربع
قسط واف

In the name of God.
Ordered the Amir Wā-
ḍiḥ, Mawlā of the Commander
of the Faithful, a quarter-
qisṭ, full-measure.

OA + 4290. Olive green. Width 3.4cm. (*Plate 15*)

From the same die Miles 1958, 181.

The few other vessel stamps of Wāḍiḥ described in the literature lack legible denominations (Casanova 1893, 155-6). The legend of Miles 1948, 102, attributed to Wāḍiḥ, differs from his normal types; it may be from the die with the names of Ītākh and 'Īsā b. Manṣūr which is known from heavy weights (Petrie, 218, Balog 1976, 679).

BAKR B. ABĪ BAKR
Executive under Wāḍiḥ

312-313 Executive stamp

Same die as the counterstamp on 310.

OA + 4096. Olive green. Width 2.4cm. (*Plate 15*)
OA + 4097. Olive green. Width 2.7cm.

From the same die Balog 1976, 748.

In the cases of No. 313 and Balog's specimen the glass flan was too small to receive the complete impression of the die. The first line of the legend in particular is entirely missing. The most complete impressions of the die are those on the *raṭl* weights of Wāḍiḥ published by Balog (see No. 310). They show that Balog's restoration of the first name on his vessel stamp as [Abū] Bakr is incorrect.

YAḤYĀ B. DĀ'ŪD
Governor and Finance Director 162–4/779–80

314 *Fals* weight of 30 *kharrūba*

امر بطبعة
هذا المثقال
الامير يحيى بن دا
ود ثلث(ي)ن خر
وبة

Ordered the stamping
of this weight
the Amir Yaḥyā b. Dā
'ūd. Thirty *kharr-*
ūba.

Beaded border. Six-pointed star flanked by trios of dots below.

OA + 4256. Green. 3.3cm; stamp 2.5cm; 5.82g. (*Plate 15*)

From the same die Fahmī 1957, 246–7; Launois 1960 II, 7.

There is another die of this denomination with the same arrangement of the legend and the same ornamental features. Specimens from it are: Casanova 1893, 40–2; Launois 1957, 223–4; Fahmī 1957, 248–9.

On both dies a 'tooth' is missing before the final *nūn* of *thalathīn*. The last two letters of Yaḥyā are run together in an unusual way to resemble final *nūn* or *ra'*; Fahmī, in fact, read the name as Baḥr. Compare, however, the only slightly less summary form of the name on the *raṭl*-system weights of the same official such as those described below.

Balog (1976, 539) has assigned another *fals* denomination, of 20 *kharrūba*, to the same Yaḥyā. The name, if it is Yaḥyā, is again written curiously; the final *yā'* would normally be taken for a *lām*. Fahmī's reading of the name of Bujayl on another specimen is certainly understandable (Fahmī 1957, 263 = Launois 1957, 358). On this type the father's name, the title *al-amīr* and the other title *mawlā amīr al-mu'minīn* which is standard on Yaḥyā b. Dā'ūd's heavy weights and vessel stamps are not present, and if the name is Yaḥyā it probably does not refer to Yaḥyā b. Dā'ūd. The use of the word *mīzān*, 'weight', in the legend, rather than *mithqāl* points to an early date, probably in the Umayyad period.

315 Ring weight: *raṭl*

بسم الله امر
الامير يحيى مولى
امير المؤمنين
اكرمه الله ر
طل واف

In the name of God. Ordered
the Amir Yaḥyā, Mawlā
of the Commander of the Faithful,
may God show him bounty, a *r-*
aṭl, full-weight

OA + 4363. The right end of the top, with a trace of a counterstamp. Length 5.3cm; height of stamp 3.1cm; 68g. (*Plate 15*)

From the same die Balog 1976, 536–7.

Balog 1976, 536, is the latest intact piece yet known on the Umayyad *raṭl* system which was superseded shortly afterwards by the *raṭl-kabīr* system (see Introduction, p. 28). On it Yaḥyā's stamp is used alone, without a counterstamp. On the other hand on Petrie, 211, the same *raṭl* stamp of Yaḥyā is used with a counterstamp of an executive named ʻAbdūya. ʻAbdūya's die was also used on vessel stamps (Petrie, 233; Balog 1976, 652). His association with Yaḥyā on Petrie, 211, makes it impossible to accept, with Balog, that he is ʻAbdūya b. Jabala who was Prefect of the *shurṭa* in Egypt in 211 and Governor on behalf of the future Caliph al-Muʻtaṣim in 215/830–1 (Kindī, 183, 189–90).

ISMĀʻĪL B. IBRĀHĪM
Finance Director 164/780–1

316 Disk weight: *wuqiyya*, with Yaḥyā b. Saʻīd

Main stamp

بسم الل[ه ا]
مر الامير [اسمعيل]
بن ابرهيم [اكرمه]
الله و[قية و]
اف

In the name of God. Or-
dered the Amir Ismaʻīl
b. Ibrahīm, may God show him
bounty, a *wuqiyya*, full-
weight.

Counterstamp below Same die as No. 317.

OA + 4303. The right hand half. Only the lower edge of the counterstamp preserved. Dark green. Length 5.9cm; 20.20g. (*Plate 15*)

From the same two dies Balog 1976, 568.

The only other *raṭl*-system weight of Ismaʻīl b. Ibrāhīm appears to be the *raṭl* published by Balog (1976, 567), which has the same counterstamp. The first example of the use of the die of Yaḥyā b. Saʻīd's stamp on a vessel stamp is described next.

YAḤYĀ B. SAʻĪD
Executive under Ismāʻīl b. Ibrāhīm

317 Executive stamp

على يدى
يحيى بن سعيد

At the hands
of Yaḥyā b. Saʻīd.

Six-pointed star below.

OA + 4346. Green. Width 2.2cm. (*Plate 15*)

See No. 316 for the use of the same die on heavy weights.

IBRĀHĪM B. ṢĀLIḤ
Governor and Finance Director 165-7/781-4 and 176/792

According to the fifteenth-century chronicler Ibn Taghrībirdī (I, 472), Ibrāhīm b. Ṣāliḥ came to Egypt in 174/790 in charge of the finances (*'alā al-kharāj*) with the new Governor, Dā'ūd b. Yazīd al-Muhallabī. In Kindī's account (133-4), which Ibn Taghrībirdī certainly uses, directly or indirectly, Ibrahīm is said to have been sent to expel (*ikhrāj*) a group of Arab soldiery which had been rioting against the Finance Director, 'Umar b. Ghaylān. Presumably at some stage Kindī's words were misunderstood, *ikhrāj* being carelessly read *kharāj*.

318-319 *Fals* **weight of 36** ***kharrūba***

خاتم فلوس
الامير ابرهيم
بن صلح اصلحه الله
ست وثلثين خروبة

Stamp for *fulūs*.
The Amir Ibrahīm
b. Ṣāliḥ, may God keep him righteous.
Six and thirty *kharrūba*.

Pentagram below.

OA + 4251. Olive green. 3.4cm; 6.94g.
OA + 4252. Olive green. 3.3cm; 7.00g. (*Plate 15*)

From the same die Launois 1957, 230; Fahmī 1957, 210-1; Balog 1976, 576.

The use of the word *khātim*, 'seal' or 'stamp', is not found on any other type, though other forms from the same root do occur (see Introduction, p. 43). Compare also the unique occurence of the synonym *ṭābi'* on No. 408. As pointed out under No. 4, the use of the plural *fulūs* in the legends of *fals* weights is uncommon. Another detail of the legend worth noting is the benediction after Ibrāhīm's name. On all the other glass pieces where his name does have a benediction it is *akramahu allāh* ('may God be bountiful to him').

There are two specimens of a 30-*kharrūba fals* weight of Ibrāhīm b. Ṣāliḥ in the Islamic Museum, Cairo (Launois 1957, 231-2 = Fahmī 1957, 212-3). On this type 'Āṣim b. Ḥafṣ is named as executive.

320 Disk weight: half-great ***raṭl (raṭl kabīr)***, with 'Āṣim b. Ḥafṣ

Central stamp

نصف
رطل
كبير
واف

Half
raṭl
kabīr
full-weight.

Left-hand stamp

امر الا
مير ابر
هيم
بن صلح

Ordered the A-
mir Ibra-
hīm
b. Ṣaliḥ

Right-hand stamp

على يدى
عاصم
بن حفص

At the hands
of 'Āṣim
b. Ḥafṣ

OA + 4430. Brown. 11 x 8.9cm; height of large stamp 3.4cm; width of stamp to right 2.0cm; stamp to left 1.8 x 1.8cm; 249g. (*Plate 15*)

All three stamps are rectangular. The impressions of the two at the sides are very faint but the identity of the dies with those of more legible specimens is certain. The command stamp of Ibrāhīm b. Ṣālih is set at right angles to the others and reads, as it were, from bottom to top.

The denomination stamp has not been illustrated but may be the one on Casanova 1893, 23. (The description of this piece is unclear; it may have also born a command stamp of Ibrāhīm b. Ṣāliḥ and an executive stamp of Mūsā b. Sābiq.) Another half-*raṭl-kabīr* denomination stamp, also used by 'Āsim b. Ḥafṣ, is described below (No. 467).

Only three intact pieces on the *raṭl-kabīr* or great-*raṭl* system have been previously published. The present one, which is in perfect condition, is the first complete half-*raṭl*. The British Museum also possesses an almost complete *raṭl kabīr* (No. 325). The system, which was introduced in Ibrāhīm b. Ṣāliḥ's first governorship, has been disucssed in the Introduction (p. 28).

At the same time a new way of arranging the stamps on heavy weights came to be used. As on the present piece, an anonymous denomination stamp was used with separate individual stamps for the Finance Director and the executive. All three types could be used in a variety of combinations. The command stamp of Ibrāhīm b. Ṣāliḥ on the half-*raṭl*, for instance, is also found on the *raṭl* (see Nos 321-324) and quarter-*raṭl* (Petrie, 208; Balog 1976, 573. Cf. Casanova 1893, 22, with executive stamp of Mūsā b. Sābiq; Balog 1976, 574). It was also used for vessel stamps (Petrie, 209; Grohmann 1925, 2; Launois 1960 II, 9. Cf. Launois 1957, 229).

'Āṣim b. Ḥafṣ's executive stamps are discussed under No. 329.

321–322 Ring weight: great *raṭl*, with ʿĀṣim b. Ḥafṣ

Rectangular central stamp

(ر)طل
كبير
واف

Raṭl
kabīr,
full-weight.

To left Rectangular command stamp of Ibrāhīm b. Ṣāliḥ, from the same die as on No. 320.

To right Rectangular executive stamp of ʿĀṣim b. Ḥafṣ, from the same die as on No. 320.

OA + 4365. Top and part of side. Green. 5.8 x 5.2cm; height of central stamp 2.0cm; height of executive stamp 1.9cm; 190g.
OA + 4418. Top and part of both sides. Green. Width 6.0cm; height of central stamp 2.0cm; height of command stamp 1.9cm; height of executive stamp 1.8cm; 296g. (*Plate 16*)

From the same three dies Miles 1963 II, 33; Balog 1976, 572, both of which are intact.

Numerous examples of the denomination stamp are known, showing that it was used under a long series of Finance Directors. Although in many cases the impression is distorted by the application of other stamps at each side the die can easily be recognized by the miswriting of the first letter of *raṭl* as *wāw*. The other published examples, on some of which only two stamps survive, are as follows:

1. With Ibrāhīm b. Ṣāliḥ's command stamp; No. 323, with Mūsā b. Sābiq; Miles 1963 II, 34, with Yazīd b. Ziyād. Cf. Casanova 1893, 44, lacking executive stamp.
2. With the command stamp of ʿAlī b. Sulaymān, Governor and Finance Director 169–171/786–7: Balog 1976, 582, and, probably, Miles 1958a, 188, both with Muʿāwiya b. Zufar.
3. With ʿUmar b. Ghaylān's command stamp: No. 339, with Hilāl b. al-Ḥusayn.
4. With Mūsā b. ʿĪsā's command stamp: Balog 1976, 588, with an executive who bears the title Mawlā al-Amīr and whose name may be Hāshim. Mūsā b. ʿĪsā was Governor of Egypt three times, in 171–2/787–9, 175–6/791–2 and 179/795, but Kindī does not say he had powers over finance except on the second occasion (Kindī, 132, 134, 137; Grohmann 1924, 129–32).
5. With unidentified command stamp: No. 330, with ʿĀṣim b. Ḥafṣ.
6. Lacking command stamp: Miles 1971, 51, with ʿĀṣim b. Ḥafṣ; Petrie, 216, with Hāshim (?). Cf. Casanova 1893, 58–9, with Hāshim (?).

Nos 325–6 are examples of another type of *raṭl* issued by Ibrāhīm b. Ṣāliḥ, seemingly also on the *raṭl-kabīr* standard. The single stamp gives the denomination as well as the names of the Finance Director and the executive, Ṣāliḥ b. Muslim (see pp. 28–30). Ṣāliḥ had a long career but his earliest other association is with Mūsā b. ʿĪsā who, as mentioned above, first acted as Governor in 171–172/787–9 but appears not to have had control of finances before his second governorship in 175–176/791–792. This makes it very probably that the *raṭls* with Ṣāliḥ b. Muslim belong to Ibrāhīm's second, and rather brief, governorship in 176/792. The precise script of the stamp would also suit the later date better. The more common types with separate denomination, command and executive stamps must mostly and probably entirely be issues of his first period of office in 165–167/781–784. That ʿĀṣim b. Ḥafṣ served under Ibrāhīm during the first governorship is attested by the appearance of both names on a reverse used on coin weights of the Caliph al-Mahdī, who died in 169/785 (see Balog 1976, 520–1). It follows therefore that the *raṭl-kabīr* standard was introduced during the first governorship.

A third type of *raṭl* of Ibrāhīm b. Ṣāliḥ is represented by a ring weight in the University College Collection (Petrie, 207). The denomination and Governor's name are on one stamp which is accompanied by an otherwise unknown executive stamp of ʿUbaydallāh or ʿAbdallāh b. ʿIrbāḍ (?), possibly the same as the ʿAbdallāh b. ʿIrbāḍ who was active much later under Maḥfūẓ b. Sulaymān (see No. 343). In spite of this possible later association of the executive the bold script favours an early date and it is likely that the type is an issue of the early part of Ibrāhīm's first governorship, from before the introduction of the *raṭl-kabīr* standard.

323 Ring weight: great *raṭl*, with Mūsā b. Sābiq

Central denomination stamp As on Nos 321–2.

Command stamp to left As on Nos 320–2.

Executive stamp to right

على يدى
موسى
بن سابق

At the hands
of Mūsā
b. Sābiq

OA + 4368. Jagged fragment; most of the top and part of the left side. Bottom of command stamp and top left of executive stamp broken off. Length of top c. 6.7cm; 107g. (*Plate 16*)

The executive stamp of Mūsā is otherwise known from two impressions on a *wuqiyya kabīr* published by Balog (1976, 607). The British Museum's *raṭl* is the first piece on which Mūsā is associated with a Finance Director. The only other type of stamp on which his name has been found is an executive stamp on which his name is followed by that of Ṣāliḥ b. Muslim (Miles 1958a, 183–4; Balog 1976, 605, from the same die. Cf. Miles 1958a, 185; Balog 1976, 604, 606).

It has been suggested under Nos 321–322 that the command stamp and denomination stamps common to those pieces and that under discussion here were introduced in Ibrāhīm b. Ṣāliḥ's first governorship and the *raṭl* with Mūsā's counterstamp is probably best assigned to that period, in spite of the fact that the denomination stamp is known to have remained is use almost up to Ibrāhīm's return to Egypt in 176 and in spite of Mūsā's association on the dual executive stamps with Ṣāliḥ b. Muslim, the body of whose career is later. Otherwise it is difficult to see how Ibrāhīm's command stamp would have survived the interval between his periods of office.

324 Ring weight: probably a great *raṭl*

OA + 4367. The left side, bearing at the top the left half of a command stamp of Ibrāhīm b. Ṣāliḥ, from the same die as on Nos 320–322. Olive green. Length 7.4cm; c. 180g.

325–326 Ring weight: great (?) *raṭl*, with Ṣāliḥ b. Muslim

مما امر به الامير
ابرهيم بن صلح ا
كرمه الله رطل ال[--]
على يدى صلـ[ـح بن]
مسلـ[ـم]

Of what ordered the Amir
Ibrāhīm b. Ṣaliḥ, may
God be bounteous to him, a *raṭl*, great,
at the hands of Ṣaliḥ b.
Muslim.

OA + 4397. Two pieces glued together. Chip of 5–10g off right side. Surface covered with silver iridescence. Otherwise intact. Four marks of a pointed tool round stamp at the quarters. Stamp faint. Brown. 7.9 x 7.9cm; 508g.
78 3–11 38. Lane-Poole, 25G. Fragment. Top and part of the sides. Stamp chipped away at bottom and left. Marks of pointed tool at top and right. Width 6.7cm; 210g. (*Plate 16*)

The one difficulty in the legend is the word after *raṭl*. No. 325 is illegible at the point and No. 326 only preserves the first two letters, which seem to be the definite article. Since the *raṭl-kabīr* system was the main one in use in the period of Ibrāhīm b. Ṣāliḥ the restoration *al-kabīr* is tentatively suggested, although the grammatical mistake of using a definite adjective with an indefinite noun, very common on the earliest stamps, does seem unusual by the last quarter of the eighth century AD. Another difficulty is that No. 325, even when slightly damaged, is heavier than might be expected at 508g. Other intact pieces on the *raṭl-kabīr* system indicate a standard of 490–500g. (see Introduction, p. 28).

As has been pointed out under Nos 321–322, Ṣāliḥ b. Muslim's association with Ibrāhīm b. Ṣāliḥ is probably to be placed in the latter's second governorship in 176/792.

ʻĀṢIM B. ḤAFṢ

Executive under Ibrāhīm b. Ṣāliḥ, Mūsā b. al-Muṣʻab (Governor and Finance Director 167–8/784–5), al-Faḍl b. Ṣāliḥ and ʻAbdallāh b. Muḥammad (Governor 189–90/805–6)

Miles (1948, p. 107) assigns to ʻĀṣim b. Ḥafṣ a first period of activity as executive some time during the two governorships of ʻAbd al-Malik b. Yazīd (133–41/751–8), which has been accepted without discussion by most scholars since. As he pointed out, an ʻĀṣim b. Ḥafṣ al-Tamīmī is twice mentioned by Ṭabarī (II, 1879, 1976) as the final link in a chain of narrators for events of 127 and 129, but the seemingly decisive evidence was his reading of the name on the reverse of two pieces of ʻAbd al Malik b. Yazīd in the American Numismatic Society collection (Miles 1948, 62–3). Later a third reverse was interpreted in the same way and, unlike the others, illustrated (Miles 1958, 101). In fact the die is the well-known one of Muḥammad b. Shuraḥbil and Chael with the legend in reverse (see Nos 171–176) and Mr Lowick, after examining all three pieces at the American Numismatic Society, confirms that they are from one reverse die. This phase of ʻĀṣim b. Ḥafṣ's career, then, can be dismissed as an illusion.

There is still a surprisingly long gap between his first real period of activity between 164 and 169 and his reappearance under ʻAbdallāh b. Muḥammad twenty years later. This last association is attested by a single *dīnār* weight (Launois 1957, 243 = Fahmī 1957, 120) but there is good reason to accept it at face value rather than try, for example, to argue that the Amir ʻAbdallāh b. Muḥammad who appears on the *dīnār* weight, and so far nowhere else, is some other person with the same very common names. On the *dīnār* weight ʻĀṣim's name appears on the centre of the obverse after *ʻalā yaday* while the reverse has a second executive formula followed by a name which is almost certainly ʻAbdallāh b. ʻIrbāḍ. In any case this reverse is linked with a third-*dīnār* obverse on which ʻAbdallāh b. ʻIrbāḍ's name is absolutely clear (Balog 1976, 629). ʻAbdallāh b. ʻIrbāḍ's only other known association is with Maḥfūẓ b. Sulaymān who was Finance Director with Aḥmad b. Ismāʻīl, ʻAbdallāh b. Muḥammad's immediate predecessor as Governor (See Balog 1976, 627).

327 Half-*dīnār* weight

Obverse

بسم الله
مثقال نصف
دينر واف

In the name of God.
Weight of half
a *dīnar*, full-weight.

Six-pointed star below.

Reverse
Marginal legend within border:

على يدى عاصم بن

At the hands of ʻĀṣim b.

Centre:

حفص

Ḥafṣ

Six-pointed star below central legend.

(Coins and Medals) 82 8-3 33. Lane-Poole, 27. Pale bluish green. 2.2cm; stamp 1.7cm; 2.12g. (*Plate 16*)

The obverse die appears not to have been published. The reverse however occurs in other contexts. It is the only reverse so far found with the *dīnār*-weight obverse of al-Faḍl b. Ṣāliḥ described below (No. 338), and it has also been recorded with a second anonymous half-*dīnār* obverse (Fahmī 1957, 121). This obverse die itself is found in combination with a reverse of ʿAbd al-Raḥmān b. Maysara (Balog 1976, 565) which in turn is linked with a *dīnār*-weight obverse of ʿAli b. Sulaymān (Balog 1976, 584. Cf. Launois II, 10).

There is a second obverse of ʿĀṣim b. Ḥafṣ which has 'ibn Ḥafṣ' in the centre with a pentagram flanked by groups of three dots below. It is found on *dīnār*-system weights of Mūsā b. al-Muṣʿab (Launois 1957, 233 = Fahmī 1957, 214; Balog 1976, 579-80).

328 *Fals* weight of 36 *kharrūba*

Marginal legend

على يدى عاصم بن حفص

At the hands of ʿĀṣim b. Ḥafṣ

Centre

مثقا

ل فلس

Weigh-
t of a *fals*.
36.

OA + 4253. Green. 3.1cm; stamp 2.3cm; 6.97g. (*Plate 16*)

From the same die Casanova 1893, 53; Miles 1948, 68; Launois 1957, 237; Fahmī 1957, 122-3; Balog 1976, 343-4. Cf. Launois 1957, 238-9; Fahmī 1957, 124-6; Miles 1958a, 106; Balog 1976, 345-6.

The figure is written in Coptic numerals. The Islamic Museum in Cairo possesses a single specimen of another type of 36 *kharrūba* with a different legend (Fahmī 1957, 127). The denomination is again written in Coptic figures. On ʿĀṣim's third known type of *fals* weight the denomination, which is 30 *kharrūba*, is written out in Arabic (Miles 1958a, 107; Balog 1976, 347. Cf. Miles 1963 II, 19).

329 Disk weight: *wuqiyya kabīr*

Executive stamp From the same die as on Nos 320-322.

Denomination stamp

[و]قية

[كبير]

[واف]

Wuqiyya,
great,
full-weight.

OA + 4304. Fragment. The end of an oval weight. Green. Length 3.7cm; 9.0g. (*Plate 16*)

Among the considerable number of ʿĀsim b. Ḥafs's executive stamps which have been published, a single vessel stamp is from a variant die although with the same arrangement of the legend (Balog 1976, 348a). Occurences of his executive stamp on larger weights have been noted under Nos 320-322. The common die was also used on vessel stamps (Miles 1963 II, 20; Balog 1976, 348b. Cf. Casanova 1893, 188-9).

A number of *wuqiyyas*, similar presumably to that from which the British Museum's fragment came, have been described (Miles 1963 I, 30; Balog 1976, 342. Cf. Miles 1963 II, 31 (?); Balog 1976, 339-41). All are roughly oval and would originally have had three stamps, though in no case does more than the edge of the third stamp survive. (Michael Bates has confirmed that none of the specimens in the Balog collection preserves legible traces on the third stamp). Balog was probably right to suggest that on such pieces ʿĀṣim b. Ḥafṣ's stamp was used twice, above and below the denomination stamp. *Wuqiyyas* with such an arrangement are known for two executives nearly contemporary with ʿĀṣim, Mūsā b. Sābiq (Balog 1976, 607) and ʿAbd al-Raḥmān b. Maysara (Miles 1948, 116). All these pieces have a rectangular denomination stamp similar to that of which the edge survives on the British Museum's fragment. None of the illustrated examples is complete or very clear but the probability is that they are all from the same die and that, like the corresponding stamps for the larger denominations, the one for the *wuqiyya* was in use under a series of officials.

330 Ring weight: great *raṭl*

Central denomination stamp From the same die as Nos 321-324, 339

Executive stamp to left From the same dies as on Nos 320-322, 329

Command stamp to right Almost completely defaced.

OA + 4366. Fragment of the top. Green. Length 5.8cm; height of denomination stamp 2.2cm; height of executive stamp 1.8cm; 76g. (*Plate 16*)

Only the bottom left-hand corner of the right-hand stamp survives. The last word appears to be *allāh*, which recalls the benediction, *akramahu allāh* at the end of the legend of the command stamp of ʿAlī b. Sulaymān, who was Governor and Finance Director, 169-71/786-7 (Balog 1976, 582-3). The die, however, is different.

ṢĀLIḤ B. MUSLIM

Executive under Ibrāhīm b. Ṣāliḥ, Mūsā b. ʿIsā, Ḥuwayy b. Ḥuwayy, Isḥāq b. Sulaymān, (Governor and Finance Director 177-8/793-4) al-Layth b. al-Faḍl, Maḥfūẓ b. Sulaymān and possibly ʿUmar b. Ghaylān (Balog 1976, 607)

It seems likely that Ṣāliḥ b. Muslim was associated with Ibrāhīm b. Ṣāliḥ during the latter's second governorship rather than his first and that he was active between approximately the years 170 and 190 of the Hijra. There is the possibility that he is the Ṣāliḥ whose name appears on copper coins of Maḥfūẓ b. Sulaymān (e.g. Fahmī 1965, 2868-2874).

331 **Third-*dīnār* weight**

Obverse

بسم الله
مثقال ثلث
دينر واف

In the name of God.
Weight of a third-
dīnar, full-weight.

Six-pointed star below.

Reverse
Marginal legend within a circle of dots:

ع[لى يد]ى

At the hands

Centre:

صا[ح بن]
مسـ[لم]

of Ṣaliḥ b.
Muslim.

OA + 4326. Pale green. 1.9cm; stamp 1.4cm; 1.27g. (*Plate 16*)

The obverse die is that of Balog 1976, 597, the reverse legend of which is described as being in three lines in a circle of small dots. One wonders whether it is not, in fact, similar to that of the British Museum's pieces, with *'alā yaday* written in elongated form in a circle. Ṣāliḥ b. Muslim's reverse dies are nearly all weakly carved and the impressions are often faint to the point of illegibility. Sometimes, as in the case of Lane-Poole's description of the British Museum's No. 332, the impression of the reverse inscription is completely overlooked. During his long career Ṣāliḥ undoubtedly used several reverse types, but from the available material it is not easy to sort out the dies.

In the present case, for instance, two *dīnār* weights of Ḥuwayy b. Ḥuwayy (Launois 1957, 23b *bis*, *ter* = Fahmī 1957, 220-1) and one of Mūsā b. 'Īsā (Balog 1976, 590) have reverses with a similar arrangement of the legend and the border of dots, but it seems impossible to establish the identity of any one of the impressions with any other.

332 **Half-*dīnār* weight**

Obverse
Marginal legend between two circles:

بسم الله مثقال نصف دينر

In the name of God. Weight of a half *dīnar*.

Eight pointed star in centre, surrounded by eight dots.

Reverse

على يدى
صلح
بن (م)سـ(لـ)م

At the hands
of Ṣaliḥ
b. Muslim.

(Coins and Medals) 81 7-6 63. Lane-Poole, 53. Pale green. 2.0cm; stamp 1.8cm; 2.12g. (*Plate 16*)

From the same pair of dies Balog 1976, 595a.

On this reverse Ṣāliḥ's father's name can be fairly clearly seen on some specimens to be written *sīn, mīm* but this does not seem likely to be anything other than a mispelling for Muslim. The obverse die is well attested but on the only other specimen of which both sides are illustrated (Balog 1976, 595b) the reverse appears to be from a different, and obscure, die. Casanova 1893, 9 (pl. I, see below), is not said to have a reverse legend but it may have been overlooked as it was in the case of the British Museum's piece in Lane-Poole's original publication. Rogers 1873, 39, appears to have had the same spelling of Ṣāliḥ's father's name. Miles 1963 II, 53, is said to have traces of a reverse.

A second very similar obverse die is known from a single specimen (Casanova 1893, 9, Plate II: another illustration No. 9 is given on Plate I, of a piece from the more common die, though only one description appears in the text).

The reverse has also been found on a third-*dīnār* obverse die with circular legend and central star which must have belonged to the same series (Balog 1976, 596a-b. Cf. Miles 1948, 95, from the same obverse die, and 96). As with the half-*dīnār* denomination a second similar obverse is known from one specimen (Balog 1976, 645). Its reverse, however, is of 'Abdallāh b. 'Uthmān.

333 ***Fals* weight of 14 *kharrūba***

Marginal legend arranged in a square

على يدى
صـ[لح] بن
مسلم
مثقال فلس

At the hands
of Ṣaliḥ b.
Muslim.
Weight of a fals

Central legend

اربعة
عشر
خروبة

of four-
teen
kharrūba.

(Coins and Medals) 1972 6-11 18. Surface badly decayed. Green. 2.5cm; rectangular stamp 1.8 x 1.8cm; 2.63g. (*Plate 16*)

Balog 1976, 598 has the same legends arranged in the same way but is from a different die. Miles 1964a, 49, is also described as having the same legends. Ṣāliḥ's other *fals* weights are for even smaller denominations, 12, 11 and 10 *kharrūba* (Launois 1957, 240-2; Fahmī 1957, 226-8; Balog 1976, 599). His are probably the last known *fals* weights in the Abbasid series of stamps.

334 **Fragment of a disk weight: probably a *wuqiyya***

على يدى
صلح
بن (م)سلم

At the hands
of Ṣaliḥ
b. Muslim.

(Coins and Medals) Or. 3711. Two impressions of the same die, that on the left largely broken off. Green. Length 2.9cm; stamp 1.8cm; 6.65g. (*Plate 16*)

The executive's father's name is very clearly written *sīn*, *lām*, *mīm*, giving Salm or possibly, by *scriptio defectiva*, Sālim. However the neat script is similar to that of stamps of Ṣāliḥ b. Muslim where the father's name is written correctly and, as in the case of a *fals*-weight of 20 *kharrūba* (Miles 1971, 46) and of the coin-weight reverse (No. 332) which have similar forms of the father's name, it seems more likely that the initial *mīm* of Muslim has been omitted by mistake than that there were two nearly contemporary officials with such similar names. Though there certainly is a Hāshim b. Sālim of about the same period (see No. 340).

Several executive stamps of Ṣāliḥ b. Muslim have been published. A vessel stamp, on which Casanova (1893, 193) read the name 'Ṣāliḥ b. Salama', may resemble the British Museum's fragment. Three different stamps have the father's name spelt correctly but legends similarly arranged to those of the British Museum's piece. One has been recorded on vessel stamps, such as No. 335 (Cf. also Miles 1963 II, 36). The others have been found on disk weights (Petrie, 250; Miles 1971, 43; Balog 1976, 593, 608). A type with *ibn* on the second rather than the third line is known on a vessel stamp (Balog 1976, 601). A minute vessel stamp with the legend 'Ṣāliḥ' has been published by Balog (1976, 602) whose attribution to Ṣāliḥ b. Muslim is probably correct, and his name may occur, as Balog suggests, on a counterstamp occurring on two *wuqiyyas* and a *raṭl* of Isḥāq b. Sulaymān, Governor and Finance Director 177-8/793-4 (Casanova 1893, 1; Balog 1976, 617, 619).

335 **Pair of vessel stamps: *wuqiyya* of fat (*duhn*)**

Executive stamp to right

[عل]ى ي[دى]
صل[ح]
بن مسل[م]

At the hands
of Ṣaliḥ
b. Muslim

Denomination stamp to left

وقية
ده[ن]

Wuqiyya
of fat.

OA + 4138. Green. Overall width 2.5cm. (*Plate 16*

From the same two dies Balog 1976, 603.

The two stamps are together on part of the rim of a vessel of approximately 2.0cm in diameter, but it is not evident how the body of the vessel was shaped. The glass flans are very small and only received the impression of part of the dies. The die of the commodity stamp appears on its own on Balog 1973, 34.

Ṣāliḥ b. Muslim is the last official known to have issued vessel stamps for commodities. Besides the present type with separate executive and commodity stamps, there is a single published specimen of a stamp on which his name appears together with what appears to be a designation for a commodity though its interpretation is uncertain (Balog 1976, 600). The great majority of anonymous commodity stamps must certainly be placed earlier than Ṣāliḥ b. Muslim on account of their script and it appears likely that the use of commodity stamps, which may have been very limited for a while, was given up for good at about this time. As has been mentioned above, he is also the last Abbasid official known to have issued *fals* weights. So it would appear that the system of glass stamps was considerably simplified towards the end of the second century of the Hijra, though there may have been some re-elaboration under the Tulunids (see Fahmī 1958). The last Abbasid *dīnār* weights are also from the last decade of the second century (see Miles 1964b).

YAḤYĀ B. JA'FAR

Amir, associated with Ṣāliḥ b. Muslim, but otherwise unknown

336 **Half-*dīnar* weight,** with Ṣāliḥ b. Muslim

Obverse

Marginal legend:

مما امر به الامير يحيى بن جعفر مثقل نصف واف

Of what ordered the Amir Yaḥyā b. Ja'far, weight of a half, full-weight.

Centre:

على يدى
صلح بن
مسلم

At the hands
of Ṣaliḥ b.
Muslim

Reverse

Outer marginal legend:

[--] بن مسلم [--]

... b. Muslim ...

Obscure inner marginal legend. Central hexagram.

93 11-11 15. Pale greenish yellow. 2.2cm; stamp 1.6cm; 2.08g. (*Plate 16*)

This is the first piece of Yaḥyā b. Ja'far to appear and no official of that name is mentioned in the relevant historical sources. Evidently he was Ṣāliḥ b. Muslim's superior and therefore it is not improbable that he was Finance Director at some time. No other example of the reverse die, which is likely to have repeated the executive formula of the obverse, has been recognized.

ḤUWAYY B. ḤUWAYY
Probably Finance Director, associated with Ṣāliḥ b. Muslim

337 **Half-*dīnār* weight**

مما امر بـ[ه]
الامير حو
ى بن حوى مثـ[قا]
ل نصف
واف

Of what ordered
the Amir Ḥuw-
ayy b. Ḥuwayy a weigh-
t of a half,
full weight.

OA + 4196. Green. 2.2cm; 2.14g. (*Plate 16*)

The other known coin weights of Ḥuwayy are all *dīnārs* and mostly have reverses with Ṣāliḥ b. Muslim as executive. There are no less than three different obverse dies of the *dīnār* denomination (1 : Launois 1957, 236 bis = Fahmī 1957, 221. Cf. Launois 1957, 236 *ter* = Fahmī 1957, 222; Miles 1964, 51. 2: Petrie, 139. 3: Fahmī 1957, 220). Balog (1976, 611-2) has published a *wuqiyya* of Ḥuwayy, on which Ṣāliḥ b. Muslim's name also occurs, and also a possible *raṭl*.

AL-FAḌL B. ṢĀLIḤ
Governor and Finance Director 168-9/785-6

338 ***Dīnār* weight,** with ʿĀṣim b. Ḥafṣ

Obverse

مما امر به الا
مير الفضل بن
صلح اكرمه الله
مثقال دينر واف

Of what ordered the A-
mir al-Faḍl b.
Ṣaliḥ, may God show him bounty.
Weight of a *dīnar*, full-weight.

Six-pointed star below.

Reverse From the same die as No. 327.

(Coins and Medals) 77 6-7 1. Lane-Poole, 26. Greenish brown. 2.9cm; stamp 2.2cm; 4.24g. (*Plate 16*)

From the same pair of dies Petrie, 206. Cf. Miles 1963 II, 35, with obverse from the same die, and reverse not illustrated.

The only other published stamp of al-Faḍl is a command stamp on a fragment of a disk weight (Balog 1976, 581).

ʿUMAR B. GHAYLĀN
Finance Director in 173/789

Reference to ʿUmar b. Ghaylān in the Arabic chronicles all go back to al-Kindī's account of how the Qudaydiyya, one of the divisions of the Arab army, raised a riot against him over their donatives (Kindī, 133). There he is described as *ṣāḥib al-kharāj*, Finance Director. However a few lines earlier it is stated that Muḥammad b. Zuhayr al-Azdī, the Governor with whom he served, had control of both 'prayer' and taxes. If this is correct ʿUmar b. Ghaylān would have been acting as Finance Director on behalf of the Governor, a situation which seems to be abnormal for the period.

Kindī does not mention that ʿUmar b. Ghaylān left Egypt after the *émeute*, though Muḥammad b. Zuhayr, who had governed for only a few months, did so. The next governor Da'ūd b. Yazīd, is only said to have been in charge of 'prayer'. He was accompanied by Ibrahīm b. Ṣāliḥ, who had been sent to put down the mutineers but whom, as has already been pointed out (p. 115), there is no reason to consider as having power over finances at that time. Thus it is possible that ʿUmar b. Ghaylān continued to act as Finance Director under Da'ūd b. Yazīd.

339 **Ring weight: great *raṭl*,** with Hilāl b. al-Ḥusayn

Central denomination stamp From the same die as on Nos 321-323, 330.

Command stamp to left

مما امر به
[ع]مر بن غيلان
[ا]كرمه الله

Of what ordered
ʿUmar b. Ghaylān,
may God show him bounty.

Executive stamp to right

على يدى
هلال بن
الحسين

At the hands
of Hilāl
b. al-Ḥusayn.

OA + 4398. Fragment. The top. Green. Length 7.2cm; height of command stamp 1.9cm; denomination stamp 2.0cm; executive stamp 1.9cm. 270g. (*Plate 17*)

This is the first known heavy weight which definitely belongs to ʿUmar b. Ghaylān, though Balog (1976, 608) has published a quarter-*raṭl kabīr* with an executive stamp of Ṣāliḥ b. Muslim which may be his.

The stamp of Hilāl b. al-Ḥusayn is the same as that on a vessel stamp also published by Balog (1976, 610), and may be that on a fragment of a disk weight described by Miles (1948, 125).

Hilāl b. al-Ḥusayn also appears on the reverse of ʿUmar b. Ghaylān's only published coin weight which is a *dīnār* weight (Fahmī 1957, 229). This reverse was also combined with anonymous obverses for the half and third denominations, which must belong to the same period (third: Miles 1948, 127; Balog 1976, 609; half: Miles 1958a, 209). The same third-*dīnār* obverse, in turn, is also found with a reverse of the two executives Hāshim b. Sālim and Nāṣiḥ (see Nos 340) and with a second one of an executive whose name Launois read as Jubayr b. ʿAbd al-Raḥmān (Launois 1960 I, 14). On the latter type the centre of the reverse is occupied by four isolated letters (*MḤAH* ?). Launois suggested that the letters might represent the name of the Caliph al-Mahdī but, apart from the difficulty of reading them so, the other associations of the obverse suggest that the reverse also must belong rather later than al-Mahdī's death in 169/785.

ʻUBAYDALLĀH B. AL-MAHDĪ
Governor and Finance Director 179/795

After a short interval ʻUbaydallāh was reappointed Governor of Egypt in 180/796, but is only said to have had control of 'prayer' (Kindī, 137-8).

340 ***Dīnār* weight,** with Ṣāliḥ b. Muslim and Hāshim b. Sālim

Obverse
Marginal legend:

مما امر به الامير عبيد الله بن المهدى اكرمه الله مثقال

Of what ordered the Amir
ʻUbaydallah b. al-Mahdī, may
God show him bounty. Weight

Centre:

دينر واف
على يدى
صلح بن مسلم

of a *dīnar*, full-weight,
at the hands
of Ṣaliḥ b. Muslim

Reverse
Marginal legend:

على يدى هاشم بن سلم

At the hands of Hāshim b. Salim

Outer border on reverse. Inner dotted border. Six-pointed star in circle in centre.

OA + 4197. Pale green. 3.1cm; stamp 2.5cm; 4.22g. (*Plate 17*)

No coin weight of ʻUbaydallāh appears to have been published; in fact the only reference to any kind of glass stamp of his seems to be Miles's listing (1964b, p. 81) of a disk weight of unspecified denomination.

On this reverse the name of Hāshim's father Sālim is written without the *alif* but on the other one which is mentioned below it is written in full. In the usual way for the time the executive's reverse is also combined with anonymous obverses for the half and third denominations (Balog 1976, 613-4). The obverse of the half-*dīnār* type also occurs with a different reverse die on which Hāshim is joined by a second executive, Nāṣiḥ (Miles 1958a, 180; Balog 1976, 615). The reverse with the two executives is found again with a different anonymous third-*dīnār* obverse which itself leads to further die links which have been noted under No. 339. Finally the same reverse was used with two different *dīnār*-weight obverses of Mūsā b. ʻĪsā (Launois 1957, 234 = Fahmī 1957, 216; Fahmī 1957, 217).

AL-LAYTH B. AL-FAḌL
Governor and Finance Director 182-7/798-802

341 **Disk weight: half a great *raṭl*,** with Ḥassān b. ʻAbd alʻAzīz

Command stamp

[امر الامير]
[الليث مولى]
امـ[ـير المؤ]
[منين]

Ordered the Amir
al-Layth, Mawlā
of the Commander of the Faithful.

Long rectangular denomination stamp

بسم الله لا ا[له الا الله]
وحده لا شري[ك له]
نصف رطل كبير [واف]

In the name of God. There is no God but God
alone, who has no partner.
Half *raṭl kabīr*, full-weight.

Below the legend: iota, omega.

Executive stamp

على يدى
حسان بن
عبد العز
يز

At the hands
of Ḥassān b.
ʻAbd al-ʻAz-
īz

Dot at each end of the last line.

OA + 4431. About two thirds, the bottom and right. At top right is part of the mark of a triangular point, almost piercing through. Length 10.0cm; height of denomination stamp 2.6cm; diameter of executive stamp 1.9cm; 165g. (*Plate 17*)

The most unusual long rectangular denomination stamp resembles that on Balog 1976, 622, and the two letters surviving of the third stamp on the British Museum's piece recall the intact command stamp of Balog's piece which is also a disk weight. The restoration proposed here seems justifiable for these reasons though in neither case can one feel certain of the identity of the die. The ring weight No. 342 has the same denomination and executive stamps as the present disk weight. The executive al-Ḥassān b. ʻAbd al-ʻAzīz was previously unknown. On his few other known pieces al-Layth is accompanied by other executives, Ṣāliḥ b. Muslim and ʻAbd alʻAzīz b. Ḥumayd (Balog 1976, 623-5).

ḤASSĀN B. ʻABD AL-ʻAZĪZ
Executive under al-Layth b. al-Faḍl

342 Ring weight: half a great *raṭl*

Denomination stamp Same die as on No. 341.

Executive stamp Same die as on No. 341.

OA + 4382. Fragment. The right side, with the edge of the top. Olive green. Length 7.2cm; executive stamp (distorted) 1.8 x 2.2cm; 154g. (*Plate 17*)

The form of the piece differs from No. 341, and Balog 1976, 622, in being a ring weight and not a disk weight. The unusually shaped elongated denomination stamp presumably took up the whole of the top, which is why the executive stamp is on the right side where the settling of the glass has caused the impression to become rather distorted. A few examples of similarly placed stamps are known, for example, Miles 1948, 117.

MAḤFŪẒ B. SULAYMĀN
Finance Director for a period beginning in 187/803

343 Ring weight: great *raṭl*, with Ibn al-Ḥajjāj

Rectangular left-hand stamp
Marginal legend arranged in a square:

[--]الامير
محفوظ
[بن سليمن]
[----]

- - - - -
the Amir
Maḥfūẓ
b. Sulaymān.

Central legend:

على يدى
[--] بن
الحجاج

At the hands
of - - b.
al-Ḥajjaj

Rectangular right-hand stamp Almost completely illegible. See commentary.

OA + 4409. Fragment, the top. Length 7.0cm; 195g. (*Plate 17*)

The piece is decayed and covered with iridescence, with the surface of the stamps in very poor condition, the right hand one preserving only a few faint traces of the legend. Such as the traces are, however, they are consistent with the stamp having been similar to the denomination stamp of Balog 1976, 626, which reads *bismillāh/ raṭl kabīr/ wāf* ('In the name of God/*raṭl kabīr*,/full-weight'). As on Balog's specimen the denomination stamp is set at right angles to the one with the officials' names.

The second stamp on the British Museum's *raṭl* is unpublished but is similar to impressions from another die of which two defective specimens survive, one on the *raṭl* in the Balog collection just referred to and one on a *wuqiyya* (Petrie, 205). Both show the lower part of the stamp and on Petrie's specimen the name of the executive's father, al-Ḥajjāj is clear. Traces of the end of his own name do survive on the British Museum's piece, possibly *alif, bā', rā'*, suggesting Jābir or some such name.

A third rather similar die of Maḥfūẓ, also with marginal and central legends, but naming a different executive, ʻAbdallāh b. ʻIrbāḍ, is known from a quarter-*raṭl* (Miles 1948, 98, attributed to Muḥammad b. Sulaymān) and a *wuqiyya* (Balog 1976, 627). ʻAbdallāh b. ʻIrbāḍ is also known from *dīnār* weights of Maḥfūẓ (Miles 1948, 128; Launois 1960 I, 15) and a third-*dīnār* weight of his own (Balog 1976, 629) and probably appears on the reverse of another *dīnār* weight of ʻAbdallāh b. Muḥammad and ʻAṣim b. Ḥafṣ (Launois 1957, 243 = Fahmī 1957, 120). Ibn al-Ḥajjāj's name, on the other hand, has yet to be found anywhere but on the *raṭl*-system weights above.

MĀLIK B. DALHAM
Governor and Finance Director 192-3/808

344 Disk weight: great *wuqiyya*, with ʻAbdallāh b. ʻUthmān

Executive stamp at top, nearly at right angles to the other stamps

على يدى
عبد الله
بن عثمن

At the hands
of ʻAbdallah
b. ʻUthman.

Cross or four-pointed star below.

Command stamp in centre

مما امر[به]
الامير مالك
بن دلهم ا
بقاه الله

Of what ordered
the Amir Mālik
b. Dalham, may
God preserve him.

Trefoil-like mark to left of third line. Marks resembling the Greek letters upsilon, omicron, lambda below.

Denomination stamp below

وقية
كبير
واف

Wuqiyya
kabīr,
full-weight.

Chevron at either side. Trefoil below.

OA + 4308. Substantially intact though the original surface has decayed and flaked away except in the centre where it remains, opaque and iridescent. Mark of a point, almost through the glass to left. 6.3 x 5.3cm; 44.6g. (*Plate 17*)

Raṭl-system weights of Mālik b. Dalham are uncommon,

the previously published corpus consisting of two broken *wuqiyyas* which only preserve the command and executive stamps. On Balog 1976, 636, the two stamps are from the dies used on the British Museum's piece but on Launois 1959, 31, they are different, though the executive stamp is also probably of ʻAbdallāh b. ʻUthmān.

As for ʻAbdallāh, the published executives' stamps are those just mentioned but he is named on a *raṭl-kabīr* stamp of al-Ḥasan b. al-Baḥbāḥ, Mālik b. Dalham's successor as Governor and Finance Director (Miles 1958a, 190) and also appears on a reverse die used with *dīnār* obverses of Mālik (Launois 1959, 30) and al-Ḥasan (Balog 1976, 643-4) as well as with an anonymous third-*dīnār* obverse (Balog 1976, 645). Balog's reading of the father's name as ʻĪsā instead of ʻUthmān is incorrect.

The denomination stamp of the British Museum's *wuqiyya* is discussed under No. 458. In spite of the surface decay the piece is of considerable metrological interest, being the first closely datable and almost intact piece which actually bears the denomination *wuqiyya kabīr*. Several anonymous ring weights marked *wuqiyya kabīr*, like Nos 460-463, have survived intact but they evidently belong to a different *raṭl* system and must be later. The weight of Mālik's *wuqiyya kabīr* is puzzling. It must have lost a few grammes and, if it is assumed conservatively that the original weight was 47.5g. and that the common ratio of 12 *wuqiyyas* to the *raṭl* obtained, a weight of 570g is reached for the *raṭl*. However the other datable pieces on the *kabīr* system all point to a *raṭl* of about 490-510g. All the other pieces in fact are from considerably before the time of Mālik and it may be that the standard of the *raṭl kabīr* had been changed in the interval. Other explanations are possible but further speculation does not seem worthwhile when the appearance of new material might make the solution obvious. The publication of the heavy weights in the great collection of the Islamic Museum in Cairo would no doubt settle many such questions.

For the appearance of what appear to be Greek letters on stamps compare the stamps of Muḥammad b. Saʻīd listed above (Nos 260-264).

ASHINĀS
Overlord of Egypt 219-30/834-44

345 Disk weight: half *wuqiyya*, with Muḥammad b. Basṭām and dated 226/837-8

مما امر به الامير ابو
جعفر اشناس مولى
امير المؤمنين اعزه
الله على يدى الامير
محمد بن بسطام -
-- مولى امير المؤ
منين سنة ست و عشر
ين و ماتين نصف وقية

Of what ordered the Amir Abū
Jaʻfar Ashinās, Mawlā
of the Commander of the Faithful, may God make him
glorious, at the hands of the Amir
Muḥammad b. Basṭām - -
- - , Mawlā of the Commander of the Faithful, in the year six and twen-
ty and two hundred. Half *wuqiyya*.

89 9-4 2. Lane-Poole, 27g. Green, with slight iridescence. Two diagonal marks on each side. 5.3cm; stamp 2.8 x 2.8cm; 33.96g. (*Plate 17*)

The reading of the digit of the date is not absolutely clear. Lane-Poole read *thalatha*, 'three', but *sitt*, 'six', seems much more likely.

This unique piece raises several problems: the explanation of its weight, the identity of Muḥammad b. Basṭām and the reading of what follows his name in the fifth and sixth lines. To deal with the metrological question first, a ring weight with similar legends (Miles 1948, 110) is evidently from the same set of dies though the digit of the date is missing. Miles classified the piece as a *raṭl*, but on his illustration the letter preceding *raṭl* is clearly *fā*, the end of *niṣf*, 'half'. There is also room in the damaged part of the stamp for the end of *mi'atayn*, needed to complete the legend. The British Museum's piece, which is in nearly perfect condition, implies a *wuqiyya* of approximately 68g and therefore a *ratl* of 816g. The weight of the A.N.S. half-*raṭl* is given as 398.53g. and since it is chipped it would originally have been not far off 408g. The weights of the two therefore fit together well, but they do not fit at all into any of the established *raṭl* systems, being a little over twice the weight of the corresponding denominations on the Abbasid standard. Balog (1976, pp. 14, 16) has listed both pieces as belonging to the Abbasid standard, tacitly assuming, in the case of the British Museum's half *wuqiyya*, that the denomination stamped on it is a mistake and that it is really a *wuqiyya* and accepting, naturally enough, Miles's definition of the A.N.S. half-*raṭl* as a *raṭl*. That the denomination is mistaken on both pieces is rather far-fetched. The stamp of the British Museum's half-*wuqiyya* is indeed too large for it to have been designed for pieces of half its size and, furthermore, in both cases the weights are rather too high for the denominations on the Abbasid standard which, supposing they have been marked in error, they have to represent.

The Abbasid *raṭl* standard certainly was in use both before and after the year 226. The intact weights of Ashinās and Mālik b. Kaydur, the issue of which must have immediately preceded those of Muḥammad b. Basṭām, are all on the Abbasid standard (Castiglioni, 22; Balog 1976, 669, 681-3, all of which, as pointed out under No. 346, are of Ashinās and Mālik). It would seem therefore that the *raṭl* system of the weights dated 226 was an exceptional and probably short-lived one. It may be called for convenience's sake the standard of Muḥammad b. Basṭām (see Introduction, p. 30).

Although Muḥammad b. Basṭām has the not unimportant titles *al-amīr* and *mawlā amīr al-mu'minīn* he is unknown to the historical sources and we do not know what official position he held. At the beginning of 226 Egypt was governed on behalf of the absentee overlord Ashinās by Mālik b. Kaydur who had been appointed in 224/839. In the course of the year Mālik was replaced by ʻAlī b. Yaḥyā al-Armanī (Kindī, 195-6). Kindī merely describes both of them as being in charge of 'prayer', giving no information about the control of finances. Glass stamps of both are however known and, in any case, it is reasonably clear that by this time the former system by which responsibility for the issue of glass weights and measures lay with the Finance Director to the exclusion of the Governor, except when the positions were united, was no longer operating fully, if at all. A possible clue to Muḥammad b. Basṭām's identity is given by Kindī who mentions that a certain Aḥmad b. Basṭām was put in charge of the militia (*shuraṭ*) in Egypt in 217, being directly appointed by the Caliph al-Ma'mūn who was briefly in Egypt to deal with the revolt of Afshīn. Kindī (192-3) preserves two separate accounts of the appointment. In the first Aḥmad b. Basṭām has the *nisba* al-Azdī and is said to be of the people of Bukhārā. In the second Ibn Basṭām, as he is called, is described as an Iranian (*min al-ʻajam*) and we are told that he was dismissed by the Governor and flogged in the court of the Congretational Mosque for taking bribes. Evidently he was called al-Azdī not as a member of the Arab tribe of Azd by descent but because he was a client (*mawlā*) of the tribe. He would have been one of the group of Iranians who accompanied al-Ma'mūn from Khurasan and Transoxiana to the West when he gained control of the entire Caliphate. Muḥammad b. Basṭām's title *mawlā amīr al-mu'minīn* is also a sign of non-Arab descent and favour from the Caliph. There is also a possibility that he was Aḥmad's brother.

As for what follows Basṭām in the legend, Lane-Poole read Abū at the end of the fifth line and *wāw*, 'tooth', *hā'*, *alif*, *rā'* on the next. The *bā'* of his Abū might be *lām* and is probably followed by *rā'* rather than *waw* but otherwise the reading is a fair one. On the American Numismatic Society weight Miles tentatively read al-Ruqʻā'ī, said to be, possibly, a *nisba* from al-Ruqʻa, a place in al-Yamāma. Neither reading nor interpretation seem probable. If Muḥammad b. Basṭām was an Iranian the obscure word or words might be an Iranian name or title.

346 Ring weight: half-*raṭl*, with Mālik b. Naṣr Kaydur

مما امر به الامير اشنا
س مولى امير المؤمنين اكر
مه الله و الامير ملك بن نصـ[ـر]
كيدر مولى امير ال[ـمؤمنين]
ابقاه [الله]

Of what ordered the Amir Ashinā-
s, Mawlā of the Commander of the Faithful, may God
show him bounty, and the Amir Malik b. Naṣr
Kaydur, Mawlā of the Commander of the Faithful,
may God preserve him.

OA + 4402. Chipped badly on face but otherwise intact except for small pieces off the bottom. 5.0 x 5.3cm; height of rectangular stamp 2.2cm; 174g (*Plate 18*)

Cf. Castiglioni, 22.

Mālik b. Naṣr Kaydur was appointed Governor of Egypt by Ashinās in 224/839 and remained in office until 226/841. Kindī (195) only describes him as being in control of 'prayer'. On his stamps his name is always written without the *alif*, but the historians give Mālik which is presumably correct as the full form.

The same die was also used on larger ring weights paired with a stamp of the Caliph al-Muʻtaṣim (Balog 1976, 663. Cf. 662). It has also been found on a vessel stamp (Balog 1976, 671). The half-*raṭl* published by Castiglioni is unlikely to be from a different die. It was, incidentally, the first heavy glass weight to be described. It is intact, or very nearly so, and the weight, which Castiglioni gave by the Milanese *peso di marco*, comes to 189.46g on the metric system, conforming to the Abbasid *raṭl* system known from quite a number of intact pieces of the third century of the Hijra, including some others of Ashinās and Mālik.

During the third century nearly all the weights and vessel stamps of identifiable officials have legends which lack any denomination. This would have caused no difficulty to a population familiar with the divisions and subdivisions of a standard system of weights and measures. The stamps without denominations were used indifferently on weights of various denominations and on vessel stamps. In many cases officials have two stamps, one large and one small, usually with similar legends. The small stamp is used on weights from the quarter-*raṭl* downwards and the large one on the larger denominations. Both usually seem to occur as vessel stamps. Specimens of the small stamp of Ashinās and Mālik have been published by Balog on a number of types: quarter-*raṭl* (1976, 669. Cf. 670); half-*wuqiyya* (681, 683-4): vessel stamp (685). On all these the name of Mālik b. Naṣr Kaydur was incorrectly read Harthama b. Naḍr Jabalī, while Nos 681-5 are also wrongly attributed to Ītākh rather than Ashinās.

MŪSĀ B. ABU'L-ʻABBĀS
Governor on behalf of Ashinās 219-24/834-9

347 Ring weight: *wuqiyya*

على يدى
موسى
بن ابى العبا
س

At the hands
of Mūsā
b. Abi 'l-ʻAbbā-
s.

OA + 4307. Fragment. Top and part of left side. Surface slightly decayed. Green. Length 3.4cm; stamp 1.8cm; 11.56g. (*Plate 18*)

No other specimen from this die appears to have been published. A second executive stamp of Mūsā, of which two examples are catalogued below, has the same legend but arranged in three rather than four lines. A third one has the same legend, again in three lines, but is square. It has been found on a broken quarter-*raṭl* and an intact half-*wuqiyya* (Petrie, 178; Miles 1958a, 193. Cf. Balog 1976, 664?). Miles (1951b, 30) described a vessel stamp on which Mūsā's name may follow that of Ashinās, and Casanova (1893, 45) what may be a similar stamp paired on a weight with a second one bearing the name and titles of the Caliph al-Muʻtaṣim (218-227/833-842). Neither piece was illustrated.

348 Ring weight: quarter-*raṭl*

على يدى
موسى بن ابى
العباس

At the hands
of Mūsā b. Abi
'l-ʻAbbās

Six-pointed star below.

OA + 4404. Green, the surface iridescent or flaked away. Two halves stuck together but otherwise intact. 4.5 x 4.6cm; 91g. (*Plate 18*)

The same die appears on a half-*wuqiyya* ring weight (Petrie, 236); for its use on vessel stamps see below.

349-350 Vessel stamp with executive formula

Same die as No. 348

OA + 4109. Pale green. Width 1.9cm. (*Plate 18*)
OA + 4291. Pale bluish green. 2.2cm.

ĪTĀKH
Overlord of Egypt, 230-5/844-9

351 Disk weight: 10-*dirham* weight

الامير ا
يتاخ عشر
ة واف

The Amir Ī
tākh. Te-
n, full-weight.

OA + 4313. Green. 3.5cm; stamp 1.2 x 1.3cm; 28.89g. (*Plate 18*)

This is only the second piece to be published as a multiple *dirham* weight, the first being a 2-*dirham* weight of rather unusual design (Balog 1976, 752a). The class as a whole has previously received little attention; it has been discussed in some detail in the Introduction (pp. 18-21). As mentioned there, it is difficult to fit weights of this class into the main official series or to date them precisely, and it may be that a number of published pieces lacking any mention of a denomination or without legends at all should be classified as multiple *dirham* weights. The particular interest of the present piece is that the denomination, if laconically expressed, is there. A tenth of its weight is 2.89g. very little below the generally accepted weight of the silver *dirham* or *dirham kayl*, 2.97g.

A weight for a single *dirham* (*kayl*) with similar coarse Kufic legends and what is apparently the same Amir's name has been attributed to Ītākh by Balog (1976, 680). The name on both does look like Ītākh and Balog's attribution is followed here but there are reasons for regarding it with some reservation. Firstly the crude script of these two pieces is distinctly different from that on the incontestably official stamps of the second quarter of the third century, for example the one such stamp on which Ītākh's name appears (only Balog 1976, 679 and 691 show the name; part of the stamp appears on Petrie, 218. Cf. Miles 1948, 102?). Second, though it might be argued that this is due to the small size of the stamps on the *dirham kayl* weights, the name on these latter is not followed by the title and benediction which appears on the official stamp mentioned above (*mawlā amīr al-mu'minīn, akramahu allāh*, '*mawlā* of the Commander of the Faithful, may God be bountiful to him'). Third, from the material published so far it does not appear that the name of one of the absentee overlords of Egypt was used on the glass stamps except when accompanied by that of a subordinate official. Perhaps then, the Amir of the *dirham-kayl* weights was another Ītākh, or the possessor of another, graphically similar name (Īnānj?).

AL-MUTAWAKKIL
Caliph 232-47/847-61

352 Ring weight: *raṭl*, with Muḥammad b. Isḥāq and ʻAbd al-Wāḥid b. Yaḥyā

Caliph's stamp to right

بسم الله الرحمن الرحيم
امر الله بالعدل والوفاء
وبذلك امر به عبد ال[له]
جعفر الامام المتوك[ل]
[على] الله امير المؤم[نين]
[اطال] الله بق[اه]

In the name of God, the Compassionate the Merciful.
God ordered justice and honesty,
and that is what ordered the servant of God
Ja'far, the Imām al-Mutawakkil
ʻalā allah, Commander of the Faithful,
May God prolong his existence.

Second stamp to left

مما امر به
الامير محمد [بن]
اسحق مولى امير المؤ
منين اكرمه الله والا
مير عبدالواحد بن
[يحيى مولى] امير المؤ
منين

Of what ordered
the Amir Muḥammad b.
Isḥaq, Mawlā of the Commander of the Faithful, may God be bounteous to him, and the A-
mir ʻAbd al-Wāḥid b.
Yaḥyā, Mawlā of the Commander of the Faithful.

OA + 4393. Green glass, but with surface almost entirely discoloured and opaque. Some chips but otherwise substantially intact. 6.3 x 7.2cm; 361g.

From the same pair of dies Balog 1976, 688; Cf. Miles 1951b, 31, probably both double-*raṭls*.

Neither die fitted completely on to the top of the piece and such legends as it had have decayed to the point where they suffice to establish the identities of the dies and little more. The best impression of the stamp of al-Mutawakkil is the one on the double-*raṭl* in the Balog collection which was first published by its previous owner M. Jungfleisch (1948). Otherwise the die is known from two vessel stamps which only show part of it (Casanova 1893, 161; Balog 1976, 687).

The reading of the second stamp has proved difficult in the past. The clearest examples are those of a damaged double-*raṭl* attributed by Miles (1971, 41) to Muḥammad b. Sulaymān and an almost complete half-*raṭl* on which Balog (1976, 385) read the names as Muhammad b. al-Ash'ath and 'Abdallāh b. . . . The weight of the latter piece, incidentally, shows that it belongs to the Abbasid and not the Umayyad *raṭl* standard. On his No. 688, where only the edge of this stamp is preserved, Balog read Sulaymān for Isḥāq, and taking it for a first name suggested the person was Sulaymān b. Wahb, known to have been Finance Director in 247/861-2. However, when all the illustrations are utilized the only obscure word is the name of 'Abd al-Wāḥid's father. Miles (1971, 41) appears to read Yaḥyā on the Corning Museum specimen, but unfortunately something has gone wrong with the printing of his transcription of the legend. 'Abd al-Wāḥid b. Yaḥyā, known as Khūṭ, belongs to the right period and the rather spiky script of the stamp under discussion resembles that of the small stamp on which his name appears (see Nos 356-7).

The question of the identity of Muḥammad b. Isḥāq still remains. His name stands first and, unlike that of 'Abd al-Wāḥid, is followed by a benediction. Clearly he is the more important. But, as Kindī (p. 199) tells us, 'Abd al-Wāḥid was appointed with powers over both 'prayer' and the finances, on behalf of al-Muntaṣir, the heir apparent who held the overlordship of Egypt for many years. Al-Muntaṣir was not of course named Muḥammad b. Isḥāq, nor could he possibly have used the title *mawlā amīr al-mu'minīn*, only applicable to those with some sort of client status. The answer may be that yet another level of delegation had been introduced for appointment to the governorship and that Muḥammad b. Isḥāq was empowered to appoint on behalf of the nominal overlord, al-Muntaṣir.

ISḤĀQ B. YAḤYĀ B. MA'ĀDH
Governor and Finance Director on behalf of al-Muntaṣir, heir of the Caliph al-Mutawakkil 235-6/850-1

353 Ring weight: quarter-*raṭl*

الامير
اسحق بن يحيي
بن معاذ
ابقاه الله

The Amir
Isḥaq b. Yaḥyā
b. Ma'ādh,
may God preserve him.

Crescent pointing upwards below.

OA + 4371. Surface decayed, but intact. 4.4 x 4.5cm; 91.6g.

From the same die Balog 1976, 692.

The die was also used on the half-*wuqiyya* denomination (Balog 1976, 693. Cf. 694) and on vessel stamps such as the two described below. No corresponding large stamp of Isḥāq has yet been found (Balog 1976, 691 is of Ītākh, not Isḥāq - compare the right-hand stamp of Balog 1976, 679, which is from the same die.)

354-355 Vessel stamps

From the same die as No. 353.

OA + 4101. Pale green. Width 2.1cm. (*Plate 18*)

OA + 4102. Pale green. Width 2.5cm.

From the same die Launois 1957, 249; Balog 1976, 695-6.

KHŪṬ 'ABD AL WĀḤID B. YAḤYĀ
Governor and Finance Director on behalf of al-Muntaṣir 236-8/851-2

356 Ring weight: quarter-*raṭl*

الامير
عبد الواحد
بن يحيي مولى [امير]
المؤمنين

The Amir
'Abd al Wāḥid
b. Yaḥyā, Mawlā of the Commander
of the Faithful.

OA + 4407. Surface decayed and partly iridescent. Chipped at the bottom. 3.9 x 4.7cm; 83g.

Cf. Casanova 1893, 41, 41 *bis*.

The impression of the die was blurred and weak to begin with and only enough survives to establish the identity of the die. For vessel stamps from the same die see No. 357. For a discussion of large stamps on which 'Abd al-Wāḥid b. Yaḥyā's name appears below that of another official see No. 352.

357 Vessel stamp

Same die as No. 356.

OA + 4347. Pale green. Width 2.1cm. (*Plate 18*)

From the same die Viré, 28; Balog 1976, 697.

YAZĪD B. 'ABDALLĀH
Governor, first appointed on behalf of al-Muntaṣir, 242-53/856-67

358 Disk weight: *wuqiyya*

بسم الله مما
امر به الامير يزيد بن
عبدالله مولى امير
المؤمنين

In the name of God. Of what
ordered the Amir Yazīd b.
'Abdallah, Mawlā of the Commander
of the Faithful.

Mark of a rectangular-ended tool on each side, arranged diagonally to the legend.

OA + 4311. Opaque, Black with buff surface discoloration. Intact. 4.7cm; stamp 2.1cm; 30.90g.

From the same die Miles, 1951b, 32.

The British Museum's collection also contains three quarter-*raṭls* and a vessel stamp from the same die (Nos 359-361, 367). The half-*wuqiyya* has also been published (Balog 1976, 718-9. Cf. Grohmann 1954, p. 145; Balog 1976, 717).

359-361 Ring weight: quarter-*raṭl*

From the same die as No. 358.

OA + 4417. Chip of several grammes off one side. Green. 4.5 x 4.5cm; Stamp 2.2cm; 91g. (*Plate 18*)
78 3-11 37. Chip off left side. Faint legend. 4.5 x 4.5 cm; 91.5g.
94 3-9 14. Chipped at bottom and one side. Surface worn. 4.4 x 4.4cm; 85.2g.

Cf. Balog, 716.

362-363 Ring weight: half-*raṭl*

بسم الله بركة مما امر
به الامير يزيد بن عبد الله
مولى امير المؤمنين
اطال الله بقاهما

In the name of God. Blessing. Of what ordered
the Amir Yazīd b. ʻAbdallah,
Mawlā of the Commander of the Faithful,
May God prolong both their lives.

OA + 4385. Chipped at bottom and right. Surface discoloured. Green. 5.0 x 5.7cm; stamp 2.6 x 2.7cm; 160g.
OA + 4406. Surface decayed. Green. 5.4 x 5.5cm; length of stamp 2.7cm; 190g. (*Plate 18*)

From the same die Petrie, 239; Balog 1976, 715. Cf. Casanova 1893, 56; Viré, 29; Balog 1976, 714.

Two states of the die are known of which only the second and more common is represented in the British Museum's collection. The existence of the variants was first noted by Petrie and later by Jungfleisch (1948, p. 3). In its original state the die has a legend of six lines, two of which were removed, leaving a blank area. On pieces in the second state it can be seen that the blank is raised above the level of the ground of the rest of the stamp, indicating not that the missing lines were, as has been said, cut out on the die but that the area was in some way filled in to block out the legend, which could of course have been partially removed before then.

Jungfleisch read the deleted portion as a Quranic injunction against fraud, but Balog was certainly right to recognize that the substance of it was the executive formula *ʻala yaday* followed by a name. His reading is *ʻalā yaday al-Ḥasan/ b. Abi 'l-Maḥāsin* ('at the hands of al- Ḥasan b. Abi 'l-Maḥāsin'). This deals satisfactorily with most of the first line though it is not entirely convincing for the second. None of the illustrated examples is very clear. Presumably the alteration was a consequence of al-Ḥasan's dismissal or demise.

The British Museum possesses specimens of the three *raṭl*-system denominations on which the stamp appears, but not the vessel stamp which is also known (Balog 1976, 720, 722. Cf. 719, 721, 723).

For convenience's sake all the published pieces with the die in the first state are listed here. Half-*raṭls*: Petrie, 237; Balog 1976, 704. *Raṭl*: Miles 1963 II, 39. Vessel stamp: Balog 1976, 705, and cf. the specimen in private hands mentioned there.

364-365 Ring weight: *raṭl*

Two impressions of the same altered die as on Nos 362-363.

OA + 4369. The top. Greenish brown. Length 6.5cm; right-hand stamp 2.5 x 2.6cm; 140.7g. (*Plate 18*)
OA + 4381. Badly chipped at the back. Opaque, black. 6.5 x 7.2cm; height of stamps 2.4cm; 350g.

From the same die in the same state Miles 1958a, 197: Balog 1976, 713. Cf. Balog 1976, 707-12.

366 Ring weight: double-*raṭl*

Two impressions from the same altered die as on Nos 362-365.

OA + 4400. The top only. Length 7.2cm; height of stamps 2.6cm; 213g.

From the same die in the same state Petrie, 238. Cf. Balog 1976, 706.

367 Vessel stamp

From the same die as Nos 358-361.

OA + 4135. Green. Width 2.1cm. (*Plate 18*)

From the same die Petrie, 229.

MUZĀḤIM B. KHĀQĀN
Governor 253-4/867-8

368 Disk weight: *wuqiyya*

مما امر به الا
مير مزاحم
اطال الله بقا
[ه]---

Of what ordered the A-
mir Muzāḥim,
may God prolong his li-
fe, - - - .

OA + 4310. Green, with some iridescence. 4.5cm; stamp 2.1cm; 31.59g. (*Plate 18*)

The last line is very badly written. Balog read the end as 'b. Khāqān', but it is difficult to accept that the benediction could come between Muzāḥim's name and that of his father. The present piece is the first *wuqiyya* of Muzāḥim to be published but the same stamp, first correctly identified by Balog, appears on a quarter-*raṭl* ring weight (Balog 1976, 726) and no less than five examples of the half-*wuqiyya*, all intact (Petrie, 203; Miles 1958a, 245; Balog 1976, 727-9).

369 Ring weight: double-*raṭl*, dated 253/867

Two impressions side by side

بسم الله بركة من الله
مما امر به الامير مزاحم
بن خاقان مولى امير المؤ
منين اطال الله بقاه
فى سنة ثلث وخمسين
و ماتين

In the name of God. Blessing from God.
Of what ordered the Amir Muzāḥim
b. Khāqān, Mawlā of the Commander of the Faithful, may God prolong his existence,
in the year three and fifty
and two hundred.

OA + 4380. The right side and part of the top. Black. Length 9.2cm; stamps 2.6 x 2.6cm; 305g. (*Plate 18*)

From the same die Balog 1976, 724. Cf. 725.

There are several impressions of a rectangular-edged tool above and below the stamps. The die was presumably used on other denominations of weight but examples have not yet come to light. However one impression of the die on a vessel stamp has been published (Balog 1976, 738 – the attribution to Aḥmad b. Ṭūlūn needs to be corrected).

3. TULUNID

AḤMAD B. ṬŪLŪN

Governor, later semi-independent ruler, 254-70/868-84

370 **Ring weight:** raṭl, dated 254/868

بسم الله بركة من الله
امر به الامير احمد بن طو
لون مولى امير المؤ
منين فى سنة
اربع وخمسين
و مائتين

In the name of God. Blessing from God.
Ordered it the Amir Aḥmad b. Ṭūlūn, Mawlā of the Commander of the Faithful, in the year
four and fifty
and two hundred.

OA + 4405. Intact but with the surface devitrifying. Two blurred rectangular impressions side by side. Green. 5.9 x 6.7cm; height of stamps 2.5cm; 377g.

From the same die Miles 1958a, 200; Balog 1976, 733.

The legend on this piece and on the two double-*raṭls* described next are only legible to a very small extent, either because of the weakness and blurring of the original impression or on account of subsequent surface decay or, as in the case of the present piece, both. However the identity of the die with that used on clearer specimens which have been illustrated photographically is easy enough to establish. The die has also been recorded on a vessel stamp (Balog 1976, 739). In spite of its condition the British Museum's *raṭl* does make it possible to correct the earlier reading of a not unimportant word, the digit of the date. Jungfleisch (1949), Miles and Balog read it as *tis*ʻ, 'nine', and there has been some discussion of the historical implications of the date 259, which is shortly after Aḥmad b. Ṭūlūn effectively declared his independence in 258. On the right-hand stamp of the present piece, however, the digit, though blurred, can be made out and must be read *arba*ʻ, 'four', the descending *rā'* being plainly visible. Aḥmad's original appointment as Governor was in 254. Of course the die could have remained in use long after the year in which it was made. Michael Bates has kindly informed me that the three double-*raṭls* in the Balog collection, which is now in the American Numismatic Society, are from the same die. (Balog 1976, 730-2. No. 730, Mr Bates confirms, is the piece originally in the Jungfleisch collection which was the first weight of Aḥmad b. Ṭūlūn to be identified and published. Balog incorrectly states that Jungfleisch published the *raṭl*, Balog 1976, 733, which was also formerly in Jungfleisch's possession.) Balog 1976, 738, attributed to Aḥmad b. Ṭūlūn and said to be dated 254 is, in fact, of Muzāḥim b. Khāqān and dated 253, coming from the same die as No. 369.

Three small circular stamps of Aḥmad can be distinguished. They occur on *wuqiyyas* and half-*wuqiyyas*. One of them is also dated 254 (Balog 1976, 734, 736, which are from one die, though Balog read the date on 736 as 259; Fahmi 1958, pl. 3, possibly a half-*wuqiyya*). The other two, which may have been in use later than the first, are not dated (the only illustrated specimens are Miles 1958a, 198 and Balog 1976, 737. Cf. Miles 1958a, 199; Balog 1976, 735).

371-372 Ring weight: double-*raṭl*, dated 254/868

Two impressions from the same die as No. 370, side by side.

OA + 4390. The left half, with about half the right-hand stamp. Stamps blurred. Green. Height 7cm; height of stamps 2.5cm, width of left-hand stamp 2.5cm; 318g.
OA + 4396. Surface flaked off or iridescent, but otherwise intact. Stamps partly illegible. Green. 7.8 x 8.6cm; right-hand stamp 2.5 x 2.4cm; 753g.

From the same die Balog 1976, 730-2 (information from Michael Bates).

No. 372 is the first intact, or, considering the surface decay, almost intact double-*raṭl* of Aḥmad b. Ṭūlūn to appear.

4. AGHLABID

ZIYĀDAT ALLĀH

373 **(*Dīnār* weight)**

غلب
زيادة
الله

May he be victorious,
Ziyādat
allah.

Oval dot flanked by crude split palmettes below.

OA + 4212. Green. 2.5cm; 4.14g. (*Plate 18*)

A similar piece of one of the Aghlabid rulers called Ibrāhīm was published long ago by Petrie (641) but has only recently been correctly identified as Aghlabid by Balog (1971, p. 175). As with the British Museum's piece its legend begins *ghalaba* ('may he be victorious'), a slogan peculiar to the Aghlabids and punning of course on the name of the ancestor of the dynasty, which appears on much of their coinage. Two glass disks in the Musée Alaoui in Tunis, described by Viré (39-40), which bear simply the name Ibrāhīm are presumably also to be regarded as Aghlabid pieces. There are said to be others in the Musée de Bardo, again in Tunis (Balog, *loc cit*).

During the period when the Aghlabids ruled in Ifrīqiyya (AD 800-909) there were no less than three rulers called Ziyādat allāh, the dates of whose reigns are as follows: 201-23/817-38, 249-50/864-5 and 290-6/903-9. It is impossible to be certain which of the three issued the piece. A similar problem arises over the one published by Petrie. Is it of Ibrāhīm I (184-96/800-12) or Ibrāhīm II (261-89/875-902)? The script itself is of no help. The Kufic used on the Aghlabid gold coinage, with which that of the two glass pieces is closely related, is extremely conservative and does not change throughout the period.

A possible indication that a later rather than an earlier date is perhaps to be favoured for the British Museum's piece is the decorative scroll beneath the text. Decorative devices rarely occur on Aghlabid coins. Among the few exceptions are certain silver pieces of Ibrāhīm II which have a scroll, generally similar to that of the glass piece but more finely engraved, at the bottom of the obverse field. The Department of Coins and Medals in the British Museum has two such pieces, both of the mint of al-ʿAbbāsiyya, one, not published, dated 282 and the other lacking its date (BMCO II, 211).

The disk of Ibrahim in University College, London, weighs 4.15g. Both pieces are therefore a little light, but not enough to make one doubt that they were produced to the *dīnār* standard.

5. UNIDENTIFIED PERSONS

Abu 'l-Ḥazan

374-380 **Token**

ابو الحزن

Abu 'l-Ḥazan.

OA + 4208. Pale blue green. 2.9cm; stamp 1.9cm; 7.09g. (*Plate 18*)
OA + 4209. Green. 2.8cm; stamp 1.9cm; 5.24g.
OA + 4329. Discoloured green. 3.1cm; stamp 1.8cm; 7.44g.
93 11-11 17. Blue green. 3.2cm; stamp 1.8cm; 8.12g.
93 11-11 18. Green, decayed. 2.6cm; 4.58g.
1965 7-31 10. Green, iridescent. 2.5cm; 4.11g.
(Coins and Medals) 90 8-4 27. Green. Decaying. 3.0cm: stamp 1.9cm; 7.98g.

From the same die Casanova 1893 V, 2; Petrie, 272-80; Launois 1960 I, 20. Cf. Launois 1960 I, 21-2; II, 20; 1969, 21.

Petrie pointed out that there is a fork at the top of the *lām* which he took to indicate a later date and the type appears to have been omitted from catalogues limited to the early categories of glass stamps. The late date may be correct but except for that one detail, perhaps an accidental flaw, the Kufic could well be of the third, or even possibly the second, century. The pieces vary in size and it has long been obvious that they are not weights.

The name has been read Abu 'l Ḥazan or Abu 'l Ḥazn with no more comment than Casanova's question mark. Of course a phrase beginning Abu 'l-, and it is difficult to suggest an alternative, immediately suggests a *kunya* but Abu 'l-Ḥazan, meaning 'Father of grief' seems a rather ill-omened name. No evidence of its use as a name has been adduced in connection with the glass weights. The problem is made more difficult by the discovery of Nos 385-386, obviously related to the present type and inscribed simply Ḥazan. Some allusion may be intended but if so its explanation is still to be found. No alternative reading of the legends suggests itself, though the last letter might be *rā'* or *zā'* rather than *nūn*.

Aḥmad b. Dīnār

381 ***Dirham* weight**

مما امر به الا
مير احمد بن د
ينر وزن در
هم واف

Of what ordered the A-
mir Aḥmad b. D-
īnar. Weight of a *dir-*
ham, full-weight.

(Coins and Medals) Pietraszewski, 370; Sawaziewicz, 9; Castiglioni 8; Rogers 1878, 11; Lane-Poole, 29. Olive green. 2.4cm; stamp 1.5 x 1.7cm; 2.95g. (*Plate 18*)

The weight is that of a *dirham kayl*.

Lane-Poole read the name on this piece and the next as Aḥmad b. Jubayr, taking it that the father's name on this one was divided between two lines thus: Ju/bayr. In Kufic, particularly of the earliest periods, the division of words between lines was freely allowed when the ductus joining leters is not broken, that is after one of the letters of the alphabet which is not joined to the following one. Numerous examples such word division are recorded in the present catalogue, for example, *d/īnar*, *kharr/ūba*. To read Jubayr, however, it has to be assumed that the ductus between *jīm* and *bā'* is broken. Such a word division is extremely unusual and must surely always have seemed ugly. There is one known example, on a glass *dīnār*-weight die of Yazīd b. Ḥātim on which the legend ends *dī/nār* (Miles 1948, 76; Launois 1957, 203; Fahmī 1957, 145; Balog 1976, 420. Cf. Fahmī 1957, 144). This exceptional case, however, need not be taken as a precedent for reading Jubayr on the present piece when there is a simpler alternative reading. The form of *dāl* used on the piece is not the *kāf*-like one of the earliest Kufic but a later variety in which the upper part of the letter consists of a single diagonal stroke, indistinguishable, in isolation, from *ḥā'* and the similar letters. The word Aḥmad provides examples of both. The letter at the end of the second line can therefore be read as *dāl*, which is not, of course, joined to the letter that follows it and Dīnār becomes a natural reading of the name, assuming that the *alif* is omitted. Such an omission of *alif* is of course common; in this case the analogy of *dīnār*, in the sense of a gold coin, frequently spelt without the *alif* until a much later date, makes the omission even more natural.

The slight difficulty in reading Dīnār in the case of the quarter-*raṭl* is discussed in the commentary on that piece.

Aḥmad b. Dīnār

382 **Disk weight: quarter-*raṭl***

مما امر به الا
مير احمد بن
دينر ربع ر
طل واف

Of what ordered the A-
mīr Aḥmad b.
Dīnar. A quarter *r-
aṭl*, full-weight.

73 3-29 37. Rogers 1878, 19; Lane-Poole, 28g. Green 6.1cm; stamp 2.8 x 2.9cm; 74.1g. (*Plate 19*)

There are shallow marks of the edge of a tool placed diagonally all round the stamp. The weight of the piece, which is in perfect condition, implies a *raṭl* of c. 296.4g - considerably lower than any of the *raṭl* standards properly attested from surviving examples.

The name of Aḥmad's father, read Jubayr on this piece by Lane-Poole as, tentatively, by Rogers before him, has been to some extent discussed under No. 381. On that piece the first letter of the name was isolated and Dīnār is an easy reading; on the present one the first letter is joined to what follows and under normal circumstances could not be *dāl*. It is not impossible, of course, that the two weights were issued by different people but they are stylistically very similar and another explanation which enables as to assume that the same name was intended may be correct. The form of *dāl* used on the quarter-*raṭl* is the same as on the *dirham* weight (No. 381) described above, that is, it is indistinguishable from *ḥā'* etc. On both pieces, but particularly the quarter-*raṭl*, a kind of pseudo-ductus is visible in places, a horizontal line joining letters that are not normally joined or even connecting separate words. Such a line is clearly visible through most of the third line of the legend on the *dirham* weight, connecting, for example, the end of Dīnār and the beginning of *wazn*. On the quarter-*raṭl* there are conspicuous connecting marks, between *rub'* and *raṭl* and between the *alif* and *fā* of *wāf*. So far as the father's name is concerned it seems possible that the connection of the first letter with the next was really due to the presence of one of the lines which may have been misunderstood as the engraving proceeded and that there is therefore no objection to assuming that the represented is in fact Dīnār, spelt once again without the *alif*.

Idrīs and Mūsā, sons of Mahdī

383 **Disk**

ادريس و موسى
ابنى مهدى

Idrīs and Mūsā,
the two sons of Mahdī.

Six-pointed star below.

OA + 4280. Dark brown. 3.4cm; stamp 2.6cm; 7.35g. (*Plate 19*)

From the same die Miles 1958a, 203.

This type must be considered in connection with one of Zakariyy and 'Īsā, the two sons (*ibnay*, 'dual') of Yaḥyā represented in the present collection by No. 387. The script of the two is so similar that it can be presumed that it was engraved by the same hand: note, in particular, the elongation of the retroflex *yā's* to neatly underline the rest of the legends, a feature not found elsewhere on glass. Incidentially, no other stamps of pairs of brothers are known. The weights of specimens of each type differ too much for them to have been intended as weights. The American Numismatic Society piece of Idrīs and Mūsā noted above weighs 7.07g. and in the case of the type of Zakariyy and 'Īsā the spread of the weights is much greater.

Balog (1976, 698) has pointed out that a Zakariyā' b. Yaḥyā is mentioned by Kindī and attributed the disks of Zakariyy and 'Īsā to him and his brother. Kindī's Zakariyā' was the scribe of 'Abd al-Raḥmān b. 'Abdallāh al-'Umarī, Qāḍī (Judge) of Egypt in 185-94/801-10, but is mentioned much later under the year 237/851-2, when he must have been an old man, as one of those fined and imprisoned for misappropriating the fortune of 'Alī b. 'Abd al'Azīz al-Jarawī (Kindī, 199-200). That Zakarriyy is a variant spelling of Zakariyā' (Zaccharias) may be accepted and Balog's identification of the two may be correct. If so, of course, an approximate dating is provided for the disks of Idrīs and Mūsā as well. Miles and Balog have both noted that a second name, and a not very common one, Ḥamza b. al-Mughīra, appears both in the list of people involved in the affair of al-Jarawī's property and on glass disks - these last, it should be noted, of variant weights and from two dies (Miles 1963 I, 78; Balog 1976, 699-700). Miles, the first to mention the possibility of the identification of the Ḥamza of the glass and the one mentioned by Kindī, discounted it on the grounds that the script of the glass disks of Hamza was of the second/eighth century. However, though the script on Ḥamza's pieces is completely different from that on those of Idrīs and Mūsā and Zakariyy and 'Īsā, Balog is undoubtedly right to date it to the third century AH. It is close to the script on the coinage of the second quarter of the third century.

Ja'far b. Sulaymān

384 **Disk**

بالله
جعفر بن سليمن
يثق

In God
Ja'far b. Sulayman
trusts.

Crescent pointing upwards either end of first line; six-pointed star either end of third line.

72 3-20 6. Rogers 1878, 20; Lane-Poole, 30G. Chip off top right. Deep blue. 3.9cm; stamp 2.8cm; 11.07g. (*Plate 19*)

The piece seems more likely to be a token than a weight. The legend with *yathiqu billāh* ('there trusts in God') and the name is of a type commonly found on seals and occasionally on later coins. See Launois 1959, 36, for a glass piece with a similar legend of 'Umar b. Aḥmad or possibly 'Umar b. Ḥafṣ.

Ḥazan (?)

385-386

حزن

Ḥazan

OA + 4210. Brown. 2.6cm; stamp 1.6cm; 4.43g.
OA + 4211. Worn. Brown. 2.4cm; 1.6cm; 3.91g.
(*Plate 19*)

The name, if it is a name, has been discussed with the related issue inscribed Abu 'l-Ḥazan (see Nos 374-380). Given the association with the other type it can be assumed that they are not weights.

Zakariyy and ʿĪsā, sons of Yaḥyā

387

زكرى و عيسى
ابنى يحيى

Zakariyy and ʿIsā,
the two sons of Yaḥyā.

Central pentagram, lacking the lower point.

OA + 4281. Pale greenish blue. 3.7cm; 11.88g. (*Plate 19*)

From the same die Petrie, 249; Miles 1963 II, 42; Balog 1976, 698.

As has been pointed out under the closely related No. 383, neither type can have been produced as weights. The weights of the previously published examples of the present type, in the order they are listed above are 10.57g, 7.10g (chipped) and 7.05g. For a possible identification of Zakariyy b. Yaḥyā see the commentary to No. 383.

Saʿīd (?) with Farwa b. Tāj (?)

388 *Fals* weight of 31 *kharrūba* (?)

Obverse

س(ع)يد
فلس واف
خروبة

Saʿīd.
Fals, full-weight
kharrūbas 31

Crescent pointing upwards above. Trident flanked by two crescents below. Beaded border.

Reverse

طبعة
فروة
بن تاج

Stamping
of Farwa
b. Tāj.

Legend in square inscribed in circle.

OA + 4201. Green. 3.1cm; square on reverse 1.8 x 2.0cm; 6.10g. (*Plate 19*)

From the same pair of dies Balog 1976, 758. Cf. Balog 1976, 757.

Specimens from the same obverse die have been published without mention of a reverse legend (Casanova 1893, 70; Fahmī 1957, 250. Cf. Launois 1957, 382; Fahmī 1957, 251). On the obverse the name has been read as Samand or Saʿīd. The second letter does look like *mīm* but no evidence has been provided that Samand is a name. It seems likely that the *mīm* is an error for *ʿayn*, the round forms being quite easy to confuse, and that the common name Saʿīd is intended. On the grounds of similarities, particularly the use of Coptic numerals, of this type with the *fals* weights of Salama, Launois (1959, 19) has suggested an attribution to Salama's near contemporary Saʿīd b. al-Musayyib, whose name appears on the reverse of *dīnār*-system and other weights (e.g. Nos 259, 272). The theory is an attractive one except for the considerable difficulty that the Saʿīd of the *fals* weights is associated with the artisan Farwa and Saʿīd b. al-Musayyib with Severus, another artisan.

Another question raised by the obverse is the correct reading of the Coptic figure. Thirty is plain but it is not clear whether the mark to the left of it is a second figure or something else, perhaps an ornament. It does not resemble very closely the only example of a Coptic figure one yet found on a coin weight (Fahmī 1957, 227). However thirty-one is not impossible as a reading and has been that of those who have expressed an opinion. One would expect the answer to the point to emerge from the weights of the pieces but they vary greatly, from 5.08g to 6.10g. At the latter figure the British Museum's piece is the only one that is reasonably close to a 31-*kharrūba* standard.

This is the only type of *fals* weight of which even some specimens have a reverse. Balog read the first name Farrūḥ but the last letter is *hā'* or *tā' marbūṭa* and Farwa, a known Arab name, is suggested here. Perhaps it needs to be established whether Tāj is a possible name at the period.

Note the traces of an earlier impression of the obverse die a little above the main one; in numismatic terms the piece has been double struck. Owing, no doubt, to the plastic nature of the hot glass such clear double impressions are rarely found on the stamps.

Sahl

389 Disk

سهل

Sahl.

OA + 4213. Worn. Green. 2.8cm; stamp 2.0cm; 4.13g.

The weight is not far below that of a *dīnār* but in the absence of other pieces from the die the possibility of coincidence cannot be ruled out.

ʿAbd al-Jabbār b. Nuṣayr

390–391 *Fals* weight of 30 *kharrūba*

على يدى عبد
الجبار بن نصير
مثقال فلس
خروبة

At the hands of ʿAbd
al-Jabbār b. Nuṣayr.
A weight of a *fals*
of *kharrubas* 30.

Six-pointed star flanked by crescents facing inwards below.

OA + 4199. A little more than half, top and right. Green. 2.5cm; 4.07g.
OA + 4254. Green. 3.2cm; stamp 2.6cm; 5.78g. (*Plate 19*)

From the same die Casanova 1893, 68; Petrie, 143; Miles 1948, 114; Launois 1957, 359; Fahmī 1957, 252; Balog 1976, 759B (information from Michael Bates).

A single specimen from a second very similar die has been illustrated (Balog 1976, 759A. The list of those described without illustration is as follows: Casanova 1893, 69; Miles 1948, 115; Viré, 31; Launois 1957, 360-1; Fahmī 1957, 253-7; Miles 1958a, 205; 1964b, 54; 1971, 47. ʻAbd al-Jabbār's weights may well be an official issue. The bold script and the use of the Coptic figure point to a date in the 760s or 770s.

ʻAbd al-ʻAzīz b. Ḥumayd

392 **Half-*dirham* weight (?)**

ما امر به
عبد العزيز بن
حميد نصف
كيل

What ordered
ʻAbd al-ʻAzīz b.
Ḥumayd. Half,
kayl.

(Coins and Medals) 54 11-2 12. Lane-Poole, 28. Slightly worn. Pale brown. 1.9cm; stamp 1.4 x 1.5cm; 1.24g. *(Plate 19)*

Lane-Poole took the last word as a blundered rendering of *dirham* but it is clearly *kayl*, an epithet applied to *dirham* weights of the standard of the ordinary currency *dirham* (see No. 407). The legend also begins *mā* rather than *mimmā*, 'of what', as he rendered it. No other weight for a half-*dirham kayl* appears to have been published, though even allowing for some wear the present piece was probably underweight. Balog (1976, 625) has published a *dīnār* weight of the Governor al-Layth b. al-Faḍl and an executive called ʻAbd al-ʻAzīz b. Ḥumayd. It is uncertain whether the latter is the same as the person on the British Museum's piece.

ʻAbd al-ʻAzīz (?) b. al-Zubayr

393 ***Dīnār* weight**
Marginal legend arranged in a square

(بسم) الله
مما امر به
عبد (العزيز)
بن الزبير

In the name of God.
Of what ordered
ʻAbd al-ʻAzīz
b. al-Zubayr.

Central legend

مثقل دينر
واف

Weight of a *dīnar*,
full-weight.

91 5-12 17. Deep blue. 2.7cm; stamp 2.0cm; 4.25g. *(Plate 19)*

The second part of the first name is virtually illegible. Of the numerous compound names formed with ʻAbd, ʻAbd al-ʻAzīz seems one of the most likely. There are other faults in the legend: *bism* appears as a large blur and the *qāf* of *mithqāl* is defective.

In spite of these faults the legends and script give the impression that the piece must be an official issue of some sort and early enough to be included in the present catalogue. Its deep royal blue colour, however, is very unusual for the early period.

ʻAbdallāh b. ʻAbd al-Raḥmān

394 **Disk weight: *wuqiyya* (?)**

على يدى
عبد الله بن
عبد الرحمن

At the hands
of ʻAbdallah b.
ʻAbd al-Raḥman.

93 11-11 16. Green, with iridescent surface. 4.4cm; stamp 1.7 x 1.7cm; 31.48g.

The inscription is very faint and impossible to reproduce but nevertheless absolutely clear. The weight would be correct for a *wuqiyya* on the Abbasid standard and the neat Kufic of the legend also points to a date in the third century.

ʻUbaydallāh (?)

395 ***Fals* weight of 18 (*kharrūba*)**

[---]
[-] عبيد الله
مثقال فلس
[ث]منية عشر
[---]

\- - - -
\- ʻUbaydallah
a weight of a *fals*
of eighteen
[- - - -]

(Coins and Medals) 80 6-3 69. Lane-Poole, 3. 2.4cm; 3.65g. *(Plate 19)*

Lane-Poole's reading of the first two lines, *bismillah/amara ʻUbaydallah* ('In the name of God. Ordered ʻUbaydallah') is certainly possible and he may have been right to attribute the piece to ʻUbaydallāh b. al-Ḥabḥāb. The script, except for being weakly engraved, is very like that of about his period and the type of legend is one that appears on his coin weights, except in omitting the name of his father. Of course the father's name might have been left out but, if so, the piece seems to be the only example of its kind. It is also possible to read *ibn*, 'son of', for Lane-Poole's *amara*. Al-Qāsim b. ʻUbaydallāh then becomes a possibility. What can be seen of the end of the first line might be the beginning of al-Qāsim but what precedes it does look like *mīm*, which is difficult to fit in with any of al-Qāsim's legends.

Lane-Poole read the end of the legend as *sana ʻAshar/mi'a* ('in the year a hundred and ten'), which is definitely wrong. At the beginning of the fourth line, where he read *sana*, *[tha]maniya* is obviously the correct reading. On the line below, where he read *mi'a* 'a hundred', only a few faint marks are really visible.

Dated stamps are not common; *fals* weights with the names of officials but without specification of the denomination in *qīrāṭ* or *kharrūba* are extremely rare. In fact the fourth line obviously does give the denomination and the fifth, if there was anything there at all, would presumably have read *qīrāṭ* or *kharrūba*. At 3.65g the piece is slightly over the weight of 18 average *kharrūba*, and appears to belong to the group of types struck to a slightly heavier standard.

ʻAlī b. (?)

396 **Ring weight**

الوفاء لله
على بن [--]

Honesty for God.
ʻAlī b. – –.

OA + 4403. Considerable loss of weight by chipping on the lower parts. Green. 4.5 x 5.9cm; 123g. (*Plate 19*)

The last letter of ʻAlī's father's name is certainly *lām*, which is probably preceded by *alif*. The beginning of the name is quite obscure.

The legend is cut by a technique which is not otherwise represented in the British Museum's collection and seems to be very unusual. On nearly all glass stamps the legends are in relief on the glass, meaning that they were cut in intaglio on the dies. Here the surface of the letters is on a level with the face of the stamp and they are made visible by being outlined by shallow depressions in the glass which must have been in relief on the die. The script can hardly be earlier than the third century AH and may even be later.

ʻAlī b. Muḥammad, with Ibrāhīm

397 Disk weight

مما امر
به الامير
على بن محمد
امتع الله
به واف على
يدى (ا)برهيم

Of what order-
ed the Amir
ʻAlī b. Muḥammad,
may God give him
joy. Full-weight, at
the hands of Ibrahīm.

Border of dots round upper part.

89 9-4 1. Lane-Poole 30Q. Small chip. Otherwise intact. Marks of pointed tool at edge of stamp at four, eight and twelve o'clock. Surface opaque. Green. 8.8cm; stamp 4.3cm; 346g. *(Plate 19)*

There is certainly no *alif* at the beginning of the executive's name and its end is very obscure but the reading Ibrahīm, suggested by Lane-Poole, may be correct.

Except in being rather shallowly cut, the legend and script resemble those of official issues of about the middle of the second century AH. The title Amir points to ʻAlī's being, if not Governor or Finance Director, then somebody of comparable status. The benediction following his name is also a sign of high rank, especially since the particular benediction is one that is otherwise only known to have been used on glass by the Caliph al-Mahdī (see Nos 298–305). However, although ʻAlī b. Muḥammad is a common name the historians do not mention any high Umayyad or Abbasid official of that name as being in Egypt in the eighth century AD. It should also be noted that the weight of the piece is aberrant; although it lacks a denomination it is obvious that it does not belong on the Ummayad *raṭl* system still in use in Egypt at the time it was most probably issued or, in fact, to any of the other established *raṭl* systems of eighth and ninth century Egypt.

There is, however, an ʻAlī b. Muḥammad who briefly played a significant role in Egyptian history at the right period, a role which might explain the unusual features of the weight. His identification with the Amir of the weight can only speculative but the possibility seems worth pointing out. The person in question is ʻAlī b. Muḥammad b. ʻAbdallāh b. Ḥasan b. Ḥasan b. ʻAlī b. Abī Ṭālib who was sent to Egypt by his father to raise support for the revolt against the Abbasids being organized by Muḥammad b. ʻAbdallāh and other members of his family which broke out in 145/762–3. The Alids' supporters' attempt to rise and gain control of Fusṭāṭ was an even greater failure than the risings in the Ḥijāz and Iraq, being scotched by Yazīd b. Ḥatim in the course of a single night. Obviously the rebels were never in control of the weights-and-measures office of the Egyptian capital, but Kindī tells us that ʻAlī b. Muḥammad had attracted considerable support before the rising and conceivably he might have had sufficient administrative control elsewhere to have issued weights. In support of this argument the weight is recorded as having been found in Fayyūm (Kindī, 111–5, 361–2; Ṭabarī III, 171–2; E.I.[1], *art.* Muḥammad b. ʻAbd allāh; E.I.[2], *art.* Ibrāhīm b. ʻAbd allāh).

To speculate further, this hypothesis could help to explain the piece's weight.Although it does not conform to the Egyptian standards it could be taken to be a *raṭl* on the standard known to have been in use in Syria in the Umayyad period which, from the few examples known, appears to have been about 335–350g (see Balog 1976, p. 21). It is not impossible that the leaders of the Alid movement intended to replace the *raṭl* standard of Egypt with the one from farther east.

ʻAmr b. ʻUbayd

398 ***Fals* weight of 30 *kharrūba***

امر عمرو
بن عبيد بمثقال
فلس ثلثين خر
وبة واف

Ordered ʻAmr
b. ʻUbayd a weight
of a *fals* of thirty *kharr-*
ūba, full-weight.

OA + 4200. Green. 3.2cm; 5.84g. (*Plate 19*)

The weight is correct for 30 *kharrūba*.

ʻĪsā b. Junāda

399 Disk weight

[---]
عيسى
بن جنادة

- - - -
ʻĪsā
b. Junāda

Six-pointed star below.

OA + 4306. The bottom two thirds. Marks of a pointed tool on the surviving three sides, the bottom one going right through. Green. 5.7cm; width of stamp 2.6cm; 33.18g. (*Plate 20*)

Unlike most people in the unidentified category 'Īsā b. Junāda issued a variety of stamps. The legend on all is similar, simply the name, which is always accompanied by the star. Three of 'Īsā's published pieces are small disks, similar in general appearance to coin weights (Miles 1948, 209; Fahmī 1957, 296; Balog 1976, 762). All are from one die, but the weights, 2.88g, 3.03g and 5.21g respectively, are so far apart and so unrelated that the pieces can hardly have been produced for any metrological purpose.

The large pieces must presumably be weights, but are difficult to relate to any of the established *raṭl* systems of the eighth and ninth centuries which the script suggests as a probable date for Īsā. When intact the British Museum's piece would have been too large for a *wuqiyya* and too small for a quarter-*raṭl* on all but one such *raṭl* system and fall in between the *wuqiyya* and half-*wuqiyya* on the apparently short-lived 'standard of Muḥammad b. Bastām'. A nearly intact ring weight in the American Numismatic Society (Miles 1948, 110) at 73.25g is equally difficult to fit in and also difficult to relate convincingly to the British Museum's disk weight.

'Īsā's published corpus is completed by a fragment of a disk weight, evidently similar in some ways to the British Museum's piece, published by Balog (1976, 763).

Muḥammad

400 Disk

محمد

Muḥammad

Eight-pointed star below.

72 3-20 12. Lane-Poole, 34g. Surface a little decayed. Dark brown. 3.2cm; 7.45g. (*Plate 20*)

Probably a token rather than a weight.

Muḥammad b. ʻAmr

401 *Fals* weight of 20 *kharrūba*

مما امر به
محمد بن عمرو
مثقال فلس وزن
عشرين خروبة

Of what ordered
Muḥammad b. ʻAmr
A weight of a *fals* of the weight of
twenty *kharrūbas*.

OA + 4255. Green. 2.9cm; stamp 2.2cm; 3.85g. (*Plate 20*)

From the same die Launois 1957, 354; Balog 1976, 775.

A specimen from the second die of the same denomination is described under No. 402. A number which are not illustrated may be from one or other of the dies (Casanova 1893, 47; Launois 1957, 355-6; Fahmī 1957, 303-6).

Muḥammad b. ʻAmr issued a second denomination of *fals* weight, of 23 *kharrūba* (Petrie, 148; Launois 1957, 352; Fahmī 1957, 300; Balog 1976, 774. Cf. Launois 1957, 353; Fahmī 1957, 301-2). The illustrated specimens are all from one die. He is not otherwise known but the neat appearance and relative commonness of his *fals* weights makes it likely that they belong to the main series of official issues. As Balog points out, the use of a rectangular stamp on the 23 *kharrūba* issue finds parallels in the early Abbasid period. The use of *wazn* in the legend of the 20-*kharrūba* types might suggest a slightly earlier date. In any case a dating of about the middle of the eighth century AD cannot be far wrong.

Muḥammad b. ʻAmr

402 *Fals* weight of 20 *kharrūba*

Same legend as No. 401, arranged in the same way, but note the extra stunted tooth of the *sīn* of *fals*.

(Coins and Medals) 1923 11-11 2. Green. 2.8cm; stamp 2.2cm; 3.88g. (*Plate 20*)

From the same die Casanova 1893, 45-6; Fahmī 1957, 307-8; Miles 1958a, 206. Cf. Rogers 1878, 4.

Maymūn

403 *Fals* weight of 33 (?) *kharrūba*

بسم الله
م{ـ}ما امر به
ميمون مثقال
فلس [illegible] واف

In the name of God.
Of what ordered
Maymūn. Weight
of a fals. 33, full-weight.

Ornament or letter at end of first line.

OA + 4283. Green. 3.2cm; 6.30g. (*Plate 20*)

Mimmā at the beginning of the second line has a superfluous 'tooth' after the initial *mīm*, perhaps a kind of anticipatory dittography from *mithqāl*. The Coptic figure for three is very clear, though the same can not be said for the thirty. The weight, however, is close to what would be expected for 33 *kharrūbas*. A 24-*kharrūba* weight of one Maymūn b. Kaʻb who may or may not be the same person has been published by Balog (1976, 383).

Yuḥannis

404–405 Vessel stamp

طبعة
يحنس

Stamping
of Yuḥannis

OA + 4108. Green. Width 4.3cm; stamp 2.2cm. (*Plate 20*)
94 3–9 7. Green. Width 3.4cm; stamp 2.2cm.

From the same die Balog 1976, 786.

The script is similar to that of the official eighth-century stamps but there do not seem to be official, or indeed other, vessel stamps with legends consisting only of *ṭabʻa* and a name, a formula which is, of course, common at one period with artisans' names on the centre of the reverse of coin weights. Perhaps Yuḥannis's stamps do not belong to the official series but represent rather a craftsman's 'signature', in which case it might be more appropriate to read *sanʻa* 'making', for *ṭabʻa*, 'here' (see Introduction pp. 42–3).

A specimen from a second die with the same legend is described under No. 406. Casanova 1893, 198–9, are evidently similar but are not illustrated.

Yuḥannis

406 Vessel stamp

Legend as on Nos 404–405.

94 3–9 8. Green. Blurred. Width 4.6cm; stamp 2.2cm. (*Plate 20*)

From the same die Launois 1960 II, 18.

Yaḥyā

407 *Dirham* weight

Obverse

درهم
كيل

Dirham
kayl

Reverse

على يدى
يحيى

At the hands
of Yaḥyā.

Dotted margin

(Coins and Medals) 85 10–7 5. Lane-Poole, 51. Green. 2.3cm; obverse stamp 1.5 x 1.4cm; 2.95g. (*Plate 20*)

From the same pair of dies Miles 1948, 124.

The reverse was overlooked in Lane-Poole's catalogue, and on the American Numismatic Society specimen Miles misread the name as al-Nahlī. The script is probably eighth- or ninth-century.

For the words '*dirham kayl*', which Balog has turned into a useful general term for *dirham* weights struck on the common standard of the silver coinage, see the Introduction (pp. 18ff). The weight of the British Museum's piece is very close to that standard which, calculated as seven-tenths of a gold dinar estimated at 4.25g, comes to 2.97g. The American Numismatic Society specimen weighs 2.92g.

Yaḥyā b. Habal

408 *Fals* weight, with Sulaymān b. ʻAbd al-Raḥmān

هذا ما امر
به يحيى بن هبل
طابع فلس{ر}
على يدى سليمن
بن عبد الر
حمن

This is what ordered
Yaḥyā b. Habal.
Stamp of a *fals*,
at the hands of Sulayman
b. ʻAbd al-Ra-
ḥman.

There is an extra 'tooth' at the end of *fals*.

OA + 4202. Green. 3.0cm; 5.59g. (*Plate 20*)

The name of Yaḥyā's father is reasonably clear and though the last letter might be *nūn* or *rā'* the only suitable name which a certain amount of investigation has revealed is the rare Habal, not, apparently, to be confused with Hubal which is written the same in unvowelled script but which was the name of one of the pre-Islamic divinities whose idols stood in the Kaʻba at Mecca (Dhahabī, p. 539; E.I.[1, 2], s.v. Hubal).

The use of *ṭābiʻ*, meaning seal or stamp, is not recorded elsewhere on glass though the synonym *khātim* is found on *fals* weights of Ibrāhīm b. Ṣāliḥ (e.g. Nos 318–319). Its occurrence here is one of the main pieces of evidence in favour of reading the problematic word which occurs on many early stamps as *ṭabʻa* rather than *ṣanʻa*. It is very unusual for a *fals* weight with a name or names on it not to have the demonination in *kharrūba* or *qīrāṭ*.

Ibn Yazīd (?)

409 *Fals* weight of 30 *kharrūba*

بسم ا[لله]
امر عـ[- بن]
يزيد مثق[ال]
فلس ثلثين خـ[روبة]

In the name of God.
Ordered – – – b.
Yazīd a weight
of a fals of thirty *kharrūba*.

OA + 4191. About two thirds, right-hand side. Green. 3.2cm; 4.25g. (*Plate 20*)

The curious 'tooth' preceding the *alif* of *amara* is presumably an engraver's error. The initial letter of Yazīd is tall enough to be a *lām* but there is no obvious name beginning with *lām* which might fit. Of the first name *ʻayn*, 'tooth', are clearly visible which offers several possibilities. ʻAbd al-Malik b. Yazīd's name seems too long for the available space and the same is true, *a fortiori*, of ʿAbd al-Raḥmān b. Yazīd. A curious *fals* weight has been published of an otherwise unknown ʿUthman b. Yazīd (Launois 1957, 383 = Fahmī 1957, 262), but the script differs from that of the present piece. There are other possibilities, ʿĪsā, for instance, or perhaps ʿAbdallāh.

Yūsuf

410 Disk

يوسف

Yūsuf.

Device above the name: two crossed lines on a base-line with a vertical extension at the left end. Dot in annulet below.

OA + 4214. Pink. Some decay. 2.2cm; 2.26g. (*Plate 20*)

This may be a token and possibly belongs to a later date, beyond the proper scope of the present catalogue.

6. ANONYMOUS WEIGHTS WITH DENOMINATIONS

Dīnār and *Dirham* Weights

411 *Dīnār* weight

مثقال
دينر
واف

Weight
of a *dīnar*
full-weight.

Dot below.

(Coins and Medals) 80 8-1 1. Lane-Poole, 45. A little worn. Bluish green. 2.3cm; 4.07g. (*Plate 20*)

Anonymous *dīnār* weights are not common and may not all belong to the main series of Umayyad and Abbasid official issues.

412 50-*dīrham* weight

على [يدى]
[----]
وزن [خمسين]
در[هم] كـ[يل]

At the hands
of - - - .
Weight of fifty
dirhams kayl.

OA + 4432. Surface decayed to some depth and mostly flaked off. Bluish green. Height 3.7cm; diameter 4.8cm; stamp 2.6 x 2.6cm; 139g. (*Plate 20*)

The restoration of the legend and the assignment of the piece to the category of 50-*dirham* weights is helped by its similarities to one in the Fitzwilliam Museum, briefly described by the present writer in an entry in an exhibition catalogue (Fitzwilliam Museum, 136b). The remains of the legend on the present piece are very like that of the other, but too faint for it to be certain that they are from one die and therefore that both were issued by the al-Nuʻmān b. ʻUmar (or possibly Jaʻfar) whose name occupies the second line on the Fitzwilliam piece. They differ in shape from the usual ring and disk weights. Originally they would have been short cylinders with flat ends. When the stamp was applied at one end the soft glass became distorted: on the present piece the bottom has spread out: on the other the sides bulge in the middle, resulting in a barrel-like profile. Both have become lopsided.

The term *kayl*, as applied to *dirhams*, has been discussed in the Introduction pp. 18ff. As noted there, almost none of the *dirham-kayl* weights, single or multiple, can be given a place within the main official Egyptian series of glass weights and measures. The script on the 50-*dirham* weights is a fairly early Kufic, probably datable to the ninth century AD, but al-Nuʻmān b. ʻUmar is not identified and the legends differ from those of the official ninth-century types. The use of the word *wazn*, 'weight', for instance, is otherwise only known from the first half of the eighth century.

At the conventional figure of 2.97g. to the *dirham*, 50 *dirham* comes to 148.5g. The surface decay on the present piece adequately explains why its weight is so much lower. The Fitzwilliam piece, itself slightly decayed, is reasonably close at 142.4g.

In describing the latter, the writer suggested that it might be of Syrian origin, mainly for the reason that in shape it bears some resemblance to the few known *raṭl*-system weights of Syrian provenance, those published by Abdel-Kader (1935) and Ettinghausen. However, atypical pieces of Egyptian manufacture do exist and since the present one was part of the collection which Dr Llewellyn Phillips formed in Cairo it is likely that both are Egyptian.

Fals Weights with Denominations in *Qīrāṭ* or *Kharrūba*

413–414 Half-*fals* weight of 9 *qīrāṭ*

مثقال
نصف فلس
وزن ت(سـ)عة
قرريطن

Weight
of half a *fals*,
of the weight of nine
qīrāṭs.

Six-pointed stars at end of first and last lines. Central hexagram in beaded circle. Central dot.

83 6-21 32. Lane-Poole 55g. Green, decayed. 2.2cm; stamp 1.8cm; 1.73g.
(Coins and Medals) 90 8-4 25. Lane-Poole, 55. Green. 2.2cm; stamp 1.9cm; 1.80g. (*Plate 20*)

From the same die Miles 1948, 150; Fahmī 1957, 388-9; Launois 1960 II, 26; Balog 1976, 833. Cf. Miles 1958a, 238.

The script is early and the use of *wazn*, 'weight', after *fals* in the legend and of *qīrāṭ* rather than *kharrūba* are early features. The issue must be assigned to the Umayyad period. For other half-*fals* denominations see No. 36. The *fals* denomination corresponding to the present type must be the type of 18 *qīrāṭ* here represented by No. 418.

Sīn of *tisʿa*, 'nine', is written with two instead of three 'teeth'. Another peculiarity is the seemingly superfluous letter, apparently *nūn*, at the end of *qarārīṭ*, the plural of *qīrāṭ*, which is here written without the *alif*.

415 14 *qīrāṭ*

[هذ]ا فلس
[و]اف اربعة
[ع]شر قيراط

This is a *fals*,
full-weight, of four-
teen *qīrāṭ*.

Beaded border. Marks below legend.

(Coins and Medals) Or. 3608. Lane-Poole, 52. Opaque. Black. 2.2cm; 2.40g. (*Plate 20*)

Lane-Poole read the first word *mithqāl*, 'weight', but the pronounced right-pointing tail of the last letter, the only one fully visible, would be extraordinary for a *lām*. The colour is unusual but the piece stands apart from the definite group of opaque or dark-coloured Abbasid pieces discussed under Nos 429-430, for the use of *qīrāṭ* rather than *kharrūba* is an indication of an Umayyad date. The piece is a little decayed but even allowing for that the weight is too low.

416 15 *kharrūba*

(م)ثقال فلس
خمس عشر
ة خروبة

Weight of a *fals*
of fiftee-
n *kharrūba*.

The *mīm* of *mithqāl* is miswritten as two 'teeth'.

(Coins and Medals) 89 6-4 70. Lane-Poole, 49. Green. 2.4cm; stamp 1.9cm; 3.02g. (*Plate 20*)

From the same die Fahmī 1957, 374.

A second very similar die is described below. The issue is evidently related to examples of 20 and 25 *kharrūba* which have similar legends in a similar bold script, probably to be dated to the early Abbasid period. There are examples of all these types in the British Museum's collection (nos 419-21, 431-4). Metrologically these issues are also related. The weights of the various denominations are generally consistent and almost all are slightly heavier than most other issues. The weights of the group as a whole imply a *kharrūba* of slightly over 2.00g. It is clear that there was a definite, though small, shift in the *kharrūba* standard used for the issue of these types. The existence of unusually heavy types of 25 and 20 *kharrūba* was first demonstrated by Miles's statistical analysis of a large number of glass weights (1964b, p. 85), but it has not previously been pointed out which particular issues are the heavy ones.
85), but it has not previously been pointed out which particular issues are the heavy ones.

417 15 *kharrūba*

Legend as on No. 416, with the same mispelling of *mithqāl*, and also with an extra tooth at the end of *fals*.

OA + 4269. Green. 2.6cm; 3.05g. (*Plate 20*)

From the same die Miles 1948, 23b; Balog 1976, 830.

418 18 *qīrāṭ*

بسم الله
مثقال فلس
واف وزن
ثمنية عشر
قيرط

In the name of God.
Weight of a *fals*,
full-weight, of the weight
of eighteen
qīraṭ.

Dotted border.

(Coins and Medals) Or. 3607. Green. 2.9cm; stamp 2.2cm; 3.55g. (*Plate 20*)

From the same die Casanova 1893, 10; Miles 1948, 148 Fahmī 1957, 371; Miles 1958a, 234; Balog 1976, 826. Cf. Castiglioni, 12; Fahmī 1957, 372; Miles 1958a, 235; Balog 1976, 827.

It has been mentioned that this type is likely to be the whole denomination of the half-*fals* weight of 9 *qīrāṭ* already described (Nos 413-414) and that the legends show that they belong to the Umayyad period. Two specimens (Casanova 1893, 10; Miles 1948, 148) are said to have possible traces of a reverse legend. This would be unparallelled at that time. The reverse of the British Museum's piece is perfectly preserved and never had a reverse legend.

419-420 20 *kharrūba*

فلس
عشرين
خروبة

Fals
of twenty
kharrūba

Six-pointed star below.

OA + 4267. Green. 2.9cm; 4.07g. (*Plate 20*)
(Coins and Medals) 83 5-10 2. Lane-Poole, 44. Green. 2.6cm; 4.08g.

From the same die Miles 1948, 144; Launois 1957, 343; Fahmī 1957, 359; Miles 1963 I, 64; Balog 1976, 822-3. Cf. Miles 1948, 145-6; Launois 1957, 344-7; Fahmī 1957, 360-5; Miles 1958a, 230.

This type belongs to the group issued on a heavy weight standard as discussed under No. 416. No. 421 is from a similar die.

421 20 *kharrūba*

Legend as on Nos 419-420. Dot above and two dots to left of six-pointed star below.

OA + 4268. Green. 3.0cm; stamp 2.5cm; 4.75g. (*Plate 20*)

The script is very similar to that of Nos 419-420 and the related types issued on a heavy *kharrūba* standard but this piece is far too heavy for a 20-*kharrūba* piece even on the heavy standard.

422 22 (?) *kharrūba*

بسم الله
هذا فلس
اربعين
خروبة

In the name of God.
This is a *fals*
of forty [*sic*]
kharrūba.

Dot or star at end of third line.

OA + 4207. Green. 2.7cm; 4.21g. (*Plate 21*)

From the same die Miles 1948, 140. Cf. 1964a, 61.

The script is very crude. Miles read *mithqāl*, 'weight', where *hadhā*, 'this', seems a little more likely. The other difficulty is the denomination in *kharrūbas*. The reading 'forty' first suggested by Miles for the piece in the Muntazah Palace does justice to what is visible on the other specimens but makes no sense. Forty *kharrūba* is almost certainly beyond the upper limit of weight for a *fals*; the largest *fals* weights are of 36 *kharrūba*. Nor do the examples of this type weigh anything like 40 *kharrūba*. Miles suggested that the intended denomination may have been 24 *kharrūba*, simply the relatively easy slip on the part of the engraver of writing *arba'īn* for *arba' wa 'ishrīn*. The weights are, however, too low for 24 *kharrūba*. The Muntazah piece weighs 4.00g, but that in the A.N.S. is very close to the British Museum's one at 4.20g and since it is chipped would originally have been a little heavier. If these two pieces represent the intended standard the mistake would have been writing *arba'īn* for *ithnā wa 'ishrīn*, a slightly more complicated error.

423 24 *kharrūba*

مثقال فلس
اربعة و
عشرين خر
وبة

Weight of a *fals*
of four and
twenty *kharr-*
ūba.

OA + 4266. Slightly chipped at bottom. 3.4cm; stamp 2.8cm; 6.26g. (*Plate 21*)

The piece is considerably overweight.

424 25 *qīrāṭ*

مثقال فلس
واف وزن
خمسة و عشر
ين قيرط

Weight of a *fals*
full-weight, of the weight
of five and twen-
ty *qīraṭ*.

Dot above end of third line. Border.

(Coins and Medals) 82 8-3 32. Green. 2.9cm; stamp 2.2cm; 4.91g. (*Plate 21*)

From the same die Miles 1948, 138; Balog 1976, 812. Cf. Miles 1958a, 226; Balog 1976, 811, 813.

Examples from two other similar dies have been illustrated. One has a crescent above and a star below as well as the mark over the third line (Launois 1957, 324. Cf. 325). Two specimens of the third, which has a defect in the legend, are described below.

The occurrence of *wazn* and *qīrāṭ* in the legends of these well-produced pieces indicates an Umayyad date.

425-426 25 *qīrāṭ*

Legend as on No. 424, but see commentary. Dot over end of third line. Border.

OA + 4262. Green. 2.9cm; stamp 2.1cm; 4.90g. (*Plate 21*)
(Coins and Medals) 82 8-3 31. Lane-Poole, 41. Green. 2.9cm; stamp 2.1cm; 4.91g.

From the same die Casanova 1893, 11; Fahmī 1957, 337. Cf. Launois 1957, 331-3; Fahmī 1957, 338-48 - said to be from several dies.

While most of the legend is competently written something has gone wrong at the end of the second line. In view of the great similarity of this type with the two others described under No. 424, there is no doubt that *wazn* is what was intended. It looks as if the *wāw* has been omitted and the two other letters shifted to the right.

427 25 *kharrūba*

هذا مثقا
ل فلس خمس
و عشرين
خرو
بة

This is a weigh-
t of a *fals* of five
and twenty
kharrū-
ba.

Six-pointed star at end of legend.

OA + 4265. Green. Some wear. 3.0cm; stamp 2.2cm; 4.82g. (*Plate 21*)

From the same die Launois 1957, 326; Fahmī 1957, 335 or 336 (illustration numbered 332); Miles 1958a, 225; Balog 1976, 810. Cf. Miles 1958a, 224.

Here is a case of a die which was later altered in a remarkable fashion. Two specimens which have been illustrated are certainly from the same die but with *khams*, 'five', replaced by *sabʿ*, 'seven' (Casanova 1893, 14; Balog 1976, 809). Most die alterations consist of removing something or adding something completely new in an empty space; to replace part of the legend must have been a rather complicated piece of craftsmanship. That *sabʿ* is the later version can be seen from the way the tail of its *ʿayn* has encroached upon the end of *ʿishrīn* below. The weights of both types conform well to the denominations appearing on them (Michael Bates has provided the information that Balog 1976, 810, weighs 4.86g rather than 5.24g).

Another die is known with the same arrangement of the legend as on the 27-*kharrūba* version of the present one (Fahmī 1957, 317; Miles 1958a, 218). A number of similar specimens of the same denomination have not been illustrated (Casanova 1893, 14 *bis;* Fahmī 1957, 318; Miles 1951b, 37).

428 25 *kharrūba*

مثقال فلس
خمسة و عشر[ين]
[خ]روبة

Weight of a *fals*
of five and twenty
kharrūba.

OA + 4263. Pale blue-green. 2.8cm; 5.02g. (*Plate 21*)

The weight would seem to indicate that the type was produced to a slightly heavy standard.

429–430 25 *kharrūba*

مثقال فلس
خمس و عشر
ين خروبة

Weight of a *fals*
of five and twen-
ty *kharrūba*.

Roughly rectangular border set in a circular border.

83 6-21 31. Lane-Poole, 39g. Edge chipped off at top and sides. Opaque. Black. 2.8cm; 3.40g.
(Coins and Medals) 81 7-6 62. Lane-Poole, 39. Under half; top and left. Opaque. Black. 2.9cm; stamp 2.3cm; 3.12g. (*Plate 21*)

From the same die Miles 1958, 223; Launois 1960 II, 24.

A second die is represented by a single illustrated piece in Cairo (Fahmī 1957, 319); several others have not been illustrated (Miles 1958a, 222; Fahmī 1957, 320-2; Miles 1971, 53). The Cairo pieces are all described as blue; the others are said to be black or brown and evidently resemble the British Museum's ones in colour. Not all opaque dark *fals* weights are necessarily closedly related to the present type. No. 415, for instance, is certainly not. However an issue of dark types of 23 *kharrūba* with similar legends, script and borders must have been in use at nearly the same time. Two dies of the issue have been recorded (Miles 1963 I, 62; Balog 1976, 816. Cf. 817-8). Balog pointed out that certain pieces of the Caliph al-Manṣūr are of similar fabric and dated the anonymous *fals* weights to his reign. The dating is probably correct but it is possible to go a little further. As has been noted under No. 197, the dark weights of al-Manṣūr have reverses of ʿAbd al-Malik b. Yazīd enabling one to suggest a more precise date for the anonymous types in ʿAbd al-Malik's second governorship (137-41/755-8).

The design with the legend framed in a roughly rectangular border inscribed in a circle is only found on these types of *fals* weight. The design itself is obviously derived from the appearance of a small circular coin weight impressed with a square stamp, a type that begins to appear, notably among 13-*kharrūba dirham* weights, early in the Abbasid period.

431–433 25 *kharrūba*

فلس
خمس و
عشرين
خروبة

Fals
of five and
twenty
kharrūba.

Crescent above, partly overlapping the *sīn* of *fals*.

OA + 4206. Green. 3.1cm; stamp 2.4cm; 4.98g. (*Plate 21*)
OA + 4264. Green. 3.3cm; stamp 2.4cm; 5.13 g.
OA + 4328. Chipped at bottom left. Green. 3.1cm; stamp 2.4cm; 4.93g.

From the same die Casanova 1893, 13; Petrie, 171; Miles 1948, 135; Launois 1960 II, 22; Miles 1963 II, 43; Balog 1976, 814. Cf. Castiglioni, 14.

These pieces and No. 434, from a very similar die, belong to the group of issues on a heavy *kharrūba* standard which has been discussed under No. 416. The following specimens have not been illustrated or in one case adequately illustrated and may be from either die: Miles 1951b, 38; Virê, 25; Launois 1957, 335-42; Fahmī 1957, 323-34; Miles 1958a, 221; Launois 1960, 23, 23 *bis*; Miles 1963a, 58-60; Balog 1976, 815.

434 25 *kharrūba*

Legend as on Nos 431-433 but the crescent is over the ductus between the last two letters of *fals* and does not overlap the *sīn*.

OA + 4205. Green. 3.1cm; 5.20g. (*Plate 21*)

From the same die Launois 1957, 334.

See Nos 431-433.

435 26 *qīrāṭ*, with the title *al-amīr*

امر الا
مير بستة
و عشرين
قيرطا

Ordered the A-
mir six
and twenty
qīraṭ.

Border

OA + 4261. Pale blue-green. 3.2cm; 5.09g. *(Plate 21)*

From the same die Miles 1963 II, 6.

As Miles pointed out the script is early; the neat layout and the letter-forms, particularly the elevated *rā'* have such a close resemblance to certain pieces of Qurra b. Sharīk that it is probable that the engraver was the same. Qurra's only known *fals* weight (Launois 1959, 2) is of the same denomination and has exactly the same legend, with the addition of his name after *al-amīr*, a legend which is unusual in lacking any word such as *fals* or *wazn* before the specification of the denomination in *qīrāṭ* and in having an *alif* at the end of *qīrāt* (for the latter see No. 92). The anonymous type must then be assigned to the last decade of the first century AH, the time when the first glass stamps of Muslim officials begin to appear. At that period there is no doubt that only one person in the official hierachy of Egypt had the title Amir, the Governor for 'prayer'. The point is made in an anecdote related by Kindī (62-3) about Qurra's incognito arrival at Fusṭāṭ to take up his post. It was not until it was realized that he was Governor with full powers and not merely a finance official that he was greeted with the title. The legends of the glass stamps confirm this. Only towards the end of the Umayyad period do Finance Directors begin to use the title. Conversely there is no well-attested example of a Governor's name appearing on the glass of the Umayyad period unless he also had control of finance. The anonymous Amir of the 26- *qīrāt* weights is thus likely to be a Governor who also acted as Finance Director. The possibilities are very limited. Qurra himself is evidently the most likely person; if our attribution of No. 1 is correct, ʻAbdallāh b. ʻAbd al-Malik b. Marwān, Qurra's predecessor, who also had full powers, might be considered. For a considerable time after Qurra no Governor acted as Finance Director.

The piece in the Ruthven collection is broken. In the second line the last two letters of *bi-sitta* are missing and Miles restored the word as Bishr, attributing the piece to Bishr b. Ṣafwān who was the Governor of Egypt in 101-102/720-721. There is no indication that Bishr acted as Finance Director and it would be surprising if his name appeared on stamps, though a piece excavated at Fusṭāṭ has also been attributed to him (Scanlon 1968, 190).

436 26 *kharrūba*

مثقال
فلس

Weight
of a *fals*.
26.

Triangle of punched dots each side of the figure.

94 3-9 16. Green; 3.1cm; stamp 2.2 x 2.3cm; 5.82g. *(Plate 21)*

From the same die Balog 1976, 808.

The weights of both the known pieces are much too high for 26 *kharrūba*, which would normally be close to 5.0g. Nor are their weights consistent with each other, Balog's weighing 5.50g. He argued that it was actually meant to be of 28 *kharrūba*, which seems even less likely when the British Museum's specimen does not conform to that standard. As Balog noted, the Coptic figure for 26 is absolutely clear: compare Salama's issue of the same denomination (No. 249).

437 20 – X *kharrūba*

[بـ]سم الله
مثقال فلس
[--] و عشر
[ين] خر(و)
بة

In the name of God.
Weight of a *fals*
of – and twen-
ty *kharrū-*
ba.

(Coins and Medals) Lane-Poole, 43. Fragment. About two-thirds of the left. Green. Length 2.2cm; 2.98g. *(Plate 21)*

The *wāw* of *kharrūba* is written 'tooth', *ra'* and was so read by Lane-Poole, but the correction seems obvious and there is room for the rest of the word below.

438 30 *kharrūba*

بسم الله
مثقال (ف)لس
[ث]لثين خروبة

In the name of God.
Weight of a *fals*
of thirty *kharrūba*.

Six-pointed star above.

OA + 4204. Green. 3.0cm; 6.02g. *(Plate 21)*

The script is rather crude and spidery but the weight is correct for 30 *kharrūba* on a slightly heavy standard.

439-441 30 *kharrūba*

مثقال الفلو
س ثلثين خرو
بة واف

Weight for *fulū-*
s of thirty *kharrū-*
ba, full-weight.

Legend in reverse

OA + 4259. Green. 3.3cm; 6.00g.
OA + 4260. Green. 3.3cm; 5.90g. *(Plate 21)*

(Coins and Medals) 88 7-12 13. Lane-Poole, 38. Green. 2.9cm; 5.10g. Cf. Miles 1958a, 217.

Nos 439 and 440 are of a reasonable weight for 30 *kharrūba*, but No. 441 is far too low and the piece published by Miles weighs only 4.13g. For the appearance of *fulūs* in legends see No. 4.

442 30 *kharrūba*

مثقال
فلس
ثلثين
خروبة

Weight
of a *fals*
of thirty
kharrūba

Rectangular stamp

(Coins and Medals) 72 6-3 18. Fragment. About a third from the right hand side. Green. Length 2.1cm; 2.00g.

From the same die Casanova 1893, 15; Fahmī 1957, 313; Miles 1958a, 216. Cf. Casanova 1893, 16 and possibly Fahmī 1957, 314-5.

443-444 32 *kharrūba*

مثقال
فلس اثنين
و ثلثين خر
وبة

Weight
of a *fals* of two
and thirty *kharr-*
ūba.

8 3 6-21 27. Lane-Poole, 37g. Green. 3.2cm; stamp 2.4 x 2.4cm; 6.25g. (*Plate 21*)
(Coins and Medals) 81 7-6 61. Lane-Poole, 37. 3.2cm; 2.4 x 2.4cm; 6.23g.

From the same die Casanova 1893, 17; Fahmī 1957, 312

445 33 *kharrūba*

مثقال
ثلثة و
ثلثين خر
وبة

Weight
of three and
thirty *kharr-*
ūba.

Border of punched dots.

OA + 4258. Green. 3.3cm; stamp 2.2 x 2.2cm; 6.52g. (*Plate 21*)

446 33 *kharrūba* (?)

[بسـ]ـم الله
مثقال فلس
(ثلاثة) ثلثين
خروبة

In the name of God.
Weight of a *fals*
of three and thirty
kharrūba

(Coins and Medals) 53 4-6 976. Rogers 1878, 8; Lane-Poole, 36. Green. 2.7cm; stamp 2.1cm; 5.70g. (*Plate 21*)

The word before *thalāthīn*, 'thirty', is oddly written. Any digit before thirty should, of course, be followed by *wāw*, 'and', but Lane-Poole's reading *thalātha*, 'three', still seems a little more likely than Rogers' grammatically better *waznuhu* ('the weight of which is ...'). In any case the weight is too low even for 30 *kharrūba*.

Without Denomination in *Qīrāṭ* or *Kharrūba*

447

بسم الله
ميزان فلس
واف

In the name of God.
Weight of a *fals*,
full-weight.

Six-pointed star over last letter.

OA + 4273. Green. 2.6cm; 4.19g. (*Plate 21*)

The British Museum's collection is well off for pieces in the not very common category of anonymous *fals* weights without denomination in *qīrāṭ* or *kharrūba* (Nos 447-454). Obviously a number of issues without any particularly close relation to each other are represented in the group. On some the legends are poorly written but on others this is not the case. To judge by the script they are to be assigned to the first three quarters of the second century AH. Whether any are unofficial issues is difficult to say. The weight standards to which such pieces were intended to conform need not necessarily have been based on the *kharrūba* or *qīrāṭ* and in cases where no more than a single piece is known from a particular die it seems preferable not to speculate on possible metrological implications.

448-449

ميزان
فلس
واف

Weight
of a *fals*,
full-weight.

OA + 4274. Lane-Poole, 40g. Cracked. Pale blue. 3.1cm; 5.74g. (*Plate 21*)

(Coins and Medals) 73 8-1 75. Rogers 1878, 7; Lane-Poole, 40. Pale blue. 3.1cm; 5.77g.

The very bold script and the use of the word *mīzān* for 'weight' in the legend suggest an early date for this issue. Lane-Poole misread *mīzān* as *mithqāl*, though Rogers had already provided the correct reading. Lane-Poole's reading presumably led Miles (1948, 133) to compare these pieces with one in the American Numismatic Society collection which, though it is not illustrated, probably does have a legend beginning *mithqāl* and belong to a different issue as its weight of 5.13g would imply. The weight of the British Museum's pieces are consistent and may indicate a standard of 30 *kharrūba*.

450

ميزان
فلس

Weight
of a *fals*

OA + 4270. Green. 2.4cm; stamp 1.9cm; 3.55g. (*Plate 21*)

Mīzān is used for 'weight', once again likely to indicate an early date.

451

ميزان
فلس

Weight
of a *fals*

Legend in reverse

OA + 4271. Green. 2.6cm; 3.99g. (*Plate 21*)

From the same die Miles 1948, 147.

The piece in the American Numismatic Society collection weighs 3.95g, very close to that of the British Museum's piece. The standard may be intended for 20 *kharrūba*.

452

مثقال
فلس
واف

Weight
of a *fals*,
full-weight.

Square border, with a loop at the centre of each side.

OA + 4272. Slightly decayed. Green. 3.0cm; 4.61g. (*Plate 21*)

453

مثقال فلس
واف

Weight of a *fals*,
full-weight.

OA + 4275. Cracked. Pale green. 3.1cm; stamp 2.5cm; 3.99g. (*Plate 21*)

454

مثقال
فلس

Weight
of a *fals*.

(Coins and Medals) 90 8-4 23. Lane-Poole 35d. Green, with olive-green stain. 3.3cm; 7.21g. (*Plate 21*)

Other pieces with the same legend and similar loose script are known, but none of the illustrated specimens is from this die.

Heavy Weights

455 Disk weight: half-*wuqiyya*

نصف
وقيه

Half
wuqiyya.

Crescent beneath legend. Rectangular border.

(Coins and Medals) 81 7-6 60. Lane-Poole, 35. Olive-green, surface part discoloured and opaque. 3.6cm; stamp 1.9 x 2.0cm; 15.74g. (*Plate 22*)

Cf. Casanova 1893, 12; Miles 1948, 175.

The weight of the piece is right for a half-*wuqiyya* on the Abbasid standard. The design and script are similar to those of the *wuqiyya* stamp, No. 456, and the two types may belong to the same set.

456 Disk weight: *wuqiyya*

وقية

Wuqiyya

Eight-pointed star flanked by crescents pointing upwards below. Rectangular border.

OA + 4314. Iridescent. Green. 3.6cm; stamp 1.6 x 1.8cm; 15.18g. (*Plate 22*)

Cf. Balog 1976, 806.

The weight is that of a half-*wuqiyya* on the Abbasid standard. In spite of its legend, however, the piece may really have been intended as a half-*wuqiyya*, for the same die is used on disk weights twice the size of this one which are the normal weight for Abbasid *wuqiyyas* (Petrie, 254-6. Cf. Balog 803, not illustrated but said to be from the same die as, presumably, 806; No. 457). Balog has suggested a Tulunid date on account of the shape of the stamp and the toolmarks on his own piece, but the plain script indicates a considerably earlier dating.

457 Disk weight: *wuqiyya*

وق[ية]

Wuqiyya.

Ornament or ornaments below. Rectangular border.

OA + 4351. Green, with opaque and devitrifying surface. Mark of a round-pointed tool on each side of the rim. 4.4cm; stamp 1.6 x 1.6cm; 30.45g.

The impression is very faint but there is some chance that the piece is from the same die as No. 456. However, as noted there, its weight places it with the other pieces from the die of No. 456.

458 Disk weight: great *wuqiyya* (*wuqiyya kabīr*)

From the stamp of the denomination stamp of No. 344.

91 7-1 523. Fragment of the edge, lacking the bottom left quarter of the stamp. Green with slight iridescence. Length 3.7cm; 8.70g. *(Plate 22)*

From the same die Petrie, 251.

Petri 251 is also a fragment, with the denomination stamp repeated twice. On other pieces it is found combined with executive and command stamps. On No. 344, for instance, it is used with a command stamp of Mālik b. Dalham and the executive stamp of ʻAbdallāh b. ʻUthmān. Other such occurrences of the stamp are on Petrie 205, with Maḥfūẓ b. Sulaymān and Ibn al-Ḥajjāj, Balog 1976, 627, with Maḥfūẓ and ʻAbdallāh b. ʻIrbāḍ and Balog 1976, 641, with command stamp of al-Ḥasan b. al-Baḥbāḥ.

459 Disk weight: great *wuqiyya*

Denomination stamp

وقيه
كبير
واف

Wuqiyya
kabīr,
full-weight.

Command stamp
Marginal legend arranged in a rectangle:

مما [امر به]
[----]
[مولى امير]
المؤمنين

Of what ordered
- - - -
Mawlā of the Commander
the Faithful,

central legend:

ا[-- الله]
على [يدى]
[----]

May God - him
at the hands
of - - -

OA + 4309. Fragment, lacking two-thirds of the command stamp. Green, surface partly opaque. Length 5.0cm; denomination stamp 1.9cm; 13.5g. *(Plate 22)*

In the centre of the command stamp part of the first letter of the name is visible offering many possibilities, *dāl, ṣād, ṭā' kāf* and of course the dotted letters similar to them.

The die of the denomination stam was also used on Petrie, 210, paired with a different and also damaged command stamp with part of an Amir's name. The name begins ʻAbd and Petrie was probably right to read ʻAbdallāh. He attributed the piece to ʻAbdallāh b. al-Musayyib, Governor in 176-177/793. The appearance of both command stamps, and particularly the arrangement of the legend on the British Museum's specimen, suggest a rather later date. ʻAbdallāh b. Muḥammad, Governor in 189-190/805-806 would fit this theory. Neither of them is reported by Kindī (135, 141-2) to have controlled finances, but a *dīnār* weight has been reasonably attributed to ʻAbdallāh b. Muḥammad (Launois 1957, 243 = Fahmī 1957, 12, and see the note on ʻĀṣim b. Ḥafṣ preceeding No. 327).

460-463 Ring weight: great *wuqiyya*

وقية
كبير
واف

Wuqiyya
kabīr,
full-weight.

OA + 4372. Dark green. Intact. 4.5 x 4.8cm; 66.7g. *(Plate 22)*
OA + 4373. Green, with surface discoloured. Chip of a gramme or two off the left edge by the stamp. 4.3 x 4.5cm; stamp 1.8cm; 65.1g.
OA + 4374. Green, with surface iridescence. 3.5 x 4.4 cm; stamp 1.9cm; 65.8g.
OA + 4375. The upper half, broken off from front to back. Green. Length c. 4.0cm; 35.1g.

From the same die Petrie, 252; Miles 1958a, 259; Balog 1976, 799-800. Cf. Miles 1958a, 258; 1963 I, 66-7; II, 47.

All recorded specimens from this common die are anonymous ring weights with only the one stamp. The script and layout of the legend are extraordinarily similar to those of several other *wuqiyya kabīr* denomination stamps, including the two described immediately above, which appear beside stamps of executives and governors of the last quarter of the second century AH. The present stamp is presumably later than the others but cannot be much later. Nos 460-2 are undamaged and their weights conform to those of a number of other intact or nearly intact pieces. Seven such specimens give an average weight of 63.33g. As Balog (1976, 799-80 and pp. 15-6, 27-8) has pointed out, such a weight is difficult to explain as a *wuqiyya* on the *raṭl-kabīr* system as we know it from intact pieces of the higher denominations. He suggests that the *wuqiyya kabīr* pieces of the present type are in fact double-*wuqiyyas* on the Abbasid standard. As far as the actual weights are concerned this suggestion raises no difficulty but it is not easy to see why a double-*wuqiyya* denomination should have become briefly popular or to accept Balog's further suggestion that the denomination *wuqiyya kabīr* is used in error on such pieces. Errors do occasionally seem to have been made in the use of stamps but in this case the error would have had to have been repeated many times and there is no example of the hypothetical correct use of the stamp. The question must for the present remain one of a number of unsolved problems concerning the heavy weights of the end of the second century AH.

464 Ring weight: quarter-*raṭl*

ربع
رطل

Quarter
raṭl.

Rectangular intaglio border.

94 3-9 15. Chip of half a dozen or so grammes from below the stamp. 4.2 x 4.8cm; 91.3g. (*Plate 22*)

From the same die Miles 1948, 153.

Presumably on the Abbasid standard.

465-466 Ring weight: quarter-*raṭl*

ربع
رطل
واف

Quarter
raṭl,
full-weight.

Star or dot below.

OA + 4383. Badly chipped on left side and bottom. Surface discoloured. Green. Height 5.0cm; 104g.
OA + 4384. Badly chipped at left and back. Surface opaque and flaking. Dark green. Length 6.1cm; 146g. (*Plate 22*)

From the same die Petrie, 175.

Petrie's intact piece weighs 188g, which appears to indicate a *raṭl* system about twice as heavy as the Abbasid one. The same die also seems to be that used twice on a disk weight together with a still undeciphered rectangular stamp which perhaps bears the names of officials (Miles 1971, 49).

467 Ring weight: half a great *raṭl* (*raṭl kabīr*)

نصف
رطل
كبير

Half
raṭl
kabīr.

89 4-14 1. Lane-Poole, 34t. Fragment of the top. Rectangular stamp with trace of larger circular stamp to right. Length 4.2cm; height of stamp 1.9cm; 77.5g. (*Plate 22*)

From the same die Casanova 1893, 60 (left-hand stamp).

On the piece published by Casanova the denomination stamp is paired with the common executive stamp of ʿĀṣim b. Ḥafṣ of which several examples have been listed (Nos 320-322, 329). It belongs with the other denomination stamps used for weights on the *raṭl-kabīr* system at or shortly after its introduction.

468 Disk weight: double-*raṭl*

رطلين

Two *raṭl.*

Stamp roughly octagonal.

OA + 4315. Surface decayed away. Otherwise intact. Green. 4.6cm; stamp c. 2.5cm; 30.14g. (*Plate 22*)

The piece is evidently a freak, far too small to be any sort of double-*raṭl*. Its weight is about that of a *wuqiyya* on the Abbasid standard.

469 Ring weight: double-*raṭl*

رطلين

Two *raṭl.*

Eight-pointed star below. Double rectangular border.

71 6-16 14. Lane-Poole 34q. Five marks of a pointed tool round the stamp. The top half. Length c. 8cm; stamp 2.2 x 2.2cm; c. 410g. (*Plate 22*)

The brief legend *raṭlayn* occurs on the aberrant piece, No. 468, described above, but otherwise has only been recorded on Balog 1976, 792, which, from the description, differs from both the British Museum's pieces.

7. ANONYMOUS VESSEL STAMPS

With Denominations of Measures of Capacity

470–478 Half a quarter-*qisṭ*

نصف
ربع
القسط

Half
a quarter
qisṭ.

OA + 4110. Green. Width 2.7cm. (*Plate 22*)
OA + 4111. Green. Width 3.0cm.
OA + 4112. Piece of rim attached. Width 3.5cm.
OA + 4113. Olive green. Width 2.2cm.
OA + 4114. Green. Width 3.1cm.
OA + 4350. Green. Width 2.9cm.
94 3-9 11. Green. Width 3.2cm.
94 3-9 12. Green. Width 3.0cm
95 12-30 6. Piece of rim attached. Green. Width 4.1cm.

From the same die Casanova 1893, 36; Miles 1948, 176; Viré, 35; Launois 1957, 270; Miles 1958a, 266; 1963 I, 69; Balog 1976, 918. Cf. Miles 1948, 177-8; 1958a, 267; 1963 II, 48; 1964a, 67; Balog 1976, 915-7.

The denomination of this and similar types still requires satisfactory explanation. Half-a-quarter for an eighth is clumsy in Arabic, which has no difficulty in saying eighth. Noting the point, Balog has suggested that *wa*, 'and', has dropped out and that we should read 'half and a quarter', i.e. three-quarters. This is proper Arabic. As Balog points out the usage does occur in Mamlūk coinage. However, the fact that there are several dies reading apparently 'half quarter-*qisṭ kabīr* (see Nos 479-481) makes the hypothesis of a mistake less likely and in any case this interpretation raises the problem of why such a metrologically curious denomination should have been favoured. There is no obvious series of other denominations in which any of these types might have been included.

479 Half a quarter of a great *qisṭ* (*qisṭ kabīr*)

[ن]صف
[ر]بع قس[ط]
كبير

Half
a quarter of a *qisṭ*,
great.

OA + 4115. Green. Width 2.3cm. (*Plate 22*)

Nos 480 and 481, both with faint and incomplete legends are from different dies of the same denomination (see Nos 470-478). No specimen of the denomination appears to have been illustrated but a number have been described (Casanova 1893, 27-32; Launois 1957, 268-9 (?); Balog 1976, 922).

480 Half a quarter of a great *qisṭ* (*qisṭ kabīr*)

[ن]صـ[ـف]
[ر]بع قس[ط]
كـ[ـبير]

Half
a quarter of a *qisṭ*,
great

OA + 4116. Pale green. Width 1.9cm.

481 Half a quarter of a great *qisṭ* (?)

[نصف]
[ر]بع قس[ط]
كبي[ر]

Half (?)
a quarter of a *qisṭ*,
great.

OA + 4118. Pale green. Width 1.8cm. (*Plate 22*)

With the Names of Commodities

482–484 *Mikyala* of lupin seeds (*turmus*) for a *fals*

مكيلة
ترمس
بفلس

Measure
of lupin seeds
for a *fals*.

OA + 4121. Green. Width 3.5cm. (*Plate 22*)
OA + 4122. Green. Width 2.8cm.
OA + 4123. Olive-green. Width 2.3cm.

From the same die Miles 1963, 70; Balog 1976, 845. Cf. Launois 1957, 308; Balog 1976, 846.

No. 484 is considerably smaller than the die and only received the impression of the central part. No. 485, which also shows only the centre of the legend, may be a product of the same die in an altered state. The die would seem to belong to the group of stylistically similar anonymous ones for different products recognizable by the bold script and extended *kāf* in *mikyala* which have been discussed in the Introduction (p. 38) where the name 'long-*kāf*' group has been proposed for them. As stated there it would appear that the group formed a set of commodity stamps which were used in combination with the stamps of executives from about 145-160 AH. This die may well in fact appear paired with an executive stamp of Qutayba b. Ziyād on a piece that was in the Fouquet collection (see No. 288).

The botanical identification of *turmus* with *Lupinus termis*, Forsk., has been discussed in detail by Miles (1951, 15). The seeds of the lupin were, and still are, used as food. *Turmus* is listed among the significant winter crops of Egypt by the mediaeval writers, who give details of how it was grown and the tax paid on it (Ibn Mammāti, 235, 264; Cahen, 146; Müller-Wodarg, 27). At the time of Napoleon's occupation of Egypt lupins, like beans and chick peas, were cooked for sale and sold very cheaply in portions, the lupins being even cheaper than the other two basic foods. The naturally bitter lupin seed needs to be subjected to a long process of soaking in water before it is fit to eat. According to Ibn al-'Awwām a kind of bread was made from the flour of lupins mixed with what and barley. (*Description*, Histoire Naturelle II, 23-4; Etat Moderne (1) 528, 704-5, (2) 410-1; Ibn al- 'Awwām II, 99).

485 *Mikyala* of lupins for a *fals*

[مـ]كيـ[ـلة]
[تـ]رمس
[بـ]فلـ[ـس]

Measure
of lupins
for a *fals*.

Omega, iota above the second line.

OA + 4124. Bluish green. 2.2cm; (*Plate 22*)

From the same die Casanova 1893, 83.

The impression of the centre of the die is all that appears on both Casanova's piece and the British Museum's. It is possible that the die is the same as that of Nos 482-484 with the addition of what appears to be the two Greek letters. The same letters are found on weights of Muhammad b. Saʿīd (see Nos 260-264) which suggests that this vessel stamp might be from about the same date. The similarity, or possibly even identity, of the die with that of Nos 282-284 supports such a dating since that type appears to belong to the group of 'long-*kāf*' anonymous vessel stamps which would have been in use during Muḥammad b. Saʿīd's governorship.

486 *Mikyala* of skinned vetch (*julubbān muqashshar*)

مكيلة
جلبان مقشر

Measure
of skinned vetch

OA + 4117. About a third broken off at bottom and left. Olive-green. Width 2.8cm. (*Plate 22*)

From the same die Petrie, 223; Launois 1957, 305; Balog 1976, 851-2. Cf. Casanova 1893, 72, 72 *bis*; Miles 1963 II, 49; Balog 1976, 850.

There is another impression of the same die paired with executive stamp of al-Muhājir in the Balog collection (Balog 1976, 549 and see commentary to No. 306). The commodity stamp belongs to the group of stamps which it has been suggested in the Introduction (p. 38) are associated on stylistic grounds and can therefore be taken to belong to a single set of stamps in use at one time. Balog's rim with the stamp of al-Muhājir is the only such illustrated piece with a 'long-*kāf*' commodity stamp and therefore valuable evidence for the date when the series was in use.

487 *Mikyala* of *dawm*

مكيـ(لـ)ة
الدوم

Measure
of *dawm*.

OA + 4125. Green. Width 2.9cm. (*Plate 22*)

From the same die Balog 1976, 869.

The *lām* is omitted from *mikyala*. Balog 1976, 868 (cf. 867?), for the same commodity, has *mikyal* for *mikyala*. The only published stamp for *dawm* with an official's name is one of ʿUbaydallāh b. al-Ḥabḥāb (Miles 1963 II, 11).

As Miles states, *dawm* certainly means the fruit of the doum (*dawm*) palm or gingerbread tree (*Hyphaene thebaica*, Mart.), a branching species of palm common in Upper Egypt. The doum palm is known to have been cultivated or at least encouraged there long before the Islamic period. According to the much later account of the *Description de l'Égypte* the leaves were used for weaving rugs and baskets and the trunks employed in carpentry. The fruit, which tastes of gingerbread, is edible and was and is eaten but has a tough rind and fibrous flesh. As a fruit it is generally spoken of with little enthusiasm, though allowed to have beneficial properties. At the present day it is given to children and helps keep their teeth clean. Its appearance on the glass, however, raises a problem when its size is taken into consideration. The doum fruit is rather large, approximately the size and shape of a goose egg, and so quite unsuitable to be sold in relatively small quantities by measure. How large the largest of the glass measures for commodities were is not, of course, exactly known but one would estimate that anything larger than a capacity of about two pints at most would have been too unwieldy and liable to break. The fragments of the walls of the larger vessels which survive attached to stamps are not particularly thick.

It seems most unlikely that the *dawm* of the stamps can refer to the whole fruit of the doum palm and for once there is virtually no possibility of an alternative reading. Miles (*loc. cit.*) has said that the doum fruit was sometimes confused with the jujube (*nabq*), for which stamps also exist, but it is not easy to accept that that could have been done by anyone familiar with the actual fruit, as the inhabitants of Fusṭāṭ and Upper Egypt must have been. The fresh jujube is about the size and shape of a small plum. Perhaps we should assume that on the stamps *dawm* does not refer to the whole fruit but to some preparation made from it.

The evidence of over a millennium later cannot of course be given too much weight, but Delile in the *Description de l'Egypte* states that a kind of sherbet was made from doum fruit which was sweet and passed for salutary (Müller-Wodarg, 64; *Description*, Histoire Naturelle I, 53-8; Klunzinger 123, 141; Ibn al-Bayṭār, *s.vv. muql, muql makkī*; Ghāfiqī, 237; Maimonides, 230).

488-489 ***Qisṭ* of olive oil**

قسط

زيت [--]

Qisṭ
of olive oil - -

OA + 4119. Green. Width 2.2cm.
OA + 4120. Green. Width 2.2cm. (*Plate 22*)

From the same die Balog 1976, 870, 873. Cf. 871-2.

The two items described next are from a very similar die though only the first letter of the mysterious last word of the legend survives. Certain pieces that have not be illustrated may belong to the same group: Casanova 1893, 47-9, where the last word is read *fīhi*, 'in it', and Miles 1948, 262-3, where it is read *wā[f]*, 'full-measure'. Balog (*loc. cit.* and 1963, 5-6) has suggested reading *zayt qinnib*, 'oil of Indian hemp'. *Wāf* would be an easy reading from the point of view of sense, but the first letter on the present type is certainly connected to the 'teeth' that follow. The fact that there are at least two and probably three 'teeth' after the first letter makes it very difficult to accept *fīhi* or, to a lesser extent, *qinnib*. With regard to the latter, although Balog provides evidence for medical appreciation of the properties of hemp oil, that is far from establishing that it was widely consumed. Since the stamps of the group are evidently quite common it is likely that they were meant for a common commodity, most probably olive oil which appears on far more stamps than any other substance. There are of course no stamps for hemp oil among those with the names of officials. But if it is reasonable to accept that these stamps were for olive oil the last word of the legend still remains an unsolved puzzle.

490-491 ***Qisṭ* of olive oil**

قسط

زيت [--]

Qisṭ
of olive oil - - .

OA + 4136. Piece of rim attached. Green. Length 2.5cm. (*Plate 22*)
OA + 4137. Piece of rim attached. Green. Length 2.7cm.

See Nos 488-489.

492 ***Mikyala* of olive oil,** for a *fals*

مكـ(يلـ)ـة

زيت

بفلس ·

Mikyala
of olive oil
for a *fals*.

93 11-11 7. Green. Width 1.8cm. (*Plate 23*)

Lām and *yā'* in *mikyala* have been transposed, and it is possible that *bā'* is omitted before *fals*. Another die with the same legend, written correctly, appears on Balog 1976, 876 (Cf. 877), and also on an almost intact handled measure, with a capacity of 60cc, in the Museum of Islamic Art in Cairo, which was published by Miles (1951b, p. 53).

493 ***Mikyala* of fennel (*shamār*)**

مكيلة

شمار

Measure
of fennel.

OA + 4126. Green. Width 2.9cm. (*Plate 23*)

On this and the only other published stamp for fennel (*Foeniculum vulgare*, Mill.), a *mikyala* of Muḥammad b. Al-Ash'ath (Miles 1951b, 25), the name of the commodity is remarkably clear. Once again the identification is discussed in detail by Miles. In the Arabic-speaking world the plant was more usually called by a name of Persian origin, *rāziyānaj*, but Ibn al-Bayṭār informs us that *shamār* was the word used in Syria and Egypt. Instructions for the cultivation of fennel are given by Ibn al'Awwām, who quotes in this connection earlier writers from more eastern parts of the Islamic world. Unlike some herbs, cumin for example, fennel is not found in the usual lists of significant Egyptian crops and perhaps it was regarded more as a garden plant. Presumably it is the seeds that are referred to on the stamps (Ibn al-Bayṭār, *s.vv. rāziyānaj, shamār*; Ibn al-'Awwām II, 260-1; Klunzinger 143).

The British Museum's piece displays the characteristic features of the 'long-*kāf*' group of anonymous vessel stamps.

494-495 ***Mikyala* of skinned lentils (*'adas muqashshar*)**

مكيلة

عدس مقشر

Mikyala
of skinned lentils.

OA + 4128. Green. 3.0cm. (*Plate 23*)
OA + 4129. Olive-green. 2.4cm.

From the same die Casanova 1893, 70; Launois 1957, 272; Miles 1963 I, 72; Balog 1976, 886. Cf. Casanova 1893, 65-9, 71; Balog 1976, 887.

Many, but not all, specimens have a faint dot below the *sin* in the second line, presumably the mark of a flaw that developed in the die. The die belongs to the 'long-*kāf*' group.

496 Black lentils (*'adas al-aswad*) for a *fals*

عدس
الاسود
بفلس

Lentils,
black,
for a *fals*,

OA + 4127. Olive-green. The surface decayed to opaque grey or flaked off. Width 4.3cm; stamp 2.5 x 2.6cm. *(Plate 23)*

497–498 *Mikyala* of black cumin (*kammūn aswad*)

مكيلة
كمون اسود

Measure
of black cumin.

OA + 4130. Green. Width 3.4cm
OA + 4131. Green. Width 3.6cm. (*Plate 23*)

From the same die Casanova 1893, 61. Cf. Casanova 1893, 60; Launois 1957, 278–92; Miles 1971, 61.

The type belongs to the 'long-*kāf*' group.

499 *Mikyala* of milk (*laban*)

مكيل[ة]
اللبن

Measure
of milk.

OA + 4132. About a quarter broken off at right. Green. Width 3.6cm. (*Plate 23*)

This is the first stamp for milk to be published. The name of the substance is very clear and although measures for it cannot have been among the most common, milk fits well into the pattern of generally used commodities found on the stamps. It is unusual among them only in being rapidly perishable.

500 *Mikyala* of *mishsh* (?)

مكيلة ال{ـ}مش

Measure
of *mishsh*.

OA + 4349. Green. Width 2.9cm. (*Plate 23*)

From the same die Petrie, 224; Balog 1963, 9 = 1976, 843b (judging by the illustrations). Cf. Casanova 1893, 93, 93 *bis*; Viré, 34; Launois 1957, 271; Miles 1958a, 273; 1971, 63; Balog 1976, 842–3a, 843c, d.

The name of the commodity appears fairly clearly written but is not paralleled elsewhere. If it is taken in a straightforward fashion several readings can be suggested but none of them is very satisfactory in the context of the vessel stamps. Casanova's reading, tentative like most others, was *naqsh*, taken to mean 'gum'. Petrie suggested, as alternatives to gum, 'dates' or 'paint' (*nuqsh* and *naqsh* respectively, it may be assumed, though the latter means painting rather than paint). Viré listed, in addition to these, *baqs* 'box' (the tree), *nafash* ('menues graines d'ombillifères s'ajoutant aux dattes fermentées lors de la distillation de l'arakabilah ainsi que celles du sésame, du pavot, du tabac etc... '), *niqs* 'ink' and *naqāsh* (said to mean thyme). Balog came down firmly for *baqs* in the sense of box wood, which was later accepted by Miles (1960, 386). Most of these suggestions are obviously far-fetched. Two seems to call for a word of explanation. Dates must certainly have been widely consumed in early Islamic Egypt but there are no other stamps for them and it is not apparent why the obscure term *nuqsh* should be used for them rather than a more common word. Box and its medical properties are noted in the pharmacopoeias but it is unlikely to have been consumed in quantity.

As the list of published examples shows, stamps of the type under discussion are common. They are therefore for a common commodity which is likely to be one that occurs elsewhere on the stamps. The reading *mishsh*, Miles's first suggestion (1958a, 273), meets this requirement but of course demands the emendation of the obvious 'text'. It has to be assumed that the mark between the *lām* and *qāf* which most commentators have naturally taken for a 'tooth' letter, though it is rather stunted and bent to the left, is no more than an engraver's error. The reading *mishsh* then offers no problem. The type has the features of the 'long-*kāf*' group of vessel stamps, to which it presumably belongs, and in connection with the reading it may be further noted that though *mishsh* is a common commodity on the stamps of officials no other 'long-*kāf*' *mishsh* stamp is known. In fact only one other anonymous stamp for *mishsh* appears to have been published, an unusual one for a half-*raṭl* of the commodity (Balog 1976, 897). If *mishsh* is read on the present type, therefore, an obvious gap in the 'long-*kāf*' group is neatly filled. The dairy product *mishsh* has been described under No. 64.

501 *Mikyala* of *sukk* (?)

مكيلة
السك

Mikyala
of *sukk*.

OA + 4133. Green. Width 2.3cm. (*Plate 23*)

From the same die Casanova 1893, 91; Miles 1951b, 41; Viré, 33; Launois 1957, 296; Balog 1963, 8 = 1976, 881; 1973, 33. Cf. Launois 1957, 297–300; Miles 1971, 60.

The name of the commodity has been interpreted in a remarkable variety of ways. Miles at first read *sukkar*, 'sugar', and Viré *sadhā[b]*, 'rue', but on the better specimens it can be seen that nothing follows the *dāl*, *dhāl* or *kāf*. *Sukk* was first put forward tentatively by Casanova who translated it *'pastilles aromatiques'*. Miles (1960, 386) later retracted his original suggestion *sukkar* in favour of *sukk* and it speciously appears in accordance with his theory that the commodities named on the vessel stamps are essentially drugs that *sukk* is listed in the Arab pharmacopoeias as a medical compound. Ibn al-Bayṭār, for instance, lists three kinds of *sukk* and their virtues. On the other hand, the classical Arabic dictionaries define *sukk* as a perfume and not as a medicine. *Sukk* is mentioned several times in the Hadith, always as a perfume. A fairly detailed description of the manufacture of the perfumed pastilles which the word seems to mean specifically is quoted in Lane's *Dictionary* from the *Qāmūs*. Dictionaries and pharmacopoeias agree that *sukk* was made from a black pitch-like substance called *rāmak* and various aromatics. Of course there is nothing to prevent perfumes and other cosmetics from having, even less from being supposed to have, beneficial effects but the *sukk* of the vessel stamps, like the other cosmetics that are named on them, such as henna, are not likely to have been distributed as widely as the existence of measures for them implies, for strictly medical use.

Although this type of stamp is quite common it is the only one on which the name of the commodity *sukk* appears. It is obviously a little surprising that something should be widely sold by measure for a brief period only. The reading itself cannot in any case be regarded as entirely certain. Launois's suggestion, *nabīdh*, 'wine', is not unattractive but although in Kufic script three 'teeth' may often stand as well for three 'tooth letters' as a single *sin*, in this case the compact grouping of the 'teeth' favours reading them as *sīn*, or of course *shīn*. Wine also brings up the question of the official countenancing of the sale of alcoholic drinks (see commentary to No. 24). To make a highly implausible suggestion, if it were the case that any of the vast number of substances listed in the pharmacopoeias was likely to turn up on the stamps one might even be tempted to propose one which certainly meets the epigraphic requirements, *shukk*, a kind of rat poison (Ibn al-Bayṭār, *s.vv. sukk, shukk;* Maimonides, 290 377).

The script of this type suggests a date in the middle of the second century. Although the *kāf* of *mikyala* is not greatly extended other features of the script make it not unlikely that the stamp does in fact belong to what we have called the 'long-*kāf*' group.

Anonymous Counterstamps

Period of Ḥayyān b. Shurayḥ

502–504

الو
فاء لله

Hon-
esty for God.

OA + 4105. Green. Width 3.5cm; stamp 1.4cm. (*Plate 23*)
OA + 4106. Surface decayed. Green. Width 2.3cm.
OA + 4107. Green. Width 1.8cm.

Vessel stamps from the same die Petrie, 227–8; Launois 1957, 256. Cf. Castiglioni, 16; Miles 1948, 189–90; Launois 1957, 257–9; Miles 1958a, 275–6.

It has been pointed out in the Introduction (p. 38) that stamps with the brief legend *al-wafā'lillah* and a few others are the precursors of the stamps with the names of executives which come into use in the late Umayyad period and that it is possible to date most of them by their appearance paired with stamps of Finance Directors. Surviving pairs are, of course, mostly on heavy weights.

The present type differs from others in having *al-wafā'*, 'honesty', divided between the first and second lines. The only clearly illustrated paired example is Balog 1976, 36, on a *wuqiyya* of Ḥayyān b. Shurayḥ. On Miles 1963 II, 3 and Balog 1976, 34, both double-*raṭls* of meat of the same Finance Director and not illustrated, the arrangement of the legend is the same. Miles 1971, 5, shows beside Ḥayyān's vessel stamp for a *qisṭ* of honey, the edge of what is probably the same stamp, though too little survives to be certain.

Period of al-Qāsim b. 'Ubaydallāh

505–506

الوفاء
لله

Honesty
for God

Crescent pointing upwards below.

OA + 4103. Green. Width 2.6cm; stamp 1.6cm. (*Plate 23*)
95 12–20 7. Width 2.5cm.

Vessel stamps from the same die Casanova 1893, 20; Launois 1957, 260. Cf. Launois 1957, 261–6; Miles 1958a, 277–80; Balog 1976, 904–8.

The dating is provided by two *wuqiyyas* and a quarter-*raṭl* of al-Qāsim b. 'Ubaydallāh in the British Museum's collection (Nos 85–87). Since the anonymous stamps perform the function of executive stamps it is plain that those of al-Qāsim's finance directorship belong to the period before the names of the executives were put on his stamps, a practice which began with Muslim b. al-'Arrāf in 119, that is, his first three or four years of office. Of the three counterstamps known to have been in use during this rather short period the first is evidently one which was introduced under 'Ubaydallāh b. al-Ḥabḥāb (Miles 1948, 32, and see commentary to Nos 85–86). A third stamp, represented by No. 507, is probably to be associated with a number of al-Qāsim's weights which are dated 118. The stamp with the crescent below, then, is likely to have come between the two and replaced the one inherited from the time of 'Ubaydallāh. Naturally, there are no executives' names on the stamps beside which it has been found.

Period of al-Qāsim b. 'Ubaydallāh

507

Pentagram within beaded border. Five dots between the points of the pentagram.

OA + 4041. Green. Width 3.1cm. (*Plate 23*)

Vessel stamps from the same die Casanova 1893, 9; Balog 1976, 209.

The association of the stamp with al-Qāsim b. 'Ubaydallāh was demonstrated by Balog (1976, 135), who published an example paired with a stamp of al-Qāsim for a half-*raṭl* of meat. It has been suggested under No. 88 that the half-*raṭl* stamp is to be associated with al-Qāsim's set of weight stamps dated 118. The pentagram counterstamp, as suggested under Nos 505–506, is likely to be the last of the anonymous series before the names of al-Qāsim's executives appear on his stamps.

Period uncertain

508

الوفاء
لله

Honesty
for God.

OA + 4104. Green. Width 2.2cm. (*Plate 23*)

From the same die Miles 1948, 187; 1963 I, 76.

No piece has been illustrated with this stamp paired with another to provide a dating.

8. WEIGHTS AND DISKS AND PIOUS LEGENDS

509 **Disk weight: (*wuqiyya* ?)**

[بر]كة
[م]ن الله
واف

Blessing
from God.
Full-weight.

OA + 4316. Intact, except for slight surface decay. Green, surface partly opaque. Mark of an oval-pointed tool diagonally at each side of the stamp. 4.4cm; 30.76g.

The small rectangular stamp is deeply impressed and the sides have sagged inwards upon it, partly obscuring the very faint legend. The weight is correct for a *wuqiyya* on the Abbasid standard. A piece with a similar legend published by Miles (1958a, 246) weighs 15.85g and may be a half-*wuqiyya*. It is impossible to tell if the die is the same. Another piece with the same legend (Miles 1963 I, 65) weighs only 4.99g.

510–511 **Disks**

بسم
الله امر
محمد بالو
فاء لله

In the name
of God. Ordered
Muḥammad hon-
esty for God.

OA + 4279. Green. 3.3cm; stamp 2.5cm; 7.00g. *(Plate 23)*
1978 10–10 4 (former registration No. Western Asiatic Antiquities 120394). Fragment. A little over half, the lower part. Decayed. Green. Length 2.6cm; 2.21g.

From the same die Balog 1976, 278.

Balog's attribution of his piece to the House of Muḥammad is, of course, incorrect. His slightly damaged specimen weighed 4.11g and was classified as a *dīnār* weight. However the divergence of weight among speimens of such types is so great that they must be regarded as some kind of token. A second very similar die is represented by a piece in the American Numismatic Society collection (Miles 1948, 215. Cf. 216–7). The weights of the three pieces in the American Numismatic Society collection are 2.88g, 2.73g and 2.31g respectively (information from N.M. Lowick).

512 **(Third-*dīnār* weight)**

بسم
الله
ربى
الله

In the name
of God.
My Lord
is God.

OA + 4277. Green. 1.7cm; 1.40g. *(Plate 23)*

From the same die Casanova 1893 IV, 2 *bis* Cf. 2.

Casanova classified the pieces in the Fouquet collection as amulets and did not give their weights. His 2 *bis* is larger than the British Museum's piece and looks as if it might be of the *dīnār* denomination.

This is the first of a group well represented in the British Museum's collection by Nos 512–521, which have the same or similar legends. Some types are plainly imitations of others in the group and there is some overlapping of ornamental or unexplained features. On several types, though not the present one, there is partial or complete reversing of the legend and other marks. Examples of all these peculiarities are described below.

The group as a whole received the attention of Jungfleisch (1950) who attempted, with little justification, to maintain that the curious marks on some of them were dates in *abjad* notation (see No. 515). However, as he pointed out, it is true that the weights of pieces in the group correspond to the *dīnār* and its fractions. Their consistency in fact approaches or equals that of the series known to be official, though there are occasional aberrant or at least unexplained pieces such as Nos 514 and 521. It is difficult on the other hand to agree with Jungfleisch's suggestion that different types within the group come from different periods. As with the issues known to be official, and most others, few dies are used. The similarities of appearance and denomination point rather to the group's having been issued at a single place at the same period.

It is not easy to be certain when, and even more where, this was. The rather weak script may be classified as Kufic but does not seem closely related to any of the varieties used on the main official series, nor to show any of the ornamental features normal in later, particularly Fatimid, Kufic. Launois (1969, 26) has remarked, not without justice, that a plain Kufic need not necessarily be very early. However, it probably is and a date in the second century for the group under discussion is strongly suggested by the frequency with which half- and third-*dīnar* weights occur in it. It is indeed a mystery why half- and third-*dīnar* weights in the official series continued to be made long after the brief issue of half- and third-*dīnār* coins came to an end in the early years of the second century of the Hijra (see Miles 1964b, 82). In the Fatimid period glass disks of *dīnār* and quarter-*dīnār* weight were issued but not halves and thirds (see Balog 1971, pp. 183-5).

To sum up, pieces of the group are likely to have been produced in the second century, over a not very long period and, apart from the normal official types, perhaps at a provincial centre.

513 (Third-*dīnār* weight)

Legend as on No. 512, but the third line written in reverse. Beaded border.

(Coins and Medals) 82 8-3 34. Lane-Poole, 56d. Green. 1.9cm; 1.44g. (*Plate 23*)

No. 514 is a larger piece, of uncertain denomination, from the same die. Lane-Poole read the third line *kayl*, translating 'measure of God', but he had not realized that the word was written in reverse. Clearly the legend is simply a variant of that of the preceding type. Launois 1960 I, 23, also from this die, weighs 2.15g and would be the corresponding half-*dīnār* denomination. She, too, did not realize that *rabbī* was reversed and read *kabbara allah*, '*Exalte*(?) *Dieu!*'

514 Disk

Same die as No. 513.

(Coins and Medals) 73 8-1 77. Lane-Poole, 47. Green. 2.2cm; stamp 1.5cm; 2.86g. (*Plate 23*)

Lane-Poole gave the weight as 65 grains (4.21g), correct for a *dīnār* but the piece is actually considerably lighter. It would pass for a *dirham* weight but one hesitates to assume it was one without further evidence for the existence of the *dirham* denomination in the group of disks to which it belongs.

515 (Third-*dīnār* weight)

بسم الله
[ر]بى الله

In the name of God.
My Lord is God.

Dot above. Omega-like mark flanked by stars below. Circle at the bottom of the *alif* of *allah*. Border.

OA + 4278. Green. 1.7cm; 1.40g. (*Plate 23*)

The ornamentation is similar to that of two types described by Jungfleisch (1950) from a *dīnār* and a third-*dīnār* weight in his possession in the article in which he argued that the marks below and the *alif* with the annulet at the bottom were letters making up, by the *abjad* system, the date AH 160. This very unlikely theory has failed to find any acceptance.

516 (Third-*dīnār* weight)

بسم الله
ربى الله

In the name of God.
My Lord is God.

Band of herring-bone ornament, pointing to right, below, with three four-pointed stars beneath.

(Coins and Medals) 80 6-3 71. Lane-Poole, 56. Green. 1.6cm; 1.42g. (*Plate 23*)

A specimen from the same die weighing 2.14g and therefore of the half-*dīnār* denomination has been published by Launois (1969, 26).

517 (Third-*dīnār* weight)

بسم ا[لله]
ربى الله
حسبى اللل[ه]

In the name of God.
My Lord is God.
My sufficiency is God.

Border.

(Coins and Medals) Or. 3610. Green. 1.5cm; 1.42g. (*Plate 23*)

518 (Half-*dīnār* weight)

Same die as No. 517.

(Coins and Medals) Or. 3609. 1.8cm; 2.15g. (*Plate 23*)

Grohmann 1925, 122, which weighs 2.14g, may be from the same die.

519 (*Dīnār* weight)

بسم الله
ربى الله

In the name of God.
My Lord is God.

Border.

OA + 4276. Worn. Green. 2.7cm; 4.20g. (*Plate 23*)

From the same die Petrie, 685; Launois 1959, 103. Cf. Castiglioni 15a = Grohmann 1925, 171.

This piece represents the first state of the die; No. 520 is from the same die in an altered state, while No. 521 is an imitation of No. 520. Grohmann and Launois read *hasbī allāh* ('my sufficiency is God'), for *rabbī allāh* and the same misinterpretation is found elsewhere in descriptions of other pieces in the same group. *Hasbī* is very far-fetched as a reading of what can be seen, but arises from an attempt to take into account what, when once understood, can easily be seen to be a peculiarity, certainly an unusual one, in the way *rabbī* is written. The almost vestigal *rā'*, is written below the level of the following *bā'* and cuts across the retroflex *yā'*. Those who have read *hasbī* have, not unnaturally, taken the *rā'* to be one of the letters of the alphabet which are connected by a ductus to the next letter.

520 (*Dīnār* weight)

Same die as No. 519, in an altered state.

(Coins and Medals) 74 7-8 35. Lane-Poole, 46. Green. 2.4cm; 4.17g. (*Plate 23*)

Petrie pointed out that the die of this piece has been altered. The first state of the die is represented here by No. 519. An eight-pointed star has been added above. The alif or *allah* in the second line is extended, first downwards and then at right angles to the left to end in an annulet. To the right of the extension are a number of indistinct marks, which may be intended for letters. Lane-Poole read them as *dīnar*, which is not entirely impossible though the *dal* is particularly suspect. Similar marks are found on other types, some, like No. 521, clearly imitations of the present one while others, for instance, are not so close. As mentioned under the latter, Jungfleisch's theory that the marks represent a date is hardly likely.

521 Disk

Legend a crude reversed copy after the die of Nos 519-520 in the altered state as on No. 520. Border. Six-pointed star flanked by dashes above.

78 12-30 315. Green. 2.8cm; 4.47g. (*Plate 23*)

From the same die Miles 1948, 214.

This piece is considerably overweight. The American Numismatic Society specimen, however, weighs 4.23g, exactly right for a *dīnār*.

Another imitation of the same original is known (Launois 1960 II, 31, weighing 4.25g). On it the main legend is not reversed though some of the additional features are. It has the star and dashes of the present type.

522 Disk

توكلى [--]
ثمرته [--]

My trust - -
Its fruit - -

OA + 4219. Yellow with black streaks. 3.8cm; 11.42g. (*Plate 23*)

The legend is probably an expression of trust in God.

523 Disk

لله

For God.

Six-pointed star below.

(Coins and Medals) Pale blue. 2.7cm; stamp 2.0cm; 5.67g. (*Plate 23*)

A piece with the same legend but lacking the star and weighing 7.74g has been published by Launois (1969, 29).

524 (Half-*dīnār* weight)

For the legend see below. Crudely hatched border.

(Coins and Medals) 73 8-1 101. Lane-Poole, 54. Green. 2.0cm; 2.14g. (*Plate 23*)

Lane-Poole read *lillah allah* / *lillah aḥad*, which gives a good idea of the letters that can be seen but makes little sense. (He translated 'To God: God is. To God: One'.) The first line may be a botched attempt at *bismillah* and the second possibly one at *allah aḥad* ('In the name of God. God is one'.).

525 Disk

نعم
الرفيق
التوفيق

A good
companion is
success.

(Coins and Medals) 82 8-3 122. Lane-Poole, 48. Opaque, black. 2.3cm; stamp 1.5cm; 3.04g. (*Plate 24*)

Cf. Launois 1959, 104.

It is possible that this type and the related one described next belong to the Fatimid period. Nearly all the specimens with the legend weigh between 3.0g and 3.1g. The weight of 67 grains (4.34g) given by Lane-Poole for this piece is incorrect.

526 Disk

Legend as on No. 525, but a different die.

(Coins and Medals) 85 10-7 6. Lane-Poole, 50. Green. 2.2cm; 3.08g. (*Plate 24*)

From the same die Petrie, 638; Launois 1959, 105.

527-528 Ring weights

الوفاء لله

Honesty for God.

Isolated letter *dāl* above

OA + 4370. Fragment of the top. Bluish green. Length 4.3cm; 58g. (*Plate 24*)
OA + 4410. Intact except for very minor chipping. Surface largely opaque. Green. 5.4 x 5.8cm; 196g.

No. 528 may be a half-*raṭl* on the Abbasid system, though its weight when complete would have been a little above average. No. 527 appears to be a larger denomination and there may have been a second stamp below the surviving one. The script of this type appears to be of the third/ninth century or perhaps even later.

529 Ring weight

الوفاء
لله

Honesty
for God.

Obscure ornament below.

OA + 4411. Surface iridescent and opaque. Original colour uncertain. 5.3 x 5.8cm; width of stamp 2.1cm; 183g.

There are two marks of a blunt-pointed tool at either side of the stamp. The stamp itself is in very poor condition. The weight would have been about right for a half-*raṭl* on the Abbasid system.

530 Disk

الوفاء
لله [--]

Honesty
for God - -

OA + 4218. Pale blue with a dark stain. 2.3cm; 2.92g. (*Plate 24*)

The end of the legend consists of a 'tooth', attached to the end of *lillāh*, a *wāw* by itself and an annulet possibly intended for *mīm*. *Al-wafā' lillah* is a standard phrase in metrological contexts, but the legend here may be a variant, *al-wafā' lil-m ...*, perhaps.

9. PIECES WITH LARGELY ILLEGIBLE OR OBSCURE LEGENDS

531 **Third-*dīnār* weight**

Three-line legend in crudely hatched border.

(Coins and Medals) 82 8-3 35. Green. 1.6cm; 1.36g. *(Plate 24)*

Except for the last line the legend is very poorly written but it is clearly an attempt to write or an imitation of *Bismi[llah]/mithqāl thulth/wāf* ('In the name of God./ Weight of a third,/full-weight').

532 **Disk,** of an Umayyad Caliph

[----]
ا [---]
[امير] المؤ
منين

\- - - -
\- - - Com-
ander of the Faith-
ful.

(Coins and Medals) 73 8-1 93. Slightly under half, bottom and left. Brown. 2.6cm; 1.88g. *(Plate 24)*

The Fatimid caliphs, of course, used the title Commander of the Faithful on their numerous glass disks. However the script of this fragment is not Fatimid but a neat early Kufic of the type found on some of the better examples of official Umayyad epigraphy, notably the post-reform coinage. It evidently belongs to the group of small disks with the names of Umayyad caliphs. The end of a horizontal line is visible before the *alif* of *amīr*, 'commander', part of *dāl*, *dhāl* or *kāf* and among the Umayyad names ʿAbd al-Malik, al-Walīd and Yazīd are the possible ones. Given the amount of space left the legend must have been a brief one; it may have resembled that on the three known disks of ʿAbd al-Malik which read *'l-ʿabdallāh ʿAbd al-Mamlik amīr al-mu'minīn'* ('Of the servant of God ʿAbd al-Malīk, Commander of the Faithful'). (Abdel-Kader 1939, 1; Launois 1959, 1; 1969, 1, all from different dies and of divergent weights.) ʿAbd al-Malik's name seems a little too long to fit in. Yazīd I is probably too early but one would hesitate to choose between Yazīd II and III and al-Walīd I and II.

533 **Disk**

Kufic legend arranged in an elaborate double rectangle. S-like mark flanked by dots in centre. Two dots at one side.

(Coins and medals) 90 8-4 28. Brown, 2.4cm; stamp 1.7cm; 2.83g. *(Plate 24)*

No glass piece with anything like this arrangement of the legend appears to have been published. Although no reading has suggested itself for the whole, a number of clearly formed letters, *hā'*, for instance, at the centre of one side and *ʿayn* opposite it, indicate that it should in fact be a legend. The forms of the letters seem early enough to justify the piece's inclusion here.

534 **Disk, possibly a third-dīnār weight**

Three lines of crude script, imitating simple, probably early Kufic.

OA + 4220. Green. 1.8cm; 1.48g. *(Plate 24)*

From the same die Miles 1963 II, 46; Launois 1969, 27.

The weights of the other specimens listed above are 1.39g and 1.37g respectively. All three therefore are around the third-*dīnār* mark. Miles 1963 II, 45, which is said to have the 'same "legend"', and weighs 2.12g may perhaps be a half-*dīnār* weight from the same die.

535 **Disk weight: 10-*dirham* weight (?)**

مما امر به
[----]
[----]
[--] واف

Of what ordered
\- - - -
\- - - -
\- -, full-weight.

OA + 4312. Surface a little decayed. Brown. 3.8cm; stamp 1.5 x 1.5cm; 29.43g. *(Plate 24)*

The legend is in a crude irregular Kufic but, such as it is, is in quite good condition. It is hoped that the illustration will enable others to decipher the parts for which no reading is offered here.

Script and colour set the piece apart from the main official series. The small rectangular stamp and the shape, higher in proportion to the width than the normal official disk-weights, are somewhat similar to those of the 10-dirham weight described above and attributed, with considerable reservations, to Ītākh (No. 351). The weight of the present piece is very close to the theoretical weight of 10 *dirham kayl*, 29.7g (see Introduction, p.18).

536 Ring weight

[م]ما ام[ر به]
[----]
[----]

Of what ordered
- - - -
- - - -

OA + 4391. Surface iridescent or flaked off. Slight chipping at bottom. Otherwise intact. Mark of round pointed tool below stamp. Green. 5.8 x 6.2cm; stamp 2.0cm; 180g.

The legend may have been in four rather than three lines. The weight appears a little low for a half-*ratl* on the Abbasid standard.

537 Ring weight

[مما امر] به الامير [-]
[--] ابقاه الل[ه على]
[ي]دى عبد
[ا]لر[شيـ]ـد [-]
[----]

Of what ordered the Amir
- , may God prolong his life, at
the hands of ʻAbd
al-Rashīd(?) -
- - - -

OA + 4387. Surface opaque or flaked off. Otherwise intact. Mark of blunt round tool above and below stamp. Green. 5.3 x 5.8cm; height of stamp 2.8cm; 178g. (*Plate 24*)

The rectangular stamp is unusual in being considerably higher than it is wide. The script is reasonably good. Its use of low, though sometimes elongated, letters and wide interlinear spaces resembles that of certain types of the late second and early third centuries of the Hijra. The piece is almost certainly an official issue of that period. However, its weight appears rather too low for a half-*raṭl* on the Abbasid standard.

538 Ring weight

Two rectangular stamps side by side with marginal legends arranged in a square and two-line central legends. Possibly impressions of the same die. For the legends see commentary.

OA + 4394. Some large chips off at edges but substantially intact. Surface decayed. Green. 7.8 x 7.8cm; stamps 2.2 x 2.3cm; 547g.

Bismillah, occupying one side of the margin, is all that is legible on the left-hand stamp. The right-hand one, which is impressed at ninety degrees to the other, shows rather more of its marginal legend: [*bi*] *smill* [*ah*/ *mimma amara*] *bihi al-a*/*mīr* - - , ('In the name of God, ordered the Amir - - '). Of the Amir's name an initial *alif* followed by three 'teeth' can be made out, offering such possibilities as Isḥāq, Ashinās and Ītākh.

The arrangement of the legends recalls that of certain stamps used towards the end of the second century AH, some of those of Maḥfūẓ b. Sulaymān, for instance. The piece would seem to have lost some 10g to 15g of its original weight, which would therefore have been about 560g, a weight that does not fit into any of the established *raṭl* standards.

539 Ring weight

Four (out of five?) lines of large but crudely written and almost completely illegible Kufic are visible. First line conceivably *bismillah*.

OA + 4392. Fragment. Right side and bottom of stamp chipped off. Mark of blunt tool on rim. Maximum width 5.3cm; 70g.

540 Stamp, dated 'year nine'

بسم الله
-- سوى
سنة تسع

In the name of God.
- - was made equal,
in the year nine.

89 5-8 1. Lane-Poole, 34k. Green, surface iridescent. Breaks at top and bottom. 3.1 x 3.5cm; stamp 2.1 x 2.1cm; 7.10g.

One of the unusual features of this piece is its provenance; it was given to the British Museum by E. A. Wallis Budge and is registered as coming from near Mosul. The donor was the well-known Egyptologist and the information that the stamp does not come from Egypt but northern Iraq must therefore be taken seriously. It looks as if it might be an official issue but is presumably unlikely to have anything to do with the official Egyptian series. Nothing similar has been published.

It is not a vessel stamp in the usual sense of the term, that is an impression on a piece of glass originally applied to the wall of a vessel; the back is flat and has never been attached to anything. It may be a weight but in its damaged state the actual weight tells us nothing. The roughly even breaks at top and bottom seem rather to indicate that it may have been attached to something by the ends. It might have been part of a handle, but if so the handle would have been very fragile for the break at the bottom is only a millimetre or two thick.

The first part of the second line of the legend appears to consist of two 'teeth' followed by *dāl* or *dhāl*. If the word ends here the last letter could of course be *kāf*. The rest of the line can be read *suwwiya* ('was made equal, made worth or rectified'). Other forms from the same root are also possible. The idea of equalization seems quite appropriate if the piece is in fact an official issue. The century of the date is presumably omitted, a usage occasionally found, notably on a type of glass stamp from Egypt dated 88, where it is now generally accepted to stand for 288 (Miles 1958a, 260-1; Balog 1976, 795-6). The script of the piece from Iraq seems too developed for AH 109; AH 209/AD 824-5 is the most likely possibility though an old-fashioned script might have remained in use even later.

541 **Vessel stamp,** of an Abbasid caliph

[----]
[ع]بد الله ابـ[و --]
[ا]لامام الـ[---]

\- - - -
the servant of God, Abū -
the Imām al- - -
\- - - - .

93 11-11 8. Green, most of the surface opaque buff. Width 2.0cm (*Plate 24*)

The titulature is characteristic of the glass stamps in the names of Abbasid caliphs used in Egypt in the first half of the third century AH, otherwise represented in the British Museum's collection by a poor specimen in the name of al-Mutawakkil (see No. 352). All the known types, which are of al-Mu'taṣim, al-Wāthiq and al-Mutawakkil are represented in the Balog collection. The script of the British Museum's vessel stamps is also very similar to that on these types but the die differs from those of all the examples which have been adequately illustrated.

542 **Vessel stamp**

[----]
[----]
[مو]لى امير
[الـ]مؤمنين

\- - - -
\- - - -
Mawlā of the Commander
of the Faithful.

OA + 4348. Blue-green. Width 1.9cm. (*Plate 24*)

The piece is evidently an official issue of the third century AH.

10. RING WEIGHTS WITHOUT LEGIBLE LEGENDS

543

OA + 4378. Chipped on bottom and side; surface decaying. Otherwise intact. Impression of oval stamp 1.3cm long. Bluish green. 2.8 x 2.8cm; 25.3g.

This piece and the next two cannot be easily fitted into any of the established *raṭl* systems.

544

89 12-11 2. Surface decaying. Otherwise intact but for very small chips. Trace of stamp on top. Bluish green. 3.3 x 3.6cm; 49.4g.

545

OA + 4377. Surface opaque and iridescent. Otherwise intact. No trace of stamp. Bluish green. 3.8 x 4.0cm; 69.3g.

546

OA + 4376. Surface slightly worn. Otherwise intact. Mark of circular stamp of 2.2cm diameter. Black. 3.9 x 4.5cm; 94.2g.

The weight and general appearance of this piece indicate that it is a quarter-*raṭl* on the Abbasid system and of the first half of the third century of the Hijra.

547-548

OA + 4388. Chipped on top and sides. Surface opaque or iridescent green. Mark of rectangular stamp. Green. 4.8 x 5.5cm; 170g.
OA + 4389. Slightly chipped. Surface iridescent. Mark of rectangular stamp. Green. 5.0 x 5.3cm; 179g.

Both would appear to be half-*raṭls* on the Abassid system, probably of the same period as No. 546.

549-550 Fragments of large ring weights

OA + 4412. Bottom corner. Olive-green. 4.2 x 4.3cm; 131g.
OA + 4413. Bottom half. Green. Length 7.5cm; 209g.

11. DECORATIVE VESSEL STAMPS

551–552

Winged horse passant to right. Trio of dots on flank of horse. Kufic legend above: *rabbī allah* ('My lord is God').

OA + 4139. Pale Yellowish green. Width 3.4cm. (*Plate 24*)
OA + 4140. Pale yellowish green. Width 2.8cm.

From the same die Erdmann 1952, coll. 123–4, 2; Balog 1974, 9.

Other early Islamic stamps with winged horses are described in the articles of Balog and Erdmann referred to above and in Erdmann 1954.

553

Horse passant to right. Kufic legend above: [*bi*] *smilla*[*h*] ('in the name of God').

1968 5–22 19. Chipped at top left. Surface discoloured. Pale brownish yellow. Length 4.5cm. (*Plate 24*)

The stamp is rather larger than other published decorative ones and the figure of the horse is in comparatively high relief, too high for the technique used, it would seem, since the upper part of the body has not come out at all clearly.

This piece was transferred to the Department of Oriental Antiquities from that of Western Asiatic Antiquities. It came to the British Museum in 1848 or 1851 with other material excavated by Layard at Koyunjik, the site of ancient Nineveh near Mosul in northern Iraq. For a stamp of completely different type which also came from near Mosul see No. 541. The pale brown colour is normal for decorative vessel stamps while it is very uncommon among the official stamps of Egypt which are nearly all green or greenish blue. That the decorative pieces were not manufactured in the same workshop as the official pieces is evident, and it may well be that they were made somewhere other than Egypt, perhaps, as Erdmann (1952, 1954) has suggested, Syria. The discovery of other pieces which have, like this one, non-Egyptian provenances, may clarify the problem.

554

Big-horned sheep passant to left. Kufic legend down left side: *bismillah* ('In the name of God'). Kufic legend partly visible to right, perhaps repeating that on the left.

91 5–12 12. The back smoothed. Pale yellow green. Width 2.2cm. (*Plate 24*)

Balog (1974, 6–7) has published a number of vessel stamps with big-horned sheep and Arabic legends but on all of them the sheep faces right. However, one facing left occurred on a piece in the Innes collection described by Casanova (1893, p. 340), who tentatively read its legend as *bismillah rabbī allah* ('In the name of God. My Lord is God').

555

Peacock passant to right. Traces of Arabic legend in front of it.

1968 5–22 20. Chipped at top left. Surface much decayed. Olive-green. Width 2.8cm. (*Plate 24*)

Balog 1974, 5, is very similar and has the Kufic legend *bism-* (beneath the bird's tail) *illah* (in front of its breast). The British Museum's piece is too damaged to tell if it is from the same die. It was transferred to the Department of Oriental Antiquities from that of Western Asiatic Antiquities, the oriental registration number being 1908 6–15 20. It was given to the British Museum by Mrs H. H. Way and the provenance is recorded as Bayt Jibrīn, in Palestine.

556

Facing human head, with high bifurcated headdress or coiffure.

OA + 4141. Pale brownish. Width 2.4cm. (*Plate 24*)

This type lacks an Arabic legend. It is included here on account of the similarity of the treatment of the face with that of another type which has a human bust in the centre and the brief Arabic legend *bismillah* at the sides (Casanova 1893, 15; Balog 1974, 12a–b).

Bibliography

Except where otherwise indicated, references to catalogues of glass stamps apply to catalogue numbers and not page numbers.

Abbott, Nabia. 1933. *The rise of the North Arabic script...*, Chicago.

Abdel-Kader, Djafar. 1935. 'Deux unités pondérales musulmanes omayyades', *Berytus* II, 139-42.

Abdel-Kader. 1939. 'Monnaies et poids en verre inédits', *Mélanges syriens offerts à M.R. Dussaud*, Paris, 399-419.

Ashtor, Eliyahu. 1969. *Historie des prix et des salaires dans l'Orient médiéval*, Paris.

Al-Azdī, Abu Zakariyyā' Yazīd b. Muhammad. 1967. *Tārīkh al-Mawṣil*, ed. ʿAlī Ḥabība, Cairo.

Bacharach, Jere L. and Henri Amin Awad. 1974. 'The early Islamic bronze coinage of Egypt: additions', *Studies in honor of George C. Miles*, ed. Dickran K. Kouymjian, Beirut, 185-192.

Bālādhurī, Aḥmad b. Yaḥyā. 1866. *Kitāb futūḥ al-buldān*, ed. M.J. De Goeje, Leiden.

Balog, Paul. 1959. 'Poids forts fatimites en plomb', *Revue belge de numismatique et de sigillographie*, CV, 171-88.

Balog, Paul. 1963. 'Poids en plomb du khalife fatimite al-Ḥākim biamr-illah frappés à Miṣr en l'an 389 H.' and 'Quelques estampilles en verre arabes du huitième siècle AD avec les noms de drogues', *Journal of the economic and social history of the Orient*, VI, 216-227.

Balog, Paul. 1970. 'Islamic bronze weights from Egypt', ibid., XIII, 233-56.

Balog, Paul. 1971-3. 'The Fāṭimid glass jeton', *Annali, Istituto Italiano di numismatica*, XVIII-XIX, 175-264, and XX, 121-212.

Balog, Paul. 1973. 'Poids et estampilles en verre et poids en bronze musulman du Musée d'Art et d'Histoire de Genève', *Gènava*, n.s. XXI, 297-311.

Balog, P 1974. 'Sasanian and early Islamic ornamental glass vessel-stamps', *Studies in honor of George C. Miles*, ed. Dickran K. Kouymjian, Beirut, 131-40.

Balog, Paul. 1976. *Ummayad, ʿAbbasid and Ṭūlūnid glass weights and vessel-stamps*, New York.

Balog, Paul. 1977. 'Pious invocations probably used as titles of office or as honorific titles in Umayyad and ʿAbbāsid times', *Studies in memory of Gaston Wiet*, ed. Myriam Rosen-Ayalon, Jerusalem, 61-8.

Balog, Paul. 1981. 'Fāṭimid glass jetons: token currency or coin-weights?, *Journal of the economic and social history of the Orient*, XXIV, 93-109.

Bates, Michael L. 1981. 'The function of Fāṭimid and Ayyūbid glass weights', *ibid*, XXIV, 63-92.

Bergmann, E. v. 1870. 'Die Nominale der Münzreform des Chalifen Abdulmelik', *Sitzungsberichte der philosophisch-historischen Classe der Kaiserlichen Akademie der Wissenschaften*, LXV, 239-266.

BMCO. 1875-90. *Catalogue of oriental coins in the British Museum*, London.

Cahen, Claude. 1972. 'Al-Makhzūmī et Ibn Mammāṭī sur l'agriculture égyptienne médiévale', *Annales Islamologiques*, XI, 141-51; reprinted in Cahen's *Makhzūmiyyāt* (Leiden 1977).

Casanova, Paul. 1891. 'Étude sur les inscriptions arabes des poids et mesures en verre (Collections Fouquet et Innes)', *Bulletin de l'Institut d'Égypt*, series 3, II, 89-121.

Casanova, Paul. 1893. 'Catalogue des pièces de verre des époques byzantine et arabe de la collection Fouquet', *Mémoires publiées par les membres de la Mission Archéologique Francaise au Caire*, VI, 3, 337-414. For references to items in this work the number of Casanova's sub-heading is only given in cases where it is not self-evident.

Casanova, Paul. 1894. 'Sceaux arabes en plomb', *Revue numismatique*, 3e série, XII, 97-126.

Casanova, Paul. 1924. 'Dénéraux en verre arabes', *Mélanges offerts à M. Gustave Schlumberger*, Paris, II, 296-300.

Castiglioni, Carlo Ottavio. 1847. *Dell' uso cui erano destinato i vetri con epigrafi cufiche, e della origine, estensione e durato di esso*, Milan.

Clément-Mullet. See Ibn al-'Awwām.

Day, Florence E. 1953. 'An Umayyad pharmacist's measuring cup', *Bulletin of the Metropolitan Museum of art*, May, 259.

Description. 1809-28. *Description de l'Égypte*, ..., Paris.

Dennett, Daniel C. Jr. 1950. *Conversion and the poll tax in early Islam*, Cambridge [Mass.].

al-Dhahabī, Muḥammad b. Aḥmad. 1863-81. *Kitāb al-mushtabih fi asmā' al-rijāl*, ed. P. de Jong, Leiden.

Dudzus, Wolfgang. 1959. 'Umayyadische gläserne Gewichte und Eichstempel aus Ägypten in den Berliner Museen', *Aus der Welt der Islamischen Kunst. Festschrift fur Ernst Kühnel*, Berlin, 277-82.

Dudzus, Wolfgang. 1961. 'Frühe Umayyadische Glasstempel aus Ägypten mit Beamtennamen in den Berliner Museen', *Forschungen und Berichte, Staatliche Museen zu Berlin*, 3-4, 18-24.

E.I.[1], E.I.[2]. *Encyclopaedia of Islam*, first and second edition.

Erdmann, Kurt. 1952. 'Zur Datierung der Berliner Pegasus-Schale', *Archäologischer Anzeiger, Beiblatt zum Jahrbuch des Deutschen Archäologischen Instituts*, (for 1950-1), coll. 115-31.

Erdmann, Kurt. 1954. 'Noch einmal zur Datierung der Berliner Pegasus-Schale', *ibid.*, (for 1953), coll. 136-41.

Ettinghausen, Richard. 1939. 'An Umayyad pound weight', *Journal of the Walters Art Gallery*, II, 73-6.

Fahmī (-Muḥammad), 'Abd al-Raḥmān. 1957. *sinaj al-sikka fī fajr al-Islām*, Cairo.

Fahmī (-Muḥammad), 'Abd al-Raḥmān. 1958. 'Al-ṣinaj al-ṭūlūniyya wal-sikkat al-ikhshīdiyya wal-jadīd fīhimā', *Al-mu'tamar al-thānī lil-āthār fil-bilād al-'arabiyya*, Cairo, 1-13.

Fahmī (-Muḥammad), 'Abd al-Raḥmān. 1961. 'Al-shārāt al-masīhiyya wal-rumūz al-qibṭiyya 'alā al-sikkat al-islāmiyya', *Kitāb al-mu'tamar al-thālith lil-āthār fil-bilād al-'arabiyya*, Cairo, 337-358.

Fahmī (-Muḥammad). 'Abd al-Raḥmān. 1965. *Fajr al-sikkat al-'arabiyya*, Cairo.

Fitzwilliam Museum. 1978. *Glass at the Fitzwilliam Museum*, Cambridge.

Forbes, R.J. 1964. *Studies in ancient technology*, IV, Leiden.

Fremersdorf, Fritz. 1975. *Catalogo del Museo Sacro ...*, vol. V, Vatican City. The descriptions of the Islamic stamps are by Adolf Grohmann.

Al-Ghāfiqī, Ahmad b. Muḥammad. 1932-40. *The abridged version of The book of simple drugs*, ed. and trans. M. Meyerhof and G.P. Sobhy, Cairo.

Grierson, Philip. 1975. *Numismatics*, Oxford.

Grohmann, Adolf. 1924. *Corpus papyrorum Raineri*, III, Vienna.

Grohmann, Adolf. 1925. 'Arabische Eichungstempel, Glasgewichte und Amulette aus Wiener Sammlungen', *Islamica*, I, 145-226.

Grohmann, Adolf. 1934. *Arabic papyri in the Egyptian Library*, III, Cairo.

Grohmann, Adolf. 1955. *Einführung und Chrestomathie zur Arabischen Papyruskunde*, I, Prague.

Hamarneh, Sami K. and Henry A. Awad. 1976. 'Arabic glass seals on early eighth-century containers for materia medica', *Pharmacy in History*, XVIII, 3, 95-102.

Herz (Bey), Max. 1907. *A descriptive catalogue of the objects exhibited in the National Museum of Arab art*, trans. G. Foster Smith, Cairo.

Hinz, Walther. 1970. *Islamische Masse und Gewichte*, Leiden.

Ibn 'Abd al-Ḥakam, Abū Muḥammad 'Abdallāh. 1927. *Sira 'Umar b. 'Abd al-'Azīz*, ed. Aḥmad 'Ubayd, Cairo.

Ibn al-'Awwām, Muḥammad b. Aḥmad Ishbīlī. 1802. *Kitāb al-filāḥa*, ed. and trans. Josef Antonio Banqueri, Madrid.

Ibn al-'Awwām, Muḥammad b. Ahmad Ishbīlī. 1864-7. *Le livre de l'agriculture d'Ibn-al-Awam (Kitab al-felahah)*, trans. J. Clément-Mullet, Paris.

Ibn al-Bayṭār, Ḍiā' al-Dīn 'Abdallāh b. Aḥmad al-Andalusī al-Māliqī. 1291 AH. *Al-jāmi 'li-mufradāt al-adwiya wal-aghdhiya*, Bulaq.

Ibn al-Bayṭar, Dia' al-Dīn 'Abdallāh b. Aḥmad al-Andalusī al-Māliqī. 1877-83. Fr. trans. by L. Leclerc, *Notices et extraits des manuscrits de la Bibliothèque Nationale ...*, XXIII.1, XXV.1, XXVI.1.

Ibn Mammātī, As'ad. 1943. *Kitāb qawānīn al-dawānīn*, ed. A.S. Atiya, Cairo.

Ibn Taghrībīrdī, Abu 'l-mahāsin Yūsuf. 1855-61 *Al-nujūm al-zāhira fi mulūk Miṣr wal-Qāhira*, T.G.J. Juynboll and B.F. Matthes, Leiden.

Jahshiyārī, Muḥammad b. 'Abdūs. 1926. *Kitāb al-wuzarā' wal-kuttāb*, ed. Hans v. Mžik, Leipzig.

Jungfleisch, Marcel. 1929a. 'Poids fatimites en verre polychrome' *Bulletin de*

l'institut d'Egypt, X, 19-31.
Jungfleisch, Marcel. 1929b. 'Les ratls discoïdes en verre', *ibid.*, X, 61-71.
Jungfleisch, Marcel. 1949. 'Un poids et une estampille sur verre datant d'Ahmed Ibn Touloun', *Ibid.*, XXX, 1-9.
Jungfleisch, Marcel, 1951. 'Notations conventionelles se rencontrant sur certains poids arabes en verre', *ibid.*, XXXII, 257-74.
Jungfleisch, Marcel 1952. 'Notations en "Abjad" sur des poids arabes en verre attribuables au second siècle de l'Hégire', *ibid.*, XXXIII, 207-13.
Jungfleisch, Marcel. 1965. 'Le système pondéral islamique dit "Kebir"', *ibid.*, XXXVIII, 1, 303-6.

Al-Kindī, Muḥammad b. Yūsuf. 1912. *Kitāb al-wulāt wa kitāb al-quḍāt*, ed. Rhuvon Guest, Leyden and London.
Klunzinger, C.B. 1878. *Upper Egypt: its people and products*, London.
Kmietowicz, Anna. 1959. 'Déneraux et poids musulmans en verre conservés dans les musées de Pologne', *Folia Orientalia*, I, 135-41.
Lamm, Carl Johann. 1930. *Mittelalterliche Gläser und steinschnittarbeiten aus dem Nahen Osten*, Berlin.
Lane, Edward William. 1860. *An account of the manners and customs of the modern Egyptians*, London.
Lane-Poole, Stanley. 1891. *Catalogue of Arabic glass weights in the British Museum*, London.
Launois, Aimée. 1957. 'Estampilles et poids faibles en verre Omeyyades et Abbasides au Musée Arabe du Caire, *Mélanges islamologiques*, III, 1-83.
Launois, Aimée. 1958a. 'Deux estampilles et un gros poids Omeyyades en verre', *Journal asiatique*, CCXLVI, 288-312.
Launois, Aimée. 1958b. Review of Miles 1958a, *Revue numismatique*, VIe serie, I, 231-4.
Launois, Aimée. 1959. *Estampilles et poids musulmans en verre du Cabinet des Médailles*, Paris.
Launois, Aimée. 1960. *Catalogue des étalons monétaires et autres pièces musulmans de la collection Jean Maspéro*, Paris. (I. Maspéro collection; II. Cabinet des médailles.)
Launois, Aimée. 1969. 'Estampilles, poids, étalons monétaires et autres disques musulmans en verre', *Bulletin d'études orientales*, XXII, 69-126.

Maimonides. 1940. *Sharḥ asmā' al-ʿuqqār*, ed. and trans. Max Meyerhof, Cairo.
Al-Maqrīzī, Taqī al-Dīn Abu 'l-ʿAbbās Aḥmad b. ʿAlī. 1270 AH. *Kitāb al-mawaʿiẓ wal-iʿtibār bi-dhikr al-khiṭaṭ wal-āthār*, Bulaq.
Matson, Frederick R. 1948. 'The manufacture of eighth-century Egyptian glass weights and stamps', in Miles 1948 (31-69).
Miles, George C. 1938. *The numismatic history of Rayy*, New York.
Miles, George C. 1948. *Early Arabic glass weights and stamps*, New York.
Miles, George C. 1951a. 'Cumin and vinegar for hiccups', *Archaeology*, IV, 1, 23-4.
Miles, George C. 1951b. *Early Arabic glass weights and stamps: a supplement*, New York.
Miles, George C. 1952. 'A three-wuqīya glass weight', *American Numismatic Society Museum Notes*, V, 179-80.
Miles, George C. 1956. 'A glass measure issued by Ḥayyān b. Shurayḥ', *Studi orientalistici in onore di Giorgio Levi della Vida*, Rome, 148-58.
Miles, George C. 1958a. *Contributions to Arabic metrology*, I, New York.
Miles, George C. 1958b. 'The early Islamic bronze coinage of Egypt', *Centennial publication of the American Numismatic Society*, ed. Harold Ingholt, New York.
Miles, George C. 1960a. 'Byzantine miliaresion and Arab dirhem', *American Numismatic Society Museum Notes*, IX, 189-218.
Miles, George C. 1960b. 'Egyptian glass pharmaceutical measures of the 8th century AD' *Journal of the history of medicine and allied sciences*, XV, 384-9.
Miles, George C. 1962. 'A Byzantine bronze weight in the name of Bišr b. Marwān', *Arabica*, IX, 113-8.
Miles, George C. 1963. *Contributions to Arabic metrology*, II, New York. (I. Benaki Museum; II. Peter Ruthven collection.)
Miles, George C. 1964a. 'Early Islamic weights and measures in Muntaza Palace, Alexandria', *Journal of the American Research Centre in Egypt*, III, 105-113.
Miles, George C. 1964b. 'On the varieties and accuracy of eighth century Arab coin weights', *Eretz Israel*, VII, 78-87.
Miles, George C. 1971. 'Umayyad and ʿAbbasid glass weights and measure stamps in the Corning Museum' *Journal of glass studies*, XIII, 64-76.
Müller-Wodarg, Dieter. 1953-8. 'Die Landwirtschaft Ägyptens in der frühen ʿAbbasidenzeit', *Der Islam*, XXXI, 174-227, XXXII, 14-78, 141-167, XXXIII, 310-321.
Muqaddasī, Shams al-Dīn Abū ʿAbdallāh Muḥammad. 1906. *Aḥsan al-tāqasīm fī maʿrifat al-aqālīm*, ed. M.J. de Goeje, Leyden.

Nāṣir-i Khusraw. n.d. *Safar-nāma*, ed. M. Dabīr-siyāqī, Tehran.
Nies, J.B. 1902. 'Kufic glass weights and bottle stamps', *Proceedings of the American Numismatic and Archaeological Society*, 48-55.
Nützel, Heinrich. 1908. 'Muhammadanische Glasstempel aus Ägypten', *Amtliche Berichte aus den Königlichen Kunstsammlungen*, XXX, 1, coll. 24-6.
Petrie, W.M.F. 1926. *Glass stamps and weights*, London.
Pietraszewski, Ignatius, 1843. *Numi Mohammedani*, I, Berlin.

Rice, D.S. 1955. Review of Miles 1948 and 1951b, *Bulletin of the School of Oriental and African studies*, XVII, 172.
Rogers, E.T. 1873. 'Glass as a material for standard coin weights', *Numismatic Chronicle*, New Series XIII, 60-88.
Rogers, E.T. 1878. 'Unpublished glass weights and measures', *Journal of the Royal Asiatic Society*, 98-112.
Sauvaire, Henri. 1879-86. 'Matériaux pur servir à l'histoire de la numismatique et de la métrologie musulmanes', *Journal Asiatique*, VIIe série, XIV, 455-533, XV, 228-77, 421*bis*-478, XVIII, 23-77, 97-163, 281-327, VIIIe série, III, 368-445, IV, 207-321, V, 498-506, VII, 124-77, VIII, 113-65, 272-97, 479-536.
Sawaskiewicz, L.L. 1846. *La génie de l'Orient commentée par ses monuments monétaires*, Brussels.
Sayre, Edward T. 1964. *Some ancient glass specimens with compositions of particular archaeological significance*, Upton, New York.
Scanlon, George T. 1966. 'Fusṭāṭ expedition: preliminary report 1965. Part I', *Journal of the American Research Centre in Egypt*, V, 83-112.
Scanlon, George T. 1968. 'Fustat and the Islamic art of Egypt', *Archaeology*, XXI, 3, 188-95.
Severus, b. al-Muqaffa'. 'History of the Patriarchs of the Coptic Church of Alexandria', ed. and trans. B. Evetts, III, *Patrologia Orientalis*, V, fasciculus I.

Ṭabarī, Muḥammad b. Jarīr. 1879-1901. *Ta'rīkh al-rusul wal-mūluk*, ed. M.J. de Goeje et al., Leiden.

Viré, François. 1956. Dénéraux, estampilles et poids musulmans en verre en Tunisie (Collection H.H. Abdul Wahhab)', *Cahiers de Tunisie*, IV, 17-90.

Walker, John. 1956. *A catalogue of the Muḥammadan coins in the British Museum*, II, *A catalogue of the Arab-Byzantine and post-reform Umaiyad coins*, London.
Wensinck, A.J., *et al.* 1933-69. *Concordance et indices de la tradition musulmane*, Leiden.

Zambaur, E. von. 1906. *Contributions à la numismatique orientale, II, Extrait de la Numismatische Zeitschrift* (XXXVII), Vienna.

Additional note

Since the completion of the text of this catalogue in 1980 a number of publications relevant to the subject have appeared. Two are particularly worth nothing:

Balog, Paul. 1980. 'Reference Guide to Arabic metrology. Umayyad, 'Abbāsid and Ṭūlūnid officials named on glass coin weights, weights and measure stamps', *Jahrbuch für Numismatik und Geldgeschichte*, XXX, 55-96.
Fahmī, Sāmiḥ 'Abd al-Raḥmān. 1981. *Al-makāyīl fī ṣadr al-islām*, Mecca.

Concordance of British Museum registration numbers

Registration No	Catalogue No
71 6-16 14	469
72 3-20 6	384
72 3-20 12	400
73 3-29 37	382
78 3-11 37	360
78 3-11 38	326
78 12-30 315	521
80 6-14 23	155
83 6-21 27	433
83 6-21 28	144
83 6-21 30	227
83 6-21 31	429
83 6-21 32	413
83 6-21 35	305
89 4-14 1	467
89 5- 8 1	540
89 8- 6 2	147
89 9- 4 1	397
89 9- 4 2	345
89 12-11 2	544
91 5-12 12	554
91 5-12 17	393
91 6-12 23	19
91 7- 1 523	458
93 2- 5 86	269
93 2- 5 87	10
93 11-11 2	220
93 11-11 4	283
93 11-11 7	492
93 11-11 8	541
93 11-11 9	232
93 11-11 11	67
93 11-11 12	1
93 11-11 13	194
93 11-11 14	293
93 11-11 15	336
93 11-11 16	394

Registration No	Catalogue No
93 11-11 17	377
93 11-11 18	378
94 3- 9 5	209
94 3- 9 6	226
94 3- 9 7	405
94 3- 9 8	406
94 3- 9 9	123
94 3- 9 10	161
94 3- 9 11	476
94 3- 9 12	477
94 3- 9 13	256
94 3- 9 14	361
94 3- 9 15	464
94 3- 9 16	436
95 3-12 2	46
95 3-12 3	97
95 12-20 3	286
95 12-20 4	47
95 12-20 5	270
95 12-20 6	478
95 12-20 7	506
1965 7-31 10	379
1968 5-22 19	553
1968 5-22 20	555
1978 10-10 4	511
1978 11-15 1	24
OA + series	
4000	7
4001	6
4002	12
4003	14
4004	15
4005	22
4006	23
4007	20
4008	25

Registration No	Catalogue No
4009	28
4010	27
4011	50
4012	55
4013	51
4014	61
4015	62
4016	59
4017	60
4018	57
4019	54
4020	56
4021	64
4022	63
4023	65
4024	133
4025	92
4026	93
4027	94
4028	95
4029	96
4030	99
4031	100
4032	101
4033	102
4034	104
4035	110
4036	105
4037	107
4038	108
4039	109
4040	106
4041	507
4042	118
4043	124
4044	120

Registration No	Catalogue No	Registration No	Catalogue No	Registration No	Catalogue No
4045	121	4091	134	4137	491
4046	122	4092	146	4138	335
4047	126	4093	166	4139	551
4048	127	4094	231	4140	552
4049	128	4095	170	4141	556
4050	142	4096	312	4158	2
4051	145	4097	313	4159	31
4052	143	4098	308	4160	32
4053	153	4099	235	4161	29
4054	154	4100	234	4162	42
4055	156	4101	354	4163	41
4056	157	4102	355	4164	37
4057	158	4103	505	4165	36
4058	159	4104	508	4166	33
4059	165	4105	502	4167	34
4060	186	4106	503	4168	71
4061	187	4107	504	4169	69
4062	182	4108	404	4170	70
4063	183	4109	349	4171	72
4064	184	4110	470	4172	78
4065	200	4111	471	4173	79
4066	201	4112	472	4174	80
4067	202	4113	473	4175	83
4068	203	4114	474	4176	82
4069	205	4115	479	4177	73
4070	208	4116	480	4178	84
4071	206	4117	486	4179	130
4072	207	4118	481	4180	43
4073	210	4119	488	4181	111
4074	211	4120	489	4182	114
4075	212	4121	482	4183	138
4076	219	4122	483	4184	149
4077	169	4123	484	4185	148
4078	185	4124	485	4186	162
4079	246	4125	487	4187	175
4080	247	4126	493	4188	178
4081	230	4127	496	4189	179
4082	254	4128	494	4190	177
4083	255	4129	495	4191	409
4084	264	4130	497	4192	188
4085	271	4131	498	4193	216
4086	160	4132	499	4194	240
4087	282	4133	501	4195	278
4088	288	4134	52	4196	337
4089	287	4135	367	4197	340
4090	281	4136	490	4198	237

Registration No	Catalogue No
4199	390
4200	398
4201	388
4202	408
4204	438
4205	434
4206	431
4207	422
4208	374
4209	375
4210	385
4211	386
4212	373
4213	389
4214	410
4218	530
4219	521
4220	534
4221	4
4222	35
4223	129
4224	66
4225	112
4226	77
4227	139
4228	163
4229	171
4230	174
4231	197
4232	192
4233	193
4234	218
4235	217
4236	221
4237	241
4238	238
4240	248
4241	279
4242	274
4243	275
4244	273
4245	298
4246	300
4247	302
4248	295
4249	292

Registration No	Catalogue No
4250	284
4251	318
4252	319
4253	328
4254	391
4255	401
4256	314
4257	250
4258	445
4259	439
4260	440
4261	435
4262	425
4263	428
4264	432
4265	427
4266	423
4267	419
4268	420
4269	417
4270	450
4271	451
4272	452
4273	447
4274	448
4275	453
4276	519
4277	512
4278	515
4279	510
4280	383
4281	387
4282	172
4283	403
4284	11
4285	26
4286	58
4287	132
4288	167
4289	266
4290	311
4291	350
4292	85
4293	86
4294	88
4295	198

Registration No	Catalogue No
4296	181
4297	189
4298	190
4299	141
4300	214
4301	224
4302	272
4303	316
4304	329
4305	245
4306	399
4307	347
4308	344
4309	459
4310	368
4311	358
4312	535
4313	351
4314	456
4315	468
4316	509
4319	38
4320	74
4321	75
4322	68
4323	115
4324	180
4325	251
4326	331
4327	258
4328	433
4329	376
4330	8
4331	9
4332	13
4333	16
4334	21
4335	18
4336	53
4337	103
4338	98
4339	125
4340	119
4341	191
4342	204

Registration No	Catalogue No
4343	213
4344	267
4345	268
4346	317
4347	357
4348	542
4349	500
4350	475
4351	457
4353	90
4354	91
4355	151
4356	152
4357	48
4358	233
4359	199
4360	262
4361	263
4362	264
4363	315
4364	307
4365	321
4366	330
4367	324
4368	323
4369	364
4370	527
4371	353
4372	460
4373	461
4374	462
4375	463
4376	546
4377	545
4378	543
4379	49
4380	369
4381	365
4382	342
4383	465
4384	466
4385	362
4387	537
4388	547
4389	548
4390	371

Registration No	Catalogue No
4391	536
4392	539
4393	352
4394	538
4395	310
4396	372
4397	325
4398	339
4399	309
4400	366
4401	45
4402	346
4403	399
4404	348
4405	370
4406	363
4407	356
4409	343
4410	528
4411	529
4412	549
4413	550
4414	285
4415	131
4416	229
4417	359
4418	322
4419	5
4420	87
4421	89
4422	44
4423	150
4424	168
4425	228
4426	260
4427	261
4428	306
4429	225
4430	320
4432	412
11474	135

Department of Coins and Medals

53 4- 6 949	242
53 4- 6 976	446
53 4- 6 1000	17
54 11- 2 12	392

Registration No	Catalogue No
70 5- 4 12	303
71 6- 1 8	81
72 6- 3 18	442
73 8- 1 75	449
73 8- 1 76	304
73 8- 1 77	514
73 8- 1 93	532
73 8- 1 101	524
74 7- 8 34	164
74 7- 8 35	520
76 11- 5 6	140
77 6- 7 1	338
80 6- 3 69	395
80 6- 3 70	3
80 6- 3 71	516
80 8- 1 1	411
81 7- 6 57	196
81 7- 6 58	116
81 7- 6 59	137
81 7- 6 60	455
81 7- 6 61	444
81 7- 6 62	430
81 7- 6 63	332
82 8- 3 27	223
82 8- 3 28	222
82 8- 3 29	259
82 8- 3 30	294
82 8- 3 31	426
82 8- 3 32	424
82 8- 3 33	327
82 8- 3 34	513
82 8- 3 35	531
82 8- 3 100	113
82 8- 3 122	525
83 5-10 1	277
83 5-10 2	420
83 6- 8 21	297
83 6- 8 22	289
85 10- 7 1	239
85 10- 7 2	290
85 10- 7 5	407
85 10- 7 6	526
87 10- 5 12	236
87 10- 5 13	296
88 7- 2 8	243
88 7- 2 9	173

Registration No	Catalogue No
88 7- 2 10	276
88 7- 2 11	195
88 7- 2 13	441
89 6- 4 68	76
89 6- 4 70	416
89 6- 4 71	176
90 8- 4 22	136
90 8- 4 23	454
90 8- 4 24	252
90 8- 4 25	414
90 8- 4 27	380
90 8- 4 28	533
91 10- 3 27	40
91 10- 3 29	291
1910 6- 9 12	39
1923 11-11 2	402
1972 6-11 18	333
1978 5- 3 1	30
Or. 3600	117
Or. 3601	244
Or. 3602	257
Or. 3603	215
Or. 3604	301
Or. 3605	280
Or. 3606	253
Or. 3607	418
Or. 3608	415
Or. 3609	518
Or. 3610	517
Or. 3711	334
–	381
–	437
–	523

Department of Egyptian Antiquities

87 4- 2 64	299

Indexes

The Indexes are arranged in English alphabetical order, ignoring the Arabic definite article (al-).

The figures in ordinary type refer to page numbers, those in italic to catalogue numbers.

Index of Proper Names

Index of commodities and denominations

Index of Arabic words and phrases

1

2

3

5

4

6

7

8

9

10

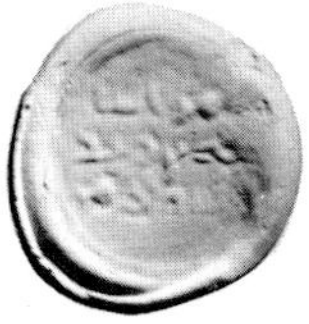
11

12

13

14

15

16

17

19

21

PLATE 2
UMAYYAD *Nos 22-44*

22

24

25

26

27

28

29

30

31

32

34

36

38

40

41

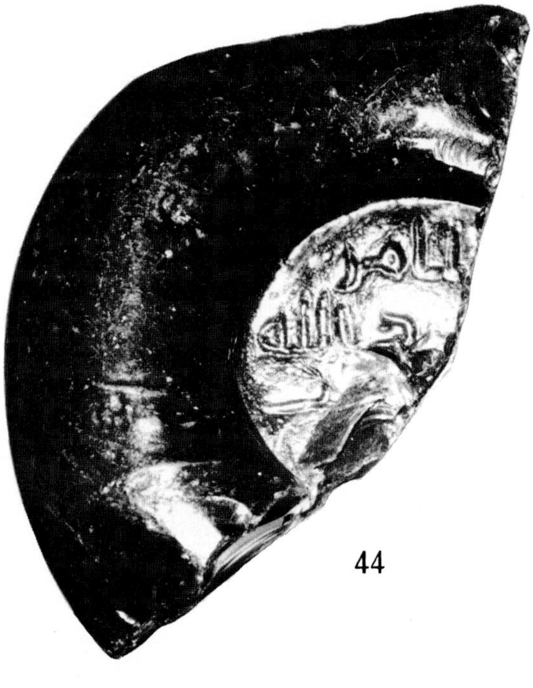
44

42

43

PLATE 3
UMAYYAD *Nos 45–67*

45

46

48

49

50

52

54

55

56

57

60

61

63

64

65

66

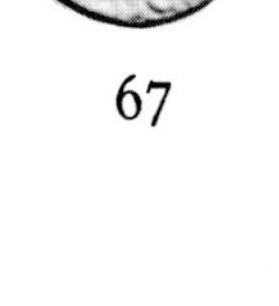
67

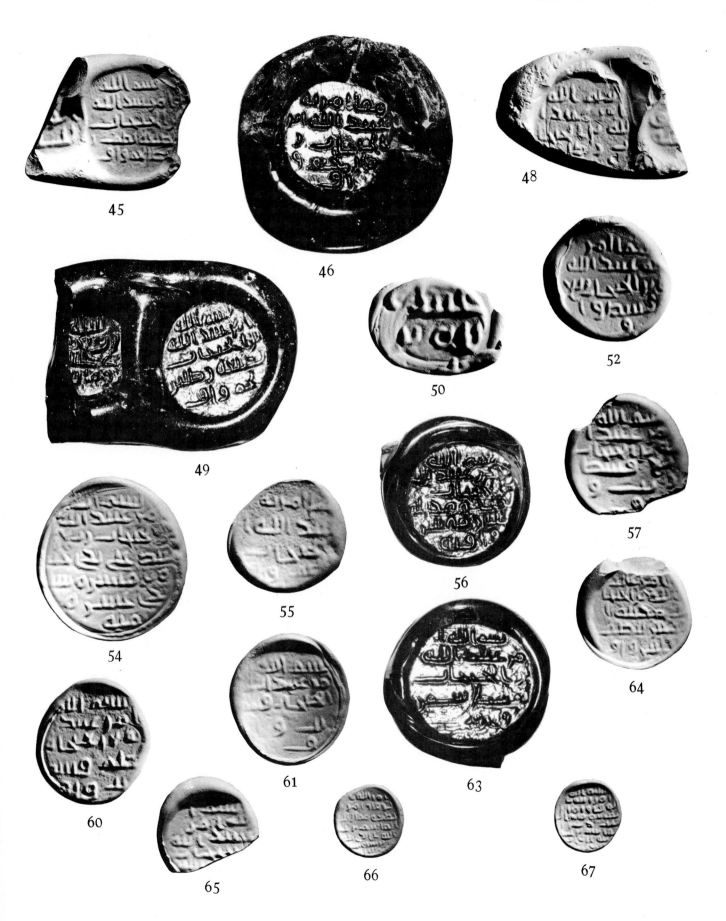

PLATE 4
UMAYYAD *Nos 68–92*

68

70

71

72

73

74

77

78

82

83

85

87

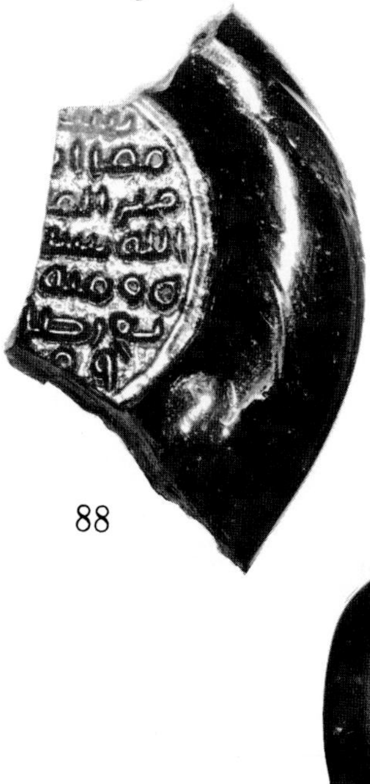

88

89

91

90

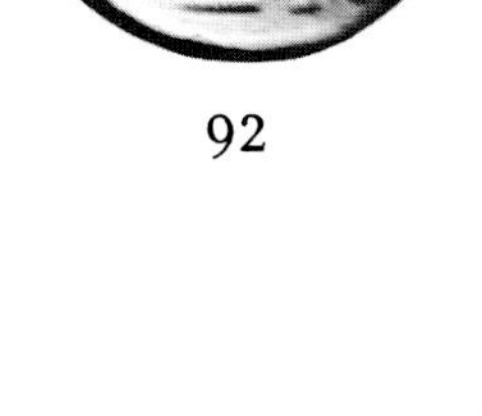

92

94

97

98

99

101

102

103

104

105

106

107

108

109

110

111

112

115

117

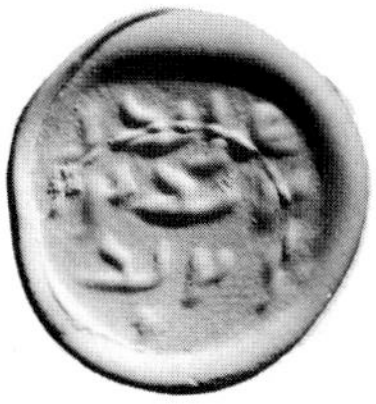
118

121

PLATE 6
UMAYYAD *Nos 124-47*

124

126

127

128

129

130

132

133

135

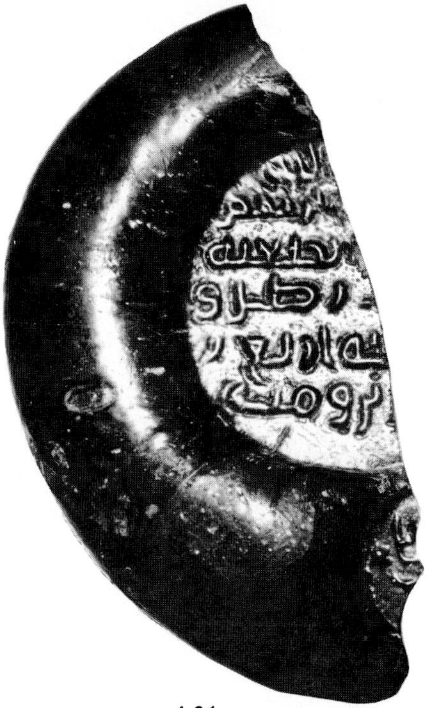
131

136

137

139

140

141

142

144

145

146

147

UMAYYAD *Nos 148-60* / ABBASID *Nos 162-66*

148

149

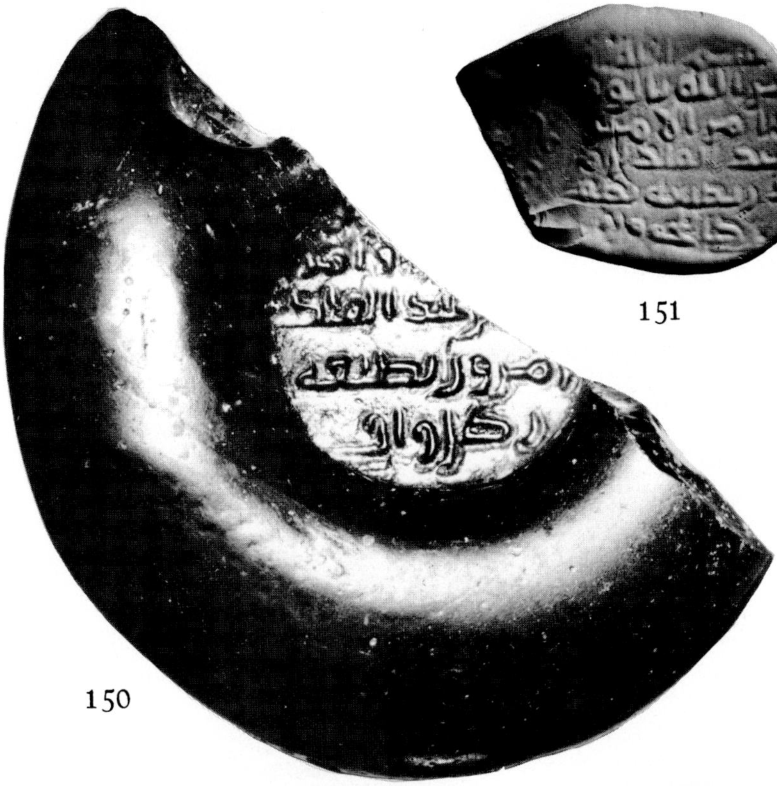

150

151

152

153

155

156

157

158

160

162

163

165

166

PLATE 8
ABBASID *Nos 168-88*

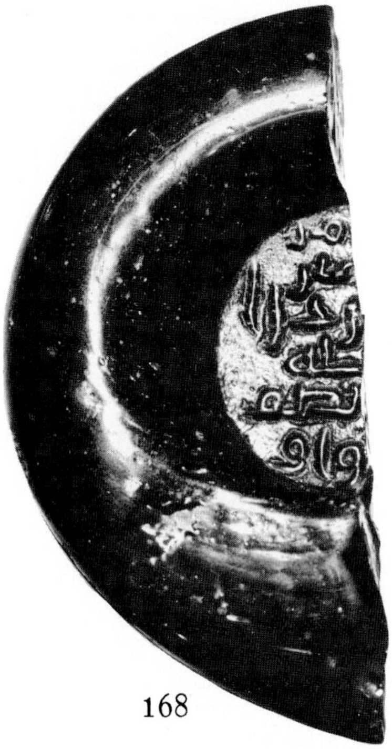
168

169

170

171

173

174

175

177

178

181

182

186

181

188

189

191

192

193

194

196

197

198

198

199

200

205

206

207

PLATE 10
ABBASID *Nos 209–27*

209

210

212

213

214

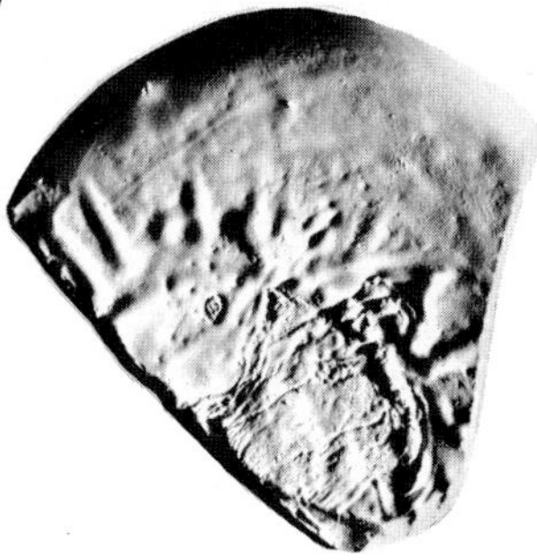
214

215

216

217

218

219

221

222

223

224

225

226

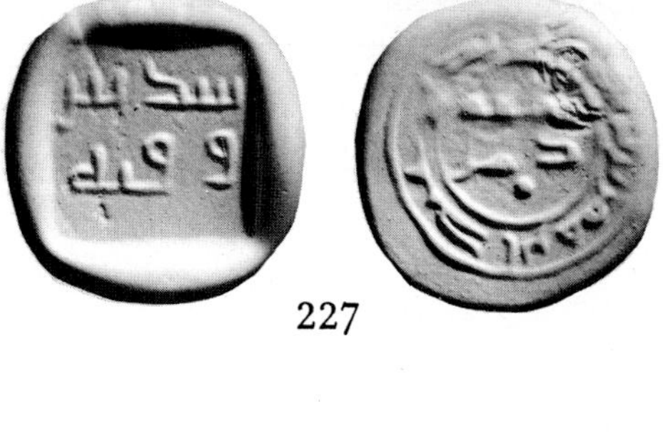
227

228

229

230

231

233

234

235

236

240

237

239

242

244

245

PLATE 12
ABBASID *Nos 246-71*

246

248

249

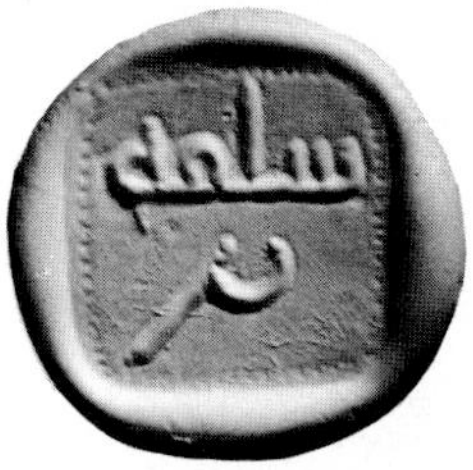
251

255

257

258

259

260

261

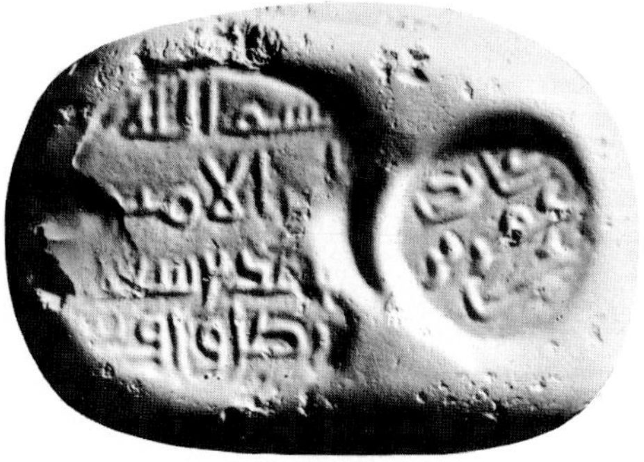
262

267

271

272

273

274

278

281

283

284

285

286

287

288

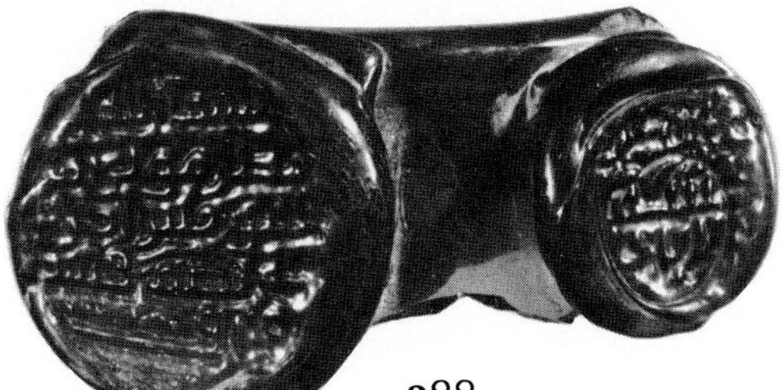
288

288

289

291

292

PLATE 14

ABBASID *Nos 294–308*

294

295

296

297

298

299

300

302

303

304

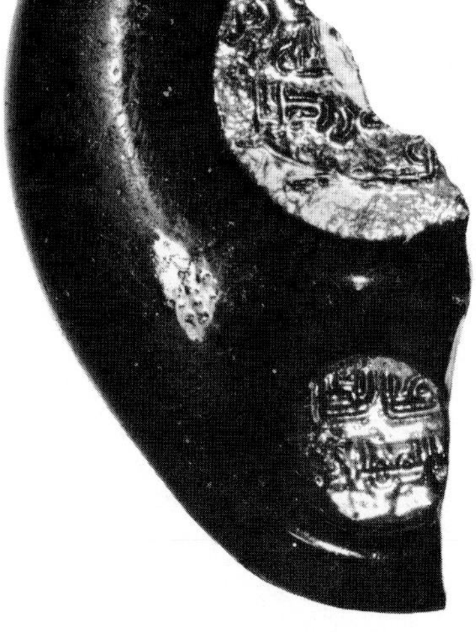

306

305

307

308

309

310

311

312

314

315

316

317

319

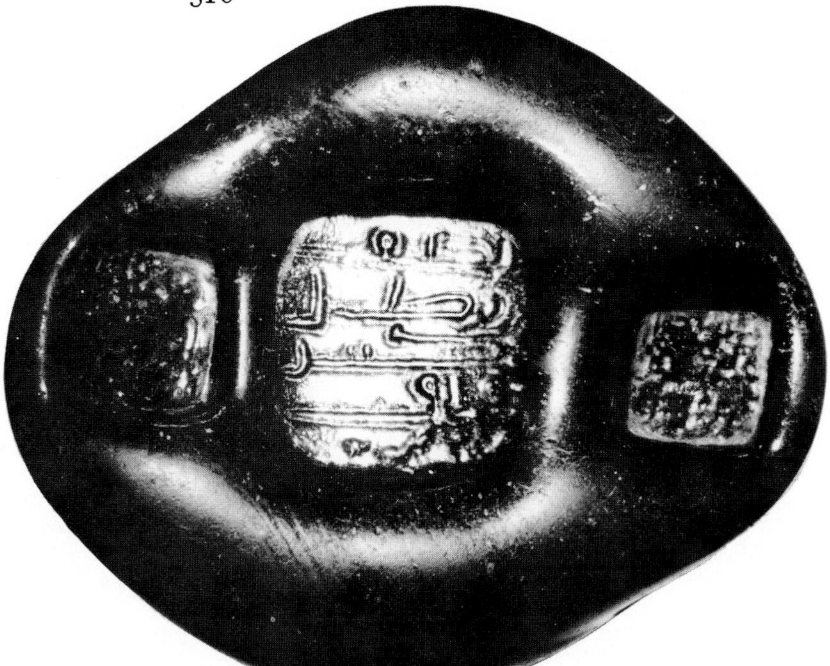

320

PLATE 16
ABBASID *Nos 322-38*

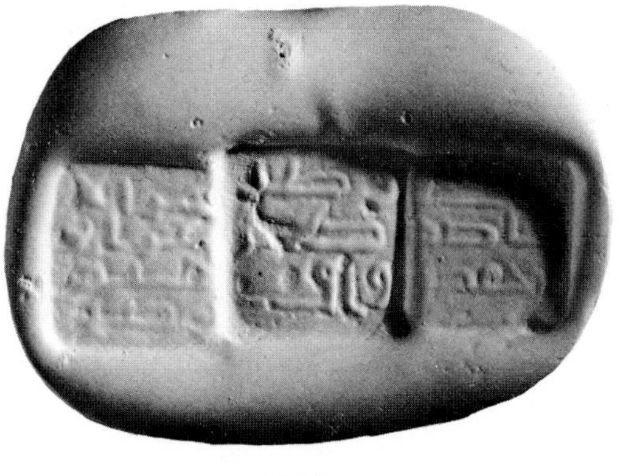
322

323

326

327

328

329

330

331

332

333

334

335

336

337

338

339

340

341

342

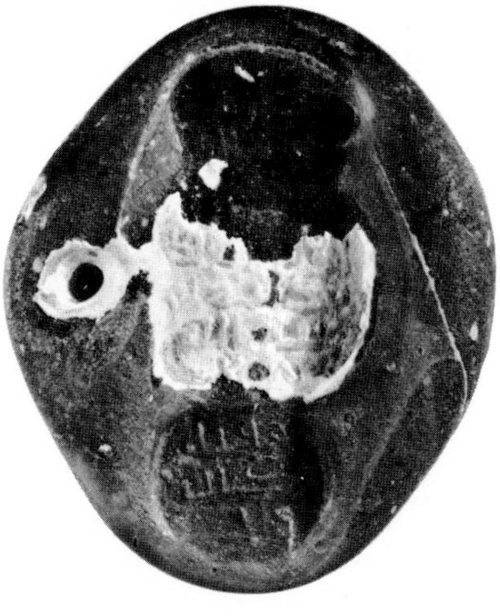

344

343

345

PLATE 18
ABBASID *Nos 346-69* / AGHLABID *No. 373* / UNIDENTIFIED *Nos 374-81*

346

347

348

349

351

354

357

359

363

364

367

368

369

373

374

381

382

383

384

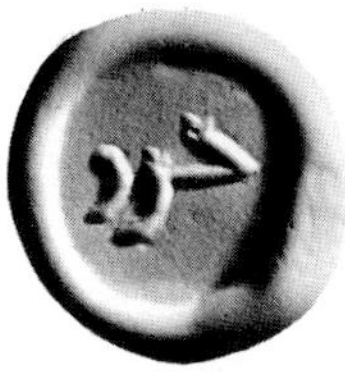

386

387

388

389

391

392

393

395

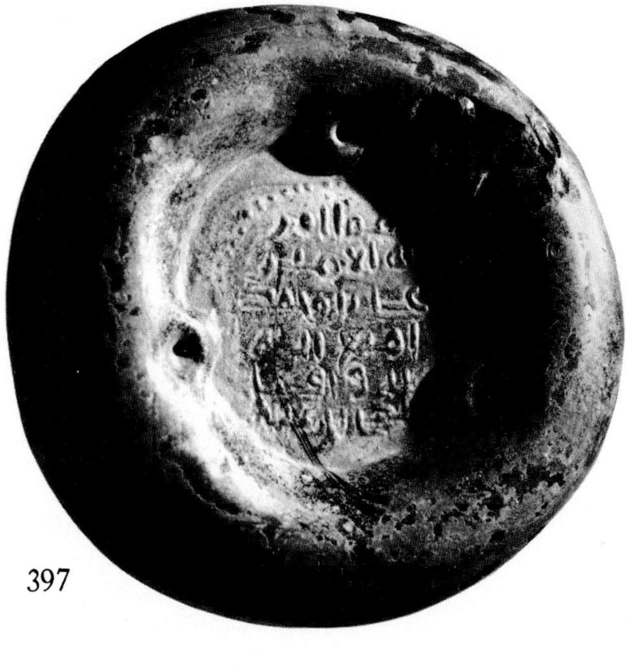

397

398

PLATE 20

UNIDENTIFIED *Nos 399-410* / ANONYMOUS *Nos 411-21*

399

400

401

402

403

404

406

407

408

409

410

411

414

415

416

412

417

418

419

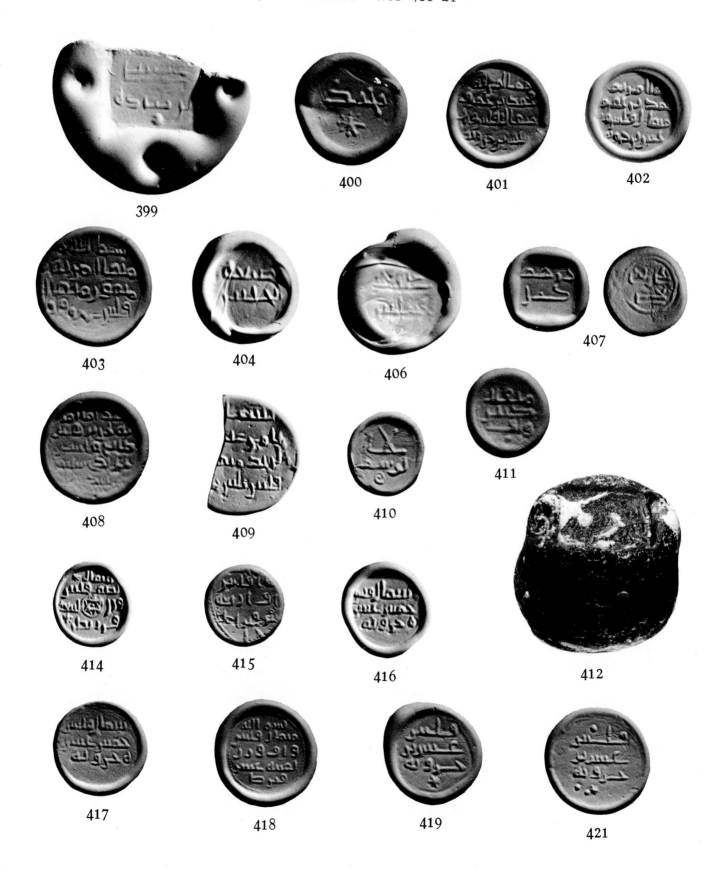

421

422

423

424

425

427

428

430

431

434

435

436

437

438

440

443

445

446

447

448

450

451

452

453

454

PLATE 22
ANONYMOUS *Nos 455-90*

455

456

458

459

460

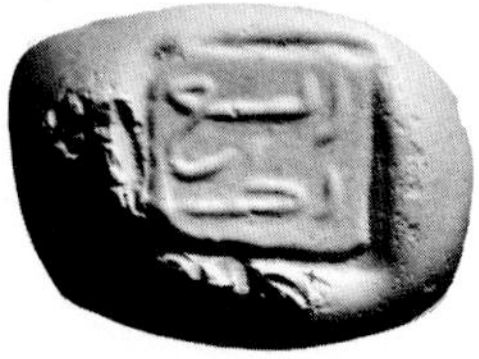
464

466

467

468

469

470

479

481

482

485

486

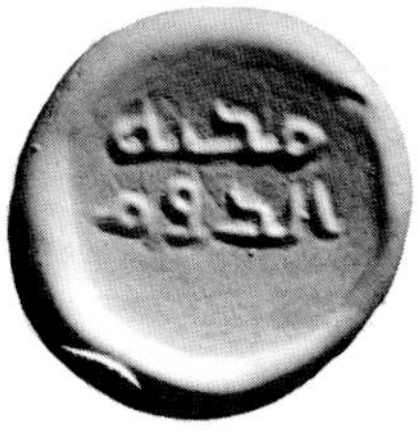
487

489

490

492

493

494

496

498

499

500

501

502

505

507

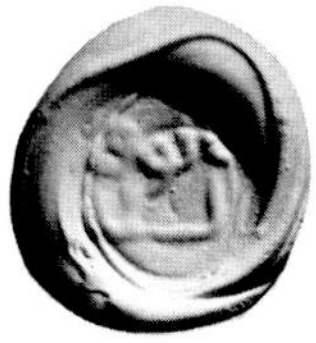
508

510

512

513

514

515

516

517

518

519

520

521

522

523

524

PLATE 24
ANONYMOUS ETC. *Nos 525–56*

525

526

527

530

531

532

533

534

535

537

540

541

542

551

553

554

555

556